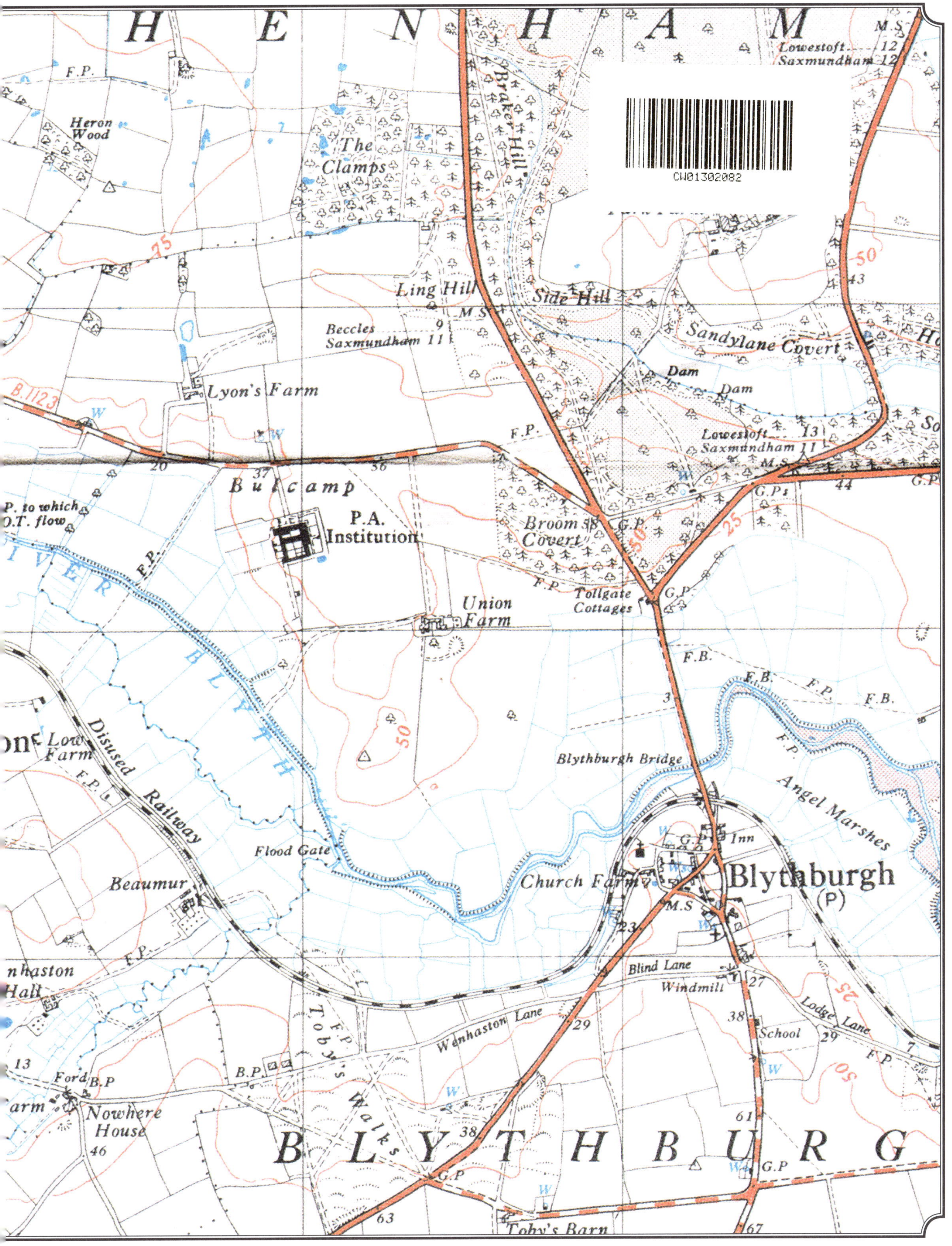

H E N H A M
M.S
Lowestoft 12
Saxmundham 12
F.P.
Heron Wood
The Clamps
Braker Hill
75
Ling Hill
Side Hill
50
43
M.S
9
Beccles
Saxmundham 11
Sandylane Covert
Dam
Dam
B.1123
W
Lyon's Farm
W
F.P.
Lowestoft 13
Saxmundham 11
M.S
20
37
56
44
G.P
Bulcamp
G.Ps
P. to which O.T. flow
P.A. Institution
Broom Covert
38
G.P
50
25
RIVER
F.P.
F.P.
Tollgate Cottages
G.P
Union Farm
F.B.
F.B.
F.P.
F.B.
BLYTH
3
Disused Railway
Low Farm
50
F.P.
Blythburgh Bridge
Angel Marshes
F.P.
Flood Gate
G.P
Inn
Church Farm
Blythburgh
(P)
Beaumur
M.S
W
23
F.P.
Blind Lane
nhaston Hall
Windmill
27
Lodge Lane
25
38
Wenhaston Lane
29
School
29
7
F.P.
Toby's Walks
F.P.
13
B.P
W
50
Ford B.P
W
arm
Nowhere House
61
38
46
B L Y T H B U R G
G.P
G.P
W
63
Toby's Barn
67

THE SOUTHWOLD RAILWAY

The Southwold Railway was never known for its speed or ease of access to other coastal towns, hence the comment on the postcard: *'Toy Rail – Takes about 3 hrs to get to Lowestoft'*. The picture shows a section of railway near Eastwoodlodge Farm at the western end of Walberswick Common, facing towards Halesworth. Two permanent way gangs maintained the permanent way and fencing over the entire length of railway.
John Alsop collection

Southwold station platform was open to the approach road with no barriers so ticket checking was nonexistent. Horse drawn vehicles are parked as local people are saying their final farewells before the departure of the train. The station was provided with adequate platform seats for waiting clientele under one of the ornate electric lighting columns installed in 1905. The building has been extended at the western end and a telegraph pole for the railway route is located by the structure.

John Alsop collection

THE SOUTHWOLD RAILWAY

PETER PAYE

Lightmoor Press

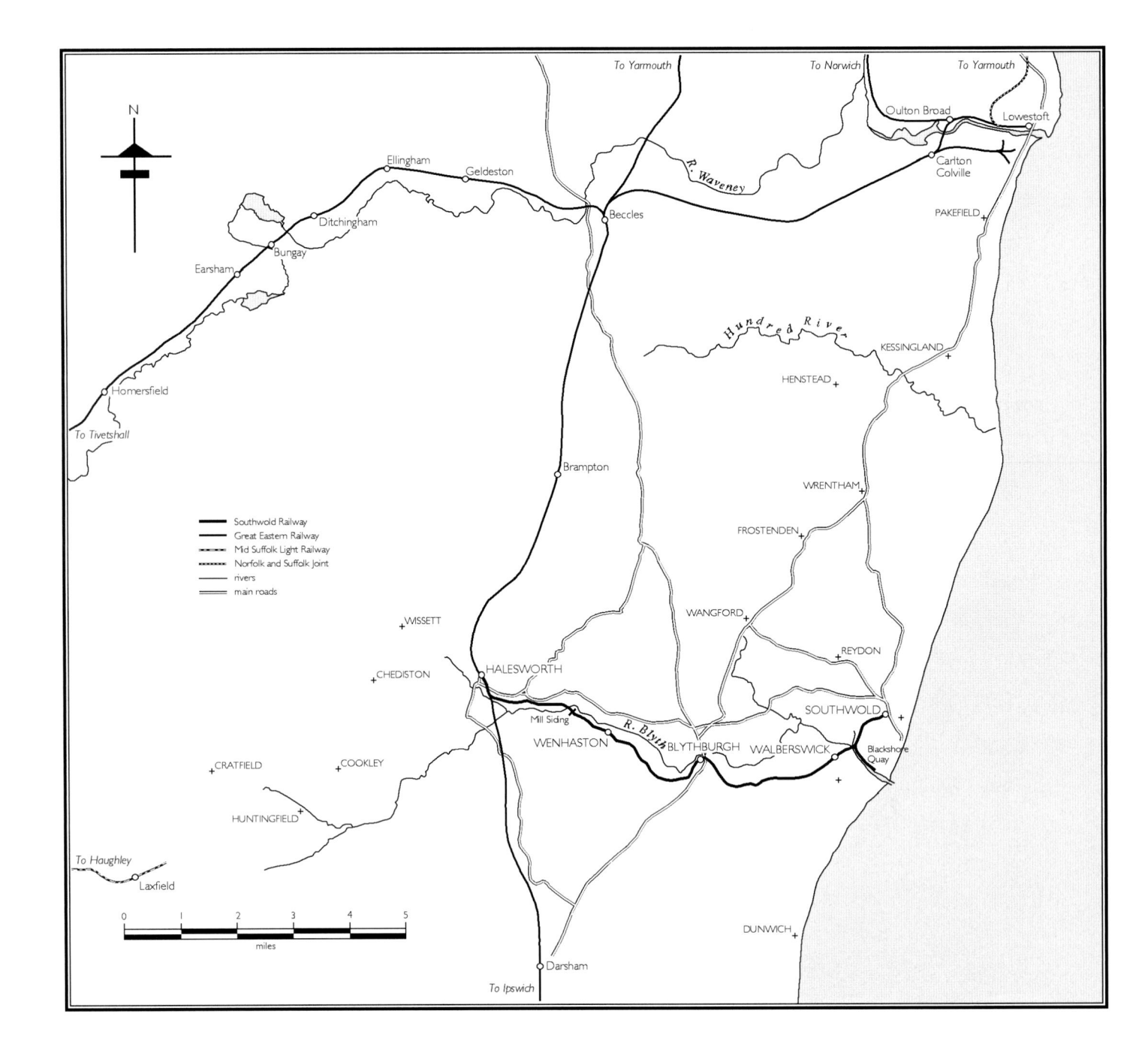

© Peter Paye and Lightmoor Press 2018
Designed by Nigel Nicholson
British Library Cataloguing-in-Publication Data. A catalogue record for this book is available from the British Library
ISBN 9781 911038 42 9
All rights reserved. No part of this publication may be reproduced, stored in a retrieval system or transmitted in any form or by any means,
electronic, mechanical, photocopying, recording or otherwise, without the written permission of the publisher

LIGHTMOOR PRESS

Unit 144B, Lydney Trading Estate, Harbour Road, Lydney, Gloucestershire GL15 4EJ

www.lightmoor.co.uk

Lightmoor Press is an imprint of Black Dwarf Lightmoor Publications Ltd
Printed in Poland; www.lfbookservices.co.uk

Contents

Introduction 7
1 Advent of the Railway 9
2 Opening of the Line 17
3 The Early Years 23
4 Consolidation 33
5 Possible Expansion and Conversion of Gauge 45
6 Great Eastern Bus Services to Southwold 81
7 Decline and Closure 85
8 The Route Described 105
9 Permanent Way, Signalling and Staff 147
10 Timetables and Traffic 159
11 Locomotives 189
12 Coaching Stock 205
13 Wagons 219
Appendices
   1 The Reg Carter Postcards 227
   2 Southwold Railway Bridges 231
   3 Southwold Railway Level Crossings 232
   4 Train Staff Regulations, September 1908, with Amendment of August 1914 234
   5 Rules and Regulations, 1st November 1918 238
Bibliography 246
Acknowledgements 246
Index 247

Close up detail of 2-4-0T No. 3 *Blyth* at Southwold circa 1906, showing the large sand box atop the left-hand side tank, the whistle position on the front of the cab and the obligatory oil can on the footplate by the smokebox. A postcard showing the complete scene is reproduced on page 143.
Author's collection

Introduction

With the coming of railways to East Suffolk in 1859, the ancient coastal town and port of Southwold was bypassed some seven miles to the west, where a station was established at Halesworth. Despite concern at being economically isolated from the outside world and agitation for this oversight to be rectified, nothing was done until 1872 when an Act of Parliament authorized the building of a tramway connecting the towns. Unfortunately money to finance the scheme was not forthcoming and the project was abandoned. Undeterred, local dignitaries and townsfolk pressed for an alternative and after consulting with one of the leading proponents of light railways in the country the Southwold Railway was conceived, culminating in an authorizing Act in 1876 which sanctioned the building of a narrow gauge line in order to reduce costs. This was hardly a satisfactory solution, forcing passengers to change trains and freight to be transshipped at Halesworth, but with Southwold harbour deficient and fishery in decline, the new line was better than nothing. The Great Eastern Railway, successor to the East Suffolk Railway, accepted the newcomer but initially demurred from providing monetary assistance, happy in the fact the new line would provide a feeder whilst carrying no threat of competition. Construction was relatively easy and the 3-foot gauge railway opened to traffic on 24th September 1879, heralding new prosperity for the town and encouraging trade to the aspiring seaside resort, which hitherto had been in steady decline. Thereafter for the five decades the railway operated the company provided a reasonable and adequate service but nagging issues always persisted with Southwold Corporation, which was undecided in its relationship with the company, at one moment supporting and encouraging, and the next severely critical of the organization.

In moments of financial difficulty the Southwold Directors attempted to get the GER in 1893, and later the L&NER in 1923, to purchase the undertaking but the problems of narrow gauge with its lack of through running facilities, the manual interchanging of goods traffic at Halesworth and latterly ageing rolling stock, weighed heavily against such action. Attempts to convert the line to standard gauge in conjunction with an extension of the Mid Suffolk Light Railway from Laxfield to Halesworth and a totally new extension to Lowestoft from Southwold combined with a new harbour scheme fell by the wayside. The railway continued to faithfully serve the community through World War One and in the years following, but by the early 1920s and with the development of local bus services its days were numbered. With no ready finance for improvements, and antiquated rolling stock and infrastructure, the company soldiered on reducing costs by cutting the wages of some staff and dismissing others, until with no resurrection in sight the Directors called time and closed the line down on and from 11th April 1929. Stock stored at various points over the years deteriorated whilst weeds and foliage grew through the permanent way. Various abortive attempts were made to reopen the railway but all failed and in 1941 all assets were taken in the drive for metal for the war effort.

This little railway was a unique narrow gauge line in several respects. First it was built to a gauge of 3 feet 0 inches, unusual for an English company; secondly it was the first narrow gauge line to close, and thirdly it displayed a marked reluctance to lie down and die after the abandonment of services in 1929. After years of frustration and legal wrangling the last rites finally came in 1994.

Passengers arriving by the Great Eastern Railway East Suffolk main line train at Halesworth and destined for Southwold crossed by a footbridge to join their train. Here the urgencies and worries of the late 19th and early 20th centuries were soon forgotten as a more relaxed atmosphere prevailed. Standing at the separate SR station they would have found a small narrow gauge locomotive painted in the same blue livery as their GER standard gauge cousins, with immaculate paintwork and shining brass and copper fittings, standing at the head of a mixed train formed of a couple of coaches, one or two vans for passengers' luggage and parcels, and several goods wagons. Travellers entered the coaches by doors at each end of the vehicle and sat on tramway style benches mounted along each side, whilst porters busied themselves loading cases, baggage and parcels on board. A wave of the guard's flag and an acknowledging blast from the engine whistle and the miniature train was set in motion. To the discerning ear the exhaust from the engine was softer and the clickety-clack of the track joints much closer, as the train rolled and swayed on its journey to the coast at an official maximum speed of 16 mph. Rumours abounded that it was possible to jump off the train to pick wild flowers from the lineside and then jump back on again as the train was in motion, but the claim was exaggerated. After running parallel with the GE main line for few hundred yards, the Southwold train crossed the main Halesworth to Southwold road by the separate Holton Road bridge before swinging east through Quarry or Bird's Folly and past Halesworth engine shed. The line entered the valley of the River Blyth and continued through fields and woods before passing under Mells Road bridge, followed by water meadows and then over the river close to Wenhaston or Kett's Mill, served by a siding. A meandering course followed before the railway bisected the only public road level crossing on the line protected by gates to enter Wenhaston station. As at all stations, trains frequently shunted wagons into and out of the siding before continuing their leisurely journey. Away from the station limits the Blyth valley broadened and the railway clung to the shelf on the southern bank just above the high tide mark. Marshland with willows, alders and reeds heralded the widening skyline, with the tower of Holy Trinity Church, Blythburgh standing as spiritual sentinel on the hill, dominating the scene before the railway swept on a long curve around the base of the contour, avoiding earth works and gradients to enter Blythburgh station, the only crossing loop on the line.

The single line Train Staff was exchanged before the train departed, passing under the London to Yarmouth road, later A12, to emerge on an embankment where fine views of the ever-widening estuary were available on the north side of the railway. By this time regular travellers would have gathered in the small guard's compartment to pass the time of day, oblivious of the passing scenery. Pulses raced as other passengers, notably holidaymakers, sensed the approaching destination, but just as the view widened so the engine started the battle against the gradient, as the railway left the riverside, with is teeming array of bird life, and climbed through woodland known as 'The Heronry' to the summit of the line to emerge on Walberswick Common. Sandy heath and low hills dominated the scene as the railway ran parallel to the locally known 'Tinker's Walk' before swinging to the left and descending through a cutting, bright with gorse in season. *'There is no finer natural feature than the brilliant expanse of blossom seen in May'*, wrote one traveller. The line then entered the small station of Walberswick, located almost a mile from the village. After the station a long straight stretch of railway enabled the engine to gather speed, Southwold Railway style, to surmount the short sharp 1 in 53 gradient heralding the approach to the swing bridge over the River Blyth, the major engineering structure on the line. The rumbling of the girders as the train crossed the navigational stream added to the cry of the sea birds wheeling over the small harbour, with a view of the short branch line serving the north bank. Away from the bridge the exhaust note of the locomotive changed as the railway crossed marshland before climbing through a deep cutting spanned by a footbridge. Here a gaggle of golfers on the Southwold Golf Course, which was bisected by the line, would often give a cheery wave to the passengers. By now travellers were gathering their belongings together as the train emerged from the cutting and slowed to a halt at the terminus as station staff called *'Southwold – All Change'*.

Except for the first Up train in the morning and the last Down train at night from Halesworth, which were designated passenger only, and a 'conditional' goods working each way, all trains were designated 'mixed', conveying both passenger and freight traffic. Thus most passengers were subjected to a slow journey as wagons were shunted on and off the train at the intermediate stations. For convenience, goods vehicles were placed behind the locomotive at the front of the train ahead of the passenger coaches with one or two closed luggage vans at the rear. The lack of continuous brake meant the driver had to skilfully apply the steam brake on the engine leaving the guard to adjust the handbrake on the coaches as necessary, resulting more often than not in a less than smooth retardation.

I have attempted in this volume to provide the complete story of this unique narrow gauge railway from conception to closure; details have been checked with available documents but apologies are offered for any errors which may have occurred. The interest generated over many years has resulted in the formation of the Southwold Railway Trust whose aims are to keep alive the memories of the narrow gauge line and open a short section of railway on the former trackbed. This being the 'Old Testament' it is for future historians to write the 'New Testament'.

Peter Paye
Bishop's Stortford

On occasions, and usually on return of a locomotive from Stratford Works, engines were turned to even wear and tear on the axles and tyres. Here 2-4-0T No. 2 *Halesworth*, facing east, and sister locomotive No. 3 *Blyth*, facing Halesworth, pass each other at Southwold on 10th September 1910. Latterly all engines reverted to running chimney first to Southwold. *LCGB/Ken Nunn*

1
Advent of the Railway

The old Suffolk port of Southwold facing the German Ocean, later the North Sea, situated at the mouth of the River Blyth overlooking Sole Bay, and midway between Aldeburgh to the south and Lowestoft to the north, was known at various times in the past as Suwald, Suwalda, Sudholda, Southwaud and Southwood. The town was of considerable importance and off Southwold in 1672 the combined fleets of England and France, under the command of the Duke of York, then High Admiral of the Fleet and later the last Stuart King, James II, defeated the Dutch in the battle of Sole Bay. By the end of the 18th and beginning of the 19th century many of the inhabitants were engaged in the smuggling industry, handling wines, spirits, silks, lace and tobacco. The Government sought to eliminate such practices and those caught by revenue officers without paying customs tariffs were imprisoned or hanged. The punishments were enhanced when the press-gang paid regular visits to the town to 'recruit' young men for His Majesty's Navy. Thus, like many other small ports, by 1815 the place was inhabited chiefly by women, children and old men. Maritime trade using the port was affected by the faulty construction of two piers in 1749 and 1752, the width between them being too great which subsequently affected the discharge of the waters of the River Blyth. The power of the river as a scouring agent was so mitigated when passing the pier heads that it scarcely affected the bar, so when the ebb streams of the river and sea met they acted as opposing forces causing the port to silt up. The decline in the importance of the harbour was of considerable concern and to counteract the loss of maritime trade Southwold Corporation actively promoted the town as a holiday centre for the discerning and by the early 19th century the fame of its broad sandy beaches was established.

Further expansion, however, required ready access to and from the outside world, hardly manageable with the poor roads giving access to the resort. With the coming of the railway the situation might have been remedied but many years were to evolve before Southwold was to benefit.

The advent of the railways in East Anglia began in earnest with the incorporation of the Eastern Counties Railway on 4th July 1836. With a share capital of £1,600,000, the company was granted powers to construct a 126 mile line from Shoreditch in East London to Norwich and Yarmouth via Colchester, Ipswich and Eye. By September £58,100 of shares had been sold but there was great concern that only one twelfth of the capital raised was of local origin. Construction of the railway commenced in late March 1837 at the London end only, as incomplete negotiations with landowners prevented a start being made concurrently at Norwich and Ipswich. The problems continued when landowners along the proposed route demanded higher compensation, and by October 1838, with 40 per cent of the capital called, only nine miles of railway was under construction. With creditors urgently pressing, action was necessary to prevent total ruin and by April 1839 Lancashire proprietors, who had taken a majority stake in the undertaking forced a decision to terminate the line at Colchester.

The first public trains ran from a temporary terminus at Mile End to Romford on 20th June 1839, with extensions each end to Shoreditch and Brentwood opening for traffic on 1st July 1840. Robert Stephenson was engaged by the ECR Directors to give engineering advice but he could only confirm that another £520,000 was required to complete the railway to Colchester. Mutinous shareholders were almost bludgeoned into meeting the calls for outstanding shares and application was made to Parliament for a further £350,000 share capital in 1840. With these assets and the added borrowing powers authorized by the 1840 Act, construction of the final section went ahead. Eventually the line was opened to Colchester for goods traffic on 7th March 1843 and for passenger trains on 29th March. The 51 mile line, of unusual 5 feet gauge, had taken seven years to construct at a cost of nearly £2½ million, the works alone, amounting to £1,631,000, had exceeded the original estimate for the whole project from London to Yarmouth.

The ECR Directors' decision to terminate the project at Colchester was of particular concern to the merchants of Ipswich and Norwich, who were fearful of isolation from the railway network and probable loss of trade. Some ECR shareholders from Norfolk and Suffolk, alarmed by the slow progress and decision of April 1839, obtained a rule nisi in the Bail Court to force the fulfilment of the company's contract with the public, but this was overruled in 1840 when Parliament refused to extend the ECR's powers beyond July of that year. Local factions then decided to take action by planning a railway linking Norwich and Yarmouth and this received the Royal Assent in 1842, to be followed the next year by a projected line from Norwich to Brandon. This situation was aggravated by the ECR plan to join up with the Norwich to Brandon line at Thetford, with the mainline by-passing Ipswich altogether and leaving the town at the end of a branch line from Hadleigh.

Objections were raised but ignored and fearful of economic isolation the traders and merchants of Ipswich produced their own scheme for a line linking the town with the ECR at Colchester. Plans were prepared by Peter Schuyler Bruff, who had already worked on surveys for the initial ECR route from London. The leading advocate for the Ipswich scheme was John Chevallier Cobbold, a member of the wealthy Ipswich banking and brewing family, who was a member of the original ECR Board of Directors. As well as connecting Ipswich with Colchester, the promoters of the scheme also intended to continue the line running north to Norwich, and the new company, entitled the Eastern Union Railway, was incorporated on 19th July 1844.

In the meantime the ECR plans for a route to Thetford were abandoned but a group of businessmen in Bury St. Edmunds were concerned that the town would be isolated from the developing railway network. In February 1844 the ECR Directors received a deputation who wished to salvage their plans, but were advised the company was unwilling to extend its line beyond Colchester. The townsfolk subsequently promoted their own line, the East & West

Suffolk Railway, and were advised the EUR would not oppose the railway provided the route went from Bury St. Edmunds to Ipswich via Hadleigh and not interfere with the direct line from Ipswich to Colchester.

The development of railways in Norfolk and Suffolk was the subject of a special investigation by the Railway Department of the Board of Trade and, in the final report of 4th March 1845, full support was given to the EUR scheme to Ipswich and the extension on the Norwich. The tract of land north-east of Ipswich towards Bury St. Edmunds finally received the attention of railway developers with the passing, on 21st July 1845, of the Act authorizing the construction of the Ipswich & Bury St. Edmunds Railway. With an initial capital of £400,000 the new concern appeared nominally independent but it was, however, an extension of the EUR, with no fewer than six EUR Directors appointed to a board totalling fifteen members. The Colchester to Ipswich section of the EUR opened to goods traffic on 1st June and passenger traffic on 15th June 1846, whilst the extension to Bury St. Edmunds was opened for goods traffic on 7th December and passenger traffic on 24th December 1846.

Meanwhile, in the autumn of 1845 a proposed railway to Hadleigh, backed by the EUR, had effectively stemmed the competitive desire of the ECR to build a duplicate line from Colchester into East Anglia. Much to the annoyance of the Ipswich company, the ECR had not abandoned the goals of Norwich and Yarmouth, but had instead taken steps to reach Norfolk via an alternative route. On the same day as the ECR was incorporated in 1836, a rival company, the Northern & Eastern Railway (N&E), received the Royal Assent to build a line over the 53 miles from Islington to Cambridge financed by a share capital of £1,200,000. The N&E, like the ECR, soon encountered financial difficulties and it was 1839 before construction commenced and even then only with the sanction of the ECR. To conserve finances the N&E route was diverted from Tottenham via Stratford, where running powers were permitted into the ECR Shoreditch terminus. Like the ECR, the new line was built to a gauge of 5 feet, and despite the abandonment of the route north of Bishop's Stortford by Act of Parliament in 1840, had reached the Hertfordshire market town on 16th May 1842, at a cost of over £25,000 per mile. In 1843 the N&E secured an extension Act to Newport, some 10 miles nearer Cambridge, but on 23rd December of the same year the ECR agreed terms on a 999 years lease for the company on and from 1st January 1844. Once the lease was in force, the ECR lost no time in obtaining powers linking Newport to the Norwich and Brandon line at Brandon on 4th July 1844. The N&E line, along with the existing ECR line, was converted to the standard gauge of 4 feet 8½ inches in the late summer of the same year; after a formal opening the previous day, the whole line from Bishop's Stortford to a temporary station at Norwich (Trowse) commenced public service on 30th July 1845.

The southern railway approach to Norwich was surveyed by Joseph Locke and built by the EUR. It ran from a junction with the Bury St. Edmunds line at Haughley, north-west of Stowmarket, and ran direct to the Norfolk capital via Diss. The line was opened in stages, initially for goods traffic to Finningham from 7th June 1848, then to Burston for goods on 11th June and passengers from 2nd July 1849, with completion throughout by 7th November of the same year. Thus, while the main routes from London to Norwich via Cambridge and Ipswich were established, a vast acreage of East Suffolk was devoid of railways. The genesis of a main line through East Suffolk began in 1851 when a local venture, the Halesworth, Beccles & Haddiscoe Railway (HB&HR), obtained powers to construct a line connecting the river ports of Halesworth and Beccles with the Reedham to Lowestoft line of the Norfolk Railway. The following year it was empowered to enter into a working agreement with that company and subsequently opened to goods on 20th November and passenger traffic on 4th December 1854. From the beginning the railway was operated by the ECR, which had leased the Norfolk Railway in 1848; by June 1855 the company was able to show a modest profit of £528. In the meantime the HB&HR Directors, encouraged by the backing they had received, proposed a southward extension to Woodbridge to join up with the EUR. The EUR connection from Ipswich, originally proposed in 1847, was never built, and so these plans were dusted down and resurrected in the hope the combined railways would provide a through route to the Suffolk capital and chief port of the county. At the same time it was proposed to re-title the HB&HR undertaking, the East Suffolk Railway. Sir Samuel Morton Peto, who had ambitious schemes afoot to elevate the status of Lowestoft, immediately recognized the new line would provide a more direct access to London than the existing routes via Norwich. He quickly became the principal subscriber and subsequently offered to lease the whole line for fourteen years on a cost not exceeding £10,000 per mile, with 3½ per cent paid during construction.

The original intention had been to route the Halesworth to Woodbridge extension via the town of Framlingham but the Duke of Hamilton had objected to the line passing through his estate at Easton and so the proposed railway was routed further to the east. The combined proposals for the ESR and EUR schemes, together with books of reference, were deposited with the Parliamentary Bill Office on 30th November 1853, with copies sent to parish councils affected by the planned railways. Included in the ESR proposal were branch railways to serve Richard Garrett's engineering works at Leiston, Newson Garrett's maltings at Snape and the town of Framlingham. Of significance was the omission of a branch railway to Southwold.

The East Suffolk Railway Act (17 and 18 Vict. Cap cxix), which received the Royal Assent on 3rd July 1854, vested all assets of the Halesworth, Beccles & Haddiscoe Railway to the newly titled East Suffolk Railway. The statute authorized the building of the main line from Halesworth to Woodbridge and the three branches. Three years were permitted for compulsory purchase of land and five years for the completion of works. The share capital of the new company was £450,000, formed of £150,000 shares of the former Haddiscoe company and £300,000 new shares, with borrowing powers for £50,000 once half of the original capital was paid up.

In 1855 the Mayor of Southwold, Alfred Lillingston, presented a petition to the ESR Directors requesting the building of a branch line from Halesworth to Southwold, but the request was rejected. The following year local businessmen, aided by Southwold Town Council and others, resolved to promote an independent branch railway and a meeting was held at Southwold Town Hall on 3rd October 1856, chaired by Alfred Lillingston. The local press reported that interested bodies were to take into consideration the best means of promoting a branch railway from the ESR at Halesworth and a resolution was passed to the effect that a committee be appointed and copies of the resolution sent to local landed gentry and Members of Parliament to seek their support. The Mayor and Corporation were requested *'to give their warmest support'* but little immediate action was taken.

After many trials and tribulations the ESR main line and branches were opened to traffic on and from Wednesday 1st June 1859 passing through Darsham, Saxmundham and Wickham Market en route to Woodbridge and Ipswich. Much to the chagrin of many, Southwold remained isolated from this railway route, which passed some 9 miles to the west at Halesworth, and a once daily horse-bus service with the vehicle painted bright yellow and operated by Mr Catton between the coastal town and Darsham proved woefully inadequate for the clientele wishing to enjoy the bracing air of the Suffolk resort. Even at this early date the town was noted for its sea bathing and a considerable number of visitors benefited from the visits during the summer season. To accommodate this clientele there were a number of commodious lodging houses, three good inns and several bathing machines, where 'private bathing' was possible without the intrusion of the general public.

The question of providing a railway connection to Southwold, however, dragged on until September 1860 when the *Suffolk Mercury* reported that a memorial had been prepared by the Southwold Town Clerk to present to Sir Samuel Morton Peto, as the *'whole town'* was *'anxious that this projected line be carried into effect'*. Nothing further transpired until November when another meeting was held but there was lack of unity in the town as to how the money for such a scheme could be raised. The gathering was of the opinion *'unless those of position and influence showed an example the project would not be realised'*. Despite the bickering, a memorial was presented to Peto in December 1860 when a printed circular urged *'gentlemen possessing property'* to add their names to the subscription list. Peto estimated the cost of the line at £60,000 but declined to support such a venture because of his financial commitments to the ESR and other schemes. Alfred Lillingston subsequently presided at yet another meeting, in which upwards of £1,000 was raised towards a railway, but the scheme collapsed through lack of finance.

The ECR, having by this time leased or taken over the working of most major railways in East Anglia, amalgamated with the Eastern Union Newmarket and Norfolk railways to form the Great Eastern Railway. The Act authorising the amalgamation (25 and 26 Vict. Cap ccxxiii) was passed on 7th August 1862 but took effect retrospectively from July 1862.

A number of independent schemes were also mooted to save the town from its railway isolation. The *Suffolk Mercury* for 16th December 1865 reported that a preliminary survey for the Blyth Valley Railway had been completed and plans deposited with the Clerk of the Peace for the County of Ipswich and Suffolk, and to the parish clerks for the parishes to be crossed by the proposed line. The next step was to obtain an Act of Parliament and it was learned that Southwold Corporation and Sir John Blois had agreed to sell land to the embryonic company. There was said to be *'enthusiastic support'* for the scheme and it was hoped *'the sound of the whistle will be heard along the valley of the Blyth within fifteen months'*, although another report quoted twelve months. On 30th December the *Suffolk Mercury* reported the proceedings of a public meeting held at Southwold and chaired by Sir John Blois. The attendees were advised the railway would commence in Southwold, at the South End near the Salt Works, and after crossing the River Blyth at Blackshore would run parallel to and never far from the river to a junction with the ESR at Holton. Intermediate stations were to be provided at Blythburgh and Wenhaston, and the Engineer appointed to oversee the construction was none other than William F. Bruff of London, son of Peter Schuyler Bruff, an eminent engineer who worked on the surveys for the ECR under Braithwaite and who later became engineer of the EUR. The project was heralded as being of *'great advantage to the Borough of Southwold and the District through which it passes'*. Doctor Beckett suggested the opening of a subscription list for shares and so the Blyth Valley line was born. Some apathy was expressed towards the scheme in a letter published in the *Halesworth Times* in January 1866, although conversely the lack of railway communication was much regretted in the summer editions of the same paper. Unfortunately, soon after the Bill was presented to Parliament it was withdrawn on advice because of inaccuracies; Sir John Blois presided over another meeting on 24th October 1866 to *'take steps for making another application to Parliament in the ensuing session'*, as prospects for success were then said to be *'much better'*. The amended plans were lodged with the Clerk of the Peace for Suffolk on 30th November and application made to Parliament but again met with failure. The scheme remained in a dormant state until the *Suffolk Mercury* of 14th October 1871 reported that Bruff was resurrecting plans for depositing in the Private Bill Office in November. Unfortunately the application met with a similar fate to its predecessors.

After frustration and seemingly endless failure to provide a railway in the latter part of 1870 and the spring and summer of 1871, consideration was being given to the building of a tramway from Yarmouth, through Lowestoft to Southwold. Despite opposition from the Lowestoft Improvement Commissioners, the project for the Lowestoft, Yarmouth & Southwold Tramways Company Limited gained strength. On 19th October 1871 at a Town Council Meeting at Southwold, the Town Clerk presented an application from the Lowestoft, Yarmouth & Southwold Tramways Company for the consent of the Corporation to make a tramway from Lowestoft to Southwold under the clauses of the Tramways Act 1870. A deputation from the promoters also attended the meeting and explained their plans were to build the tramway from Lowestoft, Halesworth or Darsham, as the Southwold Corporation should decide. After due deliberation, in early November the Council granted permission for the tramway to enter the Borough of Southwold on condition that the promoters connected Halesworth with the scheme and that the company enlarge the bridge over Buss Creek at their own expense, and sufficiently to provide for increased traffic. At the same time it was stipulated that if any other tramway company desired to enter Southwold with the consent of the Council, that company would have running powers over that part of the proposed tramway within the borough. The direction and position of the tramway within the borough was to be approved by the Council, whilst clauses were to be inserted in the Provisional Order to the satisfaction of the Council to secure fulfilment of the conditions. Two weeks later Halesworth Town Council approved the continuation of the tramway *'as far as the same affects roads under their jurisdiction'*. The Lowestoft, Yarmouth & Southwold Tramway Company Limited was duly registered on 25th November 1871.

On 18th January 1872 the Directors of the GER decided to oppose the tramway scheme when raised in the 1871-72 session of Parliament, but their opposition was in vain and the Southwold & Halesworth Tramway was incorporated by Act of Parliament on 6th August 1872 (35 and 36 Vic cap cxlvii). The statute authorized the building of a roadside steam tramway, known in the Act as tramway No. 4 commencing opposite the Swan Hotel, Southwold thence proceeding along the High Street, over Buss Creek Bridge into the parish of Reydon, then along the road leading to Wangford passing Reydon church, and continuing in a westerly direction into the village of Wangford and terminating on the turnpike on London

> **BLYTH VALLEY RAILWAY**
>
> (Incorporation of the Company – Construction of the Railway from Halesworth to Southwold – Agreements with the Corporation of Southwold – Amendments of Acts, &c.)
>
> Notice is hereby given, that an application is intended to be made to Parliament in the next session for an Act for the following, or some of the following, among other purposes.
>
> To incorporate a Company (hereinafter called 'the Company') and to enable the Company to make and maintain a railway hereinafter mentioned, with all necessary stations, buildings, approaches, works and conveniences connected therewith, that is to say:- A railway commencing in the parish of Halesworth, by a junction with the Great Eastern Railway near Halesworth Station, at or near the south end of the bridge carrying the said railway over the public road leading from Halesworth to Holton, and terminating in the parish of Southwold, at or near the road leading from Southwold Common to the Salt Works, in Southwold, at a point about 170 yards south of Park Lane, which said railway will pass from, in, through, or into the parishes or other places following, that is to say:- Halesworth, Holton St. Peter, Wenhaston, Blyford, Blythburgh, Bulcamp, Walberswick, and Southwold, or some of them, all being in the county of Suffolk.
>
> To enable the Company to purchase or take by compulsion or otherwise, lands and hereditaments in the parishes or places aforesaid, and to confer, vary, repeal or extinguish all other rights and privileges which might impede or interfere with the purposes of the intended Act, and to acquire by compulsion land and hereditaments which the construction of the railway and works may reclaim wholly or partially from tidal waters.
>
> To levy, alter existing, and grant exemptions from tolls, rates, and duties in respect of the use of the intended railway, stations and works.
>
> To enable the Company to cross, stop up, alter, or divert, whether temporarily or permanently, any roads, highways, footways, railways, telegraph poles or apparatus, sewers, bridges, works or buildings, tramways, aqueducts, canals, streams and rivers, within or near the aforesaid parishes and places which it may be convenient to cross, stop up, alter or divert for the purposes of the intended Act.
>
> To enable the Company, and the Corporation of Southwold to enter into agreements for the purchase, lease, or user of lands and hereditaments, and to enable the said Corporation to take and hold a rent-charge or rent-charges of the Company in payment thereof.
>
> A plan and section in duplicate of the proposed railway, and all lands which the intended Act will give power to purchase by compulsion, a book of reference to the plan and an Ordnance Map will be deposited with the Clerk of the Peace for the county of Suffolk, at his office at Ipswich; and a copy of so much of the said plan, section, and book of reference as relates to any parish or extra-parochial place, will be deposited in the case of a parish, with the parish clerk thereof at his residence; in the case of an extra-parochial place, with the parish clerk of some place adjoining thereto, at his residence; and each such deposit will be made on or before the 30th November, 1875, and will be accompanied by a copy of this notice; and printed copies of the intended Act will be deposited in the Private Bill Office of the House of Commons, on or before the 21st day of December 1875.

Road, opposite the Angel Inn. It then continued as tramway No. 6 in the Act, passing through some or all of the parishes of Uggeshall, Brampton, Westhall, Southern Holton and Halesworth where it was to terminate in Bridge Street at a point 470 yards beyond the bridge carrying the GER over the Halesworth to Holton Road. The project subsequently failed through lack of capital, as Southwold inhabitants were dubious of the company's intentions. A number of local residents, who had initially shown interest in the scheme and offered to purchase shares, were later sued for the balance of money required to meet the outstanding promotional expenses. The company was ultimately wound up in November 1874, despite opening a section of tramway between Yarmouth South Town and Gorleston.

Disappointed at the failure of the tramway, the first practical steps were taken in 1875 to provide a railway to Southwold at comparatively low cost. The month of October was busy for the promoters of the line. A meeting was held at Halesworth chaired by Charles Easton of Easton Hall, whilst a second was held at Southwold under the chairmanship of the Earl of Stradbroke of Henham Hall. Both men were influential local landowners and beneficiaries, and it was thought their presence and support would inspire a general feeling of confidence. Arthur C. Pain, a Civil Engineer, who had been trained by R.P. Brereton, Isambard Kingdom Brunel's chief assistant, with particular experience in light railways, and actively involved with the standard gauge Culm Valley Light Railway from Tiverton Junction to Hemyock in Devon, addressed both gatherings and explained the plan to build a light railway to a gauge of 2 feet 6 inches, which would be considerably cheaper to construct than a standard gauge line, whilst ongoing maintenance would be proportionally reduced. The argument for the railway was further enhanced when Richard C. Rapier, of the Ipswich firm of Ransomes & Rapier, announced he had constructed a locomotive as an experiment, suitable for running on the 2 feet 6 inches gauge and weighing a mere 1 tons 5 cwt. During trials it had travelled at a speed of 20 mph hauling a load of 20 tons, and this locomotive had since been sent to work in China. Both gatherings carried the resolution, *'this meeting having heard the description of the projected railway from Halesworth to Southwold, is of the opinion that the two towns and intervening district would be greatly benefited by it, and the meeting warmly approves the proposal.'* The encouraging response for the line and the backing of a number of influential and wealthy landowners led the promoters to formulate a temporary committee for the Southwold Railway. Colonel Heneage Bagot-Chester of Henstead Hall was elected Chairman, whilst Arthur C. Pain and James B. Walton were appointed Engineers, and H.R. Allen, a local solicitor, as Secretary. The first company office was based at Halesworth as all the nominated Directors came from that town. Notices of the proposal (reproduced left) were published in the local press on 12th November 1875.

The title of Blyth Valley Railway was subsequently altered to Southwold Railway. The GER raised no serious objections to the bill, regarding the railway as a feeder to their own system and obviating the need to provide a branch line of their own.

The Southwold Railway Act 1876 duly received the Royal Assent on 24th July 1876 (39 and 40 Vic cap clxxxix) and sanctioned the building of Railway No. 1, 8 miles 6 furlongs and 9 chains in length commencing near the Great Eastern Railway station in the parish of Halesworth and terminating near the Gate House in the parish of Southwold; Railway No. 2, 3 furlongs 8¼ chains in length commencing near the River Blyth Navigation in the parish of Halesworth and terminating in the same parish by a junction with railway No. 1; and Railway No. 3, 2 furlongs and 30 links in length commencing by a junction with Railway No. 1 in the parish of Southwold and terminating at Black Shore (sic) Quay in the same parish. Under the provisions of the Act the company was not to take properties numbered 20a, 20b and 20c in the parish of Halesworth without the consent of Mary Crabtree and Fanny Crabtree or other owners for the time being.

The £40,000 estimated cost of construction was to be raised by the issue of 4,000 £10 shares with borrowing powers of £13,000, once the whole capital was subscribed and half actually paid up. Three years were allowed for the compulsory purchase of land and five years for completion of works. Clause 21 of the statute permitted the company to build the railway to any gauge but not less than 2 feet 6 inches; Clause 22 allowed the railway to cross road No. 40 in the parish of Wenhaston on the level whilst Clause 23 required the company to build a bridge with 15 feet width to carry the parish road over the line in the parish of Holton St. Peter. Clause 25 stipulated that Railway No. 1 between its commencement and road No. 5 in the parish of Holton St. Peter was to be constructed according to the working plans agreed between the Engineer of the Southwold Railway and the Engineer of the Great Eastern Railway. In the event of a dispute the President of the Institute of Civil Engineers was to appoint an arbiter. In constructing the remainder of Railways No's 1 and 2 through or over land belonging to the GER the company was not to deviate from the centre line of the railway laid down upon the deposited plans without the consent of officers of the GER. All works on Railways No's 1 and 2 were to be constructed to the reasonable satisfaction of the GER Engineer and were not to interfere with the safe working of that railway. Clause 26 required the SR not to interfere with the lands and properties of the GER except when absolutely necessary for the construction of the railway, when the main line company would grant easement in accordance with Clause 27 of the statute. The Southwold Company was by Clauses 29 to 32 not to interfere with any telegraph line or equipment owned by Her Majesty's Postmaster General, whose personnel could at any reasonable time require access to railway land for maintenance and repairs of such equipment. The SR was also liable to pay compensation for any damage caused.

The Board of Trade permitted light earthworks during construction as well as a simple form of signalling provided speeds were restricted to 25 mph or less and loads were limited, all in accordance with the Regulations of Railways Act 1868.

The initial Directors of the Southwold Railway were Colonel Heneage Charles Bagot-Chester, Edward Stisted, Mostyn Price, William Martin Leake, Francis Evans Babington, George Crafter Croft and Robert William Burleigh. In mid-November 1876 Arthur C. Pain wrote to the GER headquarters advising that the Directors of the Southwold Railway were desirous of constructing the line from Southwold to Halesworth and asked for assistance in the form of a rebate in traffic exchanged with the main line company. On 28th November the GER General Manager replied the company could not entertain such a rebate.

Surveying works for the new railway commenced in the spring of 1877 and in a letter of 3rd April to Southwold Corporation permission was sought for the contractor, when appointed, to enter Corporation land. On 29th August 1877 T.H. Jellicoe was appointed Company Secretary as a replacement for H.R. Allen, who had resigned after being asked by a number of landowners and farmers to act for them in an official capacity in future negotiations with the railway company. The Board of Directors at this time included the Mayor of Southwold, J.E. Grubbe and Richard C. Rapier.

The prospectus for the proposed railway, issued on 3rd November 1877, stated a provisional contract valued at £30,000 for the construction of the line, stations and infrastructure, had been awarded to Charles Chambers of Westminster. The Bristol Carriage & Wagon Works Company had been asked to supply engines, carriages, wagons and brake vans for a price of £4,000. Included in the document was a report on traffic expectations by C.J. Wall, a former Manager of the Bristol & Exeter Railway, whom Pain had become acquainted with in his dealings with the Culm Valley line. Wall made the recommendation for the adoption of a gauge of 3 feet which, if approved, would cost more than the estimate but would provide additional carrying capacity in the rolling stock. Despite the issue of this prospectus the Directors had been unable to raise sufficient funds for the building of the railway and Chambers refused to enter into a binding contract until he was assured the necessary land would be made available. Two days after the issue of the prospectus, on 5th November, the original board of Directors resigned en masse and was replaced by an entirely new board except for Rapier and the Chairman Colonel Bagot-Chester. Initially board meetings were transferred from Southwold to Rapier's London

Southwold Railway Act 1876: front page.

office, and when Rapier was subsequently appointed Chairman on 20th December 1877 the railway business was wholly conducted from the London office with the minimum of local influence, except for minor day-to-day decisions.

As preliminary work commenced a dispute arose when the Company Engineer wished to enter adjoining land owned by the GER near Halesworth and in the parish of Holton St. Peter. A notice of treat was served on the GER on 14th April 1878 but the charge for easement could not be agreed. The matter was the subject of arbitration and Francis Vigers of 4 Frederick Place, Old Jewry, London EC, the appointed Engineer acting in his capacity as arbiter, visited both sites. His decision was not made until 10th January 1879 when he determined the SR should pay £371 to the GER in settlement of temporary easement.

In the meantime the new Chairman, with his business contacts, sought financial backing and soon obtained a £5,000 advance from the English & Foreign Credit Company so that the compulsory purchase of land could be arranged. A revised contract was then prepared. The Contractor commenced work on 3rd May 1878 and was soon ordering materials and sleepers, the latter shipped direct from Norway to Southwold. The ship *Ida Gesina* docked on 25th June and a second ship the *Ibesstina* arrived on 5th July with consignments of sleepers from Gothenburg. The Tredegar Iron Company was contracted to ship rails direct to the Suffolk port, whilst Ransomes & Rapier of Ipswich provided signalling equipment and pointwork. As the Contractor progressed, Charles List, the Southwold blacksmith, was called upon to provide many items of miscellaneous ironwork. The contract for the building of the swing bridge over the River Blyth was awarded to Mr Double, who was also responsible for the construction of Hammersmith Suspension Bridge in London and for the conveyance of Cleopatra's Needle to the Embankment in London. Then on 17th July 1878 Southwold Corporation ordered its seal to be affixed to the document for the conveyance of lands to the SR Company.

Five days later, on 22nd July 1878, Thomas Jellicoe reported the company had acquired all the land for a distance of five miles through the parishes of Southwold, Walberswick and Blythburgh and also one mile in the parishes of Halesworth and Holton St. Peter. Negotiations were in progress for the early acquisition of the remaining two and a half miles. The Contractor had ordered all the sleepers direct from Norway, whilst rails, fastenings and fencing were on order. He also reported:

> *'Eighteen thousand sleepers have been delivered to Blackshore Quay, and the remainder are being shipped. A considerable length of fencing has been erected, and a quantity more has been delivered, and is in the course of erection. The whole of the rails have been rolled by the Tredegar Iron Company in South Wales. The first shipload had been delivered, and the remainder are lying at Newport awaiting shipment.'*

Along the line two bridges had been erected and a mile and one quarter of earth works completed at the Halesworth end of the railway ready for the laying of the permanent way. Southwold station and yard and half a mile of formation at the eastern end of the line was similarly waiting the laying of track. The cutting through Southwold Common was being excavated and the spoil used to form an embankment across the marshes. On 30th July the *Harriet* docked at Blackshore Quay with a consignment of iron, believed to have been components of the swing bridge.

The GER Directors made one of their periodical visits to their system on 1st and 2nd October 1878 and between inspections at Beccles and Snape, journeyed to Southwold to view the new railway under construction. The Chairman on his return duly reported to the chief officers of the company on the adoption of 3 feet gauge instead of the 2 feet 6 inches originally proposed.

On 29th January 1879 Colonel Bagot-Chester resigned from the board. At this time Thomas H. Jellicoe was Secretary and Arthur C. Pain, Engineer. On 7th February no fewer than three vessels, the *Eliza*, the *Victoria* and the *Tertins* arrived at Blackshore Quay from Ipswich with consignments of iron rails. This delivery enabled the Contractor to complete the track laying between Southwold and Blythburgh. The rails for the western end of the line were delivered by rail direct from Newport to Halesworth GER goods yard.

In March 1879 the Chairman advised a crowded gathering in Southwold Town Hall that work was progressing satisfactorily, despite the doubts expressed by many of the attendees. He reiterated *'in a very few months you will actually see the iron horse marching triumphantly into town'*. In truth, the company was experiencing difficulty raising capital for railway No. 1, the main line, and the Contractor, despite having received plans for the two branches as early as 30th April 1878, was instructed to concentrate on the line from Halesworth to Southwold. At the Trinity Luncheon held on 10th June 1879 Charles Chambers, the Contractor, announced to the gathering that he hoped the line would be opened to traffic before the summer was over. Because of the difficulties raising capital for the main scheme no work was carried out on the branches and powers for their construction were allowed to lapse. The deposited plans showed the junction of railway No. 2 with railway No. 1 was to have been at 0 miles 33 chains from Halesworth, whence it diverged on the north side to run under the eastern arch of two arch bridge at 0 miles 30 chains before continuing under the GER line to curve sharply and terminate at the River Blyth Navigation Quay. During these early years Pain was undoubtedly the power behind the throne as far as the SR was concerned and he was subsequently appointed Manager on 30th August 1879.

Meanwhile, on Sunday and Monday 21st and 22nd July 1879, continuous rain brought flooding to the Blyth valley. The road which bisected the SR at Wenhaston was carried on a raised causeway across low-lying land between the railway and Blyford Bridge. As the river flooded so the causeway acted as a dam, causing a lake to form and inundate the causeway and the railway. The Directors were annoyed and complained to the local authority and by Friday 26th July Mr Turner, the Parish Surveyor held a meeting to arrange the repair of the causeway pending future agreement between the railway company and the Parish Council to provide a footbridge over the river, which would replace the causeway and leave the road level with the surrounding land.

As work was nearing completion arrangements were made with the Board of Trade for the railway to be inspected but correspondence was received from Messrs Cross and Ram, Solicitors of Halesworth, regarding the access road to Wenhaston Mill, which bisected the line at 1 mile 72¼ chains from Halesworth; the firm complained on behalf of their clients that the unattended occupational crossing was likely to be busy with carts proceeding to and from the mill and suggested the railway company provide a gatekeeper.

Major General Charles Scrope Hutchinson conducted the official Board of Trade Inspection on Friday 19th September 1879. In attendance were Arthur C. Pain and Richard Rapier of the SR, and J. Dutton, the GER Superintendent for the Eastern District. The railway was single line 8 miles 63.5 chains in length commencing in the Great Eastern Railway station yard at Halesworth and terminating at Southwold. Hutchinson noted the Act of Parliament obtained in 1876 was for a railway of any gauge not less than 2½ feet and that the line had been constructed with a gauge of 3 feet. The sharpest curve at Halesworth station was of 5 chains radius, whilst the steepest gradient on the line was 1 in 62. Stations were provided at Halesworth, Wenhaston and Southwold. At Halesworth the GER booking office and waiting rooms were to be used whilst an overbridge and stairs (temporary at the time of inspection) provided a connection from both main line platforms to the Southwold Railway single platform. At Wenhaston and Southwold, Hutchinson found that proper accommodation had been provided whilst the platforms at all three stations were only 9 inches above rail level. He remarked, *'Considering the character of the line and the carriages provided are all entered by steps at the ends, there being no side doors, I do not think this low height need be objected to in the present instance'*.

The signals and points were interlocked similarly to the plan adopted on the Culm Valley Light Railway in Devon (of which A.C. Pain was Engineer) and distant signals were dispensed with as the maximum permitted speed on the railway was 16 mph and the line was to be worked on the 'One Engine in Steam' method. Turning to civil engineering matters the inspector noted part of the line passed through very boggy ground, whilst there were no deep cuttings or high embankments along the formation. The two bridges over the line had spans of 20 feet and 29 feet respectively, both had cement concrete abutments whilst the former had a concrete top and the latter a timber span. The local road authorities had complained of the state of both structures and representatives from Suffolk County Council, Sir John R. Blois and the Reverend C.W. Roberts accompanied by the County Surveyor, H.M. Eaton met Hutchinson on the day of the inspection. In the case of the bridge built entirely of concrete there was a slight crack visible in each abutment but except for these the structure appeared to be properly built and to be strong enough for its purpose. The other bridge at Blythburgh constructed with concrete abutments and timber span was not considered the usual type for *'an important turnpike road'*. On examination the abutments and longitudinal beams appeared substantial but the planking on the beams measuring 12 inches by 3 inches with a 3 feet bearing which was in Hutchinson's opinion was:

'Barely sufficient to support the heavy traction engines which are used in this district having sometimes as much weight as 5 tons on a wheel. I consequently think that no time should be lost in adding another layer of 3 inch planking over the existing one.'

The fencing adjoining the bridge was considered sufficiently strong provided it received attention if the banking settled.

The two underbridges were also inspected, one of 45 feet span had a wrought iron lattice girder supported on concrete abutments faced with brickwork whilst the other with two spans of 20 feet was constructed entirely of concrete. There were also four viaducts, three constructed entirely of timber and the fourth the opening swing bridge built of iron over the River Blyth approached by four timber spans of 22 feet each.

Hutchinson noted the swing bridge was composed of two wrought iron lattice main girders 146 feet in length connected at the bottom with rolled cross (iron) girders and in the centre at the top with T irons. The bridge was supported on a central cylinder of wrought iron carried on cast iron screw piles. On the inside of the circumference of the cylinder there were rollers on which the bridge revolved offering two openings, each 60 feet wide. The shore ends of the girders rested on wooden piles. The inspector was advised the bridge would only be opened about three times during the year; that no special arrangements were considered necessary for opening and therefore the span was opened by hauling it round by means of ropes from stages erected up and down the river which received the ends of the girders when swung fully open. The bridge was opened for the inspector who commented that it *'swung very easily and appears to have been constructed well'*. Hutchinson suggested to the engineer that some improvements be made in the bearing of the ends of the girders. The bridge when in position was locked by means of the Annett's key on the end of the Train Staff, which the engine working the traffic was always to carry. The *Suffolk Chronicle* had earlier reported on 27th August 1879 the span would see little use as it was expected on average only one vessel per year would pass through.

In addition to the viaducts three culverts with timber spans were also examined. The structures appeared to have sufficient theoretical strength under load and were standing well. The wrought iron girders on other bridges gave moderate deflections when tested but the wooden girders, especially those adjacent to the Blyth bridge,

Arthur Claude Pain in 1901. He was the SR engineer but later took over as Company Chairman. He was also engineer of the Culm Valley Light Railway between Tiverton Junction on the Great Western Railway and Hemyock in Devon and the Axminster & Lyme Regis Light Railway on the Dorset/Devon border, connecting with the London & South Western Railway. *Author's collection*

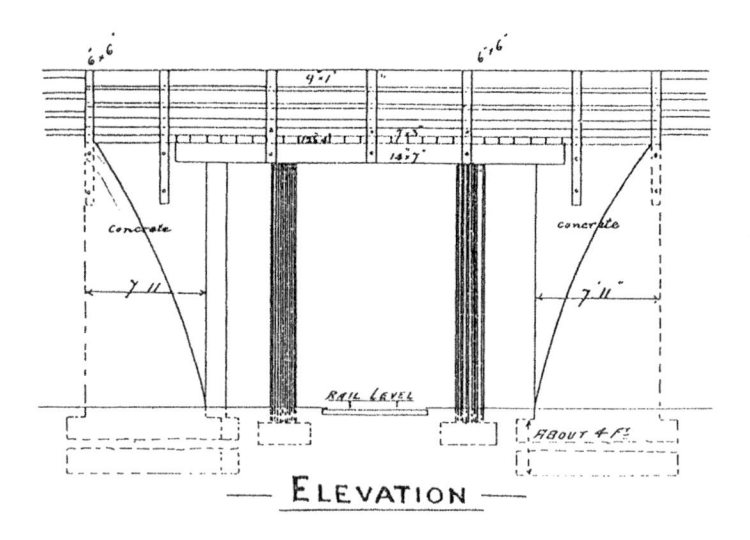

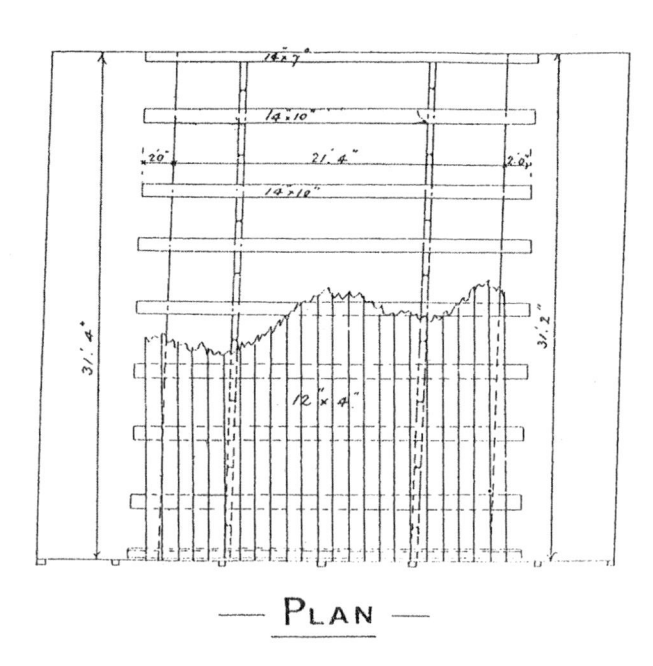

GER survey of SR overbridge at Blythburgh No. 11 at 4 miles 72 chains

were considered *'too springy'* and it was suggested this could be reduced by bolting the two thicknesses of timber composing the girders more closely together. The Major General also stipulated the provision of additional supports for the ends of the beams of the culverts at 2 miles 64 chains and 2 miles 69½ chains. The one authorised level crossing of a public road at Wenhaston station was provided with proper gates but complaints made by Messrs Cross and Ram as to the non-erection of a gate keeper's hut at the private road crossing leading to Wenhaston Mill caused Hutchinson to investigate. Whilst alluding that the road appeared to be used *'a great deal by carts going to and from the mill'* and that it would be desirable for a gatekeeper to be stationed at the crossing, he stated the BOT had no powers to make any order on the subject. Turning to the fencing alongside the railway the Major General found it was partly ordinary post and rail fence, partly a ditch without any fence and partly existing hedges. In consequence of the soft bottom where the ditch alone had been employed, the engineer was of the opinion that it would of itself be sufficient protection. Hutchinson did not agree and thought a ditch alone could not be regarded as a substitute for a proper fence. He therefore stipulated the provision of full post and rail fencing within six weeks of the date of inspection. The other requirements included:

1. Coating of the timber tops of bridges with a fireproof composition.
2. At Wenhaston station: adjustment to the facing points and interlocking of the catch siding with the signals; also provision of lamp irons on the level crossing gates.
3. Covering up the opening at the side of the underbridge at 0 miles 14 chains.

Hutchinson concluded the rolling stock for working the line consisted of two 6-wheeled tank locomotives each weighing 11 tons 15 cwt and a sufficient number of Composite First and Third Class carriages on six wheels weighing 10 tons loaded and wagons weighing 6 tons loaded. Subject to the remarks contained in his report and the receipt of a satisfactory undertaking as to the mode of working the line, the completion of the fencing and re-inspection, he was of the opinion the BOT need not object to the opening of the line to passenger traffic. The opening was subject to certain conditions, that speed did not exceed 16 mph and weight on the wheel of any vehicle did not exceed 2 tons. Because of the character of the railway and slow speed to be observed, the requirement for engine turntables was dispensed. In conclusion the railway officers were advised to keep careful watch on the concrete structures to detect any deterioration.

Some time after the inspection, H.M. Eyton, the County Survey reported the Southwold Directors *'seemed to care very little whether the bridge at Blythburgh was strong enough or not'*. He told them *'they would have to repair the structure if anything went wrong and they said they intended to do so'*. Whether the conversation was held within earshot of the inspector is not recorded. The magistrates at the Suffolk Quarter Sessions discussed the matter and subsequently wrote to the BOT and SR. The Southwold Directors undertook to take the necessary steps to improve the bridge.

In a letter dated 22nd September the BOT confirmed to Messrs Cross and Ram that they did not have sufficient powers to compel the SR Company to provide a gatekeeper to attend to the level crossing near Wenhaston Mill, though it was considered a good idea. Gates were subsequently provided but without attendance by a resident gatekeeper.

On Tuesday 23rd September 1879 an official luncheon was held at the Swan Hotel, Southwold to celebrate the completion of the railway and the planned opening to traffic the following day. Some of the speeches were less than complimentary and both the *Suffolk Chronicle* and *Eastern Daily Press* record references to the lack of local support and even opposition to the scheme. However, mention was also made of the possible extension of the line from Southwold to Lowestoft so the gathering departed in an optimistic mood.

A total of 39 acres of land had been required for the railway, including owners in Blythburgh parish selling 7 acres, Walberswick parish 6 acres, Halesworth and Holton parishes 2 acres and Wenhaston parish 4 acres from two owners. Five acres of land was rented at Southwold at £521 0s 0d per annum, one acre from Walberswick Common Land Trustees at £10 0s 0d per annum and one acre at Halesworth at £20 0s 0d per annum.

2

Opening of the Line

Heavy and torrential rain fell during the ensuing night across Suffolk and as rivers burst their banks, the line was flooded near Wenhaston Mill. It was decided the opening of the railway to traffic should proceed and the first Up train on Wednesday 24th September 1879, driven by W.G. Jackson arrived at Halesworth just after 9.00am. The driver expressed some doubts about his ability to get the return train through the flood waters, which were continuing to rise. The train made the return trip and safely arrived at Southwold a few minutes late. The *Halesworth Times* reporting the event.

'The London visitors started from Liverpool Street found the dainty little engine and carriages of the French-American pattern waiting to convey them to the ancient borough. The party at once to use an Americanism "got aboard" and gently and swiftly glided over the light railway till Wenhaston was reached. Here the party alighted and examined the pretty little station, which is a happy combination of cheapness and convenience and it is at the same time a model of what good architectural taste can do with very circumscribed materials. The motion of the carriages is remarkably easy. The carriages themselves were airy and spacious, and very superior in construction, with an alley running through them. We trust they will do much to revolutionise our present stupid and, to protect females and sometimes males, dangerous system of rail travel.'

The 'London Visitors' were lucky to get to Southwold for the flooding at Wenhaston thereafter effectively blocked the line for the rest of

The circa 1904 interior of one of the 6-wheel Cleminson coaches, which possessed large side windows as well as top lights, with passengers sitting longitudinally along the carriage sides facing inwards. Because of the intense heat generated through the glass on hot sunny days, curtains were provided but only on the south side of the vehicle. In the absence of steam heating in winter months the company placed straw on the floor for some element of warmth but the layer was always subject to occupation by spiders and other insects to the consternation of travellers. It was not unknown for mice to invade when coaches were berthed in sidings. Then there was also the risk of fire!
Southwold Museum

the day, and the remaining trains only ran between Southwold and Wenhaston. By midday a large crowd had assembled at Halesworth, intending to travel on the new railway and visit the fete and gala at Southwold. On being advised at the junction station of the flooding and cancellation of trains, many travelled forward by road. After arrival in the town they found many attractions, including horse and pony racing as well as races for children and novelty races for adults. Three triumphal arches were erected across the main road in the town and the eventful day was concluded with a torchlight procession.

After the opening of the line a luncheon was held at the Swan Hotel, Southwold; at the post-meal speeches Charles Chambers stated there was one subject which he was sorry to have to raise: that in a place like Southwold, so far removed from railway communications, there had been so much apathy and such little public spirit in the way of providing a railway to the town. *'A great deal had been done by certain people, to use the expression, "crab" or undermine the railway'*. Nothing good had been said of the railway, on the contrary much that had been expressed was, in his opinion, *'silly and ridiculous'*. The flooding which had almost wrecked the day for the SR brought a further comment in the *Halesworth Times* calling for the causeway to be removed and replaced by a footbridge, although the implications were clear: as the SR would stand to gain the most by its replacement, then the SR should bear the largest part of the cost.

A week after the opening the SR suffered its first case of vandalism when Maria Baxter, a single woman from Blythburgh, smashed the window of a railway carriage. She was apprehended and later at Halesworth Petty Sessions pleaded guilty, for which she was fined 1s 0d, plus 15s 0d damages and 8s 6d costs. Later in the year, in December during construction work on the new footbridge linking the Great Eastern and Southwold stations at Halesworth, a workman named Copping sustained injuries to his face and head when the rope lifting a heavy girder fractured causing the metal section to fall and hit the unfortunate individual. He was conveyed to Beccles Hospital and detained.

When the line opened to traffic it had been the intention to open a station at Blythburgh but additional land had to be purchased before construction could commence and the station, in the shadow of the famous Holy Trinity church subsequently opened to traffic in December 1879.

Major General C.S. Hutchinson re-inspected the railway on 23rd February 1880 and found the requirements stipulated on 20th September 1879 had been completed. During his examination Hutchinson observed a number of weak spots in the lineside hedges, which the engineer promised to rectify. He also stipulated that guard rails be provided on the viaduct over the River Blyth; at the bridge at 3 mile 61 chains and for the blocks which carried the ends of the girders on the Blyth viaduct to be secured to prevent them being shaken out of position by the vibration of trains crossing the span. The cracks in the concrete abutments of the bridges showed no signs of increasing but the inspector stipulated the careful watch continue. Subject to early completion of the outstanding work Hutchinson belatedly sanctioned the opening of the line to passenger traffic. In his report the Major General advised he had notified the County Surveyor and Mr Eaton of his intended visit but neither gentleman bothered to attend. During the inspection Hutchinson also examined the new station and siding at Blythburgh and noted the arrangements were similar to those at Wenhaston and immediate use was sanctioned.

Within a month of the opening to traffic the SR Directors had sought authority from the BOT to work the SR as a Light Railway but it was pointed out the line was not passed in the statute as a light railway. This error had to be rectified and was achieved by placing an announcement in the *East Anglian Daily Times* for three weeks. On completion of this, and after consultation with Major General Hutchinson, the BOT issued a Conditions and Regulations Certificate on 11th March 1880 for the line to be maintained and worked as a Light Railway in accordance with the 1868 Regulation of Railways Act. The BOT noted the railway, as constructed, conformed to the legal requirements and was to be operated on the 'one engine in steam or two locomotives coupled together principle' using the Train Staff for authority to travel over the single line. The Annett's key attached to this Train Staff was used to unlock and release the mechanism to operate the swing bridge. The maximum speed was revised to 16 mph, reduced from 25 mph, and the maximum axle loading was restricted to 2 tons. Subsequent Light Railway Orders of 1902, 1907 and 1913 all referred to the line being a light railway.

In the same month an inquiry was held before an arbiter, A. Garrard, at the Angel Hotel, Halesworth, to resolve the claim made by the Reverend John L. Ewen against the SR. Land owned by Ewen in the parish of Wenhaston had been bisected by the railway, which cut through his pastures in nine places and involved two tenancies. The plaintiff giving evidence reported that in order to reach all the farmed land the tenants had to negotiate no fewer than six occupational crossings. Furthermore the railway was not properly fenced, thus allowing animals, notably sheep to stray on the line, and in one instance trespass had forced a train to stop. The tenants had of necessity been forced to make good the fencing at their own expense. The waterway leading to Wenhaston Mill, which formed part of one of the tenancies, was also blocked preventing barges from reaching the mill. Ewen advised Garrard that originally the SR had promised to build a siding to the mill provided he withdrew his opposition to the Bill before Parliament. This he had done but A.C. Pain counteracted saying the offer was conditional on the landlord accepting the SRs terms and was withdrawn when the case was taken to arbitration. The tenant of the mill and twelve acres of adjoining pasture, William Scarfe Kett, had dealt with Halesworth Estate Agent Charles Duncan Smith, who acted on behalf of the railway company. Smith in evidence stated that it was his understanding the protected level crossing, which now gave access to the mill, was to have a gatekeeper, probably at the company's expense. Kett then advised that since leaving the coal trade he was not concerned with the loss of water access but the gated crossing was discouraging farmers from delivering corn to the mill. It would cost him 1s 0d per day to employ a boy as a gatekeeper and when he had accepted £50 in compensation from the SR Company it was on the understanding they would provide a gatekeeper. At the conclusion of the hearing Arthur Pain stressed that despite what was said in evidence, it was always the intention to build the siding to the mill but only bad weather had prevented the work being executed. The arbiter subsequently reserved his decision.

On 21st May 1880 T.H. Farrer, Secretary to the BOT, authorised the BOT certificate allowing the Southwold Company to raise an additional £9,000 capital by new shares issue, either wholly ordinary or wholly preferential or part ordinary and part preferential. The rate of interest paid on any preferential shares was not to exceed 6 per cent per annum. The company was also granted powers to borrow a further £3,000.

By early June 1880 the work on the footbridge at Wenhaston was completed and on 8th June the *Halesworth Times* reported it had been constructed under the superintendence of the surveyor John Turner and planned and constructed by carpenter H. Webb. Known locally as the 'Tay Bridge', the structure had a span of about 40 feet. It is uncertain who financed the project but the SR for their part deepened and widened the trackside drainage in association with the scheme.

In July 1880 much excitement was caused at Southwold station when a policeman tried to serve a warrant on 23-year-old Porter Dovey, who was accused of embezzling some of the company's money. The miscreant fled the scene and tried to hide in the nearby Buss Creek but only succeeded in falling in the water. The policeman to his credit rescued the poor individual, who was in danger of drowning. Later at Suffolk Summer Assizes, Dovey pleaded guilty to embezzling three sums of money, totalling £16 2s 6d from the SR. In his defence he claimed he had intended to pay back the money before discovery. He was sentenced to 18 months imprisonment with hard labour. Less than a week after the arrest of Dovey the driver of a train noticed *'two little urchins'* placing stones on the rail at the crossing between Holton and Halesworth. The driver stopped the train short of the obstruction and the fireman, being younger and more fleet of foot, together with the Wenhaston station master, gave chase and apprehended the pair. The eldest boy, who was variously reported as being of seven or twelve years of age, pleaded guilty to *'attempting to upset a train'* and was sentence to be detained in the local police station until 10.00pm and to receive three strokes of the birch. The other boy was considered to be too young to be sentenced.

During the construction of the railway access to three meadows, amounting to nine acres of pasture belonging to Robert Haward, a land agent and surveyor and let to his son, had been blocked. In truth an occupational crossing had been installed but no gates were provided. The crossing was dangerous to use as the approach involved negotiating an embankment and a newly excavated ditch. Hayward was adamant hay waggons drawn by two horses could only negotiate the embankment if a third horse was hitched to the vehicle and cattle often strayed onto the railway because of the lack of gates. Haward sued the SR Company for damages, which he claimed were caused by the construction of the railway, rendering the approaches to the meadows *'more difficult and dangerous'*. The Directors vehemently objected and the case was brought before Halesworth Magistrates Court in September 1880. Giving evidence Pain opined, *'he need not tell the Magistrates that in the construction of a railway there were always large numbers of claims'*. He iterated that the Solicitor was of the opinion Haward had no claim against the company. The BOT inspector had approved the works and sanctioned opening of the line and therefore the company had decided against compensation. The company, however, lost the case and was required to pay £49 19s 0d damages and 10 guineas costs, although it is unclear whether the installation of the gates and easing of gradients on the approach to the crossing were also part of the settlement. In the same month Platelayer Clarke was caught poaching a pheasant at Walberswick. Not only was he poaching but he was stealing the game out of season and was fined £1 0s 0d with 12s 3d costs and warned to his future conduct and continuing employment with the SR Company.

On 30th August 1880 Thomas Jellicoe resigned as Secretary and Arthur C. Pain, the Manager, assumed the duties combining the two posts. The SR advised the BOT on 7th October 1880 the siding serving Wenhaston Mill would be completed within one month and a request was made for inspection. The letter and plans were acknowledged the following day when the Board advised Major General Hutchinson would carry out the examination. The siding was completed at the end of October when the company wished to put it to use but as nothing further had been heard from the BOT a repeat letter was sent on 16th November seeking authority to bring the connection into use without the necessary inspection. The board advised there was no objection to the facility being used provided any recommendations of the inspecting officer were complied with. At the same time the new footbridge and railway drainage at Wenhaston encountered its first serious test when floodwater rose four feet in the vicinity of the footbridge, fortunately without adverse effect on the railway.

Major General C.S. Hutchinson again visited the Southwold line on 2nd December 1880 to inspection the new siding and connection from the main single line at 1 mile 74 chains from Halesworth serving Wenhaston Mill. He noted the points facing Up trains leading to the siding were locked and released by Annett's key attached to the Train Staff but stipulated the switch be connected by a stretcher rod firmly secured to each end. Subject to this work being completed Hutchinson agreed to the siding being brought into use.

In 1880 the number of passengers travelling on the line totalled 65,749 whilst 9,854 parcels were conveyed, goods traffic amounted to 1,485 tons, fish traffic 475 tons and mineral traffic 3,012 tons. Train mileage for the year was 30,818.

BOT Certificate authorising increase in capital.

Southwold station in the late 1890s showing the structure as originally built and before the extension. At the head of the train is No. 3 Blyth, followed by an unidentified van. The two coaches are First/Third Composites No's 1 and 5 in the cream/white livery with black lining, with the Third in the background in darker livery. The horse chestnut trees have only recently been planted and much of the area that was to become the station yard is fenced off and planted. The Swan Hotel already has an advertising sign up by the platform entrance. *Southwold Museum*

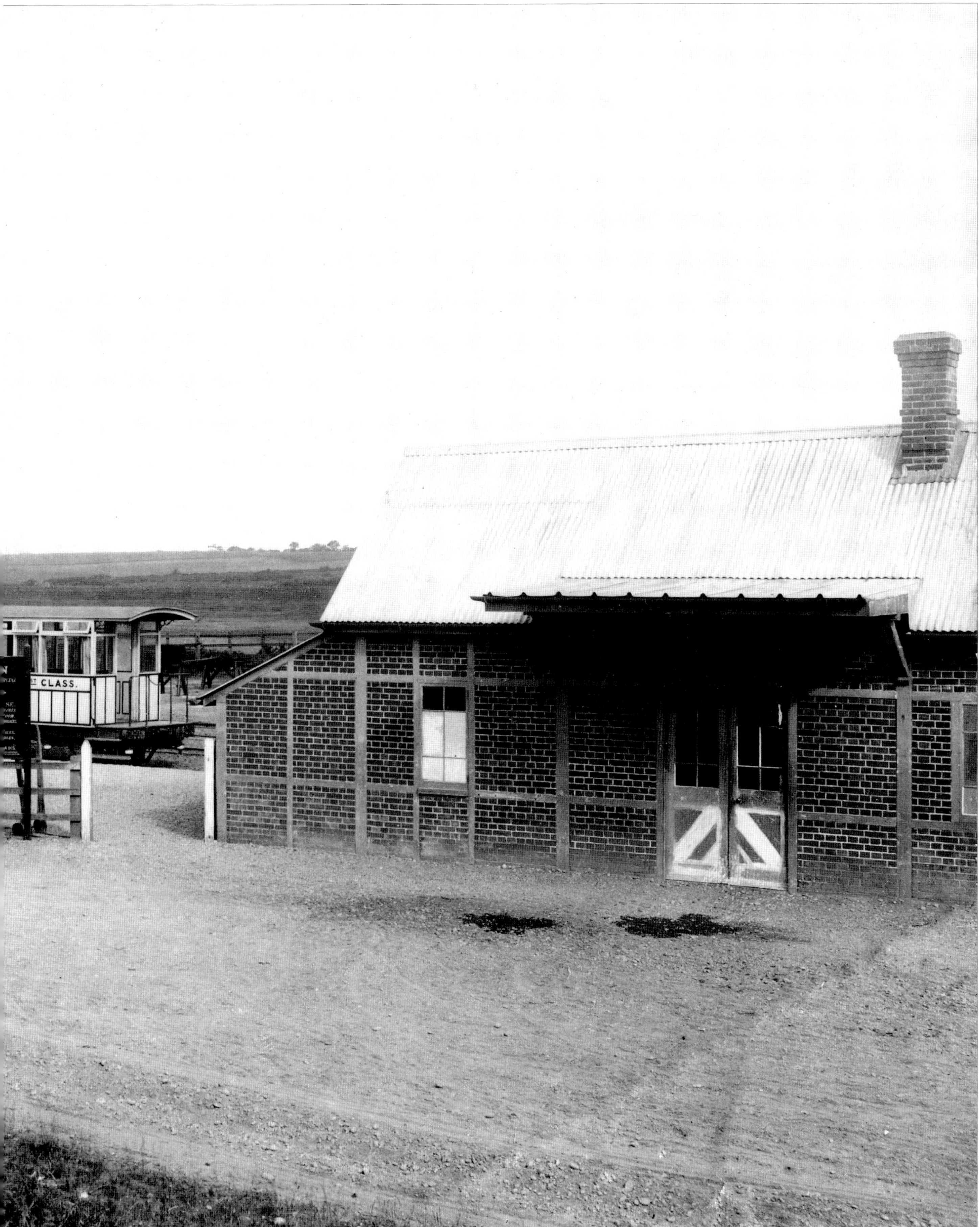
CLASS.

Walberswick station, 7 miles 46 chains from Halesworth, in the 1890s. The station was a very basic timber shed with corrugated iron roof, with a small stove to provide heating in the winter months. Two passengers are waiting for the next train, whilst a collection of boxes labelled Thompson & Stroud is heaped further along the platform and a 2-plank wagon is in the siding, its wheels apparently locked by a shunting pole through the spokes. Note that at this time the platform name sign was beyond the pile of boxes and there was a generous supply of lamp stands along the platform. The swing bridge can be seen in the distance at the end of the straight track, although all three men appear to be looking in the wrong direction for a train as the Down signal arm is lowered.

Southwold Museum

3

The Early Years

Severe weather affected train services in January 1881 when the combination of high winds and driving snow quickly filled the cuttings on the line. Services were suspended for two and a half days before the permanent way staff could clear the track of compacted snow. At the beginning of February 1881 the GER General Manager wrote to the Southwold Company asking for settlement of outstanding payments including £242 as the SR portion of the expense in respect of the provision of the connecting footbridge at Halesworth and £12 10s 0d as rental for the use of the booking office and services of the booking office staff at Halesworth for the period up to 31st December 1880, the GER staff issuing SR tickets from Halesworth. On 1st March the General Manager reported to the GE Traffic Committee that the SR Directors had replied saying they were very short of money and asking if payment could be withheld for a further twelve months. The postponement was agreed.

Increasingly trespassers used the swing bridge over the River Blyth as a quick and convenient way of crossing from Walberswick to Southwold, without entailing a long detour via Blythburgh. On 30th March 1881 matters came to a head when several members of the local stag hunt in progress on Walberswick Common chased their quarry along the railway and across the bridge, whilst an excited William Croft even tried to follow in his pony and trap. The driver of the approaching 3.31pm train ex Halesworth was aghast to see the entourage and braked his train to avoid a nasty accident. On arrival at Southwold the station master sent the engine back to the bridge for the driver to apprehend Croft, who was subsequently charged with three offences: endangering the safety of railway passengers, obstructing the passage of a train and throwing down a post and rail fence forming the boundary of the railway. Croft, evidently a gentleman with some respectability in the district, admitted guilt but the company agreed to withdraw the charges in exchange for a five guineas donation to the Railway Benevolent Fund. The Bench was delighted by the offer and applauded the attitude of the Southwold Railway Company whilst at the same time warning future trespassers would not receive such leniency and would face prosecution.

In May 1881 Driver Jackson, in charge of a train en route from Southwold to Halesworth, noticed a boy playing on the line between Blythburgh and Wenhaston. He sounded the locomotive whistle and then noticed a baby crawling towards the track. He immediately threw the engine into reverse and made an emergency brake application, whilst the fireman sounded the whistle continuously. Fortunately the train was halted only a few yards from the children. The incident was of sufficient seriousness to engender the *Halesworth Times* to publish a suitable warning to parents to stop children trespassing on the railway.

When the railway was promoted it was not the intention to open a station to serve the village of Walberswick but after petitioning by local inhabitants and a demand from walkers and picnickers using the Common the Directors relented and agreed to the provision of a simple structure located nearly a mile from the centre of the community. The station, together with a siding for goods traffic, was opened to traffic on 2nd September 1881, evidently without BOT approval. In the same year a goods transit shed was erected at Blythburgh to facilitate the storage of commodities awaiting transit of collection by tradesmen.

On 20th September a Mr Peak and a companion joined the 5.00pm train at Southwold and travelled together as far as Wenhaston, where Peak alighted to wend his way home. As he stood on the platform his friend called out asking him to accompany him on to Halesworth. Unfortunately the guard had already given the 'right away' to the driver and as the train started away Peak attempting to get back on board, missed his footing, slipped and was dragged along for several yards before the train could be stopped. Peak sustained head injuries and was taken home by horse and cart before being attended by Doctor Howard.

In mid-October 1881 a severe gale brought down two trees across the line and delayed an approaching train. Some passengers assisted the train crew to remove the obstructions so that the journey could continue. Then in December a north-easterly gale whipping off the sea blew off part of the roof of the engine shed at Southwold. The following year, in March 1882, W.G. Bridal, the Southwold station master, slipped and fell into the locomotive inspection pit as he crossed from the goods office to the station, fortunately without incurring injury. The *Halesworth Times* reported the minor incident as a warning to other users of the goods yard to take care.

The new station at Walberswick was inspected by Major General C.S. Hutchinson on 15th April 1882 and as well as examining the primitive passenger facilities he noted the single siding forming a facing junction for Up trains in the main single line, with points locked and released by Annett's key on the single line Train Staff. As the arrangements and accommodation were the same as that provided at other stations on *'this narrow gauge railway'*, Hutchinson sanctioned its opening for passenger traffic. The BOT incorrectly recorded the opening date as 1st July 1882. On 16th September of the same year the SR Directors wrote to Southwold Harbour Commissioners proposing to dredge shingle from the harbour to use as ballast on the railway permanent way. The work was to be carried out free of charge to the authorities and would at the same time help dredge the waterway, which was continually silting up, thus enabling larger vessels to dock and use the harbour facilities. The Commissioners, however, foolishly refused the offer and the Blyth navigation quickly became impassable for large vessels and much revenue was lost.

Severe storms combining with high tides during the last weekend of October 1882 resulted in Southwold being almost cut off from the outside world. Train services were initially unaffected but as the water continued to rise trains from Southwold terminated and started back from Wenhaston. By Sunday the flooding was gaining hold in the upper Blyth valley with the line inundated west of Blythburgh so that trains from Southwold could only reach that station. The company arranged for horse buses to convey passengers, parcels and mails on to Halesworth until Monday when the flooding had sufficiently subsided to permit trains to resume running between Southwold and Halesworth. Vandalism was evident one evening in March 1883 when in the darkness a plank of wood was placed across the line near Station Road bridge, Halesworth, in an attempt to derail the 8.09pm Halesworth to Southwold train. The railway was on an embankment at the point of impact and could have resulted in a serious accident. Although the driver was initially unaware of the obstruction, the guard irons on the locomotive brushed the timber aside before the train was brought to a halt and inspected for damage. None was found and the train continued its journey. The company subsequently offered a £20 reward for information leading to the conviction of the miscreants but nothing further was reported in the *Halesworth Times* to suggest they were apprehended.

Tuesday 7th August 1883 was an embarrassing day for the SR when the locomotive waiting to haul the last train from Halesworth to Southwold suffered a melted fusible plug, which allowed scalding steam to extinguish the fire and render the engine a total failure. The departure of the train had been retarded by over 30 minutes waiting for the late running GER service and the Southwold engine crew had allowed the water level in the boiler to drop. A telegraph message was sent to Southwold for assistance but this was not immediately available as steam had to be raised on the substitute engine before it could run light to Halesworth and rescue the failed locomotive and its train. Several passengers grew tired of waiting and availed themselves of road transport or walked to reach their destination. *'The majority with utmost good humour resigned themselves to their fate and waited'*, ultimately arriving at Southwold, three hours late at 11.45pm.

An annual supper was held for the company's employees on Friday 24th August 1883, paid for by *'patrons and merchants using the Southwold Railway'*. Arthur Pain addressed the assembly of twenty-five staff and thirty-five other guests and sponsors gathered at the Southwold Town Hall. The function was used as a morale boosting exercise by Pain, and he advised the gathering that from the opening of the line until 30th June 1883, a total of 235,793 passengers had been carried on the SR. He also claimed that Walberswick station was the smallest station in the country, yet *'11,083 passengers had alighted there'*. However, a source of concern was the total of passengers carried between January and June 1883, which at 22,593 was the lowest number travelling for the same period since the line opened. The reduction in the tonnage of minerals conveyed during the six months ending 30th June 1883 was offset by an increase in goods, parcels and fish traffic. He concluded:

'He believed most thoroughly in the future of Southwold, if he had not done so he would not have taken shares in the railway. Although the railway was not paying a dividend he hoped that as Southwold improved, so the prospects of the Company would also improve.'

On Wednesday 14th November 1883, Edward Court, the 17-year-old booking clerk in charge of Walberswick station, was killed in a fatal accident as he attempted to board a moving train. He had worked for the SR since the opening of the line, originally as a porter at Southwold and later on promotion to booking clerk at Southwold and then clerk-in-charge at Walberswick. On the fateful day, Court dealt with the first Up train, the 7.40am ex Southwold, which was due at Walberswick three minutes later. The young lad

Sat on top of the Southwold hill, the windmill and the lighthouse, built in 1887, will have been major landmarks for all tourists arriving by train. These two pictures were mounted side-by-side on a card, with a picture of SR No. 3 *Blyth* on the other side. *Michael Whitehouse collection*

then had two hours to while away waiting for the return working, the 9.07am from Halesworth, which arrived at Walberswick at 9.41am. As the next Up train was not due at the station until 11.03am it was the usual practice for Edward to travel by the 9.41am train from Walberswick to Southwold to help with duties at the terminus before returning on this next Up working. On the 9.07am train from Halesworth there were no passengers wishing to alight from or join at Walberswick so the driver slowed the train to walking pace to allow Court to leap aboard and join Arthur Wright in the guard's compartment. As he jumped, his foot slipped off the running board and he fell between the train and the platform and then under the wheels of the moving vehicle, sustaining fatal injuries. The train was immediately halted and the mutilated body removed from under the coach and placed in an empty First Class compartment for conveyance to Southwold. At the inquest, held later the same evening, Guard Wright testified that he had previously warned Court against the practice of leaping onto a moving train. On this occasion the lad was carrying a basket and a pair of gaiters under his arm, which might have impeded his movement. He grabbed the handrail but missed his footing and with his back to the carriage, fell between the train and the platform, being subsequently run over by the carriage wheels. The Coroner concluded no blame could be attached to anyone and the jury recorded a verdict of accidental death. Court's funeral was held in Southwold Church on the afternoon of Sunday 18th November, attended by all the railway company employees and he was afterwards interred in the churchyard.

The railway operated a train service on both Christmas Day and Boxing Day in 1883, when dense fog prevailed. The *Halesworth Times* was appreciative of the gesture and reported *'holiday traffic on the Southwold line was on a par with previous years, although the weather was such as to repel from, rather than attract to the seaside'*.

From January 1884 the company arbitrarily cut the late afternoon trains from the timetable and at the same time increased the fares, which were described as *'the dearest in the country'*. The *Halesworth Times* for 8th January placed the blame fully on thee company officers.

'The Managers, to fully understand the wants of their customers ought to remove their offices at least a hundred miles nearer. What would have been the position of the Great Eastern Railway if their offices had been on the Isle of Man. Their only means of ascertaining the wants of the locality is by visits few and far between, and which partake more of a pleasure trip.'

This vehement attack alluded to Arthur Pain, living in Surbiton, with his office in Westminster and who only spent his holidays at Southwold. The hard-hitting criticism brought an immediate response for the company reduced the fares to *'the old rate'* early in February.

The question of the fare structure was raised at the ordinary general meeting of shareholders held at the company offices at Westminster at the end of March 1884. The gathering was informed that the raising of Third Class fares by one halfpenny was unsuccessful and the rate had reverted to one penny per mile. At the meeting Southwold Corporation was criticized for failing to release further land for house building. Pain retorted:

'The Corporation told them [the company] *to make the railway, and that in return they* [the Corporation] *would let, or sell or lay out houses and gardens fronting the sea. The Corporation had done nothing, they had got the railway at a place every inch of which was building land, and not an inch of it was built upon.'*

Stung by the criticism, Southwold Corporation responded by discussing the matter on 8th April and then holding a public auction of building land on North Cliff and St. Edmund's Green on 19th June. They also responded to another of Pain's suggestions by reintroducing the weekly Southwold market, which had been aborted the previous year. By the end of the year the house building was progressing and three properties were almost completed.

In 1884 the annual staff dinner was again held in Southwold Town Hall at the end of August, with the Company Chairman Colonel Bagot-Chester as chief guest. After the meal Pain said he *'was the principal supporter in getting the line to Southwold. Had it not been for his vote which carried the scheme, the line would not have been made'*. The *Halesworth Times* reported, *'Toast and song were kept up until 1am when all not living in Southwold left by special train'*. On 3rd September Arthur C. Pain of 5 Victoria Street London SW1 was elevated to a position on the Board as Managing Director and Harry Calne, having previously been employed by the Great Western Railway, assumed the position of Company Secretary. The Chairman was Richard C. Rapier of 5 Westminster Chambers London SW1, whilst fellow Directors on the board were J.P. Cooper of Howden, Yorkshire, G. Wells Owen of 7 Westminster Chambers, London SW1 and R.A. Withall of 29 Great George Street, London SW1. Receipts for the six months ending 30th June 1884 showed an increase in passenger and parcels traffic but a slight reduction in goods and minerals. The working expenses increased in the same period as a result of the purchase of permanent way materials. Traffic for the second half of the year showed an overall increase.

The dangers of passing between moving carriages of the narrow gauge train in defiance of SR company regulations and the vigilance of guards was fully exposed on 27th September 1884 when a man named Palmer fell from a train, fortunately without sustaining injuries.

At Halesworth Petty Session in November 1884 Walter Doy, the platelayer in the employ of the SR, was found guilty of poaching two hares and was fined £2 10s 0d with 10s 6d costs. In evidence it was announced that Doy had snared the hares near the railway with the permission of Thomas Smith, who had leased the shooting rights on railway property, but on the day in question the hares were taken on the three-mile section of line crossing land owed by Sir John Blois, as his game crossed the railway. Sir John was one of the four justices on the bench and he had had to withdraw before the case was heard. The Chairman in his summing up was of the opinion the court was not exactly dealing with Walter Doy and thought the fine would be paid by *'someone else'*.

By the early 1880s Southwold Harbour had completely silted up and the two piers forming the mouth of the River Blyth were in poor condition due to lack of attention and maintenance, and in 1884 the owners of Blyth Navigation announced they were closing the canal and were disclaiming all responsibility for its condition. As a result the SR management announced they expected no further competition from the waterway authority.

Early in February 1885 a local retired tradesman was charged with poaching on the railway where it crossed Walberswick Common. When the man appeared before the magistrates at Halesworth he contested the charge and the ownership of the land was then questioned. The *Halesworth Times* reported:

A late 1890s view of an Up train waiting to depart from Southwold behind 2-4-0T No. 3 *Blyth*. The train is formed of an open wagon, two luggage vans and coaching stock in the cream/white livery lined out in black. The horse chestnut trees on the platform are in their infancy. *Southwold Railway Museum*

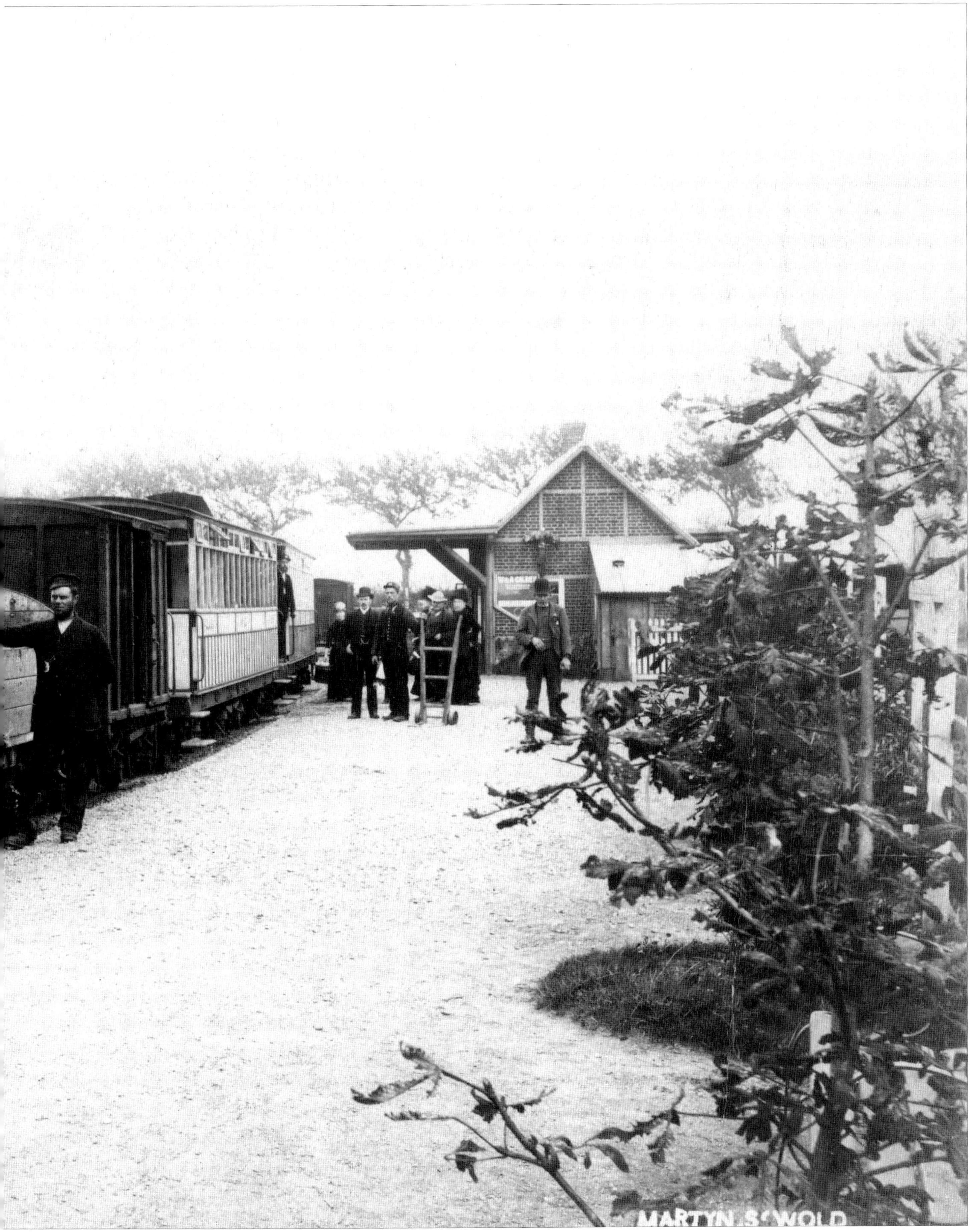
MARTYN, S'WOLD

'The natural inference was that the Lord of the Manor was the owner of the soil of the waste lands. Sir John Blois and his predecessors had for many years exercized rights of shooting over the waste-lands. When the Southwold Railway was made, a portion of the common or fen lands was separated from the rest and practically enclosed, and on that portion was let a term of five years shooting rights ending 13th May 1886.'

It was established that Thomas Smith leased the shooting rights on the railway but was in dispute with Sir John Blois where the railway crossed the common. After listening to the arguments and counter claims the magistrates found the dispute was outside of their jurisdiction and dismissed the case, much to the chagrin of by now ganger Walter Doy, who had been fined for a similar offence the previous year.

Since the opening of the line the lack of luggage accommodation in the passenger coaches meant that suitcases and other baggage, together with perishable parcels and goods items were conveyed in open wagons and suitably sheeted over with tarpaulin covers to protect the contents from the elements. To obviate the problem the company early in 1885 ordered two 4-wheel luggage vans from the Midland Railway Carriage & Wagon Company at a cost of £95 and these were delivered in the second half of the year.

The sale of plots of land at Southwold for building continued in 1885 and in early August the GER arranged for a special 12-coach train from Liverpool Street, picking up at Colchester and Ipswich to convey developers and other interested parties attending the auction. The train arrived at Halesworth shortly before midday and the passengers transferred to the 12.00 noon SR train for onward conveyance. Such a large assembly necessitated the employment of all six carriages, hauled by two locomotives and the *Halesworth Times* reported, *'The travellers were much pleased with the novelty of the railway, and with the excessive ease and comfort of travelling over the short line'*. The train arrived at Southwold at 12.30pm, whereas the booked time was 12.37pm. Similar arrangements were made to return the passengers to Halesworth in the evening.

Later in the same month ganger Walter Doy was delegated to clear out debris from the cylinder supporting the swing bridge. The cylinder, which was sunk some ten feet below the water level into the riverbed, unbeknownst to anyone had a pocket of compressed air trapped at the bottom, and when Doy entered the chamber it exploded throwing the ganger out of the cylinder. Fortunately the rest of the gang had accompanied Doy and they quickly placed him on the hand trolley and took him to Southwold station. On arrival he was treated by Dr Deck, who diagnosed he had suffered a broken left arm and had severe contusions to his head and chest.

At the annual meeting of the Southwold Railway employees held at Southwold Town Hall on Thursday 24th September the gathering was informed that during the six years of operation 377,407 passengers had been conveyed on the line, an average of 200 passengers each day, with 80,809 parcels and 2,750 tons of fish and minerals. Since 1877 seventy houses had been built or enlarged in Southwold, *'largely due to the existence of the railway'*. After the expounding of statistics the usual speeches and toasts were made to conclude the evening.

At the end of October 1885 Southwold Harbour Commissioners considered a letter received from the SR Manager asking if they would object to the railway company seeking Parliamentary powers to take over the harbour piers, extend them and dredge the waterway to enable larger vessels to berth at the port. As the subject was only one of several items on the Commissioner's agenda, the discussion was terse. The Chairman argued that because of lack of financial resources the railway company was in no position to carry out such work. It was thus resolved the Commissioners would consider funding from alternative sources.

At the shareholders' half yearly meeting held at the company office at Westminster in March 1886, it was announced that for the six months ending 31st December 1885, the 48,622 passengers conveyed represented an increase over the same period the previous year but passenger receipts had fallen. This was more than offset by increases in other receipts for goods and parcels traffic. Train mileage for 1885 totalled 30,394, whilst 72,863 passengers were carried, with 18,840 parcels, 2,577 tons of goods traffic, 622 tons of fish and 4,555 tons of minerals. It was also mentioned a new deep-water pier had been constructed near the swing bridge.

Richard Rapier, in his capacity as Company Chairman, advised those attending the Railway Employees dinner on Friday 24th September 1886 that for some time to come *'there was no probability of a dividend but they were making good progress and meeting working expenses'*. This was confirmed at the shareholders meeting held in October 1886 where a £35 reduction in receipts for the six months ending 30th June 1886 was blamed on inclement weather and a general depression in trade. Urgent repairs to carriages and the completion of the deep-water pier had necessitated expenditure of £22. At the conclusion of the meeting the Directors reported they were seeking ways of rearranging the company finances so that they could purchase rather than rent the locomotives and rolling stock.

The rapid expansion of building at Suffolk coastal towns was the subject of an article in *The Builder* magazine on 16th October 1886 which was repeated in a subsequent edition of the *Halesworth Times*. Readers might have been misled into believing the GER was about to extend their territory to Southwold. The disadvantages of transferring goods from a standard gauge to narrow gauge train were already ringing alarm bells, as the following extract reveals.

'The rapid progress of building at several watering places on the East Coast has led the Great Eastern Railway Company providing increased means of communication by the construction of new branch lines … Some of these are already in the course of construction, whilst others are about to be built. On the estate at Southwold, facing the sea, which was sold last year in several lots, building is now actively progressing … the want of adequate railway communication is a great drawback … the only means of arrival at it being by a light narrow gauge line commencing at Halesworth, where passengers have to change carriages and proceed on their journey in vehicles resembling tram-cars. Lowestoft is likewise at present only reached by a branch line running eastwards from the main line at Beccles.'

The report then entered the realms of speculation:

'In order to render the communication between the two towns more direct a new extension line is about to be constructed, commencing on the main line between Saxmundham and Darsham, running in a north-easterly direction to Southwold and Lowestoft, both places forming … integral parts of the company's London, Colchester and Ipswich section.'

During the autumn of 1886 Southwold was affected by unusually high tides, which caused flooding in the brick kiln fields. The

Council voted to finance the building of a concrete groin to prevent recurrence and appointed Arthur C. Pain, the SR's Managing Director as Engineer to oversee the work. Evidence of extra work entailed by SR staff to provide adequate connections with GER can be cited because Christmas Eve trains services from London were running late, the 3.20pm from Liverpool Street not arriving at Halesworth until 7.10pm. The 6.33pm SR departure from Halesworth departed to time conveying passengers off the 2.35pm additional train ex Liverpool Street and the 5.45pm Up train. The 8.09pm SR train also departed to time, conveying about 100 passengers off the 3.20pm ex Liverpool Street and 6.50pm ex Ipswich. However, as the 5.00pm ex Liverpool Street did not arrive at Halesworth until 9.10pm, a special train departed Halesworth for Southwold conveying about thirty-five passengers who otherwise would have been marooned at the Junction for the festivities.

Despite reasonable loadings all was not well with the narrow gauge railway for after further attempts to obtain the outstanding monies from the SR, the GE General Manager reported on 1st March 1887 the Southwold Company was experiencing serious financial difficulties. The GE was owed a total of £844 9s 10d consisting of:

	£	s	d
Land purchased by the GER for the SR	371	0	0
Mr Viger's fee	23	0	0
Proportion of the cost of the footbridge at Halesworth station	242	0	0
Interest on £371 at 4 per cent	118	8	9
Interest on £23 at 5 per cent	8	10	1
Interest on £242 at 5 per cent	78	13	0
Services of booking clerk at Halesworth for six months ending 31 December 1886	2	10	0
Shunting at Halesworth on 15th and 20th November 1885		8	0
	844	9	10

The SR had contemplated raising £10,000 by preference debenture shares and thus settle the £400 annual charge for the hire of rolling stock, as well as other outstanding liabilities. If the £10,000 could be raised, the company proposed to offer creditors half the total in preferred debentures and half in ordinary shares in place of a cash payment. The GE General Manager, however, expressed grave doubts as to the success of the proposal.

At the SR company's half yearly meeting of shareholders held at Victoria Street, Westminster on Wednesday 30th March 1887, the Directors attributed the further reduction in receipts for the six months ending 31st December 1886 to the continuing trade depression and an unusually bad fishing season. A specially convened meeting directly afterwards debated proposals to improve the company's finances by issuing four per cent preferred debentures. This, it was claimed, would enable the company to settle the arrears of interest owing on existing debentures and settle the claims of ordinary creditors with payments made half in shares and half in preferred debentures. It would also enable the purchase of locomotives and rolling stock, which were costing £400 per annum in hire charges. The money thus saved could be used to pay the interest on the four per cent preferred debentures. After due discussion the scheme was approved. In contrast, the half yearly earnings to 30th June 1887 produced an increase in gross receipts despite a modest fall in passenger traffic and the smallest reduction in fish traffic conveyed since the line opened. Parcels, goods and mineral traffic had shown a marked increase, although this had been tempered by the necessity to spend £190 on essential repairs to one of the locomotives. Despite this expenditure the balance carried forward on the accounts was greater than for the same period in 1886. For the annual staff dinner held on Friday 23rd September 1887, Southwold Town Hall was *'gaily decorated with bunting and the tables with ferns, shrubs and flowers'*. Arthur Pain cheered many when he reported the decline of passenger traffic had been arrested and *'during the late summer more passengers were conveyed to and from Southwold than ever before'*.

The attempt to raise additional capital finally met with success after months of negotiations and Henry G. Calcraft, Secretary to the BOT, signed the certificate on 28th March 1888, authorizing the SR to raise an additional £12,000 by the creation and issue of preferred debenture stock, distinguished as 1887 stock, bearing an interest of not more than four per cent per annum. The good news was tempered by the announcement in the same year the Harbour Commissioners intended to abandon Southwold Harbour, thus bringing a possible reduction in goods traffic and revenue.

In the last weeks of 1888 the Southwold Harbour Commissioners announced they were no longer able to keep the harbour open for vessels. Both the *East Anglian Daily Times* and the *Halesworth Times* reported in the New Year that the Commissioners hoped Sir

THE SOUTHWOLD RAILWAY COMPANY.

CERTIFICATE of the Board of Trade for raising Additional Capital.

WHEREAS The Southwold Railway Company have complied with the requirements of the Railway Companies Powers Act 1864.

Now therefore the Board of Trade do by this their Certificate in pursuance of the said Act as amended by the Railways (Powers and Construction) Acts 1864 Amendment Act 1870 and by virtue and in exercise of the powers thereby in them vested, and of every other power enabling them in this behalf, certify as follows :—

1. The Southwold Railway Company, hereinafter called the said Company, may for the purpose of their undertaking and in addition to the Capital already authorised to be raised by them, raise any further sum or sums not exceeding in the whole twelve thousand pounds, by creation and issue of Preferred Debenture Stock, subject to the provisions of Part 3 of the Companies Clauses Act, 1863, except where varied by this Certificate, and such Preferred Debenture Stock shall be distinguished as " 1887 Preferred Debenture Stock," and shall bear interest at the rate of not exceeding Four Pounds per centum per annum, and such Debenture Stock and the interest thereon shall rank in priority of all Debentures and the interest thereon respectively created or issued before the granting of this Certificate.

2. Sections 23 to 26 both inclusive of the Railway Companies Act, 1867, with reference to Loan Capital shall be incorporated with this Certificate, and shall apply to Loan Capital raised under this Certificate in like manner as if this Certificate were a special Act.

(8300)

BOT Certificate authorizing the raising of additional capital.

Samuel Morton Peto might renew his offer of *'30 to 40 years ago'* to renew his interest in the harbour, which presupposes the Southwold Commissioners might have once rejected an advancement to make Southwold into a major port with connections to the main line railway. Peto refused the invitation.

The half yearly report for the six months ending 31st December 1888 and published in March 1889 showed a reduction of 2,318 passengers travelling compared with the previous year. Fish traffic had also decreased by 55 tons and 1882 was the only year showing worse figures. There was an increase of 293 parcels conveyed, whilst

The approach to Southwold from the station throat in 1900 as the Station Hotel in the background is under construction and a coach stands on the Up side carriage siding. The outer home/advance starting signal arms are on the same post to the left and the inner home/starting signal arms are both on the inner post. Note there is no subsidiary arm on the outer post giving trains access to the goods yard sidings. The points were operated by a weighted lever beside the track and interlocked with the signals. The reverse of the signal arm was painted plain white. *Author's collection*

goods traffic carried showed an increase of 147 tons and mineral traffic increased by 463 tons. The total receipts for the line showed a reduction of £76 compared with the same six months period in 1887, but this was partially compensated by a decrease in expenditure of £209. In April 1889 the Manager and Secretary moved the company office from No. 5 Victoria Street Westminster, London to No. 12 in the same thoroughfare. In September the report for the six months ending 30th June 1889 revealed that 22,923 passengers had been carried, an increase of 879 over the corresponding period for 1888. All other traffic showed a similar increase, parcels by 680 items, goods 198 tons, fish traffic 7 tons and minerals by 188 tons. The Directors advised they were arranging with the creditors of the company to issue the £12,000 four per cent debentures and also announced they were gratified to learn that house building at Southwold was now progressing in East Street and on the North Cliff Estate, together with a new post office and waterworks. A new lighthouse was in the course of erection, with two *'pretty villas for residences for the principal and assistant keepers'*. At the meeting, Charles Chambers, who possessed the largest shareholding in the company, was elected to the board in succession to G.W. Owen, who had offered his resignation.

Over the years the railway suffered minor criminal activity, as on 23rd September 1889 when 17-year-old Alfred Lockett appeared before Southwold Petty Sessions charged with breaking and entering Southwold station and stealing cash and sundry items. He was duly committed for trial. On a more positive note, twenty-eight SR and GER Halesworth station staff attended the SR's annual supper held at Southwold Town Hall on Friday 27th October 1889, together with fifty guests including tradesmen and leading townsfolk. Arthur Pain announced to the gathering that the previous half year was the first in which receipts had exceeded working expenses.

On Wednesday 27th November 1889 the horse pulling an empty omnibus to Southwold station was startled as it passed a wheelbarrow and in the ensuing confusion ran up the earth bank at the side of Station Road. The vehicle overturned, throwing the driver to the ground but he escaped with only minor injuries. The only damage sustained was to the harness. It appeared that Woodgate, the regular omnibus driver, was unwell and a relief driver was in charge of the vehicle.

The injection of additional finance enabled the clearance of at least some outstanding liabilities and on 18th February 1890 the GER General Manager reported to his Directors that with the authority of the BOT the SR was raising a further £10,000 by the issuing of pre-debenture stock and, as authorised by the GE Traffic Committee minute of 1st March 1887, the GE Company accepted from the SR:

1. A certificate for 46 fully paid up £10 SR ordinary shares
2. A £450 certificate of 4 per cent debenture stock
3. A cheque for £911 16s 1d in discharge of a claim against the SR which was made up of:

Land purchased by the GER	£371 0s 0d
Mr Viger's fee or award as to payment for the land	£ 23 0s 0d
Cost of footbridge at Halesworth	£242 0s 0d
Interest up to 30th June 1889	£275 16s 1d
	£911 16s 1d

Despite the downturn of trade, goods traffic handled at Blythburgh was on the increase and in April 1890 a new siding and connection from the main single line was installed and the existing siding extended. This gave accommodation for an additional number of wagons and facilitated the easier loading and unloading of vehicles by local farmers and traders.

By clause 54 of the Great Eastern Railway (General Powers) Act 1890 (53 and 54 Vic cap cviii), which received the Royal Assent on 25th July 1890, the GER could:

'Accept in or towards satisfaction or discharge of any sum or sums of money owing to them from the Southwold Company and interest on any such sums and may hold in their own name or in the name

This photograph was presented to Guard A.E. Wright on 15th November 1887 by J. Kumbara, a representative of the Japanese Railways, as a memento of his visit to the line. 2-4-0T No. 3 *Blyth* is waiting to depart Southwold and although the print is faded it shows an immaculate locomotive with the sandbox located on top of the side tank. *Author's collection*

of one or more Directors or officers of the company or other persons appointed by the company for that purpose, preferred debenture stock and ordinary shares or stock or any of them in the capital of the Southwold Company to such amounts as the Directors from time to time see fit and may have and exercise in respect of any such debenture stock shares or stock all such and the same rights as the other holders of like debenture stock or shares or stock have or may exercise.'

The *Halesworth Times* for 26th August 1890 reported the sudden death of Duncan King, the Commission Agent, who was visiting Southwold because of ill health. As a relative was purchasing tickets at the station King collapsed and died instantly from a heart attack. The death was also announced of a SR shareholder, H.J. Debney, who also owned shares in the Southwold Gas Company, the Southwold Waterworks Company and the River Blyth Ferry Company. At a subsequent auction held at Southwold Drill Hall, Debney's ten SR £10 shares sold at par, whilst his £20 preference debenture stock sold for £15.

The annual staff dinner was held on Friday 26th September 1890 when Southwold Town Hall was decorated with flags for the occasion by the coastguards. In his usual 'pep talk' Pain advised *'times were on the mend'* with two carriages being repainted, although he confessed *'the drawback with which the Company had to contend, was the smallness of traffic out of Southwold'*! This was partly attributed to the demise of the fishing trade, which was alluded to by the *Halesworth Times* on 30th December. *'This industry has come to an end for the present, and the general verdict is that the season has been the worst on record, the outlook for the winter is exceedingly dark.'*

The Regulation of Railways Act 1889 enforced, amongst other things, major railway companies to adopt block working on all single lines except where Train Staff without Ticket and One Engine in Steam systems existed, and required the interlocking of points and signals. The statute also stated:

'The BOT may from time to time order a railway company, within a time limited by the order and subject to any exceptions or modifications to provide for and use on all their trains carrying passengers continuous brakes which acted instantaneously when applied by the driver or guard.'

The locomotives and carriages of the SR had never been fitted with such equipment and the Board of Trade required the company to adopt either the vacuum or Westinghouse brake to comply with the Act and fall in line with other British railway companies. In this respect the BOT issued the necessary order to the SR on 28th November 1890, the correspondence reiterating the wording of the Act and giving the company eighteen months to comply with the order. Anticipating the order, the SR management had sent a letter to the BOT on 13th December 1889 seeking possible exemption and setting out reasons for noncompliance, which included the possibility of the railway being categorized as a tramway. In an internal memorandum of December 1890 the company was advised no exemption could be granted.

The earning for six months ending 31st December 1890 of £2,111 15s 10d showed a deficit of £32 5s 1d compared with the corresponding period in 1889. Passenger numbers had increased by 4,552 to 54,022 and the falling receipts were caused by the failure of the fishing trade. Parcels traffic showed an increase to 1,269 and had more than doubled since the line was opened to traffic. Despite higher traffic and general expenses a balance of £599 4s 4d was carried forward to the revenue account. Train mileage for 1890 totalled 30,588, 78,655 passengers travelled and 21,952 parcels, 2,610 tons of goods, 287 tons of fish and 5,712 tons of mineral were conveyed. Thus on a weekly average 1,513 passengers travelled, 52 tons of goods traffic, 110 tons of minerals, 5½ tons fish and 422 parcels were conveyed with train mileage at 588 miles per week. It should be noted that the majority of passengers were carried in the summer months.

4
Consolidation

Mid January 1891 was particularly cold on the east coast of England and Southwold was engulfed by freezing north winds. The River Blyth was almost frozen over by the harbour mouth and the ferry service was suspended for two days. The decrepit state of the harbour was a continuing source of concern to Southwold Town Council and by early June the harbour mouth, apart from a small outlet on the Walberswick shore, was again blocked, this time by undredged shingle. The town council, frustrated that nature was engulfing both harbour and associated piers, considered taking formal possession of the harbour from the Harbour Commissioners, after they had abandoned the undertaking in 1888. They were, however, unclear as to whether they had the power to create the loans needed to fund any improvements and instead formed a committee to seek the help of the GER. The Town Clerk duly wrote to the GER Directors asking them to receive a deputation of local worthies in connection with the request for the main line company to take over the ownership of the SR and running of Southwold Harbour. After discussion at a board meeting on 16th June the General Manager was instructed to respond saying the GE Company had no parliamentary powers enabling the acquisition of the harbour and explaining that it was unlikely that such powers would be granted. It was therefore unnecessary for the deputation to waste time travelling to London.

Following the BOT decision to grant no exception to the fitting of continuous brakes, Arthur C. Pain and Henry Carne, the Secretary, had a meeting with the BOT on 8th January 1891, when they were told to advance their argument for exemption in writing. A three-page letter dated 16th January reiterated the comments made in the letter of 13th December 1889 and gave reasons for not fitting continuous brakes. The mileages between the three intermediate stations and the Mill Siding were minimal:

Station	Miles From Halesworth	Miles Between
Halesworth	0	
Mill Siding	2	2
Wenhaston	2½	½
Blythburgh	5	2½
Walberswick	8	3
Southwold	9	1

The line was operated by one engine in steam and was therefore exempt from block signalling and interlocking of points and signals. Speed was limited to 16 mph with a service of five trains a day in each direction in winter on weekdays and six trains each way on weekdays and two in each direction on Sundays in summer. The railway possessed six carriages, each holding forty passengers, of which two were equipped with hand brakes. The line had been open upwards of eleven years without an accident, although no mention was made of the death of the clerk boarding a train at Walberswick in 1883. Trains were operated with wagons at the front of the formation ahead of the passenger carriages to reduce unnecessary movement of the passenger vehicles into and out of sidings and thereby reduce shunting times. The company for financial reasons only used one locomotive at a time and could not afford more wagons, which prevented the running of separate goods trains. The distance between stations was so short and speed so slow that an accident that would be obviated by the use of continuous brakes appeared to the SR management almost impossible. There had been no difficulties experienced stopping trains in an emergency and a child straying on the line was cited as an example. Pain concluded the SR Board were of the opinion the provision of continuous brakes would not involve any additional safety, but would tend to cause accidents. However, within two days the BOT had replied that the company should press compliance with the order to fit continuous brakes to the passenger rolling stock and there matters rested.

The *Halesworth Times* in September 1891 reprinted a letter, which originally appeared in the magazine *Golden Globe*. It was penned by a lady staying at Southwold and referred to the SR, although the Directors might not have been amused.

'Figure to yourself first of all a toy train, a miniature engine, a couple of infinitesimal carriages, running right through in American fashion, with a kind of tramcar platform arrangement for the guard, and a wee little gauge line upon which a perambulator might run. One felt as if one were "playing at trains" as the baby engine puffed noisily and fussily along the wee metals; and the stations are built on a corresponding small scale, they are simply sheds lit by means of a lamp fastened against a post. But the "trainlett" takes its passengers into sunny Southwold at the appointed time, after the excellent fashion of the Great Eastern Railway trains, with which it is in connection.'

In the same month the newspaper reprinted *'A Letter From A to Zed'*, which first appeared in the 'Great London Dailies', implying that the lone station master at Walberswick was far too busy issuing and receiving tickets and dealing with the fish traffic to deal with the needs of passengers.

Thursday 15th October 1891 was a stormy day with gusting winds and driving rain. As the 1.08pm train from Halesworth to Southwold was negotiating the curve near Holton Bridge the driver noticed at the last moment a tree had blown across the line. He reversed the engine and sounded the whistle for the guard to apply the brake in the carriage. Station Master Hansford of Southwold was riding in the train and immediately applied the brake lever. Although the train halted within fifty yards, the emergency measures failed to prevent the locomotive colliding with the trunk of the fallen tree. The engine headlight was broken and the front carriage considerably scratched. A saw and axe were obtained from the neighbouring farm before the obstruction was removed from the track and only fifteen minutes delay was incurred before the train continued its journey. The *Halesworth Times* reporting the incident reminded its readers that there was no continuous Westinghouse brake fitted to the SR stock and only individual hand brakes in some of the carriages. It was of the opinion *'the railway was being operated in breach of Board of Trade Regulations'*.

On 21st October 1891 the GER and SR reached agreement regarding the transfer of land and new works at Halesworth. Under the arrangements, works including the dock walls at the end of the trans-ship shed and associated sidings were to be constructed and maintained by the SR to the reasonable satisfaction of the GER Engineer, with costs borne by the narrow gauge company. The exchange of lands was to be made with mutual convenience, each party accepting the title of the other to the respective portions of land without investigation. The document was signed by Henry Carne on behalf of the SR.

Despite the negative response from Bishopsgate certain council members continued to press for the GER to take over the SR and the ailing harbour. At a tradesmen's dinner held at Southwold in early February 1892, E.O. Debney, a former councillor, stated he was of the opinion if the GER would not help towards the development of the harbour, there were other railway companies that would. After much discussion it was proposed to create a Southwold Harbour Improvement Committee to progress possible takeover and to prevent the harbour from becoming totally silted up. Subsequent approaches were made to the GER Directors but they reiterated they had no interest in taking over the harbour or the narrow gauge line.

A hot sunny day and sparks emitted from the locomotive of a passing train on 13th June 1892 resulted in an extensive gorse fire at Walberswick, which destroyed much of the SR lineside fencing before the flames were extinguished. The following day groups of permanent way staff were repairing the fences to prevent animals straying on the railway.

The continuing lack of progress in improving facilities at Southwold Harbour was a growing concern for many of the town's inhabitants. Approaches to the SR management and the GER Directors had met with indifference and so on 20th July 1892 a deputation from the recently formed Southwold Harbour and Improvements Committee met Southwold Council and presented a petition signed by thirty-eight people. They announced that a proposal for a GER line from the Midland Railway at Bedford direct to Harwich via Colchester, thus giving access to the Continent, had been turned down. The deputation recommended an approach to the Midland Railway for a line from Bedford direct to Southwold instead of Harwich. The new line was estimated to be 8 miles shorter in distance and would include the Southwold Railway being converted to standard gauge. A connecting line to the harbour was also suggested to improve facilities at the port. The council wholeheartedly approved the scheme but in October it was reported approaches to the MR had been unsuccessful as that company had territorial agreements with the GER, a fact reported in the *Halesworth Times* for 18th October. Having failed on two occasions, local factors as a last resort proposed an independent line from Cambridge to Southwold, with running powers over the GER to Newmarket, a new line thence to Mellis, running powers over the branch to Eye and a new line thence through Stradbroke to Halesworth, and finally the purchase and re-gauging of the Southwold line. Where the promoters hoped to get the finances is unclear but for a few months the scheme lay dormant.

The eleventh annual dinner for SR employees was held on Friday 7th October 1892. At the formal speeches the Chairman alluded that the success in working the line and the comfort of the passengers was largely due to the efforts of Henry Carne, the Secretary, *'who had come from the Great Western Railway, bringing much experience with him'*. In the same month the SR staff entered into the spirit of the occasion after a wedding held at Southwold parish church. The bride and bridegroom left the town for their honeymoon on the 5.25pm train from Southwold en route to London and onward to Torquay and Cornwall. As the relatives and friends arrived at the station to see the happy couple on their way, they noted the locomotive at the head of the train was decorated with flowers. The station master rang the hand bell and after the guard signalled the 'right away', the train departed to the staccato of exploding detonators.

The question of compliance to the BOT order of 28th November 1890 was raised again on 13th July 1892 when the Secretary

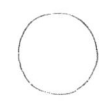

Agreement between the GER and Southwold Railway dated 21st October 1891.

enquired as to the progress the company was making in fitting continuous brakes. The SR management initially chose to ignore the correspondence, finally replying on 5th October by raising objections because of cost and the need for a third locomotive to maintain services. The BOT was evidently dissatisfied with the response for they advised on 22nd October that enforcement would become necessary if the Act was not complied with. Three days later the SR Secretary acknowledged receipt of the correspondence and the matter was put before the Directors.

As if pressure from authority was not enough to occupy the minds of the Directors and management the reputation of the railway was called into question by two items of correspondence. The *Halesworth Times* of 1st November 1892 related an account of journey to Southwold:

> 'From London to Halesworth Junction is a direct journey via Ipswich, of between three to four hours. Then there is a change into a tiny little railway, with "cars" constructed in the American pattern, drawn by a fussy tin-kettle of an engine, which emits volumes of the nastiest smoke in the world. The whole arrangement is nothing more than a steam tram-line, but it connects the outer world sufficiently well with the Southwold district.'

The integrity of the SR was again soured a fortnight later when a Southwold correspondent identifying him or herself as NEMO wrote in the newspaper, *'We have a town unique in its entrances. The journey to Walberswick is cumbersome; our railroad by its width demonstrates the mental capacity of its projectors'.*

In November 1892 Richard Rapier approached the GER General Manager suggesting that as the SR was *'experiencing difficulty paying its way'*, the GER should purchase the line or, failing that, assist it in the way of a rebate. The General Manager advised he was not against helping but *'could not see his way in the matter'*. He suggested a submission be made in writing the following summer, so that the matter could be referred to his Directors. Rapier duly submitted the application requesting £48,125 for outright purchase against an alternative 7½ per cent rebate. After initial discussions the GE board considered a 5 per cent rebate was a much more realistic figure with the option to purchase in twenty-one years but the matter was shelved pending investigations. It was considered such action would deter another railway company gaining access to Southwold harbour to develop as a seaport. Having heard nothing from the Midland Railway some Southwold townsfolk again wrote to Derby resubmitting the proposal for a direct line from Cambridge to Southwold and a development of the harbour but as before the proposal was ignored.

In February 1893 the Southwold company office was again moved, from No. 12 Victoria Street, Westminster across the road to No. 17, occupied by Arthur Pain. On 29th April 1893 a deputation of Southwold councillors visited Eye to promote the Cambridge to Southwold line and persuade local councillors to back their proposals. The resurrection of the scheme came as the result of a guarded report made indirectly from Midland Railway sources that the company was anxious to secure a port on the east coast, despite the 'official line' that it enjoyed territorial agreements with the GER This 'unofficial' leak of information was enough to lead to the formation of a promoting committee which included the Mayor of Southwold, and the presentation of a survey of the proposed route by an 'eminent engineer' Mr Stephenson. He duly reported there would be no difficulties building the line but recommended the group approach all towns connected by the proposed line to overcome any possible opposition.

The recently arrived train at Southwold finds some outgoing passengers already boarded and others waiting on the platform. There appears to be no hurry for the 2-4-0T locomotive has either to couple the 4-wheel wagon to the rear of the train or alternatively remove it and take it to the siding before running round the formation. The edge of the gravel-surfaced platform has now been planked over. *Southwold Museum*

The visit to Eye gives evidence of the seriousness of the proposal to develop Southwold harbour. At the conclusion of the ordinary meeting of the Eye Town Council on 29th April, the Mayor, Alderman Tacon informed the members of the council that he had received communication from Southwold relative to receiving a deputation of gentlemen with regard to the promotion of a railway. The Mayor thought it advisable the council members should see the deputation and accordingly they were invited to attend that day. The letter received from Southwold, dated 21st April 1893, read:

'Sir, - A scheme has been put forward in this borough with the object of promoting a Trans-East Anglian Railway, originating from the Midland system at Cambridge, and terminating in this place, which is considered to be eminently adaptable to the formation of a commodious seaport. The route proposed is from Cambridge to Bury by means of running powers over the Great Eastern Railway, from Bury to Mellis via a new line, from Mellis to Eye by means of running powers over the present line, from Eye to Halesworth by a line to be constructed, and from Halesworth by the acquisition and remodelling of the Southwold Railway. The Midland Railway Directors have already been approached by our Corporation upon the subject, and although their reply was somewhat guarded, it is confidently believed from information acquired indirectly that the Midland Railway are anxious to secure a port on the east coast, and the promoters of this scheme have every reason to believe that, if the necessary powers can be obtained, the line will be constructed and the harbour at this place developed, to the incalculable advantage of the whole of Mid Suffolk. An influential committee has been formed, with the object of enquiring into the practicability of the proposed line and the best method of promoting it, and it is at their instance that we address this letter to your Worship with the hope of ascertaining whether your Worship would be prepared to receive a small deputation to explain the objects of the scheme and the mode in which it is proposed to further it.

 'Yours & c. *John Jones (Chairman)*
      E.M.U. Adnams (Mayor)
      Henry J. Debney
      J.J. Mayhew
      J. Gurdon
      L. Stephenson
      Ernest R. Cooper (Hon. Secretary)'

The deputation consisting of E.M.U. Adnams, the Mayor of Southwold, and Ernest Cooper, the Secretary, was introduced. Adnams explained to the gathering the scheme had been surveyed by L. Stephenson, an eminent engineer and Ordnance Survey maps were exhibited to show the chosen route. Cooper mentioned the engineer had informed the committee there would be no difficulties constructing the line although much opposition was expected. If, however, the support of Eye and other towns connected with the proposed line was offered it was thought they had every chance of success. Adnams concluded saying he had been informed that the House of Commons was always disposed to passing Acts of Parliament for railways.

In reply, Alderman Tacon remarked on the desire of the Midland Railway Company to obtain a port on the East Coast, which he believed was not now so urgent as the company had access to Yarmouth. He also referred to his personal experience of the proposed line from Cambridge to Felixstowe, which had failed due to the considerable opposition of the Ipswich Dock Commission, which wanted no commercial development near the coast. He did not know whether Ipswich would oppose Southwold becoming a large port. Cooper finalized the presentation saying the Committee promoting the scheme would welcome any gentleman from Eye, either on the Committee, or to form a Committee to work in harmony with them.

The Council members briefly considered the scheme and recalled Adnams and Cooper and advised the pair that as far as they had been able to consider the matter, were favourably impressed with the idea but they were not prepared to take any furthers steps until the scheme had been developed. Adnams thanked the council for expressing their opinion; they could not expect people to jump to conclusions all at once, they only wished to learn the general feeling with regard to the project. Alderman Tacon expressed the true thoughts of his Council, remarking the GER, whilst charging high goods rates gave Eye every facility in the matter of passenger traffic. Despite such a lukewarm response the *Halesworth Times* for 6th June 1893 reported the promoters *'have every reason to believe that, if necessary powers can be obtained, the line would be constructed and the harbour developed'*. However, the saga was to continue.

In early June 1893, six teenagers, described as *'caddy boys'* and presumably employed by the Southwold Golf Club, were charged at Southwold Petty Sessions, with *'placing stones upon the metals of the Southwold Railway on 16th May 1893, and thereby endangering the safety of a train and its passengers'*. Station Master F.W. Hansford presented the case for the SR and Driver Hammond, Driver Jackson, labourer Albert Gray, twine spinner Bertie Button and Inspector Porter provided evidence. The case was, however, dismissed after the boys were given a severe reprimand and warning as to their future conduct. The same month found a newly wedded couple setting off from a decorated Wenhaston station on their honeymoon when relatives and villagers gave *'hearty cheers'* as the train left for Halesworth.

The half year report for the six months ending 30th June 1893 was most gratifying for the Directors, as it showed an increase in receipts compared with the same period the previous year. Expenses had reduced slightly and the number of passengers carried and parcels and goods conveyed showed an increase for the same period over the previous three years.

Six months ending	30 June 1890	30 June 1891	30 June 1892	30 June 1893
Passengers	24,633	24,238	27,543	28,744
Parcels	9,085	8,857	10,225	10,710
Goods tons	1,307	1,335	1,508	1,532
Fish tons	53	56	71	74
Minerals tons	2,459	3,067	2,808	2,925

After the approach by Richard Rapier in November 1892 and written submission, the GER arranged for a detailed survey to be made of the SR, including plans and elevations of all buildings, fences, gates, and permanent way features, together with alterations that the GER might institute. On 1st August 1893 the GER board heard from the General Manager that the Southwold Railway was laid to a gauge of 3 feet, was 8.75 miles in length and had two locomotives, six First and Third Class Composite carriages, fifteen goods wagons and two timber trucks. In 1892 the company had earned £3,560 with working expenses of £2,859 leaving a surplus of

£701, insufficient by £551 to cover the debenture interest. The SR Chairman had requested the GER either to rebate by 7½ per cent their proportion of receipts from traffic passing on and off the SR, or to purchase the SR at £48,125 against the original cost of £70,195. The General Manager recommended and the board duly authorised the arrangement with the SR whereby the GE would allow a rebate of 5 per cent out of GE earnings on traffic transferred on or off the SR at Halesworth, provided the Southwold Company agreed to give the main line company the option at any time during the succeeding twenty-one years of purchasing the narrow gauge line at a price to be settled by arbitration but not exceeding £48,125. This price was subject to both the GE Engineer and Locomotive Superintendent certifying that the infrastructure and rolling stock was worth that amount. Rapier considered the period of twenty-one years was excessive and suggested not exceeding ten years would be more realistic. He further opined there would be a growth in the net earnings of the SR within that timescale. Birt, the GER General Manager, reported to the Traffic Committee that he did not think the suggestion unreasonable provided the SR Directors were willing to allow a corresponding reduction in the price if the net revenue fell away.

The 1893 annual SR dinner, held in the Drill Hall on Friday 6th October, was organised by Station Master F.W. Hansford. J.J. Mayhew spoke of the *'brilliant leadership'* of Richard Rapier and added that visitors to the town always spoke in the highest terms of the civility of the company's servants, it being a well-known fact that one of the guards was a *'sort of directory and guide to the district'*. Secretary H. Carne reported he had been given the prospectus for another railway to Southwold, which was proof the present line was prospering; *'Why else would another company want to enter into competition?'* The Chairman Richard C Rapier concluded by contradicting his Secretary for he said, *'it had always been a labour of love to do all that he could for the Southwold Railway'*. He was sorry to say at present it was only a labour of love, the Directors' fees *'were still a long way up in the clouds'*.

Once again the matter of continuous brakes was raised when the BOT enquired on 16th November 1893 as to progress with compliance to the order requiring the fitting of continuous brakes. The Company Secretary replied on 16th January 1894 that the Directors had not met since November 1893 and he personally was *'laid up with an attack of influenza'* and unable to call a meeting. The BOT, probably inundated with alterations to requirements on main lines, did not respond until 30th March 1894 when they requested an urgent reply adding, *'it is now incumbent upon the BOT to consider the question of taking early proceedings to enforce compliance with the terms of the Order'*. The injury to a carrier in the goods shed at Southwold in early February could have resulted in a claim against the company but the matter was settled amicably in early April.

The half yearly report for the six months ending 31st December 1893, presented in April 1894, continued to show an increase in traffic, with 58,501 passengers travelling, whilst the carriage of parcels had nearly trebled. Goods tonnages had risen by thirty per cent despite the reduction in fish and minerals conveyed. The reduction in fish traffic was blamed on the decline in the longshore fishing at Southwold and minerals on the national coal strike. Encouraged by the upward trend the Directors announced they had ordered a further six wagons in July.

The threat of proceedings by the BOT against the company for noncompliance in fitting continuous brakes brought swift action and the company requested an early interview, which Pain and Carne attended on 10th April 1894. Despite their protestations the pair were informed there were to be no exceptions, a decision clarified in correspondence on 16th May when the BOT again asked what steps the Directors were taking to remedy the matter. The subject was placed in abeyance as no Directors meeting was to be held until September.

On 15th May 1894 William Birt the GE General Manager recommended the GE offer to consider the value of the Southwold line, together with the rolling stock, as being worth £1,000 more than an arbiter may value it for every £100 increase in the net receipts, providing the SR Directors agreed a reduction of £1,000 for every decrease of £100 in net revenue. Birt explained that by taking this action the GE would secure ten per cent for every £1,000 over and above the value of the infrastructure and rolling stock that the company would have to pay for the concern, whereas the GE could raise the money necessary for the purchase at under 4 per cent. The General Manager concluded his report stating the amount earned from the exchange of traffic was £11,000 per annum whilst the cost of working the SR was 80 per cent of gross receipts. The GE Traffic Committee broadly agreed with Birt's approach and he was advised to write to Rapier offering the amended terms. Rapier, as before, was unhappy with the offer, still considering the twenty-one years too long a period and suggesting ten years at the most, and in the event of net revenue increasing in that period the Southwold would receive some consideration for it. A request, however, was made for the GER Engineer and Locomotive Superintendent to visit the line to value the assets and rolling stock.

Members of the Suffolk Institute visited the Southwold area on 5th July 1894, the parties arriving at Ipswich to join the local contingency and catch the 10.18am train to Halesworth. After alighting they joined the *'American-carlike carriages'*, whose accommodation was *'severely taxed'* and arrived at Southwold at 11.30am. At the end of the day the SR facilities were ignored and the party was driven by road to Halesworth *'in good time for the return journey'* by GER to Ipswich.

The marriage of Walter Tuck, the Southwold Town Clerk, was celebrated in style by SR staff. On the arrival of the 2.05pm train at Southwold on Friday 6th July 1894, Station Master F.W. Hansford asked Tuck to walk into the station office and in the presence of several employees handed over a wedding present of an elegant pair of solid silver cellars together with an address:

'To Walter Charles Tuck Esq. In the presenting you with a small token of regard on the occasion of your marriage, the employees of the Southwold Railway Company trust that your journey from this junction may be without jars, collisions, delays or other accidents, that the lines may fall to you in pleasant places and that both you and your fellow traveller may reach the Great Terminus as happily and safely in all respects as when you first set out upon your journey. F.W. Hansford, A.E. Wright, H. Haycock, A. Calver, H. Ward, G. Goldsmith, G. Stannard, W.G. Jackson, J. Hammond, M. Spoor, H. Mitchell, W. Barnes, G. Adams, E. Laws, H. Sallows.'

As the 5.20pm train from Southwold to Halesworth was approaching the overbridge at Holton on Friday 27th July 1894, Driver John Hammond noted two boys looking over the parapet but as the engine passed under the arch a stone smashed the cab spectacle. One of the boys, aged twelve years, was subsequently apprehended and appeared at Halesworth Petty Sessions in August,

Railway Station, Southwold

Southwold station facing the buffer stops in 1900, soon after the opening of the Station Hotel in the right background but before the covered carriage shed was erected over the siding on the right which was protected by the simple buffer plate. The cart waiting for trade belonged the W. Doy, the SR company cartage agent. A locomotive is getting up steam on shed and the 4-wheel wagon on the run round loop has the side dropped. The platform has a gravel surface.
Author's collection

charged with *'causing a stone to fall on the engine of a railway train with the intent to endanger the lives of two men'*. After hearing the evidence, the Chairman of the Bench had no doubt the defendant threw the stone, *'it being a dangerous practice'*. The boy was sentenced to receive six strokes of the birch in the presence of his father.

On 12th October 1894 as a Down train was approaching the swing bridge, the leading wheels of the locomotive became derailed. The train crew weighed up the situation and decided to re-rail the engine using the portable jack carried on the footplate. It appeared none of the passengers considered walking to the terminus and many watched the operation. Once the locomotive was back on the track, the train continued to Southwold, where arrival was 38 minutes late. The minutes record that no passengers complained of any injuries or the late arrival!

The usual annual staff dinner was held on Tuesday 16th October 1894, at the Drill Hall, Southwold. The dinner was put back from the 24th September, the anniversary of the opening of the line, and had been delayed due to the lengthening of the summer season and the increase in traffic. Arthur C. Pain, the Managing Director, was absent as he had an appointment with Major General C.S. Hutchinson, the BOT Inspector the following day, so J.J. Mayhew officiated. He advised the gathering that *'traffic returns for 1882 still remained ahead of anything recorded since'*, whilst *'fish traffic remained at a very low ebb'* and trusted that one day the SR would provide a standard gauge line to the town and that *'improvements would be made to Southwold station'*.

The wild north-westerly gale blowing across the Blyth valley on Saturday 22nd December 1894 made for difficult conditions and as a passenger travelling on the 10.33am arrival at Southwold attempted to alight from coach No. 6 the door was snatched by the wind and the glass was smashed. This was nothing compared with the damage which was to follow, for as the wind abated in the evening an abnormally high tide overnight forced the sea to breach the coast on either side of Southwold. The onrushing water

arrive, plus parcels and mails, were safely despatched by bus. He was also advised the SR could not accept consignments of grain, oatcake, coke and coal until the line was cleared. The SR Company had hoped to run a train service between Walberswick and Halesworth from Monday 24th, Christmas Eve, but with both serviceable engines marooned at Southwold, and the third undergoing maintenance and repairs, they were forced to continue hiring buses with a service of four in each direction conveying mails and parcels as well as passengers. Walter Doy arrived on Monday to clear all small items of goods but the two trucks of timber and twelve wagons of coal had to wait until the line was cleared. The engineer arrived on site the same day and immediately summoned the entire staff, who with twelve extra men hired for the occasion, set out to reconstruct the line. On Tuesday, Christmas Day, Walter Carver started out at 7am and walked to Wenhaston to pass on instructions, issued by Arthur Pain, to Ganger Spoore. He then walked back to Halesworth and loaded one truck with sleepers. Ganger Spoore, Porters Sallows and Ferrer and the station master then pushed the wagon through to Blythburgh, where they obtained the services of a large horse to haul the wagon forward and up the gradient of Lists Bank from where they went on to the site of the breach in the road. Here they assisted with repair work until 4.30pm before walking home along the line. Ferrer remained behind to assist with the work and the three men arrived back at Halesworth totally exhausted at 7.45pm. The work continued through the Christmas period and by the evening of 27th December it was possible for a locomotive and coach to run to Halesworth to connect with the last GER service on the main line. To compensate the men for the hardship of spending Christmas hard at work on the railway and away from their families, Arthur Pain supplied the whole gang with roast beef, plum pudding and beer from the Swan Hotel for four consecutive days. The first train across the breach was accompanied by a pilotman and from Friday 28th, when the normal timetable resumed, this method of working continued. The bus service which had maintained connection with the outside world was withdrawn after the last journey on 27th December. The *Halesworth Times* voiced the thought of many on 1st January 1895 when it enthused, *'An experience of this kind in mid-winter is calculated to make us devoutly thankful for the existence of the much-abused Southwold line'*.

The half yearly results for the six months ending 31st December 1894 showed 54,990 passengers travelling, a reduction of 3,511 compared with the same period the previous year but in excess of every year except 1892 and 1893. The 16,574 parcels conveyed was a record and three times that carried in 1880. Goods traffic was still increasing, having doubled in seven years, but fish traffic, although better than the previous five years, was poor in comparison to the record amounts carried in 1884 and 1885. Mineral traffic, especially coal, was increasing annually and for the six months in question 3,842 tons were carried. As a result of the increase in non-passenger traffic the total receipts for the half year were £2,420 3s 0d, an increase of £193 8s 6d over the came period in 1893.

The night of 13th January 1895 was wild, with a howling gale blowing from the north across the Suffolk coast As the hours passed, flurries of snow filled the air and only a few hardy souls ventured abroad. By the early hours of Monday 14th a blizzard was blowing with fine snow filling every nook and cranny. The Halesworth permanent way gang with difficulty made their way to the line and commenced examining the route, whilst the Southwold gang did not have far to trudge from the terminus in the darkness to discover a six-foot drift blocking the line between the station and the cutting.

submerged Wood End marshes and initially carried away 160 feet of the railway embankment as well as flooding the bridge end of Station Road. The town was isolated and the only means of access was by boat. Even this method of transit was unsafe as the onrush of the tide continued and William Cady was drowned attempting to cross the flood by dinghy. As the sea encroached and rushed up the Blyth, the riverbanks collapsed in several places and water scoured away another 300 yards of railway embankment, leaving the rails and sleepers twisted and suspended in mid-air. Nothing could be done in the darkness but in the calm of Sunday 23rd, and in the absence of telephonic communication, Frederick Hanson the Southwold station master went to Halesworth to advise his colleague Station Master Walter Calver of the damage. A telegraph was dispatched to summon the engineer, whilst the station masters arranged for a horse drawn bus to provide a substitute service for passengers. The GER station master was advised not to book through passengers until further notice but in the meantime those passengers who did

Other permanent way staff found a drift blocking the cutting at Lists, where the snow lay between two and five feet in depth for a distance of half a mile. The position was reported to F.W. Hansford, the Southwold station master, who organised twenty staff and extra hands to clear the snow from both sites. Fortunately the snowstorm soon passed and the men cleared both blockages in time to allow the 7.30am train from Southwold to run, albeit half an hour late. At the end of the month there were even higher tides experienced at Southwold than in December 1894. Although the mail cart from Halesworth was delayed by floodwater on the road and the ferry across the Blyth was suspended, the railway was unaffected.

At the Directors meeting in September 1894, no firm commitments had been made regarding the fitting of continuous brakes and the BOT was belatedly advised of the fact on 26th December 1894. The BOT was losing patience with the SR Directors and replied on 9th January 1895 requiring an answer to their letter of 16th May 1894. With new legislation in the offing regarding light railways and a relaxation of certain provisions, including it was thought for the requirement for continuous brakes, the company replied to the BOT on 27th February 1895 stating that it was considered *'vexatious to make this company raise fresh capital for the purpose of continuous braking their trains'* and considering such expenditure as *'worse than useless'*. The BOT, however, continued to press for compliance and instructed their solicitor to write to the company. The letter dated 30th May 1895 was polite but stressed that compliance was necessary under the Act and pointed out the grave responsibilities upon the company in the unfortunate event of a fatal accident. He concluded that should the proposed bill relating to Light Railways be passed it would not relieve the SR of complying with the current legislation. The SR board again chose to ignore the diktat.

On 20th June 1895 two twelve-year-old boys, Bernard Eade and John Kett, were caught trespassing on the railway near Blythburgh and prosecuted. The case was heard at Halesworth Petty Sessions on Thursday 4th July, when W.C. Tuck appearing for the prosecution reported the boys had previously been cautioned for trespassing and proceedings were now being instituted because at the point of trespass the line was on a sharp curve, and it would have been impossible for the driver of an approaching train to brake his engine in time to avoid an accident. It was apparent that children were in the habit of placing nails, stones and coins on the rails, and the company had decided to make an example of the pair to deter others. Eade and Kett were each ordered to pay 6s 0d costs and to come up for judgement *'when called upon'*.

The report for the half year ending 30th June 1895 showed an increase in revenue from passengers and goods but a slight reduction in parcels and mineral traffic compared with the same period in 1894. Total receipts amounted to £1,561 4s 10d and the balance carried to the net revenue account was £98 0s 5d. The amount expended on the track and embankment damaged by the floods, and renewal of the points leading to Wenhaston Mill siding, however, had seriously reduced the way and works maintenance account. At this time the capital receipts of the company totalled £76,516 formed of:

	£
£10 ordinary shares	39,910
Preference shares	9,000
4 per cent preference debenture stock	11,970
5 per cent debenture stock	14,300
4 and 5 per cent loans and rental charges	1,336

Richard C. Rapier remained Chairman of the SR Company with Arthur C. Pain as Managing Director. The other Directors were Charles Chambers, the contractor and major shareholder, and his son Walter C. Chambers, both of 5 Westminster Chambers, London SW1. Henry Carne was Secretary and the company office was at 17 Victoria Street, London SW1. J.F. Clarke and J.B. Walton were the Auditors. Since the company was formed the Directors had received no remuneration and in 1895 they finally approached the shareholders to vote an undisclosed sum.

The 1895 annual dinner to the employees was held at the Drill Hall, Southwold on Friday 18th October. In the absence of A.C. Pain, Alderman J.J. Mayhew as Chairman remarked that in the sixteen years of its existence the SR had made *'wonderful progress'*. The goods traffic had increased threefold, and the passenger traffic had reached the *'highly satisfactory'* figure of 40,000 during the three summer months of the year. Increased accommodation had recently been given to the public by the enlargement of the booking office at Southwold and by the erection of a small goods office. The difficulty created by the floods in the winter had been *'well overcome'*, a temporary arrangement being made to prevent the interruption of traffic. He closed his report by congratulating Henry Carne on his complete restoration to health. Carne in response stated the *'policy of the railway company was one of caution and well considered progress. Improvement of the rolling stock and premises had to be undertaken before any thought of a dividend on ordinary shares could be entertained'*. He was *'anxious to afford the tradesmen of Halesworth and Southwold every possible convenience'*, and *'believed from the heavy nature of the summer traffic that the railway served the needs of the town, and was the chief factor in its prosperity'*.

Despite the severe winter of 1894/5 and the resultant serious damage to embankment and track, the SR was able to sustain a small increase in revenue, which was considered *'satisfactory proof the line was not only meeting the requirements of the district, but also developing the same'*. Major expenditure during 1895 included enlarging the waiting room, new booking office and lamp room and constructing a goods office at Southwold, roofing over the trans-ship shed at Halesworth, the overhaul of locomotive No. 2 *Halesworth* by the GER at Stratford and the purchase of 50 tons of steel rails for the part renewal of the permanent way. For the six months ending 31st December 1895 gross revenue from all sources was £2,567 4s 11d, an increase of £147 1s 11d on the same half of 1894. Traffic returns showed 57,287 passengers, the largest number ever carried except for the corresponding half year in 1893. Parcels conveyed totalled 16,937, an increase of 434 over the equivalent half year in 1894, 2,607 tons of goods, 171 tons more than 1894. The fish traffic totalled 414 tons, better than any half year since 1885 and an increase over the previous half year in 1894 of 28 tons. The only downturn was a fall of 252 tons of minerals conveyed to 3,590 tons. Finally, 85,711 passengers had been carried and 28,598 parcels, 4,938 tons of goods, 414 tons of fish and 6,817 tons of minerals conveyed during 1895 whilst train mileage for the year was 27,888. Outlay for maintenance of way and works in the half year ending 31st December 1895 had increased by £216 over the previous half year in 1894 because of station improvements.

On 6th July 1895 the company had responded to the BOT solicitor's letter of 30th May regretting the grave responsibility being cast upon the Directors, as the line had been worked with BOT conditions of 1880 and without accidents, an untrue statement when taking into account the death of the clerk at Walberswick on 14th November 1883 and the derailment on 12th October 1894.

It was pointed out that it was considered the BOT could exercise optional powers by the use of the word *'may'* in clause one of the Act. In conclusion the company Directors emphasized they were prepared to be taken before the Railway Commissioners as a test case. In early September the solicitor sought opinion of Council, who responded on 16th September 1895 inter alia that *'it appears to me on the facts at present before me doubtful whether the Commission will enforce the order'.* The BOT, however, continued to be adamant that there should be no relaxation in the interest of public safety and two further letters were exchanged in November pointing out that reliance should not be placed on their happy immunity in the past from accidents, or reliance on possible changes in legislation and considered other possible causes of accidents. The company responded in late January 1896 expressing the view that *'even the adoption of continuous brakes would not preclude all risk of accident and such adoption would tend in the case of SR rolling stock to increase the risk'.* The letter concluded that *'the Directors fully considered all the points raised in the letter on 30 May 1895 and that they adhered in every respect to the views expressed therein'.* Thus after considerable correspondence the company retired having earned a partial victory.

To assist with the smooth interchange of traffic at Halesworth the GER on 16th June 1896 authorised the expenditure of £240 to provide additional standard gauge sidings alongside the SR, and on SR property providing the Southwold company agreed to pay £5 per annum rental on the outlay and to the GE removing the material used at any time on one months notice. After objections from the SR, the GER authorities agreed to wave the £5 annual rental. On 18th July 1896 William Birt, the GER General Manager, duly wrote to Henry Carne, the SR Secretary, withdrawing the condition for the £5 annual payment for the material storage. Carne replied three days later agreeing to the removal of materials used at a month's notice on either side and requesting the works to be put in hand. In the same year the SR management announced plans for a proposed extension of facilities at Southwold and land was purchased at the west end of the station on 6th July. This enabled the goods yard to be extended by resiting the connection from the main single line further from the station. The sidings were subsequently rearranged and a new connection provided on the north side of the yard and another to the south of the platform forming a short bay.

The Light Railways Act of 1896 was promoted to alleviate the distress of the agricultural depression by allowing inexpensive railways to be constructed in rural areas, with the proviso that those so constructed would be released from the obligation to build to the high standards laid down by the BOT for main lines. Section 5 of the Act stated that where the Board of Agriculture certified that the provision of a light railway would benefit agriculture, the Treasury might agree to aid the building of the line out of public money. Another significant feature of the statute was that application to the Light Railway Commissioners for an order could be made by the county, borough or district through which the railway would pass, or by any company or individual. The latter was particularly relevant to the proposal for a railway in rural areas and soon various railway contractors and engineers were formulating plans to spread the railway network, if local parties were agreeable to such schemes. As we shall see the SR soon became embroiled directly or indirectly in such proposals.

In late October 1896 the report for the half year ending 30th June showed gross revenue standing at £1,559 4s 5d or £2 0s 5d less than the corresponding period in 1895. The number of passengers conveyed totalled 27,707 and parcels 12,292 whilst goods traffic showed a large increase of 550 tons compared with the same period in 1895 to 2,467 tons. Coal traffic had reduced because consumption of the fuel had fallen due to the mild winter.

As recorded earlier, annual staff gatherings were held at Southwold, the function being used as a springboard for the management to boost staff morale. The staff gathering held on Monday 9th November 1896 was, according to the *Halesworth Times*, attended by the entire railway staff plus thirty guests. Arthur Pain was in the chair and the conviviality was tempered by such topics as the desirability of easier parcels rates for small parcels, the requirements for an improved train service to Norwich and the hope the SR would extend their line to connect with the GER at Lowestoft.

At the annual SR staff dinner on Monday 30th November 1896 the deputy mayor of Southwold, E.O. Debney, praised Arthur Pain for being the *'principal instrument in the railway communication with Southwold'* having *'piloted the company through times of discouragement to their present success'.* He then asked Pain to direct the same energy and effort to reopening the harbour and inferred the *'useless body known as the Harbour Commission'* might be bought out by the expenditure of £300, after which he thought *'the Corporation would be glad enough to hand over the harbour to any person or company who might spend annually on it'.* At a comparatively small cost it might be made navigable for fishing smacks, and then *'the facility of access would bring to the railway company a large increase in fish traffic'.* Replying, Pain warmly approved and promised his best assistance to any scheme for re-opening the harbour. *'If the Corporation would lay hold of one handle of the plough, the Railway Company would seize the other'* and he concurred with Debney *'the accomplishment of the idea was within the range of possibility'.*

In December 1896 the GE announced that passenger traffic from London and stations in the suburban district booking to Southwold during the period March to October 1896 amounted to £5,700, an increase of £374 compared with the similar period in 1895.

The SR results for the half year ending 31st December 1896 showed that 57,596 passengers had travelled on the railway, an increase of 309 over the same period in 1895. The number of parcels conveyed had also increased by 1,524 to a total of 18,461 compared with 1895. Whilst goods and mineral tonnages continued to increase, fish traffic had seriously declined with only 223 tons carried compared with 414 tons in the same period the previous year. The revenue account showed total receipts of £2,580 16s 6d compared with £2,567 4s 11d in the corresponding period of 1895. Expenditure was reduced, so a balance of £590 1s 0d was carried forward to the revenue account. Following a petition signed by 250 people in favour of reopening Southwold Harbour, the mayor called a public meeting on Thursday 21st January 1897, at which he explained to the gathering that an Act of 1830 had taken away the management of the harbour from the town authorities and vested it with the Harbour Commissioners, consisting mainly of county magistrates, although ownership remained with Southwold Corporation. The Commissioners had totally failed in their responsibilities; more recently they had omitted to take adequate action to dredge the harbour, which had subsequently silted up, and had since resigned. The Town Clerk, who was the Committee Secretary, had in 1892 endeavoured to interest the Directors of the Midland Railway to take steps to obtain control of the harbour. A negative answer had been received from Derby but the Town Clerk was advised to raise sufficient money to apply for a Board of Trade Order to cancel the old Commission and to invest the powers in the hands of the Southwold Corporation. The Corporation would

ABOVE: The railway between the Blyth swing bridge and the cutting through Southwold Common was flooded on several occasions, most notably on 29th November 1897 when severe flooding across Woodend Marshes inundated the railway between the Blyth swing bridge and Southwold. After passing over the river the line descended over level crossing No 55 at 7 miles 78 chains, descending into the floodwater before rising through the cutting (hillside, far left) on the approach to the terminus. In the centre is the golf course old club house and to the right is the water tower and tower of St. Edmund's Church.
Author's collection

RIGHT: The embankment was also washed away in places as a result of the inundation. Trains terminated and started back from Walberswick or Blythburgh with passengers initially crossing the inundation by boat before a horse drawn omnibus service was instituted until repairs could be effected.
Author's collection

The rebuilding of the railway after the flooding of 29th November 1897 required the reconstruction of the embankment at a higher level above the flood plain and here repairs are well in hand using the company's wagons and a locomotive to good effect.
Author's collection

then be in a position to deal with the SR and other interested companies, if deemed advisable, or carry out the work itself. The Corporation, however, had no powers to spend Corporation funds to obtain the order so the gathering resolved to form a committee to raise the necessary funds to obtain the provisional order and at the conclusion of the meeting nearly £100 was collected.

Charles Chambers was appointed Chairman of the SR Company in 1897 on the death of Richard C. Rapier. Chambers had been elected to the board in 1889 and was an enthusiastic devotee of the railway. On bank holiday 2nd August 1897, the train services were packed with passengers seeking to spend a few hours by the sea. Halesworth station booking office issued a total of 415 return and 33 single tickets to SR stations, whilst the total number of passengers travelling was augmented by through bookings from GER stations. Brilliant sunshine and a cloudless sky resulted in most people waiting until the last possible moment to leave Southwold, so that the 7.15pm departure was formed of six crowded coaches hauled by locomotive No. 1 *Southwold*. The journey was uneventful until the engine found the weight of the formation too great to surmount the rising gradient into Halesworth station and the train came to a stand near Holton Road bridge. By the simple expedient of detaching the three rear coaches, the guard applying the hand brake and scotching them with a log to prevent them running away, the engine was able to haul the leading three vehicles of the train forward to the station. Unfortunately the log proved incapable of holding the three loaded coaches and it was unclear whether the hand brake was incorrectly applied or the engine restarting the train slightly reversed the front three coaches but to the *'consternation of the more timid passengers'* the rear three vehicles started to roll back down the 1 in 66 gradient towards Wenhaston until they came to rest on level track near Blyford. No attempt was made to reapply the hand brake. When the driver and fireman returned with No. 1 to pick up the coaches, they were shocked to find they were missing and so they continued at a slow speed until the trio full of irate passengers were found. The coaches were quickly coupled to the locomotive and the formation set off for Halesworth. To the consternation of the SR Manager a passenger wrote to the BOT complaining of the operational irregularity, otherwise the escapade might have passed unnoticed.

The *Halesworth Times* for 7th September 1897 reported the summer season at Southwold *'the best yet, with hundreds unable to find accommodation'*. There was urgent need for house building and a direct line to Lowestoft. *'The Southwold Railway had done much for the place in the last eighteen years. An extension of the line to Lowestoft would make it a thoroughfare instead of a cul-de-sac'*. In November, after council elections, Southwold Corporation unanimously accepted the report of the Harbour Committee to take over the management of the harbour and noted £142 had been raised to pay towards the application to the BOT.

A violent gale and driving rain struck the Suffolk coast on 29th November 1897 causing extensive damage and flooding to the foreshore at Southwold. The River Blyth rose to flood level and the SR was breached between the swing bridge and the Common as the rising waters undermined the embankment, leaving rails suspended in mid air. Water also breached the main road and effectively isolated the town. Fortunately a locomotive and stock were at Halesworth when the embankment succumbed, so the 1.10pm Down departure was able to proceed as far as the swing bridge beyond Walberswick station. The passengers and goods were taken across the swollen River Blyth to Blackshore in four boats, three or four to each boat, temporarily hired for the emergency. Thereafter trains operated between Halesworth and Walberswick but it was found more convenient to operate a horse bus from and to Blythburgh, a charge of 9d being made for the road conveyance. Rebuilding of the embankment was quickly put in hand and the railway reopened throughout on 8th December. To obviate the possibility of marooning all rolling stock at the Southwold end of the line, the Directors had agreed to henceforth stable a locomotive and rolling stock at Halesworth to operate the western section of the line during the winter months. The company also took remedial steps of raising the faulty embankment to a greater height during the reconstruction work.

At the half yearly meeting it was announced the balance of net revenue for the half year ending 31st December 1897 was £587, sufficient to pay interest on the rent charges and 4 per cent preferred debentures, and 1½ per cent for the year on 5 per cent debentures. Then for the half year ending 30th June 1898 the net revenue totalled £57 and rent charge interest was £39. At 31st December 1898, of the £77,000 raised in stocks, shares and loans, the company had expended £71,810. The capital receipts had increased by £20 with the 4 per cent debentures holding standing at £11,990.

On 1st July 1898 it was reported the Health Officer for Southwold Corporation had inspected the lavatories at Southwold station and the official was far from satisfied with what he found. The condition of the gentlemen's urinals and ladies' closets were foul, they were without running water, although he noted the gentlemen's facilities were fed from a large tank. It was subsequently resolved the company should arrange for a connection to be made with the mains water supply and main sewer so that proper water supplies could be made to the urinals and closets.

Passenger traffic from GER London and suburban stations booking to Southwold from March to October 1898 totalling 8,530 passengers earning revenue of £5,809, comparing favourably with Aldeburgh which only registered £3,855 over the same period. In 1899 the earnings were £7,029, an increase of £1,220. The number of passengers travelling on the Southwold Railway in 1898 totalled 93,798, parcels conveyed 31,161, goods traffic conveyed 5,346 tons and mineral traffic 6,664 tons.

The herring fishing industry at Yarmouth and Lowestoft was extremely prosperous with up to a thousand drifters coming down from the Scottish ports to finish the season. At its height the harbour facilities at both places were totally inadequate and the offloading and dispatch of fish to London and the provincial markets suffered unacceptable delays. It was imperative another harbour was found to provide additional facilities and at last after several years of petitioning Southwold was recognised as capable of providing relief to the two main ports. Thus in 1898 the BOT authorized the Southwold Harbour Order investing the maintenance and upkeep of the harbour with Southwold Corporation, the statute operative from 14th February 1899. It was reiterated the Harbour Commissioners had neglected their charge resulting in the harbour silting up; trade had transferred to the railway, while the quay, which formerly dealt with fifty to sixty ships, was deserted. However, the railway was the recipient of severe criticism when it was stated recent obstructions, which accelerated the silting up of the harbour, included the railway swing bridge, which appeared to have caused the tide to set over to the Walberswick shore and leave Blackshore Quay unapproachable.

The Southwold Express.

Another view of a mixed train departing Southwold in the circa 1904. Three children stand on the fence watching the 'Southwold Express' depart with a cloud of smoke. To the left is the outer starting signal with arm lowered and blocking the view of the third coach is the inner starting signal. In the background is the carriage shed and beyond that the Station Hotel. A lady in long white dress has been allowed to remain on the open carriage end for the departure, which is also being recorded from the end of the station platform by a second photographer.
Neil Parkhouse collection

5

Possible Expansion and Conversion of Gauge

In 1898 the first proposal was made to construct a 12¼ mile, 3 feet gauge extension line from Southwold to Lowestoft at an estimated cost of £74,734 13s 0d and an application was duly made to the Light Railway Commissioners in May. Unfortunately the document had been prepared and estimates made without any reference to the GE authorities at Bishopsgate. The submission was sensibly withdrawn before reaching the local enquiry stage when it was realised the GER would raise objections to through traffic requiring transshipment at Southwold and Lowestoft, as well as Halesworth. Across the county the seeds of the Mid Suffolk Light Railway (MSLR) were planted in October 1898 when plans for a railway linking Haughley (on the GER Ipswich to Norwich main line) to Halesworth, with a branch from Kenton to Debenham and on to a junction at Westerfield on the outskirts of Ipswich were circulated to parish councils and landowners. The idea was favourably greeted and various meetings were held at Halesworth, Debenham, Stradbroke, Stonham, Mendlesham and Laxfield in the early months of 1899.

Halesworth Parish Council approved the construction of the Mid Suffolk Light Railway in April 1899 provided no level crossings were permitted over main roads adjacent to the town, whilst in the following month some hostility was shown against the proposed Southwold & Lowestoft Light Railway. At Southwold Trinity Fair, S.W. Woollett warned that *'If such a plan were adopted, Southwold would be liable to be over-run by the riff-raff from Lowestoft and the business of the town be injuriously affected'*. He was of the opinion *'some people seemed to think such a line would be beneficial to the interests of the GER'* and *'rather suspected that the company was at the back of the project. If so, there was the possibility of injury being done to the harbour by an interference with the rights and opportunities, which the Corporation now possesses'*. The Mayor expressed the hope that proper protection would be afforded to the cliffs in the routing of the light railway. Eaton W. Moore did not regard it *'as a step in the right direction'* to tack Southwold on to Lowestoft. There was a scheme afloat to carry a light railway from Haughley to Halesworth. If this were carried into effect, then it seemed to him it would be possible to develop the scheme, which he had advocated for the last fifteen or twenty years, in securing a connection with the Midlands, for it would be possible to get communication with the rest of the country if there was anything like direct communication to Cambridge. He hoped the MSLR scheme might be carried out, but he *'deprecated the linking of Southwold with Lowestoft as proposed'*. Certainly at a meeting of the Central Committee of the MSLR held at Ipswich on 26th May 1899 it was estimated the new line would be carrying 1,262 tons of inward and 140 tons of outgoing goods traffic from Halesworth, Southwold and district.

During the spring of 1899 the railway company arranged for a telephone pole route to be installed alongside the line from Halesworth to Southwold, but the passage of the route across the swing bridge was the topic of discussion between the SR and Southwold Town Council after the local authority raised objections. The Secretary of the railway company wrote on 21st June 1899 that he was not aware it was necessary to ask the permission of the Town Council to put a telephone wire along their line of railway and that if it was necessary at any time to pass a ship by the swing bridge, the company would arrange for its passing. The matter was considered at the Council meeting on 14th July when it was resolved an answer would be forwarded stating the Council had no desire to put any obstacle in the way of the railway company, but they considered the telephone wire across the bridge to be an infringement of their rights to the harbour, and that provision had to be made for passing the wire under the river or providing unions enabling easy disconnection and reconnection, and subject to the approval of the Corporation.

In a review of the *'Southwold Season'*, the *Halesworth Times* for 29th August 1899 reported *'the little railway line'* had successfully and efficiently handled *'colossal traffic'*. However, there was still controversy regarding the proposed extension to Lowestoft forcing the Mayor, J.J. Mayhew, to call a meeting on 14th September. He thought:

'They would do good by joining hands with Lowestoft, where they would meet with the GER and the Midland and Great Northern Railway. They had no fear of invasion by trippers, as they had no attraction for them'.

Arthur Pain was then called upon to address the gathering and explained that twenty years ago the SR was opened from Halesworth and this year had carried 98,000 passengers. The distance by Halesworth and Beccles to Lowestoft was 25 miles against the 12 miles by the proposed railway. At Reydon there could be a station, also sidings for brick traffic between Frostenden and Cove Hithe. A station would be constructed at Wrentham and at Henstead there would be another stopping place, with another at Pakefield, with the termination in South Lowestoft, near Wellington Terrace, alongside the GER. The cost of the line was estimated at £74,000 and the company would undertake to convey fish traffic onto the GER line or to fish salesmen at Lowestoft market. J.T. Hughes moved the resolution approving the new line, with the Reverend C.H. Sutton seconding; the resolution was adopted unanimously amid loud applause. The resolution was duly passed to the Light Railway Commissioners with the mayor adding he would represent the town at the inquiry.

In 1899 the inhabitants of Walberswick complained of the poor location of their station, which required intending or arriving passengers to undertake a walk of over half a mile along an unlit bridle path known as Tinker's Walk to reach the centre of the village. The villagers submitted a petition requesting relocation of the station nearer the main road but when the Directors replied the suggested site would entail a much longer walk, the matter was dropped. In the same year telephonic communication was completed between Halesworth with Southwold and connecting the intermediate stations.

Those attending the half yearly meeting held in March 1900 heard that receipts for the six months ending 31st December 1899 had shown satisfactory increases in all classes of traffic. The number of passengers conveyed was 71,357, an increase of 7,243 more than the corresponding period in 1898; parcels traffic 19,563, an increase of 1,219; 3,565 tons of goods traffic up by 399 tons, and minerals 4,475 tons an increase of 545 tons. In twenty years the passenger traffic had increased by 32,000 and parcels, goods and minerals had grown threefold. Receipts were £468 above the comparable period in 1898. Six new 7-ton capacity wagons had been added to the rolling stock total and a telephone route had been erected, which greatly enhanced communications especially with train operation. It was prematurely announced the enquiry into the Southwold to Lowestoft extension by the Light Railway Commissioners was expected shortly, the local press adding the line would bring *'material advantage to our long suffering fishing industry'*. On a sadder note, the death was also announced of Henry Carne the *'much valued and esteemed'* SR Secretary, who had served in that capacity since 1884. Carne had been suffering from a severe illness for over a year and was only able to discharge his duties at intervals. His funeral was held on Saturday 31st March 1900 at St. Edmund's Church, Southwold. Among the mourners were the station masters at Southwold, Blythburgh, Wenhaston and Halesworth, Guard A.R. Wright and several other members of the railway staff. The new Secretary appointed was Henry Ward, who transferred to the line from the Great Northern Railway. Ward had previously been in the employ of the SR before seeking promotion to the main line company.

After many months of negotiations behind the scenes the solution to the impasse with the GER was clarified and in May 1900 an amended application was submitted for a Light Railway Order to convert the existing SR to 4 feet 8½ inches standard gauge and operate the undertaking in accordance with the 1896 Light Railways Act. To obviate objections being raised, the application restricted construction to the 9 miles from Southwold to Kessingland, where it was to join the GER authorised line from Lowestoft to Kessingland. The estimated cost of the revised scheme was £48,583, together with £35,666 to convert the existing Southwold to Halesworth line to standard gauge. Powers were to be sought to enter into a working agreement with the GER and for the GER to subscribe. However, after being notified on 6th June 1900 the GER board gave notice they would oppose such a scheme. At this period Charles Chambers was Chairman of the SR with fellow Directors Arthur C. Pain, Walter C. Chambers and W. Steele Tomkins of 28 Victoria Street, London SW.

Many visitors to the Halesworth Horse and Flower Show held on Thursday 19th July, as well as other SR passengers, were delayed when a locomotive derailed, reportedly because of the intense heat of the day buckling the rails. A gang of platelayers was summoned to carry out repairs after rerailing the engine and traffic was resumed after one and a half hours.

A further complaint was made to the BOT on 21st July 1900 by an irate passenger who considered the actions of the guard passing from one coach to another by using the outside steps while the train was in motion was highly dangerous and set a bad example. Lieutenant P.G. Von Donop was delegated to visit the railway to investigate; he thought the report was exaggerated but considered the suggested solution of a central bridge, walkway or drop plate over the coupling would be equally as dangerous on the many curves of the line, whilst passengers would be tempted to use them. The agreed final solution was to lengthen the exterior steps on each coach.

The pleasures of Southwold and the quaintness of the SR was expounded in the *Woolwich Herald* of 24th August 1900 and repeated in the *Halesworth Times* on 4th September:

'From London's busy city visitors make the journey from Liverpool Street, 104 miles in three and a half hours by the Great Eastern Railway. At Halesworth, eight and a half miles from Southwold, passengers change carriages and meet with a pleasant surprise. Leaving the leviathan engines which tear across the country, often at the rate of a mile a minute, the visitors enter a tramcar, drawn by a small engine, which runs on a narrow gauge railway, and is often pronounced – from the novelty and quaintness – to supply the most pleasurable part of the journey. The visitor will not be long in Southwold before he will recognize familiar faces, notably from Woolwich, Greenwich and Lewisham districts – faces in most instances of people who have secured their apartments through the Herald, which every week contains columns of advertisements of seaside apartments.'

The article concluded by advising the reader of the *'capital golf club'* with golf tickets being issued from Liverpool Street on production of a *'Southwold Golf Members card for 12s 6d (return) available for eight days'*.

Despite the glowing publicity afforded in the *Woolwich Herald*, in deepest Suffolk things appeared very different; for some time the inhabitants of Southwold had been dissatisfied with the GE main line train services to Halesworth and the connections with the SR. After due representation arrangements were made for the Town Clerk of Southwold and others to meet the GE Directors on Tuesday 2nd October 1900 regarding improvements in the service. The following day the GER board included in their agenda the possible changes but more importantly the continuing request by the SR for the line to be taken over. At the meeting the board members were advised the capital of the SR at 31st December 1899 was £76,626 and the operating profit for the year £2,128, which at 3 per cent represented a capital of £70,933. It was considered the *'sum of £60,000 was not an exorbitant sum to pay for purchase, provided the permanent way, stations and rolling stock were in fair condition'*, although the line was reportedly only valued at £27,322. The GER Engineer was requested to conduct a re-examination of the line and report on the cost of converting the existing railway to standard gauge with sufficient land to enable the line to be doubled at a future date. He was also instructed to report on the cost of constructing an alternative single track standard gauge line between Saxmundham or Leiston and Southwold, again with the provision for future widening.

Southwold Town Council held a special meeting on the evening of Friday 2nd November to receive the report of the deputation, who reported the GER Directors knew a great deal more about the matter than they did and asked for their requests to be submitted in writing. In the debate that followed, Alderman Adnams said a greater part of the visitors to Southwold and goods came from London and *'sometimes on occasions like bank holidays, passengers were left on the platform at Halesworth until their Southwold train came back again'*. Adnams reiterated he had no wish to say anything derogatory about the SR; the company had arrived in the district when badly wanted, had been of great assistance and helped the little town to expand. The time had, however, arrived for a better service and if the GER could see their way to help the town, then the Council ought certainly to support them. He had drawn up a resolution:

'That the Corporation of Southwold thank the Directors of the Great Eastern Railway for their courteous reception of the deputation sent to interview them with reference to a more convenient train service to this borough. That in the event of the GER Company providing a railway to their standard gauge, so as to place Southwold in direct communication with London, this Corporation will use its best endeavour to assist them in carrying out the enterprise. The Corporation in passing the resolution wished it to be understood that it applies to negotiations that may take place without necessary delay.'

Alderman Adnams concluded by saying *'they wanted the proper gauge'*, to obviate the trans-shipment of goods, and *'a more direct communication with London so that visitors would not have to stop at every station coming up or down'*. Alderman Debey seconded the resolution saying it had been asserted the GER intended coming through the common, but from information he had, this was not their intention. The resolution was carried fourteen for and two abstentions.

The GER Engineer's survey was completed in time for the following GE board meeting on 7th November 1900. At that meeting the General Manager reported that Pain, whilst initially accepting the £60,000 offer, had advised that his Directors were willing to sell the line at a fair and reasonable price to be agreed, or in the event of disagreement to be settle by arbitration. The Engineer then reported on the alternative line. The route proposed a railway penetrating more sparsely populated tracts of Suffolk than the Blyth valley. It commenced 27 chains north of Saxmundham Junction signal box and ran mostly on gradients of 1 in 100 for just over 10 miles to a terminal at Southwold. Stations were proposed at Westleton, Dunwich and Walberswick before the River Blyth was crossed on a swing bridge. Alternative approaches and sites for a terminus were proposed at Southwold, one running close to Walberswick parallel to Salt Creek, along the base of Skilman's Hill then through Strickland Place to terminate near the Post Office. The second proposed route ran to a point between the Southwold Railway bridge and Blackshore to terminate about 3½ chains south of the SR station. The cost of the new line was estimated at £145,445, against £158,887 for the purchase and rebuilding of the Southwold line (£98,887 for regauging and £60,000 for purchase), which would not be an 'express' line. As the GER had more important projects including capital improvement works in the London District, the Engineer advised against construction of the new line and the GER board after discussion resolved that no further steps would be taken at present to purchase the SR.

In the meantime the SR continued with their extension proposals and the Light Railway Commissioners duly held an enquiry at Southwold Town Hall into the application for the Light Railway Order on 18th December 1900, with the GER now taking no steps to oppose. The application was to widen the line to standard gauge and extend it to Kessingland. The estimated cost of conversion was £35,000 and the extension £48,000. For much of its length the new line would run through the Gooch estates, the trustees of whom had originally objected but were now convinced of the benefit it would bring to the district. Giving evidence Arthur Pain said the present SR narrow gauge line was worked as a light railway with a speed limit of 16 mph. On the new line it was proposed to provide a station at Reydon, which would also serve Wangford; a siding at South Cove for general goods traffic and the brickworks; a station at Wrentham and another at Hestead for Benacre and Sotterley. It was proposed to effect a junction with the GER at Kessingland where there would be a common station for both companies. Pain thought that after a very short time of opening of the extension, the company would be earning £13 to £14 per mile per week on the whole of their lines, against present earnings of £12 per mile per week. East Suffolk County Council, Kessingland Parish Council and the East Anglian Light Railway Company opposed the scheme, all of the objections relating to the provision of level crossings where the proposed extension would cross roads and another proposed railway. Counsel for the East Anglian Light Railway Company thought a bridge would be the better alternative. Pain strenuously objected, arguing that manned level crossings with adjacent stations were all that was needed. Despite their eagerness for improvements in railway communication Southwold Corporation raised an objection feeling that the railway company would have great difficulty raising the necessary capital if both schemes were pursued at the same time. In addition to the estimates given, the Town Clerk argued that a further £30,000 would be required for standard gauge rolling stock. He felt the widening should be completed before the extension was started. Conversion was necessary if the standard gauge Mid Suffolk Light Railway was to become an effective feeder, especially for Southwold fish trade dispatches to the Midlands. One witness added that Southwold herrings sold at 6d per hundred, whilst they sold in Lowestoft for 4s 0d per hundred. W.J. Noble, counsel for the promoters, argued it would be extremely unfair if the SR Company *'should be compelled to reconstruct an unremunerative line and also be debarred from making a remunerative extension.'* He asked that the Order be passed in the form presented.

On 3rd January 1901 it was revealed the Commissioners had reserved their decision. The GER advised the SR should not be allowed to purchase land authorized in the GER 1900 Act for the extension to Kessingland, that the clauses authorizing the Light Railway to make junctions with the GER and for the GER to subscribe to the undertaking be deleted.

As early as 1901 the narrow gauge line was being viewed with some ridicule by railwaymen; at a joint GER and SR dinner held for Halesworth employees at the King's Arms Hotel, Halesworth on the evening of Friday 15th January, the Chairman for the evening, the Reverend A.R. Upcher, referring to the Southwold Railway said to laughter *'it continued in its ancient form, for although other railways had tried to swallow it up, it refused to be swallowed up'*. Further criticism came at Southwold's Trinity Fair held on Monday 3rd June 1901 when at the Mayor's luncheon Alderman J. Beckett was reported as saying the town wanted a better outlet:

'The place was always looked upon as one of the ends of the earth. There was only one way into it, and they needed a better way out of it. If they could develop in the direction of Lowestoft by having a direct line, it would be an advantage to both places.'

He trusted facilities would offer themselves a better railway, and that they would do their utmost to promote it.

Evidently the Alderman was ignorant of proposals for such a connection; at the end of February a meeting of the Roads &

2-4-2T No. 1 *Southwold*, delivered in 1893, prepares to depart Southwold with an Up train consisting of a tarpaulin covered 4-wheel open wagon, SR 6-wheel open No. 28 then two further 4-wheel opens, the two luggage vans and coaching stock. The carriage shed was completed in 1904 and the electric platform lights installed in 1905. *Michael Whitehouse collection*

Bridges Committee of East Suffolk County Council heard that the Light Railway Commissioners had decided to grant the application, made in May 1900, for a Light Railway Order in respect of the proposed extension of the Southwold Railway to Kessingland. In settling the Order, the Commissions required that provision be made prohibiting the company from constructing the railway across the main road at Kessingland, except for the purpose of effecting a junction with the authorized line of the GER, when that was constructed to Kessingland. At the same meeting, the members while discussing motor cars recommended the numbering and registering of vehicles and the abolition of the 12 mph speed limit.

Indeed by May 1901 the Light Railway Commissioners had sanctioned the light railway from Lowestoft to Kessingland and Lowestoft Corporation were applying for powers to construct a tramway to Pakefield which they proposed to lease to the East Anglian Light Railway Company, who would then construct their line from Kessingland to join up with the Lowestoft Tramways. If the light railway was constructed it was decided the GER would abandon its powers for a railway and final agreement to the abandonment was made at a meeting on 30th July 1901.

The Light Railway Commissioners approval of the SR extension proposals required the forwarding of documents to the BOT and this was achieved on 23rd July 1901. The long drawn out process to obtain the Light Railway Order thus appeared to be nearing a conclusion but the SR Directors in their euphoria were at a loss as to where they might raise the necessary capital. The presence of brick-fields near the route of the proposed railway near Frostenden and the possible potential traffic held little sway with financiers, and later in July 1901 the Directors approached the Gooch Trustees, the principal landowners, to enquire if they were willing to finance the building of the line.

Meanwhile the day-to-day affairs of the SR continued and the balance of the net revenue for the half year ending 31st December 1900 of £1,121 was sufficient to pay interest on the rent charges, 4 per cent on the preferred debentures and 2½ per cent for the year on the 5 per cent debentures. For the following half year to 30th June 1901 the net revenue totalled £703 and the rent charge interest of £42. By this time the Capital & Counties Bank Limited of Southwold was the company bankers.

The *Halesworth Times* for 20th August 1901 published a description of Southwold and District, previously published in another journal, which emphasized the quaintness of the SR, and of a management trying to improve matters by expanding and modernizing.

'But if you go by rail, the trains are convenient enough for the holidaymaker with plenty of time on his hands. You change at Halesworth, the Clapham Junction of this part of Suffolk. The trains do not always connect, but an hour or so to dispose of gives you an excuse to wander into the quiet little town ... Southwold now has its own railway line – a narrow gauge, a 'toy' railway they call it down there – is gaining faster and faster in popularity. The Great Eastern goes but within eight and a half miles of the town, the local line carries you practically to its front door, while the name of almost every station you pass simply forces you to alight. ... Sunny Southwold ... is easy to reach from London, now it runs its own trains to Halesworth; somewhat less than four hours from Liverpool Street. Brand new red brick hotels and villas show how quickly Southwold has profited by the improvements in railway services.'

The initial response for financial backing for the northern extension, especially from the Gooch Trustees, was far from encouraging. At the BOT hearing held on 17th October, the National Electric Traction Company Limited objected to the extension on the grounds that the SR was authorized to build its line across a road in Kessingland, with the proviso that this part should not be built except to make a junction with the proposed but now abandoned GER branch from Lowestoft. At that time the National Electric Traction Company had an order before the BOT for confirmation of a line along this road. As it was later objected to, the Chairman considered it only with regard to public safety, but in the end the committee allowed the level crossing to remain. The question of continuous brakes on rolling stock was again raised but Arthur Pain pointed out that completely different rolling stock would be obtained and adequately fitted.

At the Halesworth Railway Employees Dinner attended by GER and SR employees early in 1902, Superintendent George Andrews of the GER referred to the great boon the SR was to the district and hoped to see the day when it was standard gauge. Station Master William Culver, replying on behalf of the company, acknowledged

LIGHT RAILWAYS ACT, 1896.

SOUTHWOLD LIGHT RAILWAY ORDER, 1902.

ORDER

MADE BY THE

LIGHT RAILWAY COMMISSIONERS,

AND MODIFIED AND CONFIRMED BY THE

BOARD OF TRADE,

AUTHORISING THE CONSTRUCTION OF A

LIGHT RAILWAY IN THE COUNTY OF EAST SUFFOLK BETWEEN SOUTHWOLD AND KESSINGLAND, AND THE CONVERSION OF THE GAUGE OF THE EXISTING SOUTHWOLD RAILWAY, AND THE WORKING THEREOF AS A LIGHT RAILWAY UNDER THE LIGHT RAILWAYS ACT, 1896.

Presented to both Houses of Parliament by Command of His Majesty.

LONDON:
PRINTED FOR HIS MAJESTY'S STATIONERY OFFICE,
By DARLING & SON, LTD., 34-40, Bacon Street, E.

And to be purchased, either directly or through any Bookseller, from
EYRE & SPOTTISWOODE, East Harding Street, Fleet Street, E.C.,
and 32, Abingdon Street, Westminster, S.W.;
or OLIVER & BOYD, Edinburgh;
or E. PONSONBY, 116, Grafton Street, Dublin.

1902.

Southwold Light Railway Order 1902 - front page.

the assistance they had always received from the GER staff at Halesworth *'without which it would be utterly impossible for them to cope with their increasing traffic'*. During 1901 they had carried no fewer than 110,839 passengers, taken 33,537 parcels, and conveyed 7,363 tons of goods traffic and 10,600 tons of minerals. He concluded saying the BOT had now sanctioned the order to put the line on wider gauge and it was hoped the work would commence shortly after the Light Railway Order was received.

The Light Railway Commissioners duly issued the Southwold Light Railway Order on 4th April 1902, authorizing the Southwold Company to construct a railway 9 miles and 6 chains or thereabouts in length commencing in the Borough and parish of Southwold by a junction with the Southwold Railway running in a westerly direction across Buss Creek, thence in a northerly direction past Reydon South Cove and Wrentham to Henstead, thence turning in an easterly direction and terminating at Kessingland at a point on the northern side of Church Road about 14½ chains from the southern end of Wash Lane. The statute restricted the construction of a railway across the public road, numbered 31 on the plan, in the parish of Kessingland except for effecting by agreement with the Great Eastern Railway, a junction with the railway when constructed from Lowestoft to Kessingland authorized by the Great Eastern Railway (General Powers) Act 1900 (63 & 64 Vic cap cx).

Clause 5 of the order authorized the Southwold Company to convert the gauge of their existing railway to the standard gauge of 4 feet 8½ inches and construct the new line to the same gauge. Subsection (a) of the clause permitted the company to raise the bridge in the County of East Suffolk and parish of Holton carrying the road from Holton to Mells over the existing railway and alter the approaches to the said bridge on both sides thereof commencing in the said road on the northern side of the railway 1.20 chains or thereabouts from the point over the centre of the existing railway and terminating on the southern side at a point 5.40 chains or thereabouts from the said point. Clause (b) allowed the company to raise the bridge in the County of East Suffolk in the parish of Blythburgh carrying the road from Ipswich to Lowestoft over the existing railway on the east side of Blythburgh station and alter the approaches to the said bridge on both sides thereof commencing in the said road on the northern side of the existing railway 3.60 chains or thereabouts from the point over the centre of the existing railway and terminating on the southern side at a point 4 chains or thereabouts from the said point.

Clause 6 permitted the existing railway to be worked as a light railway, whilst clause 7 required the line to be constructed to a gauge of 4 feet 8½ inches, with steam motive power *'or such other motive power as the Board of Trade may approve'*. Three years were permitted for the compulsory purchase of land and five years for the completion of works. The Southwold Railway was not permitted to take land numbered 32 or 33 in the parish of Kessingland without the prior consent of the Great Eastern Railway or compulsory purchase ten or more houses which were occupied by persons belonging to the labouring classes, without the consent of the local government board.

Clause 18 required the railway to cross the undermentioned roads by single span bridges with a clear headway of 10 feet above the surface of the road.

No. of Road	Parish	Span	Height
24	Reydon	20 feet	15 feet
35	Reydon	20 feet	15 feet
36A	Reydon	20 feet	15 feet
25	Wrentham	25 feet	15 feet
21	Kessingland	20 feet	15 feet

In each case a clear height of the springing of the arch was to be no less than 12 feet above the surface of the road. The following clause required the company to erect bridges to carry public roads over the new railway or existing line as under.

No. of Road	Parish	Width of Roadway
6	Henstead	20 feet
3	Benacre	20 feet
27	Kessingland	20 feet
31	Kessingland	20 feet
5	Holton	that of the roadway over the existing bridge
5	Blythburgh	that of the roadway over the existing bridge

Level crossings with gates were required to be provided over public road No. 30 in the parish of Reydon, 18 in the parish of South Cove, 12 in the parish of Wrentham, 17 in the parish of Henstead and 12 in the parish of Benacre, and at others determined by the company or as required by the Gooch Trustees on the Benacre Hall Estate. Where gates were erected the company was required to provide a *'proper person'* to open and close the barriers.

Clause 21 of the statute stated that where no gates were erected, cattle guards were to be placed at each side of the road to prevent cattle or horses entering upon the railway. On the railway approach to the level crossing at a distance of 300 yards a white post was to be erected, 5 feet in height, bearing the speed limit for trains over the crossing. Similarly at a distance of 50 yards on each road approach to the crossing the company was required to erect notice boards cautioning the public to 'Beware of Trains'.

For the protection of Southwold Corporation, the company was not to interfere with the sewerage farm and dykes numbered 8 and 9 in the parish, nor was Buss Creek to be altered or obstructed. The interests of Blythling Rural District Council were also protected,

As part of the modification to the line for possible conversion to standard gauge the overbridge No. 11 at 4 miles 72 chains carrying the London to Yarmouth trunk road over the line at Blythburgh, was raised to provide increased loading gauge clearance with a higher square span and improved fencing. *Author's collection*

as the centre line of the railway was not to be constructed nearer than 60 yards from the road known as Quay Lane in the parish of Reydon, whilst the centre line of the railway where it crossed the road known as South Cove was to be no nearer than 88 yards from the top of the road which the railway crossed.

Clause 27 included provision for the protection of the Trustees of the late Sir E.S. Gooch, wherein the company was required to construct and maintain sufficient passenger and goods stations with convenient approaches to serve the villages of Wrentham and Henstead. In addition, at Wrentham station a *'sufficient siding of at least one hundred yards in length'* was to be built alongside the station, with *'ample facilities for the reception and delivery of goods to and from the neighbourhood'*. At South Cove a *'sufficient goods station with sufficient siding of at least one hundred yards'* was also to be provided. The passenger station was to be provided with *'suitable covered waiting rooms and sanitary facilities'*.

The provisions of working, established in clause 34, limited the axle loading weight to 12 tons but if rails of 60 lbs per yard were used this could be increased to 14 tons. Because of its status as a light railway the speed limit on the new and existing lines was restricted to 25 mph. This was further restricted to 15 mph on gradients steeper than 1 in 50 and 10 mph when passing over curves of 9 chains radius or less. On the approach to ungated level crossings speed was also limited to 10 mph within a distance of 300 yards on the approach to such crossings. The Board of Trade could reduce this further if local conditions warranted such action. Clauses 36 and 37 included the special conditions if steam traction was abandoned in favour of mechanical or electrical power.

Under the provisions of the Light Railway Order, the Southwold Railway was empowered to raise additional capital not exceeding £85,000, to finance the new works. The shares could be either ordinary or preference or both but dividend on preference stock was not to exceed 5 per cent per annum. Borrowing powers of £28,333 were permitted once half of the £85,000 was raised and the whole amount promised.

The schedule appended to the Light Railway Order and signed by G.W. Balfour, President of the Board of Trade and Herbert Jeckyll, Secretary, stipulated the rails used on the permanent way should weigh at least 56 lbs per yard, whilst on curves of 9 chains or less a checkrail was to be provided. If flat bottom rails and wooden sleepers were used, the rails at the joints were to be secured to the sleepers by fang bolts or other through bolts, coach screws or double spikes on the outside of the rails with a bearing plate, whilst rails on curves with radii of 9 chains or less were to be secured on the outside of the outer rail to each sleeper by similar bolts and also tied to gauge by iron or steel ties at suitable intervals. No turntables were necessary but if tender engines were employed on the line they were to be restricted to a speed limit of 15 mph if running tender first. With regard to the signalling, at places where trains were required to cross or pass each other, a home signal was to be provided for each direction of travel at or near the entrance points to the loop line. If the home signal could not be seen from a distance of a quarter of a mile, a distant signal was required, to be erected at least that distance in advance of the entrance points and home signal. The signals were to be worked from the stations and proper interlocking was required between signals and points to ensure conflicting signals could not be lowered or cleared at the same time. Platforms were to be provided at ground level but there was no obligation for the company, unless provided for in the clauses, to provide shelter or other conveniences for the travelling public.

The SR intended to provide as substantial facilities at Southwold as existed with the narrow gauge save that the locomotive shed was to be demolished and replaced by a new structure further to the west beyond station limits with direct north facing access to the main single line. The Order was subsequently confirmed in the *London Gazette*.

At the meeting of Southwold Town Council held on 3rd October 1902, the letter drafted by the Town Clerk to the Directors of the SR suggesting the provision of railway accommodation to the quay at Blackshore was approved and sent. Later the 21st October issue of the *Halesworth Times* contained a reprint of an article on Southwold which had appeared in the *Hampstead & Highgate Express* in September, concluding:

'I warrant that when that famous toy train, which plies between our haven of repose and the junction which suggests Liverpool Street and work again, bears you away, the sweet sorrow of parting will be with you also as the eye is strained to catch a farewell glimpse

The rebuilt Walberswick station looking towards Halesworth circa 1927. A flatbed wagon covered with a tarpaulin can be seen in the near siding.
Author's collection

at Southwold the restorer, with its stately church, the townlet's pride and its neighbouring lighthouse, which, as the owl, blinks perpetually throughout the livelong night to warn the mariner.'

The inhabitants of Walberswick, having had their application for relocation of the inconveniently sited station refused, later expressed dissatisfaction at the inability to purchase a full range of tickets, including those for long distance destinations, from the booking office, which was essentially a simple wooden building on a low gravel platform. The company relented and in October 1902 a new booking office and timber waiting shelter replaced the existing structure. In the same year, a drawing dated 10th June 1902 had specified the proposed covering of the buffer stops end of the bay platform road at Southwold to form a carriage shed. The work involving the erection using old rails as stanchions, was not completed until 1904 and greatly improved the conditions of staff involved with the routine maintenance and repair of the coaching stock.

The ordinary half yearly meeting was held as usual at the company offices at Victoria Street, Westminster in late October 1902, with Charles Chambers as Chairman. Receipts for the six months ending 30th June 1902 totalled £2,268 against £2,304 for the corresponding period in 1901, a decrease of £64. The working expenses had been £1,703 (excluding £212 for the Southwold and Kessingland Extension Order), against £1,601, an increase of £102. The percentage of working expenses to gross receipts was 75.08 compared with 69.48 for the same period in 1901. Chambers confirmed to those present that the BOT had confirmed the order for the extension to Kessingland and for widening the gauge. Since the line opened in 1879 there had been continuous growth of business; the number of passengers carried had increased from 26,079 to 35,242 in the current year, parcels had increased from 3,887 to 13,197, goods tonnage from 606 to 3,018 and minerals from 1,390 to 4,974 tons. The company had an authorized capital of £134,000 of which £85,000 was held in stocks and shares and £28,333 on the loan account. There had been no increase in rolling stock during the year but the whole of the permanent way, station buildings and other works, plant, locomotives, carriages, wagons, machinery and tools had been maintained in good working order, condition and repair.

In their quest to raise the necessary capital to convert the existing line to standard gauge, the Directors asked the holders of five per cent debentures to surrender their holding and accept the equivalent in four per cent debentures and ordinary shares. The debenture holders initially objected to being held to ransom but the majority then reluctantly acceded to the request. Other efforts to raise funds were less successful and the board meeting held on 27th August 1903 was a sombre affair, for whichever way they turned the Directors were unable to raise capital for the Kessingland project. The conversion of the existing line was the major priority as it was realized the existing railway was antiquated, offering sub-standard comfort to passengers and suffering delays caused by the trans-shipment of goods traffic. Little encouragement came from Southwold Corporation or from local people and the future of the railway was the subject of serious discussion. At this meeting Arthur C. Pain was elected Chairman as replacement for Charles Chambers who had passed away. The Directors also offered an invitation to Sir Thomas Gooch to become a Director and thereby possibly extract some finance for the Kessingland line but in a letter dated 30th September 1903 the offer was declined, though the baronet promised to release land for the railway on preferential terms. Thus encouraged the quest for money continued.

On 13th April 1904 two boxes of oranges consigned to Mr Blowers were delivered to Wenhaston station. One of the boxes had a damaged corner and it was soon discovered that some of the fruit had been stolen. After investigation, brothers John and Sidney Cooper were brought before Halesworth Petty Sessions on Thursday 26th April and charged with stealing thirty-six oranges. E.R. Cooper appeared for the SR and Percy Dyer, the Wenhaston station master, gave evidence, which was supported by two girls who had seen the incident. The father of the boys offered to pay for the oranges but the accused pleaded guilty and the bench decided to deal with them under the First Offenders' Act, binding the father over in £5 to bring them up for judgement when called upon. The Chairman hoped the father would exercise more control over the boys, for if they came before the bench again they would be severely dealt with.

The GER introduced a bus service from Lowestoft to Southwold on 18th July 1904. The half yearly meeting was held most unusually in Southwold Town Hall on the afternoon of Thursday 1st September 1904. The Chairman, A.C. Pain, said that he and the Directors had pleasure in meeting the shareholders in the town and hoped that in future one of the half yearly meetings would be held in Southwold. The attendees were presented with the report and accounts for the half year ending 30th June 1904 and compared to the corresponding half year for 1903 the working expenses over gross receipts had improved from 73.12 per cent to 72.06 per cent. After paying the fixed charges and 4 per cent on preferred debentures they were able to pay 5 per cent on debentures. Passenger numbers had risen by 649 although passenger receipts had reduced by £20 due to more passengers making shorter journeys. Goods traffic had increased by 722 tons with receipts up by £145. This was due to an increase in general traffic and materials for the building trade. Adnams & Company had recently established a business at Eye and beer was now being conveyed from Southwold to that town. There had also been an increase in coal traffic and minerals where tonnage had increased by 480, resulting in an increase of £35 in receipts. The total receipts amounted to £2,359, an increase of £47, whilst working expenses were £1,725, an increase of £131. Concluding, Pain said the Directors hoped the Mid Suffolk Light Railway, which would run to Halesworth, would soon get over its difficulties for from that line they expected additional traffic to Southwold, by which the town and the SR would benefit. Nineteen days later, and after many trials and tribulations, the MSLR opened for goods traffic between Haughley and Laxfield.

No dividend was paid in 1904 on ordinary or preference shares but the debenture and rent charge interest was met. During the last week of December 1904 the East Coast suffered from destructive gales and severe flooding, which occurred at Ipswich quays, Woodbridge and Southwold. The GER East Suffolk main line was under water on the 29th and by 4.00pm on 30th December Southwold's sea defences were breached in four places, the water two hours later inundating Southwold and Reydon bridges, rendering the roads impassable. The bad weather continued during the first week of January 1905 culminating with the combination of gale force winds and high tide on Saturday 7th damaging the centre cliff at Southwold and flooding the harbour at Blackshore. The water rose at Blythburgh threatening to endanger the railway whilst Southwold and Reydon bridges were again flooded; the valley between them resembling a lake and leaving Southwold as an island. The first trains, 7.30am

A mixed train stands at Southwold behind 2-4-0T No. 3 *Blyth* in 1906. In this posed scene station staff and footplate crew face the camera. To the left a carriage is stabled in the goods yard sidings whilst another coach occupies the open sided carriage shed constructed of length of scrap flat bottom rail with corrugated iron roof on the right. The original gravel covered platform had been covered in timber planking by this date.

Ian Pope collection

ex Southwold and 8.43am return from Halesworth, managed to complete their journey, as did the 10.55am from Southwold. By the time the 1.12pm ex Halesworth was en route the line was flooded to a considerable depth between Walberswick and Southwold, and passengers had to alight at List's Cottage and travel by boat to connect with another train east of the inundation. Train services were subsequently suspended for the remainder of the day until the water subsided and track repairs were completed.

The Suffolk Agricultural Show was held at Chediston Park, Halesworth on Thursday 8th and Friday 9th June 1905. Prior to the event the GER carried out considerable alterations to infrastructure and amenities in order to cater for the influx of farmers and the public attending the event. The Southwold Railway contributed to the total of 4,203 passengers arriving by rail, with 343 recorded on the narrow gauge line on Thursday and 428 on the Friday.

During 1905 Arthur C. Pain continued as Company Chairman, with fellow Directors Walter C. Chambers, W. Steele Tomkins and Herbert W. Chambers. Early in the year Southwold Gas Company had approached the SR with an offer to supply gas lighting as replacement of oil illumination at Southwold station. The Gas Company obtained their supplies of coal by sea in the absence of any railway connection and the SR Directors were unhappy with this arrangement, which denied them potential traffic. They could hardly criticize the Gas Company for the cost of transferring coal from standard gauge wagons to narrow gauge SR at Halesworth and then offloading for a second time into horse drawn carts for the short trip to the gas works, would have made the operation unremunerative. The Directors were dissatisfied with the quotation and the Secretary was instructed to seek estimates for other forms of illumination. The outcome was a generous quotation for electric lighting, which was readily accepted and this was installed later the same year.

As the 3.40pm Halesworth to Southwold train, composed of three passenger coaches and a number of wagons containing coal, was approaching Walberswick on Monday 4th September 1905, the wheels of the third carriage in the formation derailed. The train was halted and passengers in the derailed vehicle transferred to the front two coaches, which the locomotive took on to Southwold. The derailed coach was removed from the line thus releasing the loaded coal wagons, which were then taken on to the terminus by the engine, which had returned. As a result of the incident the 5.40pm Southwold to Halesworth train was delayed for an hour, so some passengers intending to join connecting GER services at Halesworth were conveyed from Southwold by motor car or other conveyances. A second derailment occurred on Friday 3rd October at Southwold when a locomotive left the rails, resulting in the 5.30pm departure not leaving until 8.45pm. A number of passengers remained on the train until the stock was taken forward to Halesworth by another engine whilst several others deferred their journey until the following day.

Despite the report and accounts indicating a decrease in total receipts for the second half of 1905 compared with previous years, the Directors decided at the SR March 1906 half yearly meeting to announce the commencement of works to widen the line to standard gauge and advised they had already accepted a tender for the rebuilding of the swing bridge over the River Blyth.

After several years of inactivity largely brought about by lack of finance, the proposed improvements to Southwold Harbour received attention. At a Local Government Board of Enquiry held on 6th June 1906 it emerged the improvements involved the extension of both piers and dredging of the river. The works were expected to cost £50,000 against which the Treasury might make a grant of £15,000. The preferred contractor was W.R. Fasey & Son, who had recently carried out dock extensions for the GER

Safety is ignored at Southwold as a member of staff crosses the line in front of the arriving train. Guard Wright looks back at the photographer as the locomotive is passing the open-sided carriage shed. The platform is crowded with intending passengers for the return working to Halesworth and those waiting to meet arriving travellers off the incoming service. An unidentified locomotive sits in the engine shed with its smokebox door open. *Author's collection*

at Lowestoft. The inspector spoke favourably of the scheme and having invited remarks heard from the only respondent Arthur Pain, who after briefly explaining the proposed improvements on the SR, *'cordially supported the scheme'*.

On Thursday 21st June 1906 members of Halesworth Urban Council visited Southwold harbour to hear of the proposed developments, some travelling by the 8.43am departure to Walberswick where at 11.00am they met more adventurous councillors who had rowed down the Blyth from the town. After lunching at the Bell Inn and hearing a presentation of the proposed improvements, there was discussion on the feasibility of opening up the river for traffic to Halesworth before the party returned by train. The following month the agreement between Southwold Council and W.R. Fasey & Son, the contractor to the harbour was signed. The Mayor handed over the key of the harbour office to Anthony Fasey, who after thanking the Council handed over a half sovereign, the cost of the conveyance. The Mayor stated the coin would be placed upon the Mayoral chain and handed down to later generations as a reminder of the harbour transfer. Fasey stated a large quantity of material had already arrived at Southwold station and a barge-load of timber was on the way; he hoped to start pile driving during the first week of August, the ceremonial driving of the first pile subsequently being carried out by Lady Stradbroke.

In July 1906 the MSLR Directors held a meeting with A.C. Pain to discuss the possible connection between the two railways at Halesworth. The railway by this time had been extended from Laxfield to Cratfield several miles short of connections with the GER and SR The 'Middy' was already gaining an infamous reputation with contractors and no tenders were received for the construction of the extension beyond Cratfield.

Troubles continued on the SR, however, for on 27th August 1906 the leading wheels of the locomotive hauling the 8.40am train from Halesworth, due at Southwold at 9.17am, derailed en route. After some effort by the train crew and use of sleepers and packing the engine was reversed and the offending wheels re-railed. The train continued its journey, arriving at its destination at 11.00am.

The half yearly meeting of shareholders was held on the afternoon of Thursday 13th September 1906 at 17 Victoria Street, Westminster, but beside Arthur Pain, the Chairman, the only others present were the three co-Directors W.S. Tomkins, W.C. Chambers and H.W. Chambers, together with one of the Auditors, J.B. Walton, and Henry Ward the Secretary. The Chairman reported the total receipts to 30th June from all sources totalled £2,027 against £2,076 for the corresponding period in 1905, a decrease of £49. The working expenses had been £1,592 against £1,602, a decrease of £10. After taking credit for the balance brought forward from the December half year and the payment of fixed charges and the interest of the 4 per cent preferred debentures and 5 per cent debentures, the balance had been carried forward to the next half year. Pain advised the reconstruction of the swing bridge over the River Blyth was progressing satisfactorily and tenders for alterations to the three road overbridges had been accepted. All were to be completed by the end of 1906, enabling the gauge of the railway to be widened to standard gauge early in 1907 and made available to all classes of traffic. The proprietors would be gratified to learn the harbour works, to which the Government had granted a sum of £15,000, had commenced and completion was expected in autumn 1907. The Chairman, in moving the adoption of the report, congratulated the shareholders on the event which had take place since the last meeting and one for which they had been hoping since the line opened for traffic – the handing over of Southwold harbour to a company which had the means for carrying out an extension to the pier, and the construction of jetties and wharves in the river for the accommodation of fishing vessels, more particularly the Scottish fleet. That the scheme was bona fide and likely to be carried out was demonstrated by the Treasury grant. Since the harbour scheme had been initiated the Railway Directors had been carefully making preparations for the reconstruction and widening of their line; during the last few months they had authorized the construction of the new swing bridge over the River Blyth. Considerable difficulties had been encountered but these had been overcome and work on the other three bridges was to proceed as a tender had been accepted. An advantage of the conversion to standard gauge was the ability to carry passengers and freight through to Southwold from London, without changing trains or trans-shipping luggage. To finance this new work the Directors were prepared to receive applications for £11,660 of 5 per cent debenture stock at par, payable at 10 per cent on application and the balance at any time convenient to the subscribers, in sums of £10 or multiples of the same, on or before 1st February 1907. This stock formed part of the company's authorized borrowing powers of £16,000. The Chairman added that expending this money would practically build a new line and it would not be long before proprietors of preference stock amounting to £9,000 and ordinary shareholders would reap the benefits. J.B. Walton added he had long been in agreement with the Directors that it was important to widen the gauge and until that was achieved they would make little headway. Passenger traffic had practically been at a standstill for six years, whilst goods traffic also showed a decline. In reply, the Chairman said increases and decreases in receipts depended very much on the prosperity of the country. The nation had been through a long depression following the South African War, and finances and trade had not been good. The Southwold Railway had experienced the downturn, not only with fewer visitors to Southwold but an arrest to growth in the town. The company did all they could to stimulate traffic, which would be enhanced on completion of the harbour scheme.

In the meantime in August 1906 the Directors of the Mid Suffolk Light Railway had approached the Southwold Company to support their scheme for an extension of their standard gauge line from Cratfield to Halesworth. The MSLR line from Haughley to Laxfield had opened to goods traffic on Tuesday 20th September 1904 and the company was desperate to extend to Halesworth. The original intended route via Huntingfield and Cookley approaching the town from the west was found to be unsuitable because of marshy ground and with the proposed station a quarter of a mile from the GER station, whilst the second approach authorized by a Light Railway Order of 23rd February 1905 ran in a north-easterly direction keeping south-east of Cookley church and then proceeded to Halesworth, skirting north-west of the town before terminating in a field north of the GER station on the west side of the East Suffolk main line. Because the approach to the main line from the north was on a 1 in 70 gradient with the actual physical junction between the two railways on a 1 in 86 gradient, by which the MSLR trains would have to cross the Up and Down GER lines to exchange goods traffic in the Up side goods yard, the GER objected. Financial problems meant no construction was carried out and so the proposed alteration in gauge by the Southwold Railway gave the MSLR new incentive and a proposal to approach Halesworth from the south-west and pass over the GER East Suffolk main line to run alongside the SR for half a mile to terminate at a station on the south-east side of the GER Halesworth station was acceptable. Combining with the SR to gain access to the town and possible running powers to Southwold was thus too good an opportunity to miss.

In mid November 1906 the Directors of the Mid Suffolk Light Railway announced they were contemplating applying to the Light Railway Commissioners to deviate their proposed route from Laxfield to Halesworth to bisect the Bramfield Road, near Mells, and cross the GER about 25 yards north of Mells level crossing to a junction with the SR probably crossing the Holton Road just east of the narrow gauge line to terminate on the east side of Halesworth station. In the same month the SR Directors realised the powers granted by the 1902 Light Railway Order were nearing expiration. None of the £85,000 capital had been raised or the £28,333 borrowing powers taken up but the railway was in desperate need of an injection of capital to continue. Thus an application was made to the Light Railway Commissioners for a further order to raise additional capital by the creation of mortgage debentures or debenture stocks. As if monetary problems were not enough the elements added to the difficulties. On Boxing Day Wednesday 26th December 1906 strong winds brought blizzard conditions to the Suffolk coast and the cuttings along the railway quickly filled with drifting snow. The initial Up service weathered the storm and made it to Halesworth but the first Down working encountered atrocious conditions and arrived two hours late at Southwold, as conditions worsened. An attempt was made to run the 11.00am and 2.30pm trains as one service but when snowdrifts were encountered between Walberswick and Blythburgh the locomotive crew sensibly reversed the train and propelled back to Southwold before conditions further deteriorated, arriving at 5.40pm, after which the services were abandoned. Snow continued to fall during the night but conditions had improved on the morning of the 27th and services commenced by mid-day.

In 1904 the SR Company had purchased a field on the Down side of the railway near Halesworth, where a fine seam of shingle was available for excavation suitable to ballast the railway. Initially no excavation was carried out until supplies of shingle ballast from Southwold beach was near exhaustion but in July 1906 a siding had been installed and the pit opened for traffic. The new siding and connection with the main single line at Halesworth were inspected by Lieutenant Colonel P.G. Von Donop on 1st February 1907.

The inspector noted the connection, facing Up trains and located a quarter of a mile from Halesworth station, led to a ballast siding. The points were worked from a single-lever ground frame locked by an Annett's key on the single line Train Staff for the Halesworth to Southwold section and Von Donop found the arrangements satisfactory. Despite financial problems in early January 1907 work was completed on the reconstruction of Holton Road overbridge as part of the programme to widen the infrastructure for conversion to standard gauge.

The Light Railway Commissioners public enquiry into the MSLR Halesworth deviation application was held in the Corn Exchange, Halesworth on Tuesday 26th February 1907, with the Honourable A.E. Gathorne Hardy as Chairman, assisted by Colonel Boughey. W.H. Smith, the Solicitor, represented the MSLR, whilst the GER as leading objector, was represented by Mr Courthorpe Monroe, instructed by Mr T. Chew. H.A. Mullard represented Blything Rural District Council, F.R. Coope, the Southwold Harbour Company and Arthur C. Pain, the Southwold Railway. W.H. Smith advised those present that the deviation now requested by the MSLR crossed the GER main line by a bridge and ran alongside the Southwold Railway for half a mile to terminate at a station on the south-east side of the GER Halesworth station. The estimated cost was £29,818, and any running on the SR was at the behest and agreement of the Southwold Company. The only objection voiced by the local authority was that of Blything Rural District Council who objected to a level crossing where the railway bisected a road in the parish of Wenhaston. A.C. Pain representing the SR told those present of the MSLR approach six months previously, asking whether the two companies could work together in the interests of the district and he would therefore not offer any detailed opposition. Hederstedt, the MSLR Engineer, said the SR had powers to alter their gauge from 3 feet 0 inches to standard gauge 4 feet 8½ inches, and if the latter alteration was made in Halesworth yard the Mid Suffolk could gain access to the town. The GER contingent was obviously concerned with the intended plan and Courthorpe-Munroe offered an unqualified opposition to the scheme. Counsel for the company argued that the Directors opposed such plans as the original scheme for the MSLR, advanced in 1900, was entirely changed. No more was the MSLR to be a feeder to the GER system, as indeed was the Southwold Railway. The MSLR and

The connection from the main single line to the siding serving Bird's Folly ballast siding and Halesworth engine shed in 1936 looking towards Halesworth. The siding to the ballast pit was installed in 1906 and the connection thence to the engine shed in 1914.
Author's collection

The swing bridge and associated fixed span over the River Blyth were widened to take possible standard gauge in 1906/7 and 1914 respectively. By 1938 the structure was difficult to cross but the generous loading gauge offered as a result of the reconstruction is evident.
Author's collection

SR combined would now provide serious competition for cross-country traffic and the amalgam of the two companies was *'surely a matter for Parliament to consider'*. It was an attempt by the MSLR and SR to effect a 'pool' with a view to competing against the GER in the matter of coals, fish and other goods between Southwold and Ipswich. The construction of a harbour at Southwold, for which the Government had given a £15,000 grant, included the provision of a railway connection to link up with the Southwold line. It was known that the fishing trade would increase at the port and if such traffic was sent via the SR and MSLR, the Lowestoft fish trade would suffer and the GER incur reduced receipts. *'Under these circumstances the MSLR and SR, instead of acting as feeders to the GER, would be robbers.'* Concluding the evidence for the GER, Walter Hyde, the Assistant General Manager, stated the MSLR scheme would create wasteful competition, whilst John Wilson, the GER Engineer, estimated that the promoters' engineer would require an additional £6,000 to £7,000 above estimates to complete the scheme. At the conclusion of the hearing, and much to the dismay of the Mid Suffolk and Southwold Directors and officials, the Light Railway Commissioners announced that *'in their opinion there was insufficient commercial justification or evidence to support the deviation'*. They *'could not consent to the alterations'* and proved against the scheme. To the SR the decision was another setback in the proposal to convert their line to standard gauge and extend to Kessingland, added to which Halesworth Council rescinded their offer of a £5,000 loan.

Despite the ruling, the SR Directors decided to advance their cause and the money earned from the debenture holders enabled a start to be made on the conversion to standard gauge. Initially the infrastructure required alteration and as advised at the half yearly meeting in 1906 a contract was placed with Francis Morton & Company Limited of Garston to carry out the first major task of widening work, that of rebuilding the swing bridge. The original timber piers were replaced by steel structures, whilst the curved bowstring girders were replaced with those of an angular configuration with a reduced number of supporting cross pieces; the work being completed in 1907. Three other bridges received attention at this period: the Southwold Road underbridge at Halesworth, Corner Farm overbridge and Blythburgh overbridge.

By April 1907 rapid progress was being made on the Southwold harbour scheme with the contractor excavating 3,000 cubic yards of earth each day, a dredging machine aiding progress. The works manager had not the slightest doubt the harbour would be ready for the fishing season in October. During a visit to various locations on their system on 14th May 1907 the GER Directors visited Southwold Harbour. The group were accompanied by E.R. Cooper, Secretary of the Harbour Company, and from their subsequent comments it would appear they were not impressed for they observed, *'it was obvious from the size of the proposed harbour, the depth of water and width of entrance, that the accommodation would only be suitable for fishing boats or small traders'* and *'would not pose any threat to the prosperity enjoyed at Lowestoft'*. They paid little respect to the SR for they travelled to and from Halesworth station by *'motor bus'* and on 3rd July 1907 the GER Directors expressed concern that the SR was asking the Light Railway Commissioners for an extension in time to convert the line to 4 feet 8½ inch gauge.

The *Halesworth Times* of 17th September 1907 commented on the prospectus of the London & Southwold Trading Company Limited, which intended to develop estates and carry on the business of Lightermen and Wharfingers, for which they had purchased valuable freehold premises at Blackshore. The company already had extensive building operations in Southwold and contemplated a regular service of cargo boats, as since the *'making of the Southwold Railway, the harbour had been neglected and the entrance allowed to silt up'*. An inducement to future shareholders was the hope of attracting a Scottish syndicate owning 400 herring drifters who could not get sufficient accommodation at Yarmouth and Lowestoft. They had visited the harbour two years ago and promised to send their fleet to Southwold if the harbour was deepened and made suitable. It was noted Messrs Fasey & Company had, with the help of the £15,000 Government grant, deepened the harbour to 18 feet, extended old piers and built a new structure as well as a spacious fish market, all of which would open in October. Later at a Southwold Town Council meeting on 4th October the Council Engineer reported £55,816 had been expended on the scheme and once dredging had taken place the harbour would be ready for the herring fleet.

On 27th September 1907, the Light Railway Commissioners duly granted the Southwold Light Railway (Borrowing Powers &C) Order 1907, authorising the company to exercise the powers of borrowing on mortgage not exceeding £10,000 originally authorised in section 49 of the 1902 Light Railway Order. Section

Southwold Light Railway (Borrowing Powers) Light Railway Order 1907-front page.

The water pump installed in 1908 can be seen in this post-closure view though the back wall of the later Halesworth engine shed. View from the cab of No. 3 *Blyth*.
Author's collection

52 (Debenture Stock) of the 1902 Order was repealed by clause 6 of the new order and permitted the company to create and issue Debenture Stock. Clause 8 permitted the powers to convert the gauge of the existing railway and time permitted to construct the new line to Kessingland, to be extended to 4th April 1909 or *'until such time as the Board of Trade may approve'*. Later in the month the *London Gazette* advised the BOT had recently confirmed the order made by the Light Railway Commissioners for the Southwold Light Railway (Borrowing Powers etc) Order 1907 amending the borrowing powers of the SR Company and for other purposes.

Fasey's purchase of the harbour from Southwold Corporation and the formation the new Southwold Harbour Company was also confirmed by BOT Order issued in 1907 whilst the government grant was increased to £21.000. Litigation, however, delayed the opening of the harbour to the fishing fleet until the following year. The anticipated arrival of up to three hundred fishing vessels annually, with their owners and crews anxious to offload their catches and despatch rapidly to markets, demanded the revival of the scheme for a rail connection to Blackshore Quay, originally planned in the original SR Act of Parliament but abandoned soon after the line was built. Fasey wrote to the SR management on 26th July 1907 offering to build the line to the harbour, which would be capable of being converted to standard gauge if the SR converted from their 3 feet gauge. The SR Directors were, however, suspicious of the move and regarded the offer as possible competition; the Board thought the installation, whilst bringing traffic to the railway between Blackshore Quay and Southwold and Halesworth, would also encourage the transfer of other traffic to coastal shipping for onward transit instead of via the SR and GER to London and other destinations. As an alternative proposal, the SR Board advised Fasey that the railway company would install the siding and connections once the contractor had completed the Quay. This counter proposal was unacceptable to Fasey and months of haggling over transit and conveyance rates ensued before the SR in a report in March 1908 advised agreement had finally been reached. Despite the concordance, the immediacy of the siding and connection had been lost and no construction was carried out, although authority was given for the siding at Blythburgh to be converted to a crossing loop by the addition of points at the Halesworth end of the station.

The SR half yearly ordinary general meeting was held in April 1908 as usual at Victoria Street, Westminster when Arthur Pain advised total receipts for the six months ending 31st December 1907 totalled £3,085 13s 8d against £2,988 3s 0d for the corresponding period in 1906. The working expenses were £1,603 against £1,617; the percentage of working expenses to gross receipts being 51.96 against 51.45. After paying the fixed charges and interest on the 4 per cent preferred debentures and 5 per cent debentures, the balance was carried forward. A resolution formally adopted empowered the Directors to issue £10,000 five per cent debenture stock under the Light Railway Orders of 1902 and 1907 on such terms and at such times as they thought fit. Later in the month William Parker, a labourer of Halesworth, was summoned for *'furious drivin'* (*sic*) on the highway at Wenhaston. Albert Sivyer, station master at Wenhaston, giving evidence reported that Parker had driven into one of the level crossing gates at his station causing damage estimated at 2s 6d. Halesworth Magistrates Court duly fined Parker 7s 6d with 8s 6d costs.

Whilst work was proceeding on providing the passing loop at Blythburgh to increase line capacity – a necessary requirement if additional fish traffic was to be handled – history was made at Blythburgh Quay on Saturday 25th August 1908 when the barge *Star* discharged a consignment of antique tiles. These were consigned to J. Trueman, engaged in restoring an old house near the church, and was the first cargo delivered at the quay for almost forty years, the last consignment being coal for Trueman's father.

The second half yearly meeting of shareholders was held at Victoria Street, Westminster on 4th September 1908. Pain advised the gathering that, like other railways, the SR had been affected by the depression in trade. Despite this threat 34,790 passengers had been carried against the 32,698 conveyed in the corresponding half year in 1907 resulting in additional receipts of £31. The number of parcels conveyed showed a reduction with 14,095 against 14,428 the same period in 1907. The parcels traffic was, however, steadily increasing from 3,887 conveyed in 1880 to the present figure of 14,095. Goods tonnage showed a slight increase to 2,241 tons, whilst mineral traffic showed a decline to 3,341 tons from 4,150 tons in the same period in 1907. The total receipt from all sources was £1,998, a decrease of £70 from the same period in 1907. Working expenses had again shown a saving – £1,426 against £1,400 for the first six months of 1907. The profit for the half year of £572 together with the profit of £619 earned in the period ending 31st December 1907 enabled the company to pay the interest on 4 per cent preferred debentures and on 5 per cent debentures. Pain advised the attendees that the company was arranging for a passing loop at Blythburgh to be completed before the autumn fishing season to enable goods and passenger trains to pass. They had also agreed with the GER for fish rates from Southwold to be the same as Yarmouth and Lowestoft so that boats unloading in the new harbour would have fish sent to London on the same terms as the larger ports. He reiterated it would be greatly to their advantage if the SR was converted to ordinary standard gauge but it was very difficult until the money market had improved to secure capital for carrying out the work. Later in the month on 29th September came the encouraging news that the Mid Suffolk Light Railway was opened to passenger traffic between Haughley and Laxfield.

Further widening work was carried out on the SR main single line in 1908 when the concrete underbridge by Halesworth ballast pit received attention. Ditches on the Up side of the line were filled in and new fences erected from Halesworth as far as Wenhaston Mill. Similar work was executed on Southwold Common. A well was sunk at the Ballast Pit siding equipped with a chain pump to enable locomotives to be topped up instead of at the water mill stream, thus leaving the main line clear during widening and ballasting work. The all-important improvements at Blythburgh were completed in the autumn when the buffer stops at the west end of the siding were removed and points installed, making a loop line suitable for crossing trains thus allowing increased line capacity. The previous single line section from Halesworth to Southwold was divided into two with the new sections Halesworth to Blythburgh and Blythburgh to Southwold, each with its own single line Train Staff. Passenger trains were prohibited from crossing at Blythburgh as no second platform was provided alongside the Down or north side loop line and in the event of passenger and goods trains passing at the station, the passenger train was required to always use the south

On several occasions SR locomotives were sent to the GER Stratford for heavy maintenance. Here 2-4-0T No. 3 *Blyth* is loaded on GER flat wagon No. 21986 after receiving general repairs between 13th February and 8th May 1909 and is waiting transit to Halesworth on 19th May 1909. The actual transfer at Halesworth required the use of a GER steam crane to lift the locomotive on or off the wagon. *LCGB/Ken Nunn*

The Station, Blythburgh.

By 1908 a loop line was provided at Blythburgh to enable trains to cross on the single line, although as no second platform was provided it was only possible to cross either a goods train and a passenger train or two goods trains. The loop is in the foreground as 2-4-2T No. 1 *Southwold* is halted at the platform. The First Class saloon of the Composite coach behind the 4-wheel open wagon is devoid of passengers although the compartment door from the end balcony is open. The loop line served the goods loading platform. Some licence has taken place for a spire has been added to Holy Trinity Church.

Author's collection

or Up side loop line where the platform was located. Lieutenant P.G. Von Donop inspected the facility on 13th October 1908 and expressed satisfaction with the new arrangements.

On 6th February 1909 a parcel consigned by rail by Mr Campling of Beccles to Mrs Campling of Majuba House, Wenhaston was received at Wenhaston station by the 8.49am train and placed in the waiting room, where it was last noticed at midday, after which it disappeared. The police were informed of a possible theft and subsequently Inspector Berry and PC Mills arrested Peter Youngs, a tramp from London, in Chediston Street, Halesworth claiming he had bought the items for 6s 6d from a man who had a grey pony and cart outside the Star Inn, near Blyford. Youngs was taken into custody and charged with stealing the parcel containing three pairs of cord trousers, six linen collars and a blue woollen cap, valued at £1 3s 4d, the property of the Southwold Railway Company. He was remanded at Halesworth Magistrates' Court to appear at the Petty Sessions where he was found guilty and sentenced to twenty-one days' hard labour.

The half yearly shareholders' meeting was held at Victoria Street, Westminster in early April 1909 with Arthur Pain presiding; the receipts shown below for six months ending 31st December were presented to show comparisons.

After paying the fixed charges and interest on 4 per cent preferred debentures and 5 per cent debentures a balance of £1,130 was carried forward. The attention of those attending was drawn to the low percentage of working expenses to gross receipts, which Henry Ward, the Secretary, remarked was the *'lowest recorded'*. Arthur Pain in his report stated various works had been made in connection with the widening of the line but lack of finance had precluded widening the entire route. It was also a disappointment that so little fish traffic had been conveyed by rail since the opening of the harbour. Considerable quantities were landed at Southwold but the bulk of the tonnage was purchased by foreign buyers and was sent away by sea, the same complaint being made at Lowestoft and Yarmouth. One good factor was that the railway carried many women who had arrived at Southwold from Scotland for gutting the fish as well as conveying considerable amounts of boxes, barrels, salt and the *'hundreds of one things necessary for the fishing trade'*. It was hoped the Harbour Company would take steps, as promised, to provide rail connection from the harbour to the SR main line, in time for the next fishing season.

The *Halesworth Times* of 18th May 1909 reported that *'great satisfaction'* was expressed by the announcement that the Mid Suffolk Light Railway was depositing plans for an extension

Comparison of Six-monthly Receipts for Second Half of Year							
Year	1908	1907	1906	1905	1904	1900	1880
Passengers	67,904	65,493	67,109	66,880	71,797	68,645	39,670
Parcels	22,243	21,763	21,503	21,538	21,963	19,789	3,967
Goods (tons)	3,382	2,853	2,761	2,570	3,453	3,340	1,354
Mineral traffic (tons)	4,300	4,696	4,196	4,039	4,607		1,682
	1908	1907					
Total receipts	£3,150	£3,085					
Working expenses	£1,612	£1,603					
Working expenses to gross receipts	51.17%	51.96%					

BELOW: Sharp, Stewart 2-4-0T No. 2 *Halesworth* collects a wagon on the run round loop at Southwold on 10th September 1910. The locomotive is in good condition and boasting GER blue livery after having been to Stratford Works for general overhaul earlier the same year. *LCGB/Ken Nunn*

View from the verandah end of a coach across a wagon of coal as 2-4-0T No. 3 *Blyth* heads the 11.10am mixed train from Halesworth to Southwold on 10th September 1910. It was not unknown on windy days for coal dust to infiltrate into the passenger compartments unless the end doors were closed, and even then the seating often presented passengers with a liberal coating of dust. Ahead of the locomotive is one of the many occupational crossings with white painted gates. *LCGB/Ken Nunn*

to Halesworth from a point some two miles east of Laxfield. It optimistically forecast *'the extension would open up a large district to the sea at Southwold, Lowestoft and Yarmouth'*.

A meeting of the Southwold Trader's Association was called on the evening of Wednesday 25th August 1909 *for the purpose of supporting an application by the SR Company to the Treasury for a grant towards widening the line'*. The gathering was advised a sum of £20,000 was being requested and after further discussion it was proposed to send a petition to the Treasury pointing out that is was most essential for the welfare of Southwold and more particularly to assist with the development of the harbour, which had recently been constructed at great cost. It was the opinion of the Association the railway should be widened to standard gauge without loss of time and with the promise of an autumnal visit by a large number of Scottish and other fishing vessels using the port to discharge herrings, every facility should be provided to the increasing industry. The conversion of the railway to Halesworth to a gauge of 4 feet 8½ inches would provide proper railway accommodation. Two weeks later Southwold Corporation had also made similar representation to the Treasury, an action quickly replicated by Halesworth and Blythling Councils.

The first Down working on Friday 27th August 1909 was delayed after one pair of wheels on the locomotive derailed as it was running round the train. After using the re-railing jack and some baulks of timber the engine crew managed to re-rail the engine and the train finally arrived at Southwold a few minutes after 11.00am, nearly two hours late.

The pressure for conversion of the Southwold Railway to standard gauge continued unabated and at a constituency meeting in Southwold held by Liberal MP Edward Beauchamp on the evening of 6th October he was reported as saying he was endeavouring to get an allowance from the Treasury for the assistance of the Southwold Railway. The action was allied with a development Bill which was being sought for economic development of the United Kingdom to help schemes including improving facilities for transport. However, if the Bill were successful Beauchamp thought only £5,000 would be forthcoming.

Tuesday 26th October 1909 proved a momentous day at Southwold for forty sailing craft and fifteen steam drifters entered the harbour before 4.30pm and others followed soon after to disgorge herring and oilier fish. The work of unloading and gutting was carried on well into the evening with 300 girls working under the glare of naphtha lamps ready to send the haul to market via the SR. That same night an SR fireman, named Moore, living at Reydon, was woken about midnight by a noise outside his house. Looking out of the window he saw what he took to be a man without a hat gesticulating and talking rapidly in a foreign language. He heard the word balloon but not realising the person was in distress, went back to bed. The person gesticulating was none other than Mademoiselle Marvingt of Nancy in France, who together with an engineering friend Monsieur Gamier had flown 300 miles from Nancy in a balloon, crashing when it became entangled in telephone wires on the Lowestoft Road. A neighbour went to the assistance of the Frenchwoman and the local police soon found the balloon and the injured engineer. The crash caused excitement in Southwold and as the news spread there were many willing hands to get the balloon down from the wires and surrounding trees. The balloon had suffered little damage and by 2.00pm was packed and loaded into a Southwold Railway wagon. The French couple were then driven round Southwold by Captain Simpson and purchased several postcards as souvenirs before departing on the 5.25pm train, due at Halesworth at 6.02pm, there to connect with the train for Liverpool Street.

At the SR Board meeting on 24th September 1909 the Chairman reported that on 28th July a small strip of land, 1 rood 7 perches in extent on the north side of the railway near Southwold station, had been leased from Southwold Corporation for a term of seventy-five years at an annual rent of £1, to accommodate a new engine shed. No work was carried out on the site, however, and it was 1914 before developments were made at Halesworth.

During the early spring of 1910 William Robert Fasey reopened negotiations with the SR regarding the branch railway to Blackshore Quay. He was of the opinion that if the railway company provided the necessary permanent way materials he would complete the installation by the autumn. The matter was the subject of discussion at the half yearly meeting held at Victoria Street, Westminster on 22nd March 1910 when the following details were also debated on the relevant returns for six months ending 31st December.

	1909	1908	1880
Passengers	67,895	67,904	39,670
Parcels	22,818	22,243	3,967
Goods (tons)	3,580	3,382	1,354
Minerals (tons)	3,399	4,300	1,682
Total receipts	£3,179	£3,150	
Working expenses	£1,598	£1,612	
Working expenses to gross receipts	50.25%	51.17%	

After paying the fixed charges and interest on 4 per cent preferred debentures and on the 5 per cent debentures the balance of £1,777 was carried forward to the next half year. A.C. Pain apologized that the board had decided not to declare a dividend on preference or ordinary shares. It was also announced the Directors had been in communication with the Southwold Harbour Company, and that company had promised before the fishing season commenced in the autumn to lay down sidings from the harbour to the railway, with the junction close to the swing bridge. The Harbour Company was prepared to execute the work at their own cost and the railway company had undertaken to install proper siding accommodation. The Chairman enthused that it offered the prospect of not only fish traffic, but also stone and coal being conveyed direct from the harbour to SR stations and possibly stations on the GER system. Pain concluded that as the line had been worked safely without loss of life or limb for so many years the Directors of the railway company wished to recognize the service of their employees by awarding the entire staff two days' pay in recognition of *'the care and attention with which the traffic had been worked'*. Changes were made to the railway management when Henry Ward was appointed to the joint role of Manager and Secretary, a position he was to hold for the remaining operating life of the line.

The branch railway was debated at the meeting of Southwold Town Council on Friday 5th August when the Estate Committee reported the Southwold Harbour Company was arranging to carry the line from the existing SR across the Corporation marshes to the quay and was asking permission to cross the area at a nominal rent. After discussion the wayleave was duly granted at an annual rent of £5, the Harbour Company taking all risk of injury to cattle, and making all necessary arrangements with tenants occupying the marsh.

Southwold station and goods yard looking towards the buffer stops on 12th July 1911. The left-hand arm on the inner home signal when clear permitted trains into the platform; the arm with the white background is the Up starter. The spectacles for both arms are at a lower level on the post, whilst a windlass was used to hoist the oil lamp level with the spectacle. *LCGB/Ken Nunn*

A busy scene on the approach road to Southwold station circa 1910. Gypsy girls approach to sell their wares to unsuspecting visitors after the arrival of a Down train. Amongst others, three hotel horse-drawn omnibuses, an open landau, and a pony and trap line up to take alighting passengers to their hotels, boarding houses and holiday establishments, although there is a glimpse of a motor car to the extreme right. By this date the station building, amassed with advertisements, had been enlarged. *Author's collection*

Sharp, Stewart 2-4-0T No. 2 *Halesworth* resplendent in GER blue livery at Southwold shed on 20th July 1911. Locomotive Foreman W.G. Jackson is in the cab. 2-4-2T No. 1 *Southwold* to the left is undergoing repairs and maintenance. *LCGB/Ken Nunn*

Whatever may have been said at the half yearly meeting, the proposal made by Fasey in the spring, offering to build the connecting line to the harbour, was still not acceptable to the railway company. Yet further delay was incurred as the Directors deliberated on the offer and it was 21st September 1910 before a counter proposal was submitted offering to build the branch line and in return pay Fasey 1d per ton for all traffic placed thereon, provided Fasey granted the company a 21-year lease on the branch. The SR Directors also appealed to the GER Board suggesting the main line company construct the standard gauge line, including the branch to the harbour, and provide rolling stock on loan in return for five per cent debentures. To further the case, Arthur C. Pain arranged a meeting with Walter Hyde, the GER General Manager, and with several of his officers a joint inspection was made of the line. Needless to say the GER Directors refused to have anything to do with the conversion of the SR to standard gauge. In the same year enhancements at Southwold included new ladies' and gentlemen's toilets, whilst W.H. Smith & Son provided a new bookstall, which proved popular with the travelling public.

During an unsettled period of inclement weather rain fell continuously from 4.00pm on Wednesday 30th November for thirty-six hours resulting in flooding of the Blyth valley. The SR line was breached on Friday morning, the water laying several feet deep between Blythburgh and Wenhaston. A train service was operated between Southwold and Blythburgh and thence passengers were conveyed by road. As the water subsided the repairs to permanent way were quickly effected and by 1.00pm on Saturday the normal train service resumed. Then on 9th December 1910 excessive rain fell across much of East Anglia, again causing the rivers to rise and break their banks. On the GER the Snape, Framlingham and Waveney Valley branches were flooded at various locations, whilst the SR suffered temporary stoppage of traffic as the waters of the Blyth engulfed the line at Wenhaston, Blythburgh and near the swing bridge. Local roads were also flooded and delayed the bus services.

W.H. Hyde, the GER General Manager, duly reported to his Directors on 3rd January 1911 of the results of his visit to the Southwold Railway. He advised that Fasey, the contractor appointed to work on Southwold Harbour, had reported he was hampered by the lack of adequate railway facilities but the harbour had been constructed at a cost of £80,000 of which £21,000 had been a government grant. Fasey, frustrated by the local Directors dithering, wished the GER to purchase the SR to give the harbour a good rail service. It had been suggested the GER reconsider purchasing the line at an estimated price of £80,000 to £90,000 as it was an impediment that the railway and harbour had different owners. The railway had been offered for sale in 1900 at £60,000, with any disagreement in price going to arbitration. It was, however, Hyde's opinion that should the GE take over the railway it would require bringing up to standard, which a decade earlier had been estimated at £100,000. Despite some preliminary work being carried out on conversion to standard gauge, such as widening of the track bed and some bridges, the General Manager thought the cost of purchase was *'unremunerative to his company'* as the new works had not materially reduced the cost of conversion to standard gauge. In addition, the provision of new standard gauge rolling stock would render the line unremunerative. While the SR receipts of £5,241 for the year ending June 1910 were sufficient to pay the fixed charges of preference and debenture share dividends, the GE working expenses would be greater, and unless there was a large increase in traffic, losses would be incurred for a great number

The 10.55am mixed train to Halesworth is waiting to depart from Southwold behind 2-4-0T No. 3 *Blyth* on 12th July 1911. In the background a Moy's 6-wheel coal wagon is waiting to be unloaded. *LCGB/Ken Nunn*

of years. When Hyde had visited the harbour the previous autumn the only activity was coal being discharged from two sailing colliers, while during the fishing season most catches that were landed were exported and *'did not touch the railway'*. He doubted the harbour would become a serious rival to either Yarmouth or Lowestoft without very large expense in dock and other accommodation. Under the circumstances Hyde did not recommend any action and on 6th January 1911 the GE Board approved of the General Manager's report and advised the SR Directors accordingly.

At the annual dinner for employees of the GER and SR held at Halesworth on Friday 3rd February 1911, A.E. Smith voiced the thoughts of many and surprised some of those present when he urged the Directors of the GER to take into consideration the advisability of following the example of the Midland Railway in taking over the London Tilbury & Southend line by entering into negotiation with the Southwold Railway and Mid Suffolk Light Railway companies to develop them.

The half yearly meeting of the SR shareholders was held as usual at the company's office in Victoria Street, Westminster on 29th April 1911 with A.C. Pain presiding and fellow Directors W. Steele Tomkins, W.C. Chambers, Herbert W. Chambers, J.B. Walton, Auditor and H. Ward, Secretary. Total receipts from all sources amounted to £3,218 8s 0d, against £3,179 16s 9d for the corresponding period 1909, an increase of £8 11s 3d. The working expenses were £1,680 against £1,598, an increase of £82, the percentage of working expenses to gross receipts was 52.21 against 50.25 for the corresponding period in 1909. After expenses and interest, a dividend of 5 per cent per annum was awarded on preference shares and 2 per cent per annum on ordinary shares with the balance carried forward.

William Robert Fasey refused the counter proposal made by the SR regarding the harbour branch and in the early months of 1911 shocked the SR Directors by offering to purchase the Southwold Company outright for £50,000, provided the railway was converted to standard gauge by the autumn. The demand was obviously out of the question and so after much negotiation the two parties declared a truce, came to their senses, ceased the wrangling and negotiated a working agreement for building and operating a future Harbour Branch. At the conclusion of negotiations it was agreed Fasey would make the necessary application for the Light Railway Order leaving the SR to construct and work the line, and the agreement was signed on 30th November. At the beginning of October a combination of a severe gale and exceptionally high tides had brought flooding to the north end of Southwold and the town was again cut off from the outside world as the only road was under two feet of water. Fortunately the SR suffered only minor inconvenience and maintained a service.

Fasey, as owner of Southwold Harbour Company, duly applied to the Light Railway Commissioners in November 1911 for powers to construct a light railway from Southwold Harbour to a junction with the existing Southwold Railway.

'William Robert Fasey carrying on business under the style of the Southwold Harbour Company applied to make and maintain light railways

'Railway No. 1, 7 furlongs and 5 chains in length commencing by a junction with the Southwold Railway at a point 9 chains in a north easterly direction from the eastern end of the swing bridge, thence in a south easterly direction across the marsh lands and along the bank of the River Blyth to Southwold Harbour

Southwold station circa 1912 with the horse chestnut trees increasing in size. Several people are walking from the platform after the departure of a train. The tall electric lighting columns, dating from 1905, appear out of place at such a moderately sized station. *Author's collection*

terminating on the New Quay, 6 yards from the north-west side of Sterry's coal depot.

'Railway No. 2, 10 chains in length commencing from the junction with Railway No. 1, 125 yards from the south west corner of Blackshore Quay and passing in a north westerly direction terminating on that Quay at or near the northern end thereof.

'The said railways are intended to be constructed on a gauge of not less than 3 feet and it is proposed to run thereon engines, carriages and trucks adapted for use on the Southwold Railway propelled by steam, electrical or other mechanical power. Other powers included the right of compulsory purchase of the necessary lands, to levy tolls and charges and enter into agreement with the SR It also intended to give the SR powers to raise funds by creation and issue of new ordinary or guaranteed or preferred or deferred shares or stock and by borrowing.'

The inquiry into the order for the construction of the light railway was held in Southwold Town Hall on 5th February 1912 when a large number of townspeople attended. Mr Kennedy appeared for the promoters and E.R. Cooper opened the proceedings. He pointed out the total expenditure on the harbour to 31st March 1910 was £83,796, a quarter of which had been advanced by the Board of Trade. The railway was about 1¼ miles from the harbour and the need of connection between the two was paramount. The Board of Agriculture had certified the making of the light railway connecting the harbour with the main line was a necessary means of communication and that state assistance should be given. In response to the applications the Treasury had shown their willingness to contribute a sum of £2,700 provided the company undertook to keep the line open for a period of seventy-five years, and that the railway form part of the harbour undertaking, in the event of re-purchase during that period by the Southwold Corporation.

The length of the proposed line was 7 furlongs and three chains, and the land on which the railway was to run was held entirely by the Harbour Company or Southwold Corporation, who were consenting parties to the undertaking. Arthur C. Pain, Chairman of the Southwold Railway, said his company had been approached by the Harbour Company relative to the construction of the line, as the owner of the line running into Southwold. It was proposed to make the embankment of mud taken from below the high water mark in the river, and to ballast it with shingle taken from the harbour mouth. The total estimated cost of the line was £4,771 and it would not be a passenger line. The cost of construction would be borne half by the railway company and half by the Treasury. E.E. Grubbe, Mayor of Southwold objected to the use of shingle from the harbour and produced photographs showing the alteration caused to the beach by the removal of shingle by the Harbour Company. The Chairman pointed out the removal of the shingle was outside the jurisdiction of the inquiry and, as there was no objection to the line, the order would be granted. He would, however, see that the clause allowing the shingle to be used only for ballasting was observed, the amount required for this purpose being so small that it could not have any material effect on the foreshore.

Fasey then made another plea for a takeover to the GER and on 8th March 1912 the GE board were advised by the General Manager of the latest application for purchase. The harbour had recently been improved at a cost of £85,000 of which £21,773 had been provided by the government. Fasey of Fasey & Sons had said the scheme was not completed and paid only 2 per cent; another £100,000 was required to complete the quays and piers. To raise the money he had concluded an agreement with a syndicate, which was intending to take over both the harbour and the railway by floating a company to raise capital, though it was difficult with the current state of the English money market. Fasey preferred to sell all the property to the GER for £90,000, providing his firm had the contract for the extensions. The General Manager was of the opinion the passenger traffic showed few prospects, but the harbour might be developed for goods traffic provided the GER owned both the harbour and the railway. After a lengthy discussion the GE board, however, declined Fasey's offer.

The half yearly meeting of the SR was held on 29th March 1912 at Victoria Street, Westminster with Arthur C. Pain, the Company Chairman, presiding. He explained the hot summer of 1911 had encouraged people to visit the seaside with the result that passengers carried between July and December constituted a record. For the six months, 71,704 passengers had travelled, an increase of 3,840 compared with the similar period in 1910. Other increases included 1,581 parcels and 118 tons of merchandise. There was, however, a decrease of 208 tons in minerals conveyed but a net increase of £267 in receipts. The decrease in minerals was because coal and stone traffic for roads was now brought into the harbour by shipping. In the present three months of the half year there had been encouraging increases; minerals carried in January and February 1912, up by 230 tons compared with 1911, while receipts on 27th March showed an increase of £124 compared with the same period in 1911. Pain explained there was no reason to be anxious about competition from the harbour and the tendency was that more coal and stone would be conveyed by rail. Profits totalled £2,112 for the year 1911, of which £544 came from the first half and £1,578 from the December half. The following statistics were presented.

Six months ending 31st December	1911	1910
Passengers	71,704	69,059
Parcels	24,757	23,514
Goods (tons)	3,654	3,530
Minerals (tons)	2,920	3,382
Total receipts	£3,354 14s 6d	£3,218 8s 0d
Working expenses	£1,767	£1,680
Percentage working expenses to gross receipts	52.81	52.21
Total train mileage	17,694	16,262

A special meeting was convened immediately after the half yearly meeting for the purpose of approving the draft of the Southwold Harbour Light Railway Order. Pain referred to the competition from the harbour; the tendency of late had been to get stone of a much harder quality for the making up of roads, and in consequence much came from abroad, especially Belgium. From Southwold Harbour the stone was distributed by road across the surrounding district in waggons hauled by traction engines. The SR Directors had, however, been approached by the East Suffolk County Council Surveyor, who wanted the stone loaded into railway wagons at the harbour. Bearing in mind the fact that more seaborne coal might be distributed by rail if the branch line was constructed, he thought they could favourably look upon the proposals of the Harbour Company. In view of the possibility of the SR being widened to standard gauge in future, he urged the new branch be so constructed that it would be easily converted from narrow gauge. The estimated cost was now £5,400 of which the Treasury was granting £2,700 towards the scheme. The £2,700, which the company had to find, would be raised by 5 per cent debentures, being a second charge on the undertaking. The agreement on which he desired the meeting to sanction was drawn up firstly to ensure the Harbour Company paid the cost of the order and secondly, because the Treasury made it a condition when advancing half of the cost, the line should be constructed and worked by the railway company. Asked if there was any chance of the GER taking over the SR, Pain said the matter had been discussed and if the GER desired to buy the line the Directors were willing to sell on fair and reasonable terms. At the conclusion of the meeting the motion for approval of the order and agreement was duly approved.

At the same meeting Arthur Pain finally surrendered his position as Engineer, but kept a watching brief on affairs by appointing his son Claude to succeed him. During the same year the goods shed at Southwold was turned to a new position, ninety degrees from its original site, to provide more room for freight facilities, as complaints were made of lack of covered accommodation.

At the end of April 1912 most of the staff of the SR, together with many of the GER staff from Halesworth station, were invited and entertained by S.E. Hayward (the proprietor of the Marlborough Hotel) and his wife to a staff supper. The guests also included the town postmen and corporation employees. Hayward said he was pleased to renew the experiment of three years ago and congratulated staff of both companies for maintaining the rail service during the recent coal strike. A special train was arranged to take guests back to Halesworth at the end of the soirée. In April, Fasey again attempted to get the GER to purchase the harbour, previously having asked £70,000 for the harbour provided the GER paid him £100,000 to complete the works. He was now asking £45,000 but on 3rd May 1912 the board again refused to entertain the request. The General Manager again raised the matter at the board meeting on 12th June but it was agreed the Directors would adhere to their previous decision.

During the late spring an application was received from the Anglo American Oil Company for a license to store 1,000 gallons of petroleum spirit in a building to be erected on the SR Company premises at Halesworth. After approval of the building by the sanitary inspector Halesworth Council sanctioned the application. At this time the embryonic Halesworth Light Railway was promoted, the project commencing at a junction with the Mid Suffolk Light Railway at Cratfield and passing through the parishes of Cratfield, Linstead Magna, Huntingfield, Cookley, Halesworth and Wisset, and terminating by a junction with the GER at Halesworth. The line was to be constructed of standard gauge and was considered necessary to improve trade in Halesworth. The promoters also sought powers to lease or purchase the MSLR; Halesworth Urban Council demurred from approving of the scheme until formal application was made to the Light Railway Commissioners but after seeing an amended plan of the railway they cast their approval early in July. The public enquiry with Colonel Boughey, a Light Railway Commissioner, as Chairman was held on Tuesday 16th July at Halesworth Corn Hall when the gathering was advised the necessity for the railway was because powers obtained by the MSLR for acquiring land between Laxfield and Halesworth for an extension had expired. Mr Berry for the promoters explained 5,000 adults in the area had approved of the scheme whilst Mr Foxlee the engineer for the concern explained that estimated cost were £36,109, or about £6,000 per mile. Mr Mullens from Blythling Rural District Council urged that gates be placed at all level crossing, but after discussion with Boughey it was thought gates would only be necessary where cattle bars

The eastern end of the station layout at Southwold shortly before World War One, with the engine shed to the left and the small goods shed and loading platform (occupied by a tarpaulin-covered wagon) are to its right. 2-4-0T No. 3 *Blyth* is on the run round loop whilst the main station building, in its final form, has GER posters displayed above the platform seats and a parcels weighing machine is set into the platform beside the parcels office door. At this period No. 3 faced Halesworth but was later turned to face Southwold. *Author's collection*

prove inadequate. Boughey concluded the Commissioners would be prepared to grant the order when formal application was made and approved. No mention was made of a possible extension to Southwold by converting the SR line from narrow to standard gauge but one of those giving supporting evidence for the scheme was Mr Peck, a clerk employed by the Southwold Harbour Company. Not all approved of the scheme, for on 12th August the General Purposes Committee of West Suffolk County Council turned down an application for a £5,000 grant saying the railway would not be of the slightest benefit to West Suffolk.

In the summer of 1912 a small circus made a two-day visit to Southwold and pitched tent on the Common. A young lion, suitably caged, was transported by rail to Southwold for onward delivery to the circus. It was loaded onto Walter Doy's lorry with strict instructions given that *'carriage forward'* charges amounting to £8 or £9 were to be collected before the circus proprietor could take delivery of the animal. The proprietor refused to accept the charges and as no money was handed over, the lion was deposited back at the station. Faced with the problem of keeping an unwanted animal, the station master designated Aldis, who was a general handyman acting as porter during the summer season and served as a platelayer in the winter months, as temporary guardian of the lion. Aldis, nicknamed 'Old Fogey' by his colleagues, was sent to the local butchers to purchase one shilling's worth of cheap meat, whilst the cage was placed in the waiting room and the room locked up. Apparently Aldis was delegated the task as animal keeper on the recommendation of his earlier seafaring

Porter W. Aldis in uniform; he was previously employed as a platelayer. *Southwold Museum*

experiences, when he was said to have fed sharks at various times whilst leaning over the edge of the ship. When Aldis returned to the station he carefully affixed a piece of meat on the end of a shunting pole and gingerly approached the cage to feed the lion. This process continued until the lion was satisfied. It soon became evident that the waiting room, which also served as the booking hall, was not the best of places to keep a caged beast and when passengers arrived to purchase tickets the cage was covered with a wagon tarpaulin sheet. The rudimentary covering failed to disguise the smell and complaints were made of the *'disgusting odour'* filling the room. The waiting room was normally kept locked between the running of trains but unbeknown to the station master and Aldis, Junior Porter J.A. Stedman had obtained the key and provided his friends with a private viewing of the lion, whilst the rest of the staff were away for their mid-day meal. Fortunately, after a satisfactory first night performance, when receipts were above average, the circus proprietor was able to afford the carriage charges for the lion, together with the additional cost for animal feed and charges for the second delivery. Aldis was upset when the lion was delivered to its rightful owner and claimed he should have been entitled to *'danger money'* when feeding the beast.

Delays to GER services on Saturday 31st July 1912 caused late running but the SR maintained connections at Halesworth by running the last Down service early on Sunday morning. Then on 26th August 1912 torrential rain fell across large swathes of East Anglia resulting in serious flooding which affected many GER lines including the East Suffolk main line and the Framlingham and Waveney Valley branches. The

SR managed to run a normal service on Monday 26th but after the passage of the last train, breaches were made in the line when the Blyth burst its banks and flooded the line near Wenhaston and Blythburgh. Train services were subsequently suspended and replaced by a horse bus service. The telephone wires were also brought down during the night by falling trees so that communication with Southwold was broken. Normal trains services resumed on 28th August.

Grove Thomas Moore, the relieving station master at Blythburgh (later referred to as Deputy Station Master), before leaving the station at 9.30pm on 3rd September 1912, checked all doors were locked for the night but on returning the following morning he discovered the outside door and window of the waiting room open. The inside door had been forced open, and on checking, Moore found 9s 8d was missing from an unlocked drawer, as was a gentleman's bicycle. Another drawer, containing papers, had been forced and the contents littered about. The theft was soon reported, whereupon it was noted bicycle tyre tracks led to the main road. The police were surprisingly speedy in their investigation for in the afternoon Moore went with Police Constable King to Yarmouth Police Station where he found his bicycle. Herbert Haylock, foreman platelayer, confirmed the cycle belonged to Moore. Subsequently, George Henry Millar, a ship's steward from Newcastle, was charged with breaking and entering the railway station at Blythburgh on 4th September and stealing the sum of 9s 8d and a bicycle the value of £6, the property of Grove Thomas Moore. Millar (also referred to as Miller) was remanded in custody and brought before Saxmundham Petty Sessions. Detective Arthur Boulton reported that he had arrested Millar as he was attempting to sell the cycle in Great Yarmouth. When charged, the prisoner made no reply but afterwards on a train journey confessed he was sorry he had robbed a workman. He was committed for trial at the following East Suffolk Quarter Sessions where it was revealed the 31-year-old ex-miner had thrice been convicted of similar offences under the names of Morrison and Murphy. He was sentenced to four months imprisonment with hard labour.

On 14th September 1912 a boy named Stannard was walking near the railway at Walberswick when he noticed two men and a woman cross the line; one of the men pulled up a post and hurled it on to the rails, before placing it in an upright position between the sleepers in the track. The three then went away over Walberswick Common. On hearing the sound of a locomotive whistle Stannard ran and informed George Cotton, a gamekeeper of Walberswick, who at about 4.15pm was walking on the road linking Blythburgh with Walberswick. He ran to the railway and saw the notice board and pole, about 9 feet in length, standing between the rails before approaching Thomas P. Pilcher, who was sitting with another man and the woman having tea on the Common. He asked what right he had to go onto Sir Ralph Blois' property and pull up the post? Pilcher stated he had moved the post for a joke and Cotton told him to replace it but the miscreant went and pulled up the post and flung it against the fence. Subsequently the case was brought before the Petty Sessions at Halesworth when Thomas P. Pitcher of 12 Milner Street, London was charged with placing a wooden post and notice board on the Southwold Railway at Walberswick on 14th September. F.J. Rodwell prosecuted for the SR and E.R. Cooper appeared for the defence. After hearing from Stannard and Cotton, Cooper stated the post being merely stuck in the ground would have fallen down at a touch adding that the driver of a train would have been able to see the post at a distance of 200 yards. Rodwell for the railway company stated they had no desire to press the case; when the information was laid they had no idea the charge was of such a serious nature. The company only desired to let the public know that they could not allow such doings. The Bench, addressing the defendant, had come to the conclusion no jury would convict in this case. Pilcher had been guilty of a very foolish joke, which he acknowledged. Under the circumstances the case was dismissed.

As a result of the application by the Southwold Harbour Company for an order to build a light railway to Southwold Harbour, the Light Railway Commissioners conducted a public enquiry on 2nd December 1912 where few objections were raised and the scheme was allowed to proceed.

The GER bus service from Lowestoft to Southwold was withdrawn from the road in January 1913. At a meeting of Southwold Town Council in the first few days of January 1913, the Estate and Works Committee reported on the application by the SR Company for permission to hire a strip of No's 1 and 2 Buss Creek Marshes on the north side of the railway station, also a strip of the road and Common on the south side, in order to facilitate the construction of the new harbour branch. It was thought the additional land at

Southwold Harbour Light Railway Order 1913 – front page.

The SR was associated with many happy events and here on this pre-1914 occasion a couple stand on the end verandah of a coach at Southwold before setting off on their honeymoon. To the left Guard Wright stands beside luggage van No. 13. *Author's collection*

the station was for sidings to accommodate the extra traffic expected from the harbour. After inspecting the lands the Committee recommended the refusal of the land off the entrance road whilst it was not advisable to disturb the allotment holders on No. 2 Buss Creek Marshes. It was recommended the railway company be offered 1 rood and 20 perches of No. 1 Buss Creek Marshes, being a strip about 40 feet in width at a ground rent to be confirmed. At the same meeting the Gas Company was offered No. 6 Buss Creek Marshes on a perpetual rent of £20 per annum with the right to run a siding from the railway to serve the premises. The *Halesworth Times* subsequently reported on 11th March that as the Harbour Railway crossed Wood End Marshes, Southwold Town Council had stipulated the railway company should agree terms with the existing tenants for rearrangement of their holdings and compensate them for any loss incurred. A.C. Pain had also agreed to consult with his son Claude to ascertain if there was a possibility of reducing the area of allotment land required at Southwold station yard.

The company half yearly meeting was held in early April at Victoria Street, Westminster, London, with Arthur C. Pain, the Chairman of the Directors, presiding. The report showed in the six months ending 31st December 1912, 66,400 passengers had been carried compared with 71,704 in the corresponding period in 1911, parcels showed 25,691 against 24,757, goods 3,262 tons against 2,920 tons. Total receipts amounted to £3,268 9s 6d against £3,345 14s 6d, a decrease of £77 5s 0d attributed to the wet weather. The working expenses totalled £1,827 compared to £1,767 an increase of £60. The percentage of working expenses to gross receipts was 53.90 against 52.81, but the Directors duly declared for the half year a 2 per cent payment on ordinary shares per annum, carrying forward the balance to the next half year. Because of the alterations and amendments made in the draft order authorizing the harbour branch and in the working agreement approved at the special general meeting held on 29th March 1911, it was necessary for the proprietors to re-approve the order and agreement. Herbert W. Chambers and W. Steele Tomkins, the retiring Directors, were re-elected and a special general meeting was then held to approve the provisional draft order made by the Light Railway Commissioners upon the application of the Southwold Harbour Company, which related to the connecting of Southwold Harbour with the SR. In mid-May the Light Railway Commissioners advised in the local press that an order had been made for the construction of a Light Railway in the Borough of Southwold, in the County of Suffolk connecting Southwold Harbour with the Southwold Railway, asking that objections and amendments be lodged with the Board of Trade by 3rd June 1913.

The SR and the Southwold Harbour Company subsequently reached full agreement on the working schedule on 28th July 1913, and the document was signed by Arthur C. Pain and Henry Ward for the SR and William Fasey for the Southwold Harbour company in the presence of Thomas Eustace Hayaman, Cashier, of 52 Poppleton Road, Leytonstone, London NE.

In the meantime in May 1913 the threat of possible hostilities found the Suffolk and Norfolk Yeomanry conducting exercises near Halesworth; in the event of an invading army, the Norfolk Yeomanry were delegated to hold all the crossings over the Halesworth to Southwold railway. However, the competition from closer quarters was of more concern to the SR Board and in June Southwold Town Council granted licences to Messrs Petherick and G. Doy to operate wagonettes between the harbour and the town. The United Automobile Services Limited applied for licences for four motor buses but a petition from a representative cross-section of tradesmen asked for the application to be refused until as good a service as provided lately by the GER was to be operated. At present there was no bus to Southwold until 3.25pm and that departed again at 4.15pm, being of no use to the trade of the town. It was thought a bus ought to run from Lowestoft to Southwold to reach the town before lunch-time. After discussion the motion was carried. By 4th July 1913 the Council were advised that Mr Hutchinson, Manager of United Automobile Services, had arranged for a *'car'* to reach Southwold before lunch and that the summer service of ten buses each way would shortly commence.

As a result of a railway disaster at Colchester on Saturday 12th July 1913, in which the Cromer to Liverpool Street express collided with a light engine, GER services were severely delayed. The SR rearranged their timetable so that all trains connected at Halesworth, including the service booked to reach Southwold at 8.30pm Saturday which arrived at 4.00am on Sunday morning.

The Southwold Harbour Light Railway Order was duly confirmed by the Board of Trade on 25th September 1913, noting the estimated cost was £4,772 and the document authorised the building of:

'Railway No. 1, 7 furlongs 5.10 chains or thereabouts in length, wholly situated in the Parish and Borough of Southwold in the County of Suffolk, commencing by a junction with the Southwold Railway at a point 9 chains or thereabouts measured in a north-easterly direction from the eastern edge of the swing bridge by which that railway is carried over the River Blyth, proceeding thence in a south-easterly direction across the marsh lands adjoining and on the east side and along the bank of the said river and Southwold Harbour and terminating on the New Quay at Southwold Harbour at or near a point thereon 6 yards or thereabouts measured in a north-westerly direction from the north-west side of Sterry's Coal Depot.

'Railway No. 2, 1 furlong or thereabouts in length wholly situated in the said Parish and Borough of Southwold, commencing by a junction with Railway No. 1 at a point 125 yards or thereabouts measured in a southeasterly direction from the south-west corner of Blackshore Quay passing thence in a north-westerly direction along and terminating on that Quay at or near the northern end thereof.'

The railway was to be constructed and maintained on a gauge of 3 feet unless the Southwold Company was authorised to convert the railway to a gauge of 4 feet 8½ inches. In the event of the Southwold Railway changing gauge the harbour line was to be similarly altered. Whilst the new line was built to a gauge of 3 feet, similar rails to that used by the Southwold company were to be used as permanent way but if conversion to 4 feet 8½ inches was made the rails were to weigh 56 lbs per yard.

Three years were allowed for the compulsory purchase of land and five years for the completion of works. Where the railway crossed a road leading to the harbour, notices were to be erected 200 yards on each rail approach denoting the speed limit of trains, whilst 50 yards on each road approach to the crossing the company was to maintain notices cautioning the public to 'Beware of Trains'. Under clause 21 of the Order the railway company was not to take or use any sand or shingle from the foreshore of the Borough of Southwold between the northern breakwater of Southwold Harbour and the northern boundary of the company's freehold land, except for the purpose of ballasting the permanent way, without the consent of the Town Clerk. The Southwold Company, with the authority of three-quarters of their shareholders, was permitted to provide not exceeding £2,700 towards the full cost of £89,700 for the scheme, whilst on completion the harbour railway was to be considered part of the harbour undertaking and not part of the Southwold Railway.

The proposed Blackshore Quay Branch of 1878 was shown on a tracing sent to Chambers, the contractor, on 30th April 1898, consisting of a single line diverging from the main single line immediately north of the swing bridge and running between the river bank and the waterfront houses of Blackshore Quay, whereas the new authorized scheme routed the line behind the houses.

During 1913 a total of 108,677 passengers travelled on the SR, and 41,462 parcels, 7,334 tons of merchandise and 6,474 tons of minerals were conveyed. Gross receipts were £5,401 and expenditure £3,568, leaving a net profit of £1,803, enabling a 2 per cent dividend to be paid on ordinary shares.

Anticipating the requirement to handle an increasing amount of goods traffic once the harbour branch was open to traffic, the Directors ordered another locomotive capable of hauling heavier trains. On the arrival of this Manning, Wardle & Company Limited 0-6-2 tank locomotive named *Wenhaston* to the fleet in 1914, the SR Company was in a dilemma, however, for accommodation at the 64 feet long engine shed at Southwold was restricted to three locomotives. Accordingly, soon after the locomotive entered service, sanction was given for the construction of an engine shed and associated siding to the east of the existing ballast pit siding at Bird's Folly at Halesworth. The building had a dual function, that of accommodating the fourth locomotive and enabling an engine to be based at the Halesworth end of the line to operate a shuttle service in the event of the line being flooded at any intermediate point.

Early in April 1914 the Estates Committee of Southwold Town Council agreed to a strip of land near Southwold station – comprising a section of Buss Creek, two whole allotments and part of three others, in all totalling one rood and thirteen perches – to be rented by the SR at a rate of 4s 0d per rood, amounting to £10 12s 0d per annum, for station improvements. In return the company was required to make arrangements with the various tenants and compensate them for disturbance as well as fencing in the ground, moving the gate and the gateway at the entrance to the marsh, and extending the surface water drain beyond the gateway. The Committee also agreed to the company extracting ballast from

The curve of the harbour branch constructed by Howard Farrow in 1914 descending away from the main line in the 1930s. The connection to Blackshore Quay can been seen to the right.

0-6-2 No. 4 *Wenhaston*, built by Manning, Wardle & Company Limited and delivered in 1914, awaits departure from Halesworth.
Ian Pope collection

a strip of land staked out in the cutting on the approach to the station but restricted the cut back to 12 feet instead of the 25 feet applied for. The ballast excavated was to be charged at 9d per cubic yard subject to the material not being used for works outside the borough and the footbridge left secure. Whins were to be cut for a path along the railings as existing and new whins were planted on the new face of the cutting with concrete posts installed to mark the Corporation boundary. The matter was raised at a meeting of the whole council after a letter was received from the SR stating that for certain reasons the company was compelled to abandon some of the proposed alterations at the station but they would carry out the work if the Council would agree to the company having a strip of land 20 feet in width from the ditch to the main road. The council terms regarding the strip of land in the cutting were also agreed whilst it was thought short lengths of steel rails could be used for marking the boundary instead of concrete posts. Permission was also sought for the temporary use of a strip of land from the council property to the cutting near the white gate so that a new line of rails could be installed, the land being fenced in. The Council agreed to the amendments early in May.

The *Haleswarth Times* for 19th May 1914 advised its readers of pressure to build the Halesworth Light Railway from Halesworth to Laxfield to link up with the Mid Suffolk Light Railway to facilitate traffic passing between East and West Suffolk, and of the proposed meeting of the County Council on 26th May, where a resolution was to be made to authorize the Council to apply to the Local Government Board for financial assistance. Every householder in the locality was asked to further the aims by sending a postcard to J.B. Chevallier at Aspall Hall, Debenham. At the meeting the resolution was made to apply to the Light Railway Commissioners to authorize the advancement of the light railway, either as a loan or part share capital, a sum not exceeding £15,000. In furtherance of the scheme Alderman Canon Abbay optimistically said when the railway was completed it would open up the coast to the Midlands, and Southwold would become the second Felixstowe. E.W. Moore added the completion was absolutely necessary for the progress of the district and reminded those present that when the Midland Railway Company was approached to run a line to Haughley station they declined, on the grounds there was territorial agreement with the GER. Moore was of the opinion the agreement had been broken by the building of the Mid Suffolk line and if the new line was completed the Midland Railway could run right through to Southwold. After debate the Council referred the matter to their Finance Committee for examination and report.

The shock of the outbreak of World War One on 4th August 1914 had little initial impact on the SR, save that a national call for volunteers to fight the Germans resulted in a considerable number of Southwold men and others from the local villages lining up in the Market Square for recruitment on the evening of Thursday 3rd September. Earlier in the day a large crowd gathered in the Market Place to accompany a contingent of the National Reserve who had volunteered for service and were leaving for Bury St. Edmunds, each man being presented with a packet of tobacco by the Mayor before they marched to the station. After a farewell smoking concert on Saturday 5th September, during which patriotic songs were sung, the Mayor called for more volunteers and on Monday 7th September fifty-four volunteers marched to the station behind the Town Band, watched by the women and children of the town, to catch the 10.15am train en route to Halesworth and on to Ipswich. This was to be the forerunner of many departures over the next few years of hostilities as more and more joined the colours. The crowd, which packed the entire station enclosure, cheered as the train departed. As the weeks advanced so it became clear that the little railway was to undergo considerable change. In concord with the main line companies the Southwold Railway came under Government control and, being located in a vulnerable position on the East Coast, was virtually handed over to the War Department. The first change came with the drastic reduction in holidaymakers to Southwold and, more importantly, the resultant reduced revenue. The holidaymakers were replaced by large numbers of troops stationed in the area as the district was considered a likely site for invasion by German troops. The military authorities were concerned that in the event of the enemy landing, the swing bridge over the River Blyth would be of vital importance and they demanded the key on the single line Train Staff so that the bridge could be made inoperable at any given time, irrespective of whether a train service was operating or not. J.R. Belcher, the Engineer argued forcibly that the Train Staff was essential for the safe working of the railway, which could be an advantage to the defending troops. He declined to surrender the instrument and

The call to arms on the outbreak of World War One found thousands of volunteers enlisting in the armed forces. Southwold was no exception and on 7th September 1914 crowds gathered to watch young and not so young men line up in the market square before marching to the station behind the Town Band to catch the train to Halesworth. Here the volunteers walk down the station approach road to the platform and a waiting train.
Author's collection

the key remained safely with the railway company officials, on the strict understanding that in the event of an emergency the key was to be handed over immediately to military personnel. Additional military traffic, both personnel and stores and equipment, brought considerable traffic to the line, and indeed much needed revenue; on many occasions during the hostilities two locomotives were kept in steam and worked consecutive trains in the same direction under the Train Staff and Ticket method of operation, a practice almost unheard of in peacetime. At certain periods a locomotive was also maintained in steam overnight so that in the event of an emergency a train could be operated with the minimum delay.

A boat crowded with Belgian refugees put in at Southwold harbour on Thursday 15th October 1914; after receiving food and drink they were taken to the town by motor car and there found free lodgings. In obedience to Government edicts the following day the group were transported to Halesworth by Grey Car charabancs to catch a special train to London, the SR playing no part in the transfer.

Reminiscing about the period of hostilities, Miss Daniel, the Second Mistress of St. Felix School at Reydon, related that in December 1914 when the Germans bombarded Scarborough from the sea, a message was received from the War Office that all schools near the coast were to evacuate their children as quickly as possible from the danger area. As St. Felix was a boarding school for girls, this meant a frantic rush was made to send the pupils home and by the time all scholars were prepared for the journey there was less than half an hour before the next train was due to depart from Southwold. Miss Daniels went ahead of the party to warn the station master of the impending arrival of extra passengers; upon being advised that all spare coaches were kept at Halesworth as a wartime precaution she asked if any empty coal trucks were available to convey the girls. When he stated there were some wagons available he must have thought the Second Mistress had taken leave of her senses, when she demanded, in view of the emergency, that they be made available and be coupled to the train. Just as the station master was about to refuse the request, the girls arrived at the station and he quickly made arrangements for the engine to attach some empty coal wagons to the formation. The pupils were soon accommodated, the fortunate ones in the carriages, the others in the coal wagons. The train departed a few minutes late but arrived with its begrimed passengers in time for connections to be made with the GE main line services at Halesworth.

During the war large numbers of troops were stationed at Henham Park, near Blythburgh and special trains were operated for those who had weekend passes. The trains departed Blythburgh on Saturday evenings for Halesworth and returned on Sunday evenings, with connections to and from London and Lowestoft. The mass movement of troops during the hostilities was usually made at night or in the early hours of the morning so that members of the public were unaware of the transfer of men and equipment. The troops would march from Henham Hall to Blythburgh station where a train was waiting to convey the men to Halesworth for transfer to GER services. During this period Blythburgh goods yard handled considerable consignments of food and materials for the camp at Henham Hall but equally much was taken by road from Halesworth GER goods yard to save double handling. One young soldier, billeted at Walberswick, was going on leave but, leaving his lodgings too late to catch the train at the station, decided to take a short cut across Walberswick Common to the nearest point on the line. Hearing the train approaching he waved his kitbag above his head, whilst running through the gorse to attract to driver's attention. The driver immediately slowed the train to a walking pace to enable the soldier to clamber aboard and enjoy his short furlough.

The SR having agreed to construct the harbour branch and work the line for the Southwold Harbour Company found the war effort had delayed the start on construction. The railway company had obtained a Government grant of £1,000 towards the cost, for which the equivalent of 5 per cent debenture stock was issued. Howard Farrow carried out the work in 1914 and the line was opened for traffic the same year. Because of hostilities, fish traffic from the newly completed harbour branch reduced considerably but the connection was of the utmost importance conveying materials for the construction of seashore defence works. In the same year

St. Felix School moved to Reydon in 1902 having previously been domiciled in the South Green area of Southwold. The arrival and departure of boarding pupils at the beginning and end of each term provided significant revenue for the SR and here a number of girls with parents are seeing friends off on the train – a scene no later than 1905 as platform oil lamps have yet to be replaced by electric lighting. *Author's collection*

the side spans of the swing bridge were again reconstructed when a contract was placed with Joseph Westwood & Company Limited. After testing for navigational purposes the bridge was rarely opened and in the final years of operation, and later after closure of the railway, was only opened once a year for an annual test.

The Manager reported at the SR board meeting on 24th March 1915 that the engine shed at Halesworth was completed and in use. The structure had cost £135 and the connection to the shed was off the ballast siding from the main line, which had been installed in July 1906, the connection for the shed being formed of an extension from the trap points in the original siding.

A fleet of German airships flew along the Suffolk coast in the early hours of 16th April 1915 to attack GER targets, and bombs were dropped on Southwold and Halesworth before the craft swept north to attack Wells in Norfolk. In the raid on Southwold, 6-wheel wagon No. 31 sustained damage by an incendiary bomb and two lineside sheds were damaged. A young man dragged the bomb away from the wagon and doused the flames with earth, thus preventing damage to other rolling stock. On the same day bombs were also dropped at Maldon in Essex. Oddly, the SR minutes quote the attack taking place on 14th April.

A long-running dispute between Southwold Town Council and the SR was settled in July 1915 when the Town Clerk reported he had obtained counsel's opinion regarding the ballast taken from the cutting on Southwold Common by the SR. He had also had a meeting with Claude Pain and a letter had subsequently been received from the SR Secretary stating they were willing to pay the Corporation without prejudice the sum of £50 in full settlement. Later at a meeting of Southwold Town Council in December the gathering discussed a further letter from the SR Secretary stating the rent of £10 per annum for a strip of land 25 feet wide was exorbitant but agreed the price would be fair if the strip was 30 feet wide. A discussion followed where it transpired the railway company had continuously increased the portion of land they suggested acquiring from 20 feet to 25 feet and now 30 feet. The Council was adamant the portion of land should remain at 25 feet at a perpetual rent charge of £10 per annum.

Early in January 1916 the River Blyth encroached into Feny Road opposite the salt works at Southwold and the railway company staff repaired the breach with planking and filling, the Southwold Town Council surveyor supplying the planking. When, however, the company approached the council for a grant towards the cost of labour the application was refused. On Thursday 13th January a north-westerly gale caused the highest tide for twenty years to sweep up the East Coast resulting in extensive flooding at Yarmouth, Lowestoft, Southwold and Aldeburgh. The SR was breached at several points and passengers were left stranded at Halesworth or Blythburgh. The flooding subsided the following day and after inspection of the line by permanent way staff the first train departed Southwold at 3.00pm for Halesworth to resume the service.

On 26th February 1916 at 6.00pm a call was made for the Halesworth & District Volunteer Training Corps to occupy predetermined emergency posts and by 7.30pm guards were mounted on all GER railway bridges from Halesworth station to Sibton Road, Bramfield and also on two SR bridges at Blythburgh. The Company Commander reviewing the response praised the turnout from Wenhaston and Bramfield but was scathing of the poor attendance at Halesworth where only half the men were present. Soon after, Charles Henry Fitzhugh, the Southwold station master, was charged with failing to obscure lights after dark at the goods office. In evidence P.C. Cotterell reported a bright light was shining seaward whilst Inspector Ruffles said he had previously cautioned Fitzhugh. The station master in defence stated on the night in question he went to the goods office after hearing some movements within, opened the door, switched on the light and found one of the porters sitting down. At Southwold Magistrate Court, Fitzhugh was subsequently fined £2 0s 0d with 10s 0d costs.

The annual meeting of the SR shareholders was held at the company's London office on Friday 24th March 1916 with A.C. Pain as Chairman; other Directors present were W. Steele-Tomkins, W.C. Chambers and Herbert W. Chambers, with H. Ward as Secretary. The attendees were advised the statistical returns were presented in a modified form to meet the situation arising out of the Government control of the railway and the arrangement as to compensation payable during such period of control. Total receipts for the year ending 31st December 1915 were £6,123 offset by £4,352 expenditure, miscellaneous net receipts from rents and interest amounted to £189, resulting in a total net income of £1,960. Adding this to the balance of the last account £7,365, the total of £9,325 was offset by a deduction of £943 interest and fixed charges leaving a balance of £8,382. From this balance the Directors recommended a payment of a full 5 per cent dividend on preference shares and 1 per cent on ordinary shares leaving a total of £7,533 to be carried forward. The Chairman explained this was the second annual meeting which they had had since the outbreak of war and the line remained under Government control; the company had succeeded in coping with all military requirements, which had been considerable as large numbers of troops were stationed in the town, all of whom had to be supplied with food and munitions, much conveyed by train. Being near to the coast was a liability as damage might be incurred by attacks from hostile aircraft or bombardment from the sea. All necessary precautions had been taken but an incendiary bomb had fallen on Southwold station, fortunately causing little damage. At the conclusion of the meeting Stanley Alexander Young was elected Auditor in place of J.F. Clarke who had passed away.

A severe blizzard swept across Suffolk on the evening of Tuesday 28th March 1916 causing widespread damage. Several trees alongside the railway between Walberswick, Blythburgh and Wenhaston were blown down across the line so that services on Wednesday were cancelled until the blockage was removed. Eventually the route was cleared and the first train reached Halesworth at 12.40pm. Later in the year the SR asked Southwold Town Council to reduce the £12 rental on a strip of land on the north side of the railway station but the application was declined at a meeting in early June.

The SR could do nothing regarding the shortage of coal supplies in Southwold in December 1916 for the company relied on deliveries to Halesworth. Southwold Town Council reported on the 12th that coal merchants were refusing orders, as it was impossible, owing to delays in transit to get coal delivered in reasonable time. The military also notified that unless coal was delivered they would commandeer private supplies, as *'the cooking of soldiers' food was paramount'*. Complaints were made to the BOT who replied the GER blamed lack of fuel movements on pressure of military traffic. Had the SR been at fault the coal could have been transferred from Halesworth by horse and waggon.

Further destruction was caused at Southwold between the hours of 11.00pm and 12.00 midnight on 25th January 1917 when a German warship bombarded the coast with sixty-eight shells. Some houses and two coaches on the SR were damaged in the raid. On a far lighter note the *Halesworth Times* reported that on the evening of Saturday 3rd February at a performance of the pantomime *Babes in the Wood* by the Chums, a company drawn from members of a local battalion, the SR came in for some ridicule when the curtain rose on a scene representing Southwold station with robbers spreading consternation among the passengers and frightening the life out of the guard. On 2nd April 1917 Walberswick station was officially closed as an economy measure for the duration of the war; the timetable starting on 19th February published in the local press omitted Walberswick whilst all timings at other stations remained unaltered. The station was closed to all traffic from 10th February in order to release a man to join the colours but there is no record of who enlisted and it is believed the station master was transferred to Southwold. A further charge of showing a light during the blackout at Southwold was made against William George Colman, the foreman at T. Moy & Company coal merchants. He pleaded guilty for failing to screen the light in his office in Station Road citing *'the worry of being so short of coal'* with customers continually after him. The bench inflicted a fine of 10s 6d with 5s 6d costs.

The SR annual general meeting was held on 26th March 1917 at the company offices in Victoria Street, Westminster, London. The Chairman A.C. Pain presented the annual report for the year ending 31st December 1916 and referred to the unfortunate prolongation of the war; the railway was still under Government control and was fully occupied carrying military traffic. The revenue account showed railway receipts of £7,864, miscellaneous net receipts £208, offset by £5,951 expenditure, leaving a net total income of £2,121. To this was added £7,858 from the last account making a total of £9,979. From this was deducted £1,092 for interest payments leaving a balance of £8,887. The Directors recommended the payment of a full dividend on the preference shares and one per cent on ordinary shares leaving a balance of £8,038 to carry forward. Walter C. Chambers was re-elected a Director and J.J. Mayhew re-elected Auditor.

In April of the same year the SR was involved in an unusual repatriation exercise. The German Emperor had agreed to the safe passage of some 680 Belgian and Dutch nationals, including seamen, stranded in Britain, provided some of the ships conveying the group used the port of Southwold for embarkation and none other. The ship, the SS *Zeeland* of 850 tons, sailed from Flushing and arrived off Southwold at 12.00 noon on Monday 4th April 1917; the ninety-eight Dutch passengers were conveyed by the 1.05pm ex Halesworth train arriving at Southwold at 1.42pm and then marched across the Common to the harbour to join the ship. In the meantime another locomotive hauled a train of vans and wagons conveying luggage to the quayside. The party was ferried by three patrol drifters between the harbour and the vessel, which subsequently sailed in the early hours of Tuesday morning, this being the only sailing from Southwold. Daylight sailing was necessary to afford the vessel a safe passage.

The SR often had to strengthen trains because of wartime contingencies to allow for special traffic such as when members of the Third Battalion Suffolk Volunteer's Regiment were instructed to parade at Halesworth station at 8.20am on 28th May 1917 to proceed by the 8.40am train to Southwold, arriving at 9.17am for trenching instruction. In the meantime the incident of repatriation via Southwold was reported in Parliament and the national press and as a result of the publicity the SR approached the BOT for permission to run passenger services on the Harbour Branch. Colonel Druitt duly inspected the line on 25th September 1917 and found all to his satisfaction. He sanctioned use of the branch provided it was operated on the One Engine in Steam method of working and that trains only ran during the hours of daylight. The points to Blackshore Quay were also to be padlocked when no train was required to use the branch. No passenger trains were, however, operated.

It is interesting to note that up to the period 31st December 1917 only one unknown member of the SR staff was released from railway employment, which was a reserved occupation, to serve in the armed forces, compared with thirteen from the neighbouring Mid Suffolk Light Railway.

By the end of the hostilities the Southwold Company had abandoned plans for the extension to Kessingland and the conversion to standard gauge. The rolling stock had been used consistently throughout the war without adequate maintenance and all vehicles were badly in need of refurbishment or, better still, replacement. Locomotives, carriages and wagons were antiquated but the company had no resources to order new stock and thus the dwindling finances were used to keep the existing equipment in working order. From 1918 one passenger coach was sent away annually to Wisbech for rebuilding, until five of the six vehicles had received attention.

The SR was indirectly involved in a bizarre incident on 7th February 1918. H.A. Havers, a booking clerk employed by the GER at Halesworth, was suspicious of four men wandering around railway property and immediately advised the police. The constabulary arrived with commendable speed and with Havers leading the way subsequently apprehended the men, after ascertaining they were escaped German prisoners of war from Brocton Camp, Shropshire, who were making their way to the coast. Whether they intended to reach Southwold via the SR was not recorded.

Walberswick station reopened for traffic on and from 1st July 1919 after its wartime sojourn. A general railway strike affected SR services in October 1919 when local staff withdrew their labour. However, management arranged for a volunteer crew to operate two services in each direction, with the first train departing at 10.10am on Tuesday 26th October, when a large crowd gathered to give it *'a hearty send off'*.

The company's annual general meeting was held as usual at Victoria Street, Westminster with A.C. Pain presiding and supported by fellow Directors W.C. Chambers and H.W. Chambers, with Henry Ward as Secretary. Railway receipts for the year ending 31st December 1919 totalled £11,243, with miscellaneous income of £368 offset by £9,481 expenditure leaving a total net income of £2,130. After adding this to the previous year's balance and deducting adjustments and interest a final balance of £9,057 was achieved. The Directors recommended the usual 5 per cent and 1 per cent dividends to preference and ordinary shareholders, after which a sum of £8,208 was carried forward. Pain advised those present the railway was still under Government control and amalgamation of the larger railways was mooted. The success of Southwold on which the railway largely depended had been dealt a severe blow by the hostilities and, as with other East Coast resorts, once flourishing hotels were closed. It was hoped as time went on and money became easier, such restraint would disappear. At the conclusion Pain acknowledged he had been associated with the railway for forty years.

At a meeting of East Suffolk County Council on 13th July 1920 J.B.T. Chevallier moved that the County Council approve the proposed extension of the Central Essex Light Railway (Ongar to Sible Hedingham) to Long Melford and Haughley, and if the Mid Suffolk Light Railway were extended from Laxfield to Halesworth it would form a new direct route from London from Yarmouth, Lowestoft and Southwold. He urged they seek help from the Ministry of Transport, Finance Committee, to further consider the question initially raised on 26th May 1914 to make the Light Railway Commissioners authorize the Halesworth Light Railway by way of loans not exceeding £15,000.

At a special meeting of Southwold Town Council in early October members strongly approved of the conversion of the narrow gauge SR to standard gauge and the extension of the present line to

Six-wheel Moy's coal wagon No. 1507 in faded red oxide livery and black underframes at Southwold on 12th July 1911; one of three owned by the fuel company to run on the SR system. The Cleminson system aided the vehicle to negotiate the relatively sharp curves on the line and thus reduced track, flange and tyre wear. The company introduced two new wagons in 1922 and the original three, including No. 1507, were sold to the SR to augment their fleet.

LCGB/Ken Nunn

Sharp, Stewart 2-4-2T No. 1 *Southwold* shunting at Halesworth on 17th January 1920. The coaches behind the locomotive retain the open ended verandahs and have yet to be rebuilt.
LCGB/Ken Nunn

connect with the Mid Suffolk Light Railway as suggested in a letter from the BOT and Ministry of Transport. It was also suggested a deputation be sent to consult with Government department if they thought it necessary.

In early February 1921 under emergency business at a meeting of Southwold Town Council, Councillor Critten asked if it was possible to make any further progress towards the widening and extension of the SR. The clerk read correspondence he had had with the BOT and it was decided to write a letter to the Ministry of Transport to see if any information could be obtained or if further particulars were required. A month later the Southwold Council meeting heard that a letter from the Ministry of Transport notified that in the opinion of the Ministry the conversion of the SR to standard gauge was not of sufficient national importance as to warrant state financial aid. Councillor Critten moved the motion and the council agreed to ask the East and West Suffolk County Councils to receive a deputation, with a view to joint action in securing the extension of the Mid Suffolk Light Railway from Laxfield to Halesworth, which would strengthen the case for the conversion of the SR. An application by the SR for a strip of land at nominal rent to allow the widening of the platform at Southwold station was referred back to allow the inspection of the site by the Committee. An ominous sign of the poor standing of the railway was that ten £10 shares auctioned at the Angel Hotel, Halesworth on Thursday 3rd March 1921 were sold for a pitiful £22.

The annual meeting of the SR proprietors was held at 17 Victoria Street, Westminster, on Friday 8th April 1921 with Arthur C. Pain as Chairman, with other Directors W.C. Chambers and H.W. Chambers together with H. Ward, the Secretary in attendance. The annual report for 1920 advised the company was still under Government control and as such the statement of accounts was presented in a modified form. Receipts of the railway totalled £16,230 against expenditure of £14,468 leaving a balance of £1,762. Miscellaneous receipts from rents and bank interest amounted to £373 resulting in a net income of £2,135. This was added to the £8,208 balance from the last account making a total of £10,343 and after deduction of £898 left a balance to carry forward of £9,445. From this balance the Directors recommended payment of full 5 per cent dividend on preference shares and a 1 per cent dividend for the year on ordinary shares, thus carrying forward £8,596 to the next year. The Chairman stated that it was probably the last time they would meet as a controlled railway, the Government relinquishing their role in August. Whilst the line had been under control there had been little to report about the growth of traffic or development and he thus could only compare 1920 with 1913, the last full year before the outbreak of hostilities. Comparing the years mentioned it was curious to note the result of increases in fares and tolls. Despite this, the increase in parcels carried was 16,818 and in general merchandise 2,179 tons. There had also been an increase of 200 First Class and 5,919 Third Class passengers. Granite and slag traffic for road making had grown by 1,418 tons and coal by 3,054 tons. The company, however, could hardly expect to retain the last items, when shipping, which was non-existent during the hostilities, resumed deliveries to the harbour. Pain said it was clear that owing to the very large increase in working costs, £10,870 in 1920 over that in 1913, there would have to be a large reduction in wages paid to the staff. It was hardly conceivable that on such a small system as the SR the increase in wages alone between 1913 and 1920 should amount to £5,124 in addition to the costs of stores, materials and other items. Although the country was in the middle of a very serious coal strike, he was still hopeful that the common sense of the British working-men would find a remedy, and that when the company took over the railway from the Government some basis for the reduction in working costs would be agreed otherwise the results must inevitable be very serious, both for the employees and the company. Pain concluded that by next year when the railway was in their hands *'they would be better able to cater for the public than at present'*. At the conclusion of the meeting, W.C. Chambers was re-elected Director and Stanley Young re-elected as Auditor.

Southwold Corporation, however, was increasingly concerned with the condition and state of the *'antiquated'* railway and the effect it was having on visitors to the town, although it appears they had no wish to make any financial contribution towards any modernization. At the council meeting in early April the estate committee reported they had inspected the piece of land required by the SR Company for their improvements to Southwold station but recommended the application be deferred until the Managing Director A.C. Pain had time to visit Southwold and discuss the future policy of the company as it affected the improvements and conversion of the line to standard gauge. The Town Clerk reported that he had been supplied figures showing that it was impossible for the company to raise sufficient capital at the present time for the conversion to standard gauge and that the running expenses had heavily increased, wages having risen from £1,300 to over £5,000 per annum, that they could not undertake large scale improvements. Three councillors complained that the last GER train from London with a connection for Southwold was 3.20pm from Liverpool Street and they thought it essential in summer months that a connection be provided off the 5.00pm train from Liverpool Street as well as a Sunday service. It was suggested the granting of the piece of land be withheld until the company agreed to run the additional trains but it was eventually decided to withhold granting the application until the Council had met Pain. Council members then approached the SR board seeking a meeting with the Company Chairman to discuss possible improvements, including the conversion to standard gauge. After due discussion Arthur C. Pain declined to entertain the delegation, *'as there would be no advantage in such discussion at the present time'*. The Directors were well aware that since the transfer of the SR Company office to London, the Southwold Corporation had shown little interest in the line and therefore could expect no appeasement; they continued to show indifference thereafter.

On 1st August 1921, unbeknown to the engine crew and guard, the rear two wagons of a Down train became detached at Tinker's Farm. The rest of the train continued to Walberswick where the normal station stop was made. In the meantime the two wagons loaded with coal had started to roll on the falling gradients and crashed into the rear of the train in the station, damaging the rolling stock and tearing up the track. A large number of passengers were waiting to travel from Southwold to Halesworth and beyond, and were considerably distressed when station staff informed them that services were suspended because of the accident. The return working, the 5.23pm ex Southwold, would have made the final connection of the day with a GER train for London, and when it was found there were over twenty passengers for Liverpool Street and other stations south of Ipswich, a motor lorry was hastily requisitioned to run to Darsham station exclusively for these passengers. They just managed to catch the London train but had to leave their luggage behind, to be forwarded on the next day. The Southwold line was cleared in time for local passengers to catch a relief train, which arrived at Halesworth some two and a half hours late. As there were no injuries to passengers the company considered it unnecessary to advise the BOT but the incident was reported by the National Union of Railwaymen and an enquiry ordered. There was great concern the lack of continuous brakes might be raised again. At the subsequent BOT enquiry into the incident, conducted by Colonel Pringle, the train crew and station staff were held responsible for the accident and were reprimanded for inattention, the footplate crew and guard subsequently being fined by the company for *'lack of attention to duty'*. The Colonel also calculated that to maintain the scheduled running time of 37 minutes for the journey between Halesworth and Southwold meant trains were exceeding the permitted maximum speed limit of 16 mph between stations. He therefore advocated an increase in time allowance for the journey or, failing that, the provision of a brake van at the rear of every train. The SR management could ill afford to comply with the latter recommendation and elected to increase the train running time to 41 minutes with effect from the timetable starting on and from 21st November 1921, and thereby operate within the maximum speed limit.

Lineside fires were not unknown and on Tuesday 9th August 1921 a spectacular blaze with dense black smoke threatened to engulf Blythburgh station, the fire being readily advanced by a light breeze. Fortunately the conflagration, covering an area of 100 yards by 50 yards, was doused before reaching the railway.

Government control of the SR ceased on 15th August 1921, leaving the infrastructure and rolling stock in a seriously run down condition and finances in a precarious state. In order to maintain train services economies had to be made and the staff reluctantly accepted salary and wage reductions in the autumn of 1921 in order to keep the company solvent. The staff having received little thanks for their loyalty during the years of hostility and thereafter were rather embittered to find that from 1918 to 1921 ordinary shareholders received a dividend of 1 per cent, raised to 2 per cent in 1922, whilst preference share holders continued to receive a 5 per cent payment.

At a meeting of Southwold Town Council on the evening of Friday 2nd December 1921, the committee appointed in regard to the proposed conference dealing with the Southwold Railway and an improved train service reported they were awaiting information from the Ministry of Transport as to the position of the SR in relation to the 1921 Railways Act within the grouping of the various railways.

East Anglia experienced extreme weather on Tuesday and Wednesday 3rd and 4th January 1922, when heavy snow obliterated the landscape. The inconvenience to local transport was exacerbated on the Wednesday when further precipitation combined with high winds resulted in drifting of snow. Roads were impassable and a serious drift, reportedly 7 feet in depth, filled the cutting between Walberswick and Blythburgh resulting in the cancellation of all SR train services. The line was eventually cleared by Thursday but not before the 7.30am ex Southwold and the 8.40am return from Halesworth were cancelled, the first Up train leaving at 10.30am. On the neighbouring GER Waveney Valley line drifts blocking the railway between Bungay and Harleston were eventually cleared by snowplough. Yet further dislocation was caused by snow on Monday 16th January for when the 7.30am train departed from Southwold the locomotive ran into a drift blocking the cutting near the golf course. The train was reversed back to the station and permanent way men cleared the blockage in time for the train service to run by mid morning.

In the same month Southwold Town Council considered a letter received from A.C. Pain regarding the widening of the line to standard gauge, in which he reiterated that:

'no railway is in a position to consider the question of more capital expenditure until all the accounts for the period 19th August to 31st December 1921 are available. When available he was willing to meet members of the town council.'

In May 1922 Southwold Town Council interviewed A.C. Pain, without much success. The SR Chairman informed the committee that for financial reasons it was impossible to entertain the widening of the line. It was proposed, however, to provide a connection with the 5.00pm GER train from Liverpool Street on Fridays and Saturdays and during the high summer season to run one train in each direction on Sundays. This subsequently operated from 10th July until 1st October inclusive, departing Southwold at 5.19pm and arriving at Halesworth at 6.00pm, returning from the junction at 8.00pm with arrival back at Southwold at 8.41pm.

In July 1922 both Halesworth Urban Council and Southwold Town Council voiced complaints concerning the rateable assessment of railway property, the former especially of the two stations, resulting in lower rate payments. Sheldrake, the parish clerk, advised the reduction was as a result of a ruling made at the national conference of railway and rating authorities, which had agreed to a general reduction of railway assessments of 31 per cent throughout the kingdom. At the same time Southwold Town Council complained of the failure of W.R. Fasey to complete work on Southwold Harbour. The solicitor for the bankrupt estate asked if the council would be prepared to exercise the option of taking over the harbour, as they were entitled to do under the Southwold Harbour Order Confirmation Act of 1907, but the invitation was declined.

As late as November 1922, local people (including Southwold Railway staff) were still urging the early completion of the unfinished portion of the Mid Suffolk Light Railway from Laxfield to Halesworth with a petition reputedly 19 yards long and containing 1,900 signatures. The document was presented to Halesworth Council at their November meeting when it was agreed to send the document to their MP, Mr Lyle-Scott. The clerk to the council later confirmed the petition had been forwarded, with the promise to arrange with the Ministry of Transport for its presentation to Parliament.

At a special board meeting held on 10th November 1922 the GER board were advised Southwold Harbour was now in the hands of the receivers and had been offered to the GER with the plea that the Midland Railway were considering purchasing. The board was advised that to be of any effect the MR would have to obtain running powers from Cambridge to Halesworth and convert the SR to standard gauge. With the impending grouping the General Managers of the NER, GNR and GCR were all consulted and considered the possibility of the MR achieving their aim as *'somewhat fantastic'*. The Harbour was offered at a price of £20,000, needing as much again spending on it, plus the possibility of continuous dredging. As Lowestoft harbour was only 12 miles distant the GER board at one of their last meetings before the impending grouping of the railways resolved the question of acquiring the harbour would not be entertained.

GER Milnes Daimler omnibus No. 1 in all-over dark chocolate brown livery. One wonders what the group on the cart behind were thinking of this new form of transport.
Southwold Museum

6

Great Eastern Bus Services to Southwold

THE GER WAS ONE OF the first railways to realize the potential offered by petrol engine powered omnibuses to provide a feeder to their rail services. Often stations were remote and inaccessible to most passengers, who had to rely on walking or hitching a lift on a carrier's waggon to the nearest railhead. The GER already operated a few horse-drawn buses, but these were sporadic and not reliable. The new buses, running to scheduled timetables, gave the passenger an increased confidence in the railway and a feel that the company was providing for the needs of the travelling public. As we shall see, the SR as well as the GER benefited from a bus service which outwardly was in competition with both lines but actually provided a feeder facility for the more adventurous traveller.

When in 1903 powers to construct a light railway from Pakefield to Kessingland were transferred to Lowestoft Corporation, the GER Directors announced at a meeting on 4th November that the company intended to operate motor cars (*sic*) between Lowestoft, Kessingland and Southwold. The Mayor of Lowestoft asked the GER to take over powers to construct and work the railway and run a local motor car service between Kessingland and Southwold. The board declined the mayor's proposal and the General Manager pointed out the GER wished to run a through Lowestoft to Southwold service; if the railway was constructed anyone could still run a through motor car service over the entire route. For some years the GER authorities had contemplated running a road service between Lowestoft and Southwold via Kessingland but were also eager to find suitable vehicles which could undertake regular journeys over unmade terrain without unduly high failure. On 2nd February 1904 three Milnes Daimler motor buses with seating for thirty-five passengers (stated to be sixteen inside and nineteen outside, although this had changed by delivery) were offered to the company at a price of £900 each with a ten per cent discount if all three were purchased. The matter was passed to the Traffic Committee who duly authorised the purchase of the buses. The *Halesworth Times* of 20th October 1903 had already broken the news, for it reported:

'The Directors of the Great Eastern Railway have decided to run a fast service of motor (road) carriages between Lowestoft, Kessingland and Southwold. These carriages will be constructed on the lines of the carriages now being run by the Great Western Railway between Helston and the Lizard. Since these cars have been running they have been closely watched by officers of the Great Eastern Railway sent to Cornwall for that purpose, and it is in consequence of the favourable reports received in regard to them that the Directors of the Great Eastern Railway have resolved to try the experiment between Lowestoft and Southwold. It is understood that the order of the carriages will be immediately placed, so that no delay may occur in giving effect to the decision of the Directors.'

The *Halesworth Times* reported Southwold's Whit Monday sports would be held on 23rd May 1904, and as well as the SR running additional trains they predicted *'in all probability the first of the Great Eastern Motor Cars will be run from Lowestoft'*. This was premature but on 19th July the newspaper carried an article and front page advertisement announcing the Lowestoft to Southwold bus service had commenced on 18th July 1904 with two journeys daily in each direction, calling at Lowestoft, Kessingland, Wrentham, Reydon and Southwold *'conditions of the roads permitting'*. Three buses built by Milnes Daimler had been purchased for the service each costing £1,000. They carried eighteen passengers outside, sixteen inside and two by the driver. Very soon three return journeys were operated over the 12 miles between Lowestoft and Southwold and five between Lowestoft and Kessingland, timed to connect with trains and prepared to stop anywhere en route to pick up or set down passengers. The time allowed for the Lowestoft to Southwold journey was 1 hour 40 minutes. Later the service was increased

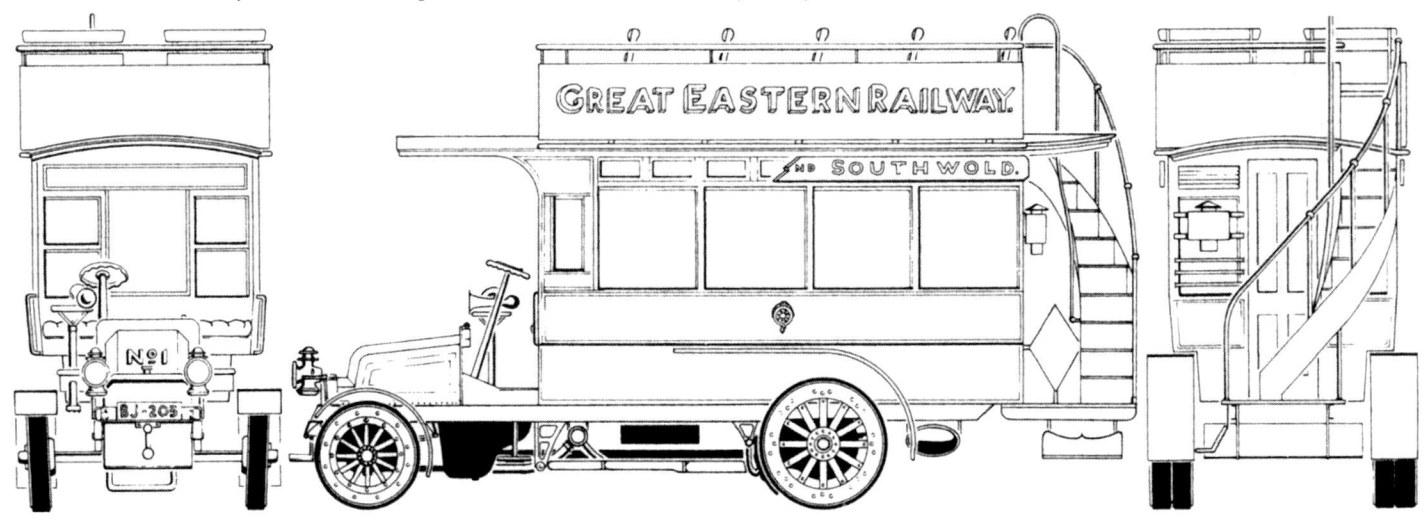

GER Milnes Daimler omnibus used on the Lowestoft to Southwold service.   *D.B. West, courtesy GER Society*

to sixteen return journeys. Another service, operating between Lowestoft and Oulton Broad, also commenced on 18th July 1904. The standard finish of all Milnes Daimler omnibuses produced at this period was a dark chocolate brown, and the GE did not change the livery except for adding Great Eastern Railway on the top deck modesty sheets, the GE crest on the lower deck waist panels and siting destination boards above the downstairs fanlights on the main windows. After their first overhaul the livery was changed to red and off white, and this remained the pattern for the rest of the fleet until its demise. The three vehicles received fleet No's 1, 2 and 3, carrying Suffolk (East) registration numbers BJ 203/4/5.

The top deck of these vehicles provided eighteen seats in the usual two side-by-side formation, whilst on the lower deck sixteen passengers were seated side by side in line on the opposite sides of the body. The two remaining passengers sat beside the driver. Later, after altercations with the travelling public, luggage space was added to some vehicles, situated behind the driver and seats were forfeited. On market days assorted sizes and types of luggage, wares and even livestock were crushed in with the passengers and tempers became frayed. Rigid leaf springs and solid tyres gave a very hard ride on the many unmetalled roads but the arrival of a bus at an appointed stop always attracted a large crowd of people. Many were intending passengers but for some it was a social occasion where souls could meet and exchange gossip.

By the end of September the service was considered reasonably successful; the receipts totalled £1,050 whilst the working expenses including interest on capital, renewal of tyres and depreciation amounted to £815. This also included a sum of £180 for cutting down and trimming trees along the route and training of drivers. The GER thus earned a satisfactory profit of £235. A garage was authorised in October 1904 to be established at the end of the yard at Denmark Road, Lowestoft at a cost of £400, but when the building was completed in December the cost was £330. The building was constructed of corrugated iron on brick foundations.

Ten new buses were ordered on 18th October 1904 and the Milnes Daimler vehicles were allocated around other garages, but by 18th July 1905 none of the new vehicles had been delivered and the GER Locomotive Superintendent submitted a report explaining the delay and expected them to be delivered by 1st August. Delivery and testing resulted in the late introduction of routes from Colchester to West Mersea, Colchester to Nayland and Clacton to St. Osyth. Other routes introduced in the same year included Ipswich to Shotley, Chelmsford to Writtle, Chelmsford to Danbury and Chelmsford to Great Waltham on 9th September and Norwich to Loddon and Beccles, this latter destination on market days only. Two further vehicles for the Ipswich to Shotley route, ordered on 8th March 1905, were expected by mid August. The Directors had, however, already inspected two buses, one for the Clacton to St. Osyth service and the other for the Lowestoft to Southwold route. The 1905 deliveries and immediate allocations were:

Omnibus No.	Trial Trip	Handed Over	Initial Allocation
4	4 July	31 August	Lowestoft
5	14 July	31 August	Lowestoft
6	26 July	31 August	Lowestoft
7	2 August	11 August	Clacton
8	11 August	18 August	Ipswich
9	14 August	18 August	Ipswich
10	16 August	25 August	Loddon
11	20 August	25 August	Loddon
12	23 August	1 September	Colchester
13	26 August	6 September	Chelmsford
14	30 August	7 September	Chelmsford
15	1 September	6 September	Chelmsford

GER Milnes Daimler motor bus No. 3 at Southwold soon after introduction in 1904, working the Lowestoft to Southwold route.

Author's collection

GER motor bus registration BJ 416 operating the Lowestoft to Southwold service at Southwold. The GER operated a service linking the towns from 18th July 1904 until January 1913, when it was taken over by United Automobile Services. *Southwold Museum*

On 27th October 1905 the General Manager reported that of the fifteen buses in service the three Daimlers were out of order and the remaining twelve required modifications to the springing. The services required two vehicles on the Shotley route, two to Mersea, four to Danbury and one as a mobile spare. The loss of the three buses had resulted in the suspension of the Loddon route, which expected to resume when all vehicles were available. The Oulton Broad and Clacton routes were operated during the summer months only. The three buses allocated to the Lowestoft to Southwold service had performed satisfactorily and on 7th November, James Holden was suggesting the purchase of another six vehicles to cover all services. It was resolved a committee visit the Motor Show at Olympia to inspect various buses with a view to purchase.

On 5th December 1905 James Holden was asking for guarantee of a reliable service on the Lowestoft to Southwold route as well as Ipswich to Shotley and Chelmsford to Danbury. The Motor Committee decided as a result of the visit to Olympia to place orders for six new buses, with three each from Maudsley Motor Company Limited and J. Thorneycroft Limited. Two buses from each firm were to be delivered in April 1906 and one from each in May, at a cost of £900 each. On 19th December James Holden reported all services would be temporarily suspended until the reliability of the vehicles had improved but that the Lowestoft routes would be reinstated from 26th December with five vehicles allocated. On 3rd January cars No's 7, 9 and 11 departed Ipswich for Lowestoft to take up duties on the Southwold route. A series of disastrous gales and associated flooding in the last week of December 1904 and the first weeks of 1905, which breached sea defences at one stage caused the suspension of Lowestoft tram services. Even the GER bus route was affected with vehicles having to take a diversionary route more inland through Kirkley Streets.

Early in January 1906 Lowestoft had an allocation of five buses and the cost of the garage had increased to £585 with a further £100 for a petrol store and £9 for sundry items. By 16th January the General Manager reported to the GER board that the Southwold services were again operating satisfactorily, but by 20th February a different story was emerging and several breakdowns were reported, especially involving bus No 11. Due to mechanical fault another failure in April resulted in a passenger missing a train at Lowestoft.

For the rest of the year the buses on the Lowestoft to Southwold route operated satisfactorily but as Christmas approached heavy frost caused problems compounded by heavy snow on Boxing Day, when lengthy delays were incurred and subsequent days proved just as troublesome. The latter days of January 1907 found bad weather and roads turned to quagmires affecting the service, although few journeys were cancelled. However, failures continued to dog the fleet and after a relatively successful period of operation Bus No. 18 lost a tyre whilst working the 9.25am service from Lowestoft to Southwold.

On 16th April 1907 it was established that work on all the GER bus garages had cost £2,675 against an estimate and allocation of £2,930. Further troubles afflicted the GER Suffolk bus services, for on 20th May 1907 No. 2 failed with a drive shaft fracture working the 11.00am Lowestoft to Southwold services, whilst No. 17 suffered a blocked carburettor working the 5.00pm from Southwold to Lowestoft. No. 17 was in trouble again on 22nd July with a broken pump shaft working the 8.15am Lowestoft to Southwold and again on 19th August with the same fault working the 6.40pm Southwold to Lowestoft service. September 1907 saw another spate of failures. No. 16 succumbed to a seized engine working the 12.40pm Lowestoft to Southwold on 2nd of the month. The following day No. 2 had a slipping clutch whilst working the 10.30am Lowestoft to Southwold; then on 28th September No. 17 had a broken crosshead on the 8.15am Southwold to Lowestoft run and two days later the same bus had a compression failure working the 12.40pm ex Lowestoft. The same vehicle was again in trouble on 18th October with low compression working the 5.30pm from Lowestoft to Southwold, whilst No. 2 had problems with the differential on 23rd October working the 11.05am service from Lowestoft to Southwold. Three days later No. 17 failed with sparking plugs on the 5.30pm Lowestoft to Southwold working. The failures rate then reduced slightly, with only one stoppage of No. 18, due to a steering gear fault whilst working the 11.05am Southwold to Lowestoft on 19th November 1907. In 1907 the first casualty was the Clacton to St. Osyth route, which had been a seasonal service for summer holidaymakers.

The New Year brought no respite for the GER bus service, which was affected for three days by bad road conditions and alternative coastal fog and then high winds. On 7th January 1908 No. 2 suffered carburettor failure on the 7.10am Southwold to Lowestoft working and again with the same problem on 25th January on the 5.30pm Lowestoft to Southwold. The first day of February found No. 3 failing with a blocked fuel pipe on the 5.30pm Lowestoft to Southwold whilst No. 18 had a seized governor on the same working on 21st February. The same bus failed with a fuel pump blockage on 18th March working the 7.10pm ex Southwold. Two months then passed before No. 16 suffered magneto failure on 28th May working the 11.15am Southwold to Lowestoft service, whilst No. 17 had a steering defect on 26th June working the 12.40pm from Lowestoft to Southwold.

In 1908 a new route was opened from Bury St. Edmunds and Stanton, but troubles continued in Suffolk when on 25th July of that year bus No. 10 collided with a car when working the 1.00pm ex Southwold, whilst on 17th August No. 2 failed with a slipping clutch on the 10.30am Lowestoft to Southwold working. On the last day of the month Bus No. 1 excelled itself by failing twice with the same differential problem, initially on the 4.50pm from Lowestoft to Southwold and then on the 6.40pm return working. On 9th September No. 17 was again a failure with transmission trouble on the 10.50am from Southwold to Lowestoft. No further failures were reported on the Southwold route until 4th December when No. 18 suffered a circulating pump defect whilst working the 11.05am from Southwold to Lowestoft.

On 21st January 1909 the GER Traffic Committee observed that as the bus service from Lowestoft to Southwold was popular in summer it should continue on a daily basis to the close of the 1909 summer timetable but thereafter run during the summer months only. Unfortunately the failures continued with breakdowns on 22nd, 25th and 28th May caused by a broken tappet spring, slipping clutch and over oiled plugs respectively. On 19th June the vehicle working the 9.25am Lowestoft to Southwold service suffered loss of water coolant whilst on 24th August the vehicle on the 1.00pm Southwold to Lowestoft working collided with a horse and cart. Six days later the 2.20pm Southwold to Lowestoft sustained a pump failure and on 16th September the bus on the 7.30pm Southwold to Lowestoft lost a front wheel. The following day the 9.10am ex Lowestoft suffered a seized bearing, on 24th the 4.00pm Lowestoft to Southwold had a water leakage and the following day the bus on the 11.20am Lowestoft to Southwold ground to a halt with fuel blockage. With all these failures in traffic it is a wonder the travelling public had faith in the service but at the end of September the Lowestoft Harbour Master was petitioning for the bus service to Kessingland and Southwold to be retained; on 7th October the GER board relented and agreed to continue the service to the end of the year.

Evidently by this time the GER management was irritated by the continuing failures of its bus fleet and attempts were made to find interested parties who might purchase some vehicles. Amongst others an approach was made to the City of York but the Town Clerk advised early in November that the Corporation were not interested in motor omnibuses as they were installing electric tramways. At the end of the year the Lowestoft to Southwold bus service was withdrawn although other routes from Norwich to Loddon, Ipswich to Shotley, Chelmsford to Danbury, Chelmsford to Great Waltham and Chelmsford to Writtle continued into the new year. In 1909 the Colchester to West Mersea route was absorbed by the local firm of A.W. Berry.

The Lowestoft to Southwold bus service resumed for the summer of 1910 but again failures dogged the system as under:

23 July	5.40pm	to Lowestoft	Broken crank shaft
25 July	1.00pm	to Lowestoft	Hot bearings
30 July	4.00pm	to Southwold	Contact breaker
4 August	10.50am	to Lowestoft	Drive coupling
9 August	6.40pm	to Lowestoft	Main bearings
22 August	2.25pm	to Southwold	Sparking plugs
12 September	5.40pm	to Lowestoft	Sprocket
13 September	7.20pm	to Lowestoft	Seized governor
13 September	11.20am	to Southwold	Gearbox
19 September	10.50am	to Lowestoft	Heavy loading
1 October	9.25am	to Southwold	Timing gear
6 October	5.30pm	to Southwold	Dense Fog
7 October	9.25am	to Southwold	Radiator leak
17 October	5.30pm	to Southwold	Carburettor
22 October	7.10pm	to Lowestoft	Drive pinion

In July 1911 the GER bus service between Lowestoft and Southwold was increased in frequency but was withdrawn at the end of the year, re-emerging for the next summer. GER motor bus traffic from Lowestoft and Southwold was delayed when two large trees were blown down across the road at Frostenden, which brought down telegraph posts and wires when record rains affected East Anglia on 26th August 1912. The GER management had lost patience with their experiment and in January 1913 the route between Lowestoft and Southwold was taken over by United Automobile Services. The same year also saw the Chelmsford routes absorbed by the National Steam Car Company. After World War One the Norwich to Loddon service was taken over by United Automobile Services whilst the Eastern Counties Road Car Company became the new owners of the Ipswich to Shotton route on 1st April 1922. The GER also ceased interest in the Bury St. Edmunds to Stanton route in 1922.

7

Decline and Closure

As a result of the 1921 Railways Act, the GER was amalgamated with the Great Northern, Great Central, North Eastern, North British and several smaller railways to form the London & North Eastern Railway. The Southwold Railway was not included in the provisions of the Act and was therefore excluded from the 1923 grouping of the railways, remaining independent of the L&NER. Neither was it on a par with the narrow gauge Lynton & Barnstaple Railway, which became part of the Southern Railway, or the Vale of Rheidol and Corris lines which became part of the Great Western Railway empire. In the rural outback of Suffolk the year was not a happy one, the SR Directors again reduced staff salaries and wages for the company to remain solvent.

Despite the decision of the GER board the new L&NER management at Liverpool Street considered the possibility of acquiring Southwold Harbour and actively encouraged the building of a sugar beet processing factory at Southwold. Under the proposals the company also considered taking a controlling interest in the SR to encourage movement of goods to the transfer railhead at Halesworth. However, an urgent resurrection of past documents confirmed the poor condition of the narrow gauge railway and associated harbour, and the relatively close proximity of sugar beet factories at Cantley and Ipswich nullified the proposal – and with it the last possibility of assistance to the SR was lost. Then in September 1923 Walberswick Common Land Charities served notice on the Southwold Company to remove the railway from their land. The Company Solicitor advised the Directors to ignore the writ and nothing more was heard of the matter.

The 1923 annual general meeting of the SR proprietors was held at the offices of the company at 17 Victoria Street, Westminster on 13th April chaired by Arthur C. Pain. After moving the adoption of reports the Chairman advised that during the war, the raising by the Government of wages and fares had had a detrimental effect in the recovery of trade. The railway companies were blamed but it was not they who had increased the wages and fares, and this had doubled the working costs resulting in strikes. As regards the SR, he reminded the proprietors that in 1922 the early part of the year was like midsummer and summertime was disappointing with poor weather, resulting in a reduction in visitors. Southwold, Walberswick and Reydon were largely reliant on tourist traffic although the latter had an increase in house building. He then stressed the encouragement of the development of Walberswick, at what was *'a charming little spot'*. There was the advantage of a large area of about 60 acres of common land only available for the grazing of cattle but which was made use of in the summer by local residents and visitors. He reminded those attending that when the railway was first built it was not thought worthwhile to provide a station but visitors to Southwold found the breezy stretch of common and gorse-land attractive and spent afternoons there, with the result that a small platform and siding were installed by arrangement with the Common Land Charity Commissioners. This was later improved by the provision of a shelter but despite the company's best efforts the local community had not made a road from the station to either the church or in the opposite direction. The company had offered to provide ballast for the construction of the roadway but this had been ignored. Pain ventured that *'if local people would take heart of grace and make the roadway'* the railway company would provide reasonable assistance. Unfortunately, what traffic did come across the common was confronted with a dangerous route, especially in darkness, and any traffic arriving by rail had great difficulty in being conveyed to the village. Because of this indifference the railway company had been forced to make a road across other people's land and it was thought with hindsight it had been unwise to provide the station without binding people to make their own access road. He strongly urged a rethink and understood that the Charity Commissioners would offer every facility for the development of land both for the road and future building development. Pain also pressed for people letting apartments in the neighbourhood to consider their charges for the coming season to ensure a steady clientele. Regarding the accounts a little money had been withdrawn from the reserve to pay the 2 per cent dividend on ordinary stock

A family group on an outing to the sea stand on the timber boarded platform at Southwold. The carriage is in the original condition with open verandah end but is painted in the all-over maroon livery.

The driver of 2-4-0T No. 2 *Halesworth* appears to be preoccupied as his train pulls into the platform at Southwold. The two coaches on the train – a Composite and a Third, in maroon livery – have been rebuilt with end verandahs filled in and doors provided at each end of the vehicle on the south side only. Southwold station was provided with electric lighting in 1905 and one of the ornate columns is on the left. Most of the platform has now been given a hard surface.
Author's collection

(up from 1 per cent the previous year) after payment of 5 per cent on Debenture and Preference shares. The report was unanimously adopted. Arthur Pain was again elected Chairman and Stanley A. Young, Auditor.

In May and June 1923 Halesworth Council asked Southwold Borough Council to take action regarding an approach to the L&NER to extend the Mid Suffolk line to Halesworth thereby opening up through communication between Southwold and the Midlands. Such action still required the conversion of the SR to standard gauge and by July it was thought there was not the slightest possibility of the company completing such a scheme with or without Government support. Certain factions thought the time was commercially ripe but others were realistic in their outlook, truthfully advising that the company had no intention of developing Southwold whilst further developing facilities at Lowestoft. One councillor was of the opinion light railways were *'getting out of date'* and it would *'be better to convert the Middy into a trunk road'* (such action was taken by the L&NER in the early 1930s but aborted because of technical difficulties).

On 6th July 1923 Southwold Town Council had discussed the possible development of lands from the railway boundary to Saltwater Creek for the construction of a sugar beet factory but no reference was made of the possible use of the SR in the project. Later in November the Mayor stated the scheme was developing and subject to arrangements with the SR, which at the time was causing a hitch, he was hopeful the scheme would commence. By early December the East Suffolk Development Syndicate indicated they intended to exercise their option to take over the lands offered by the Town Council and with their *'exceptional financial backing'* would formulate a scheme materially affecting the whole of agricultural Suffolk. They would extend the railways based on the 3 feet gauge of the SR with Southwold as its base. However, by 12th of the month the Syndicate intimated the lands they had agreed to buy were insufficient for the size of the proposed factory, and they would require additional lands. The Chairman stated at a public meeting that Southwold had been chosen for the site of the factory because of rail and water facilities. Realising the existing Southwold line was not sufficient for their purposes they were proposing to make a circular railway about 45 miles in length embracing 200,000 acres of land. Despite the backing of the National Farmers Union the scheme made no progress and by early February 1924 the Syndicate advised they had decided to delay the Southwold sugar factory scheme pending a decision on the government taxation of sugar. The grandiose scheme made mention of the proposed circular line being worked with Sentinel Cammell steam railcars and locomotives and wagons as used on the Jersey Railway because of the exceptionally low running costs.

Despite the proposal for the sugar beet factory, no mention was made of the possible growth of traffic or indeed extension of the line at the SR 1924 annual general meeting held in April at the company offices at 17 Victoria Street, Westminster. Once again Arthur C. Pain presided, supported by Walter Chambers and Herbert Chambers Directors, Claude Pain and Henry Ward, the Secretary. The annual report with statement of accounts advised that because of unfavourable weather during the previous summer and the reduction in fares collected, the passenger receipts showed a loss of £535 compared with 1922, whilst fishing receipts and other passenger sundries had reduced by £151. Railway receipts were £7,395 against expenditure of £7,276 leaving a balance of £119. The proportion under section 11 of the 1921 Railways Act was £732 with miscellaneous receipts of £374 leaving a total income of £1,225. It was therefore regretted they could not recommend a payment of dividend on Preference and ordinary shares. Pain alluded that many people visiting the area now preferred to travel by road instead of rail, largely due to the high cost of fares. Strikes and wage costs had had a detrimental effect and unless the seasons became more favourable they would not recover. On a brighter note, mineral traffic, although costly to convey, showed a slight profit. At the conclusion W. Chambers was re-elected a Director and J.J. Mayhew Auditor. In summing up, H.J. Chambers observed that Arthur Pain was really the father of the railway, having been the engineer before construction.

After the failure of the GER road services early in June 1924 approval was given for buses to run from Lowestoft to Southwold in

T. Moy & Sons 6-wheel coal wagon No. 1511 with Cleminson wheel arrangement and curved ends stands at the company's Peterborough works before despatch to Halesworth and the SR in January 1922. The vehicle is in red oxide livery with white lettering. *Author's collection*

Operating in competition against the railway, United Automobile Services Limited commenced bus services between Halesworth and Southwold in the early 1920s. Initially buses were not permitted into Southwold town centre but from the summer of 1928 this prohibition was lifted and the Eastern Counties Road Car Company, successor to United Automobile, further hastened the death knell of the narrow gauge line. This competitive vehicle, much more modern and comfortable than the SR coaching stock, complete with security box on the roof for the conveyance of Royal Mails, was photographed in 1929.

Author's collection

competition with the railway. The *Halesworth Times* for 11th June reported:

'The new 74-seater buses used by the United Automobile Services Limited on the Southwold to Lowestoft route which had only been provisionally approved by Southwold Corporation were the subject of a letter from the Roads and Bridges Committee of the County Council to the Corporation stating in their opinion the vehicles were unsuitable.'

Despite this edict the Council decided to allow the buses to run pending a decision, which the bus company stated they were expecting from Lowestoft Corporation, who had not objected to the use of the vehicles. The decision could be considered premature but the new fleet of comfortable buses certainly encouraged a new breed of passenger who had no wish to travel from Lowestoft to Halesworth, there to ride on the ramshackle railway to the sea. A few weeks later at the end of August a double deck bus working from Lowestoft to Southwold overturned whilst travelling along the main road at Wangford. The *Halesworth Times* for 27th August reported that the vehicle in question and another bus travelling from Southwold to Lowestoft met near the Plough Inn. *'Whether the wheels of the vehicles touched cannot be substantiated, but the driver of the bus destined for Southwold apparently lost control of the steering'*, with the result a wheel dropping into the ditch at the road side causing the conveyance to overturn. Apart from shock and evident fright the occupants were not seriously injured.

Heavy rain on the night of Tuesday 21st October 1924, which continued through to the next day, caused flooding near Wenhaston. The 10.05am Southwold to Halesworth train on Wednesday 22nd October managed to reach its destination although the water was up to rail level. However, within the next hour the water rose by 2 feet making the return journey impossible. The SR arranged for a replacement bus service to convey passengers to and from Southwold for the rest of the day. When the water had subsided, damage to the track was not as serious as predicted and permanent way staff made good the minor subsidence under the track by packing and replacement of sleepers enabling services to resume on the Thursday.

Because of the parlous financial state of the Southwold Company, in 1924 the Ministry of Transport advised that the statutory requirement for monthly returns of earnings and outgoings was to be waived but an annual return was still required. On the SR matters deteriorated further, for staff wage and salary cuts made in 1921 and 1923 were augmented by yet further reductions in 1925. At the same time some bonus and pension payments to retired staff were reduced.

Saturday 4th July 1925 was not the best day for the Southwold Railway. The 1.00pm train ex Halesworth, well filled with passengers from main line services and several half-day excursion tickets, departed to time but within a few yards the engine ran into a siding and demolished the stop blocks before coming to a stand with the leading wheels derailed. Fortunately no passengers complained of injury but *'several were alarmed'*. Railway staff immediately ran to the scene and passengers were detrained before the footplate crew and guard with others attempted to re-rail the locomotive. After several attempts this was achieved using the re-railing jack on the engine and sleepers as packing, and after the train was backed into the station to pick up passengers it finally departed for the coast three hours late at 4.00pm. No doubt there were red faces at the subsequent local inquiry into the accident, initially for station staff not checking the points were reset for the main single line and secondly for the driver and fireman for not keeping a good lookout as the train left the station.

The annual general meeting of the SR shareholders held in the company's office at Victoria Street Westminster in March 1926 was a sobering affair, for Arthur Pain as Chairman referred to the significant reduction in receipts brought about chiefly by road competition but also the escalating of costs during World War One, a factor which continued until the ultimate closure of the railway. Walter C. Chambers, Herbert W. Chambers and Secretary H. Ward were also in attendance. The report and accounts showed receipts of £6,476 against expenditure of £6,222, whilst miscellaneous receipts from rents and interest totalled £372, leaving a net income of £628. The Directors regretted that in consequence of another bad season they could not recommend dividend payments on preference or ordinary shares. Like many railway companies the SR had suffered a reduction in receipts and as a result the entire SR staff had agreed to a reduction in working expenses in various ways, including a reduction in wages; as a result the company had practically been able to cover the net loss in receipts. To the outside observer the *'writing was on the wall'* with no hope of recovery.

For a number of years the competing bus service between Halesworth and Southwold operated by United Automobile Services Limited consisted of four trips daily on Mondays to Fridays, augmented to five each way on Saturdays and Sundays, compared to the four weekday trains in each direction and one return trip on Sundays. In addition, the bus fares were cheaper at 10d for the full journey from Southwold to Halesworth against the railway charge of 1½d per mile. On 11th April 1926 the bus company virtually signalled the death knell of the narrow gauge line when it introduced an improved frequency timetable. Although the rail journey between Southwold and Halesworth took 41 minutes against the 46 minutes by road, the bus travelled nearer the centres of population and for many offered an almost door-to-door service, although it still terminated on the town boundary. Stung into action the railway company then threw caution to the wind and met the challenge head-on by increasing the rail service to six trains in each direction on weekdays and four each way on Sundays, although the latter was operated during the summer season only.

The general strike of 1926, whilst causing stoppage of services on the main lines, had little effect on the SR where all staff remained on duty. However, for a short period the service was reduced from four trains to three in each direction by the withdrawal of the 2.24pm ex Southwold and 3.35pm return from Halesworth.

The optimistic future outlook was shattered by a serious accident which occurred on the morning of 24th December 1926 at Wenhaston, when Station Master Harold B. Girling, aged 36 years, received fatal injuries during shunting operations at the station. At 10.30am on the day in question Girling was shunting a train with the assistance of the guard when it was decided to loose shunt two wagons into one of the sidings. After turning the points leading from the main line to the sidings, Girling gave a hand signal to the fireman for the train to be propelled towards him and then stepped between two of the wagons as they reached him to release the coupling. While he was doing so, he either slipped or caught his foot in a check-rail with the result that he fell and was fatally injured as the wagon wheels passed over him before the train could be brought to a halt. He died from his injuries in Halesworth Hospital on 26th December. J.L.A. Moore, the inspecting officer, conducted the official BOT enquiry into the accident at the end of January 1927. After visiting Wenhaston and hearing the evidence of the witnesses, including engine driver Nelson Cornelious Fisk and fireman Alfred George Stannard, Moore was of the opinion the accident was caused by possible misadventure on the part of the station master taking the considerable risk by going between the vehicles for uncoupling purposes whilst they were in motion. His motive for so doing was a matter of conjecture and he may have acted without realising the danger involved, or it might have been that an underline bridge located ten to twelve yards from the points on the main line made it impossible for him to deal with the coupling in the position where the train had come to a stand after drawing clear of the points. The bridge was formed of two longitudinal girders directly under the track with the transverse sleepers laid across them and supporting the rails. During his visit Moore noted that the space between the sleepers was not filled in, nor was any pathway provided at the side of the line across the structure. It was therefore impossible to reach a wagon or a coupling if the train came to a stand on the bridge and the shunter would therefore be compelled either to uncouple while the train was setting back or to stop the train especially for the purpose. The inspector opined that it would never be known if the bridge had a direct bearing on the accident

The open landscape and wide vistas of the Blyth valley are evident as 2-4-0T No. 3 *Blyth* runs into Southwold station with a mixed train passing the carriage siding to the left. The inner home signal arm is lowered to allow the train into the platform, whilst the other arm on the post is the Up starting signal. *The late Dr I.C. Allen*

A celebratory departure from Southwold in the 1920s, including balloons. Before the increase in car ownership the SR played an important role in the social life of Southwold residents and visitors, as well as other communities served by the line, with comings and goings associated with happy and sad occasions.
Author's collection

but was of the opinion that it presented a considerable danger in view of the closeness to the points leading to the yard. He advised the Southwold Company *'would be well advised to have the structure fully boarded under the rails with a suitable pathway on either side of the line to enable shunters or others to pass along the side of the train if necessary'*. Moore then commented on the couplings used on the rolling stock. He noted they were of the non-automatic type, with a single link secured by a pin through each buffer. The pins were of a special design to prevent them from working out of position whilst the vehicles were in motion. The inspector stated: *'whilst effective, they undoubtedly added to the difficulties of coupling and uncoupling at stations and render the use of the shunting pole impracticable'*. Moore was surprised to find that the SR Rule Book contained no clause warning staff as to the dangers of uncoupling vehicles in motion and in conclusion recommended the company take action to rectify the matter. At the earlier inquest, held under the chairmanship of H.C. Goldsmith, deputy coroner for the Stowmarket district, the jury returned a verdict of 'accidental death', adding the rider that 'the SR ought to supply extra help to men in charge of stations during busy seasons'.

Despite the increase in train services to counteract the effects of the bus competition receipts continued to deteriorate. The decline in the railway's fortunes was self evident when it was announced that the number of passengers carried in 1926 was over 10,000 less than the number travelling in 1925, leaving the company with a net debt of £4. Only 81,704 passengers travelled on the line in 1927, when gross receipts were £7,122 against expenditure of £6,371, leaving net receipts at £751. From 1923 until 1928 no dividends were paid on ordinary or preference shares, although on the preferred debenture stock interest was paid in full until 30th June 1928 and on the five per cent debenture stock until December 1925.

In 1927 there was a surprising upturn in trade, especially with goods traffic with 18,460 tons being conveyed, the highest since World War One, which together with increase passenger revenue, produced net receipts of £751. The upturn encouraged the SR management to finance minor alterations at Halesworth and Wenhaston to facilitate ease in shunting operations, and especially at the latter site to obviate unnecessary movements near the underbridge. Colonel A.C. Trench duly carried out the official BOT inspection of alterations at Halesworth on 17th July 1928. He found that an additional connection facing traffic from Southwold had been installed at the outer end of the station yard connecting the main line with the existing goods transfer siding. The permanent way was formed of 30 lbs per yard flat bottom rails spiked to the timber sleepers laid on shingle ballast, which was standard for the railway. The points on the main line were operated by a hand lever and locked for the main line except when released by the key on the Halesworth to Blythburgh single line Train Staff. The trap points were operated by rodding from the same lever. Trench was satisfied with the arrangements but required the provision of a stock rail at the points on the main line and the company engineer promised early attention to this.

The Inspector then travelled to Wenhaston to examine the additional connection facing traffic from Halesworth, which had been installed at the Halesworth end of the station between the existing siding and the main line. Again the permanent way was of 30 lbs per yard flat bottom rails spiked directly to the timber sleepers. The points were operated by a hand lever and locked for the main line except when released by the key on the Blythburgh–Halesworth single line Train Staff, whilst the trap points were operated by rodding from the same lever. Trench noted that the additional double signal shown on the site drawings was not provided as the locking of the points by the Train Staff obviated its use. As at Halesworth, a gauge tie was required on the stock rails at the points on the main line and again the engineer promised early provision. Colonel Trench sanctioned use of the new connection and concluded *'in view of the small amount of traffic on the road and railway I am satisfied that no appreciable inconvenience will be caused by the proximity of the connection to the level crossing'*.

In the summer of 1928 Southwold Borough Council authorised the Eastern Counties Road Car Company, successor to United Automobile Services Limited, to pick up passengers within the town's boundary. This was grim news for the railway authorities for passenger traffic levels were again decreasing. The antiquated and outdated train was no match for the shining and comfortable buses and to counteract the competition and anticipated loss of revenue

The evening shadows lengthen on 2-4-0T No. 2 Halesworth at Southwold, whilst 2-4-2T No. 1 Southwold to the right has already been withdrawn from traffic. In the background on the left, behind the railway wagons, are some of Moy's horse drawn coal delivery carts. Author's collection

the company reduced fares by issuing special return tickets in the summer months only.

In the same year encouraging news came from the L&NER Divisional General Manager who wrote promising to regard the SR as a light railway and afford the company the protection under the Road Transport Bill being prepared for Parliament This was of little consolation to the SR Directors for the railway continued to lose money. The desperate situation was all too evident and companies which had promoted their products in association with the railway or who had provided much needed traffic, notified their intention of withdrawing custom from the ailing line. Adnam's, the local Southwold brewer, withdrew their advertising from the fixed upper lights of the coaching stock, a feature existing for as long as many could remember. Thomas Moy, the fuel merchant, terminated the tenancy of the coal ground in Blythburgh goods yard and even threatened to remove coal and coke traffic from the railway altogether, saying it was cheaper to transfer fuel from railway wagons direct to road lorries at Halesworth instead of the wasteful off loading into narrow gauge wagons and then off loading for a second time once the destination of the consignment was reached. Amongst others, Shell-Mex Oil Company terminated the tenancy of land at Halesworth. As the downturn continued locomotive No. 1 *Southwold* required extensive repairs and overhaul but financial constraints precluded any expenditure when three other locomotives could maintain the services, and No. 1 was withdrawn from traffic to be used for cannibalisation to keep No's 2 and 3 in running order.

The additional facilities at Halesworth and Wenhaston came too late to rescue the company from its dire financial position and in order to cut costs the wages and salaries of railway staff were further reduced in December 1928. Naturally some were incensed by such action and immediately sought alternative employment after giving many years of loyal support to the Southwold Company. The Directors finally admitted the inevitable in their report of 31st December, that the financial position was *'causing considerable anxiety'*, and it was decided the railway could not stay open to traffic *'without outside assistance'*. The competitive bus company had increased the service to ten journeys in each direction with the added facility of picking up passengers within the town boundary. The railway authorities complained bitterly to Southwold Corporation, to be advised that *'times were changing'* and *'in the public interest it was their prerogative to grant advantageous facilities'*. Thus the year had seen railway passenger numbers reduce by over 25,000 despite the reduction of the return fare from Halesworth to Southwold and vice versa from 2s 3d to 1s 6d and further reduced to 1s 0d in the summer months.

As the new year progressed, so matters further deteriorated and rescue plans were formulated. On 28th February 1929 the Directors again approached Southwold Corporation for assistance, either in the form of a grant or an imposition of restrictions on the competing bus services. The Corporation, however, after due discussion, advised the Directors they *'had no powers to subsidise the railway or interfere with the facilities of the bus company'*, which was *'running smoothly in the public service'*. Furthermore, the Southwold Corporation, whilst fully admitting they had insufficient finances to save the line, agreed the closure would adversely affect the conveyance of freight and cause hardship to redundant employees.

Whilst negotiations were in hand with Southwold Corporation, the SR Chairman and Walter Chambers, one of the Directors, wrote to Mr Wilcox, the L&NER Divisional General Manager asking if the main line company would take over the narrow gauge railway. The mood at the SR half yearly meeting held on 22nd March 1929 was morbid and the Chairman reported to the gathering that he *'feared the end was coming'*. Southwold Corporation could provide no assistance and to date no reply had been received from the L&NER regarding possible takeover of the line. *'Matters were now approaching the extreme point in the negotiations and unless assistance was given, the Southwold line would be closed.'* Curiously, at this meeting Claude Pain was appointed a Director, a move which would release his father and W. Chambers from attending future board meetings and leaving himself and Herbert Chambers as a quorum of two to settle any outstanding business. Despite

This winter 1928 view of a train arriving at Southwold through a carpet of snow is evidence that the Suffolk coast suffered its fair share of adverse weather; on several occasions snowdrifts blocked the SR. The carriage shed to the left, completed in 1904, was only clad as and when the finances allowed, although doors were never fitted. *Southwold Museum*

With the rebuilding of the coaching stock and elimination of the verandah ends with the exception of coach No 2, as all platforms were on the Up or south side of the line the opportunity was taken to remove the doors on the Down side of the vehicles. As finances were also stretched the offside of the coaches received minimal attention to painting and lining, thereby saving costs and the effect can be seen with these coaches at the platform at Southwold in their final year of use. Note that, as evidenced by in this rare view of the north side of a luggage van, unlike the carriages the vans had a door in each side. *Southwold Museum*

the futility of the cause it was agreed to send a further letter to Southwold Corporation seeking assistance. Later, in a statement to representatives of *The Times*, Henry Ward, the Manager and Secretary, explained the company earned a small amount from a certain amount of goods traffic but relied mainly on passenger services for revenue.

The SR board met again on 27th March 1929. The gathering was in sombre mood for no correspondence had been received from Southwold Corporation or the L&NER and it was agreed it was impossible to continue in operation. Ward was instructed to advise the company servants that their employment would be terminated with effect from 11th April, although a few would be engaged beyond that date on a daily basis to carry out the abandonment procedure. As a last resort it was agreed to send a letter to the Board of Trade seeking assistance. A letter was also sent to the L&NER to advise of the decision taken at the meeting but no reply had been received by 2nd April and an urgent meeting was subsequently sought with Wilcox, the Divisional General Manager. The interview was held on 4th April, when all ways of retaining the railway were discussed and Wilcox promised to place the matter before his board and tender a reply the following day; although not minuted, the L&NER board had already decided to refuse assistance to the SR. From previous investigations made by the GER and later by district engineering staff from Ipswich it had been established three of the locomotives were aged machines, which would require early replacement, the coaching stock was life expired and even required oil lamps for night-time illumination, whilst nearly all goods wagons were ageing and required expensive refurbishment. The permanent way was poorly maintained and the expense of converting to standard gauge was prohibitive, and all could be encompassed more cheaply by road transport! Internal correspondence showed a complete argument against any form of administrative, engineering or financial help or assistance, and it was their conclusion that nothing could be achieved in saving the line. Buses were providing adequate and more comfortable connections to and from Halesworth, whilst road transport could deliver fuel and goods without the recourse to trans-shipment into and out of railway wagons at the junction. The BOT had in the meantime replied to a letter of 27th March advising they had no funds to assist the company; on 5th April, true to his promise, Wilcox politely replied to the effect the L&NER could not provide financial help to the Southwold Company. The SR Directors were crestfallen and Ward was instructed to *'go to Southwold and make the necessary arrangements for closure'*. The manager also telegraphed a terse message to the Southwold Corporation, Estate, Works and Repairs Committee who were meeting the same day. *'Assistance from the L&NER definitely declined: railway closing 11th instant. Ward: Southwold Railway'*. The Committee had fully expected the news and whilst expressing concern over the freight traffic concluded they must adhere to their original decision.

Notice of the impending closure of the line was sent on the same day to the Ministry of Transport, all railway companies, the Postmaster General, W.H. Smith & Sons, the newsagents, the cartage agents Day & Belcher, and tenants of the station yards. Notices were also dispatched for publication in the *East Anglian Daily Times* and the *Halesworth Times*. The company's intention to close the railway in what many considered was indecent haste, meant that no advance notice of closure was printed and made

Five staff pose for the camera on an open wagon at Southwold during the last week of operation. The trellis fence behind the weighing machine is the railway boundary with Station Road.
Author's collection

A passenger on the last train was Major Debney, standing on the left, who as a boy had travelled on the first train half a century earlier. The other traveller was J.S Hurst, the Southwold Borough Surveyor. *Southwold Museum*

available for the public and it was still possible for unsuspecting travellers to purchase on 10th April tourist return tickets, available for a return journey up to six months from the date of issue. There was, however, no need for such publicity for newspaper reporters from the local and national press arrived to interview the staff and produce lengthy reports in local papers and short snappy reports in the national dailies. Railway enthusiasts also made the journey to Suffolk to ride on the unique 3 feet gauge line before its demise, whilst Pathé News recorded the *'last train on the Southwold Railway'* for posterity, but actually filmed the scenes a few days before actual closure. Gaumont Pictorial also filmed the closure.

On the last day of service, Thursday 11th April 1929, a bitterly cold wind was blowing across the Blyth estuary. The last Up train from Southwold departed at 5.23pm hauled by 0-6-2 tank locomotive No. 4 *Wenhaston* in the charge of brothers John and Alfred Stannard. Several hundred people gathered at the station to watch the departure and about 150 passengers travelled on the train. There was a carnival atmosphere tinged with a little sadness and before departure a laurel wreath was attached to the front coupling of the locomotive. Sharp to time the station hand bell was rung, the guard waved his green flag and *Wenhaston* departed slowly away from the platform with the train, conveying two additional coaches to accommodate the anticipated heavy loading for the return journey. One of the passengers, Major E.O. Debney, had travelled on the first train in 1879 and with others had tales to tell of the little railway. A lady, who as a child had stood on a rubbish tip near Blythburgh Church to watch the passing of the first train, made a special journey to be as near as possible to the same spot to watch the passing of the last trains. All too soon the train arrived at Halesworth and *Wenhaston* ran round the formation, past the platform thronged with well-wishers before again coupling to the coaching stock. The plaintive whistles from L&NER locomotives passing on the main line were answered by a farewell toot from the whistle of *Wenhaston* as the locomotive steamed away from the junction for the last time. Each of the intermediate stations was thronged with local villagers and sightseers, and, as dusk was setting in before the train completed its journey, the guard attempted to relieve the situation by lighting the lamps in the coaches but found that none had wicks. Prolonged whistling announced the arrival and departure of the train from Wenhaston, Blythburgh and Walberswick, and as the tail lamp on the rear coach disappeared into the darkness station staff snuffed the light in the platform oil lamps for the last time. More prolonged whistling from *Wenhaston* through the deep cutting and onto Southwold Common heralded the approach to the crowded Southwold terminus. As the train drew to a halt at the platform the crowd sang *Auld Lang Syne* and many were reduced to tears.

The *Halesworth Times* of 12th April described the event:

'Tragedy and comedy were mixed when scores of people gathered at Halesworth to see the Southwold Railway close down after a life of fifty years. When the frail train started its last journey its four carriages were jammed with 150 people. As the train steamed out, the little booking office was besieged by people asking for tickets as souvenirs. The train had gone on 10 yards when a woman grabbed her small son's hat and started to collect money for the engine driver. Everyone showered silver into the hat. All along the line from Halesworth to Southwold there were crowds of villagers waving farewell to the train. At Wenhaston, Blythburgh and Walberswick the villagers were anxious to make the last journey to Southwold, but there was no room for them. On arrival at Southwold a wreath

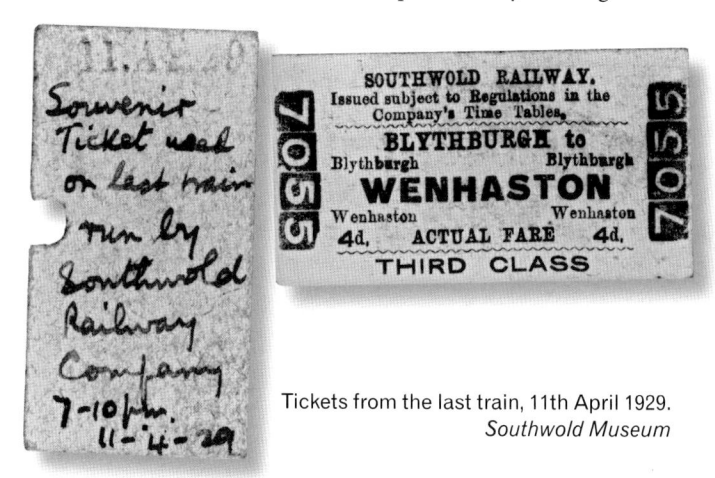

Tickets from the last train, 11th April 1929. *Southwold Museum*

was placed on the smokebox of the engine. Villagers were keen to find souvenirs, and porters had to watch the train to see that people did not steal cushions, such as they were, from the carriages. People did not know whether to cheer or cry, for the closing down of this railway has caused a great deal of distress. The employees of the railway, numbering thirty, received notice of its closing down only two weeks ago.'

After the arrival of the last train *Wenhaston* shunted the stock and then ran light to shed to the echo of three rousing cheers from those on the platform. The crew carried out disposal duties, threw out the fire and retired for the night. The abrupt closure of the line without adequate public announcement meant there were several consignments of coal and general goods at Halesworth awaiting delivery to the intermediate stations, whilst there were small commodities at Walberswick and Blythburgh requiring onward transit to Halesworth for transfer to the L&NER. Accordingly Henry Ward instructed that *Wenhaston* be kept in steam to clear the outstanding traffic. It was also decided to transfer as much rolling stock to Halesworth for storage, where it would hopefully be sheltered from the ravages of the prevailing winds from the sea and possible vandalism. The clearance of traffic and arrangements of stock took a week to accomplish and William Fisk remembered there was great difficulty placing all the stock in the sidings at Halesworth to ensure the locomotive was clear to run back to Southwold each evening. There was no room for van No. 14, which remained in the engine shed at Southwold. The task was finally completed by the morning of Saturday 20th April, when *Wenhaston* returned to Southwold shed for the last time. *Wenhaston* joined *Halesworth* in Southwold shed, whilst *Blyth* had already made the journey to Halesworth, to be stored in the engine shed by the ballast siding. The cannibalized remains of No. 1 *Southwold*, withdrawn in 1928, still rested on the blocks outside Southwold shed but during the first week of May 1929 an offer was made for the scrap metal and the 2-4-2 tank locomotive was cut up at its final resting place.

In the meantime, Bertie Girling, the Southwold station master, was instructed to audit the account books at all stations and clear any outstanding bills. He also supervised the disconnection of signal wires and closure and locking of station buildings. After the passage of *Wenhaston* to Southwold shed on 20th April, all level crossing gates were permanently locked across the railway and left open to road or occupational path. At the end of the week the remaining thirty staff were discharged from their duties.

The L&NER continued to offer through passenger bookings from their stations to Southwold only, by arrangement with the Eastern Counties Road Car Company, which operated a bus service from Halesworth station to Southwold Market Place and return, in connection with the principal train services on the East Suffolk line. Some journeys were extended through to and started back from the ferry terminal at Southwold. Arrangements were also made by the company for road delivery of goods train traffic and parcels between Halesworth and Southwold, and the intermediate villages formerly served by the SR.

Certain residents of Southwold expressed strong opposition to the abrupt closure and were of the opinion the line should re-open at least for goods traffic. Following an application by debenture holders to the Magistrates of Halesworth, Henry Ward, the SR General Manager and Secretary, was appointed Official Receiver of the Southwold Company by the Halesworth Bench on 9th May 1929. In a fit of pique at the beginning of May, Southwold Borough Council had corresponded with the Ministry of Transport seeking guidance and possible financial assistance to enable the railway to recommence operations. The Ministry duly replied saying they regretted it was beyond their powers to render financial assistance and compel the railway company to maintain a service. In the event of the railway reopening to traffic the Ministry would do everything in their powers to settle the legal question amicably. The Secretary of the Southwold Borough Council had written to Henry Ward at his London office on 8th May to enquire if the SR Directors were willing to sell the railway and if so what was the asking price? Ward, having suffered years of indifferent relationships with the local authority, realised the turmoil the closure had brought to the council chamber. Many partially blamed the Southwold authority for lack of support when the railway company badly needed such assistance and he was terse in his reply, advising the letter had been incorrectly addressed, as he was now 'Receiver of the Company'. In the meantime, Claude Pain resigned his position as Company Engineer as it was considered irregular for him to hold that post at the same time as being a board member.

The closure also generated a profound article by Charles F. Klapper, an erudite writer on both road and rail transport, in the *Locomotive Magazine* for 15th May 1929. Klapper had carefully analysed the

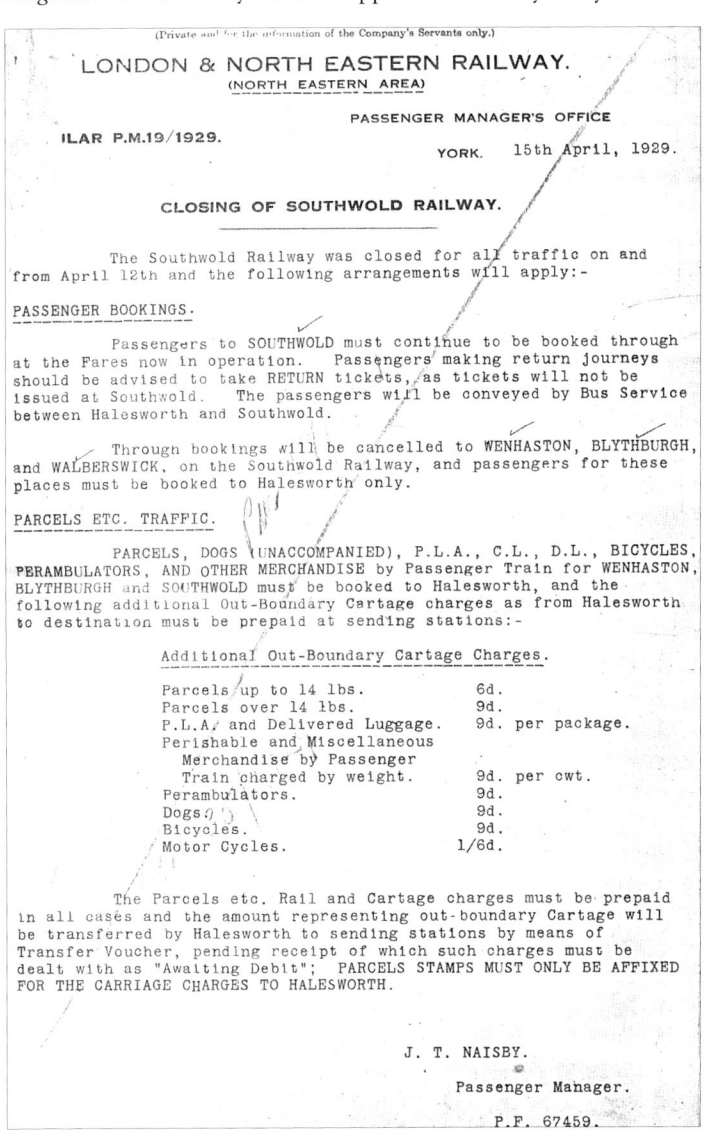

```
(Private and for the information of the Company's Servants only.)

        LONDON & NORTH EASTERN RAILWAY.
                  (NORTH EASTERN AREA)

                              PASSENGER MANAGER'S OFFICE
  ILAR P.M.19/1929.
                              YORK.  15th April, 1929.

              CLOSING OF SOUTHWOLD RAILWAY.

        The Southwold Railway was closed for all traffic on and
 from April 12th and the following arrangements will apply:-

 PASSENGER BOOKINGS.

        Passengers to SOUTHWOLD must continue to be booked through
 at the Fares now in operation.  Passengers making return journeys
 should be advised to take RETURN tickets, as tickets will not be
 issued at Southwold.   The passengers will be conveyed by Bus Service
 between Halesworth and Southwold.

        Through bookings will be cancelled to WENHASTON, BLYTHBURGH,
 and WALBERSWICK, on the Southwold Railway, and passengers for these
 places must be booked to Halesworth only.

 PARCELS ETC. TRAFFIC.

        PARCELS, DOGS (UNACCOMPANIED), P.L.A., C.L., D.L., BICYCLES,
 PERAMBULATORS, AND OTHER MERCHANDISE by Passenger Train for WENHASTON,
 BLYTHBURGH and SOUTHWOLD must be booked to Halesworth, and the
 following additional Out-Boundary Cartage charges as from Halesworth
 to destination must be prepaid at sending stations:-

           Additional Out-Boundary Cartage Charges.

        Parcels up to 14 lbs.          6d.
        Parcels over 14 lbs.           9d.
        P.L.A. and Delivered Luggage.  9d. per package.
        Perishable and Miscellaneous
          Merchandise by Passenger
          Train charged by weight.     9d. per cwt.
        Perambulators.                 9d.
        Dogs.                          9d.
        Bicycles.                      9d.
        Motor Cycles.                  1/6d.

        The Parcels etc. Rail and Cartage charges must be prepaid
 in all cases and the amount representing out-boundary Cartage will
 be transferred by Halesworth to sending stations by means of
 Transfer Voucher, pending receipt of which such charges must be
 dealt with as "Awaiting Debit";  PARCELS STAMPS MUST ONLY BE AFFIXED
 FOR THE CARRIAGE CHARGES TO HALESWORTH.


                                     J. T. NAISBY.

                                     Passenger Manager.
                                        P.F. 67459.
```

L&NER Notice advising closure of the Southwold Railway.

railway's problems basing his findings on the official SR finance returns. He offered a suggestion as to how the SR might reopen and pointed out that other minor railways could close if warnings went unheeded as road competition intensified. He reiterated what others had said regarding the drab uncomfortable wooden seating endured by passengers travelling in the elderly Southwold coaches, when compared with the modem motor buses. Poor connections between the SR and L&NER at Halesworth, and the infrequency of the narrow gauge service, particularly on Sundays when compared with the buses, added to the problems. Klapper also criticised the labour intensive trans-shipment of goods and coal facilities at the junction and the lack of a refreshment room at Southwold station, where summer visitors might have used such facilities whilst waiting for a train. He finally noted that more vigorous and locally based management of the railway might have achieved better results. Klapper then suggested possible solutions, urging a faster and more frequent service of trains was necessary to compete against the buses. Steam or petrol railcars were offered as an alternative for passenger traffic whilst a geared steam tractor or small diesel locomotive would suffice for goods traffic. Further improvements would be made if the trans-shipment shed at Halesworth was converted to high and low level docks; the purchase of four transporter wagons to convey standard gauge wagons on narrow gauge stock was also advocated. He considered the net result of the introduction of these measures would lead to an increase in both passenger and goods traffic whilst reducing labour costs.

There was no reaction from the SR Directors but the following month EA Phillipson, a regular contributor to the *Locomotive Magazine*, responded stating he was not in favour of mixing steam and diesel traction or indeed the introduction of a steam railcar, favouring instead a Sentinel type geared steam locomotive and better designed lightweight coaches operating a more frequent service. He questioned Klapper's estimates and suggested a truck tippler to mechanise the trans-shipment at Halesworth. He was also of the opinion that a two-train service would require station improvements and increased staffing levels. To raise the existing 16 mph speed limit to the 25 mph of the standard gauge light railway would necessitate easing of the curves and other permanent way improvements. Phillipson was not in favour of transporter wagons but saw no difficulty in operating mixed trains and favoured an extension of the line.

Klapper was quick to respond and stated coal consumption figures were based on the operation of Sentinel railcars on the Jersey railways and the Derwent Valley Light Railway. The delay to mixed trains en route was the cause of reduction in passenger numbers. The suggestion of a truck tippler was good but the writer wondered where all the finance for new stock and extensions was to be obtained. Phillipson replied almost immediately, defending at some length his ideas. He repeated his defence of mixed trains advising that as most goods traffic went through to Southwold, shunting delays at intermediate stations was negligible. He admitted his proposals would cost much money but reiterated the need to extend the system.

A group of creditors petitioned the legality of the Halesworth Magistrates to appoint the former General Manager and Secretary as Official Receiver, and on 25th June 1929 Mr Justice Maughan considered the case. During the deliberations, the unusual position of the company was revealed. The Directors desired to wind up the business but there was no jurisdiction in any court to enable them to proceed and therefore Parliamentary approval had to be sought.

His Lordship therefore had no option but to order the appointment of Ward as Receiver, although he ruled that by the powers vested he could not sell the statutory undertaking or dispose of the rolling stock, permanent way or other assets, neither could he sign any cheques. The infrastructure and rolling stock nevertheless had to be taken care of and that he considered was *'the receiver's sole duty'*.

Henry Ward took some time to contact the Directors but in July 1929 the news came that the company was willing to consider an offer for the controlling interest in the railway. By September Ronald Shepherd, a light railway engineer and former debenture holder had formed a syndicate and made a bid. He proposed to retain the narrow gauge line and operate a fast and frequent passenger service using petrol driven railcars, as used on many French secondary lines, with goods traffic hauled by a high pressure vertical boiler geared steam 'Sentinel' locomotive, which was more economical on coal and water, and of a type being introduced by the British main line companies. The problem of trans-shipment was to be overcome by using transporter wagons conveying standard gauge vehicles, as used on the Ashover Light Railway in Derbyshire and several narrow gauge lines in Austria and Germany. The L&NER authorities were agreeable to such arrangements and for the installation of the necessary ramps to effect the transfer at Halesworth. Subject to the raising of the necessary capital, Shepherd hoped to take over the SR and commence operations early in 1930. Shepherd's report maintained the argument for a narrow gauge railway as standard gauge was not considered viable unless the population of Southwold increased from 3,500 to 25,000. The report was supplemented by photographs of transporter wagons in use and details of the bridges which required to be strengthened.

The proposal received considerable support in Southwold but little financial backing was evident. The inhabitants were divided in their loyalties, for a competitive scheme had been advocated by Mr Belcher, one time locomotive engineer of the Southwold line with a forceful nature. He envisaged conversion of the line to standard gauge and an extension to the former Mid Suffolk line at Laxfield, passing by way of Cratfield and Huntingfield and joining the SR route from the south near Halesworth engine shed. Belcher considered this would place the SR and Southwold Harbour in a much more favourable position for through goods and passenger working. The proposer admitted he had made no approach to the L&NER, who at that stage were questioning the future of the Mid Suffolk Light Railway after reluctantly agreeing to take over the ailing undertaking in 1924, and would have certainly turned down any suggestion of the connection. At about that time another proposal to reopen the line came from William J.V. Nicholls, the discharged Wenhaston station master, who also suggested electrification, but he could attract few, if any, sponsors. Thus with the support for the resurrection of the SR divided, none succeeded and negotiations ceased in October 1930.

As the railway remained in a somnolent state, with weeds growing through the trackbed, it was very evident that no external faction intended to resurrect the railway. An SR board meeting on 26th November 1930 merely noted Claude Pain's directorship was irregular whilst he held the post of engineer, but since he had resigned from the post he was officially appointed a Director of the defunct company. The appointment of Ward as Receiver was also mentioned, as was the strange position of the company. The various offers of assistance were touched upon, as were the help of Lieutenant Colonel Boston and P.C. Loftus, neither of which were worth pursuing. The company solicitor thus advised an Act

Wenhaston station rapidly became overgrown following closure, although the nameboard (advising travellers *'for Blyford and Bramfield'*) and lamp stands were still standing when the photographer visited.
John Alsop collection

of Abandonment be obtained but there were no funds to pursue this course and no action was taken. The infrastructure and rolling stock of the railway thus continued to slowly deteriorate, with the legal conundrum of who could take any action to either improve or scrap.

It is doubtful if abandonment of the company was pursued with any great diligence, as the value of scrap would probably have been lost in legal expenses, the Receiver would lose his position and the debenture and shareholders would gain little. As it was, Southwold Corporation which owned much of the land on which the line was laid, as a consequence of the impasse was losing valuable rent because of the dereliction and eventually demanded a more impartial receiver than Ward; after negotiations E.G. Naughton, the Town Clerk of Southwold, was appointed Official Receiver in March 1933, the position subsequently being inherited by his successors H.A. Liquorish and H. Townsend. In the meantime, W.R. Fasey & Son, having expended £60,000 on the harbour scheme, had sold out to Southwold Corporation in 1932.

As the years progressed nature began to take over the route of the railway so that visitors found a picture of desolation. Halesworth station was surrounded by the decaying rolling stock, the platform giving the impression a rail service might be resumed. Hedges, bushes and brambles bounding the line between Halesworth and Blythburgh, growing unkempt and uncut, invaded railway property; willow herb, ragged robin and other marsh-loving flora spread across the rusting rails in many places and the section of the line near Wenhaston became waterlogged. Beyond Blythburgh, as the railway skirted the River Blyth and then crossed the sandy heath through Walberswick, the permanent way was fairly free of vegetation. The neglected stations and other infrastructure fell into disrepair, timber boarding rotting away and windows smashed showing damp interiors full of rubbish. At Wenhaston the ghostly arm of a signal post with both arms at danger was equalled at Walberswick where the signal post also survived alongside a decaying shed. The trackbed through Blythburgh station had been invaded by a chicken run whilst coal heaps and attendant fuel offices in black sheds had spread in the abandoned and forlorn yard at Southwold. The few railway enthusiasts who visited the line to inspect the remains found little to photograph. However, in the summer of 1936 at least one such party obtained permission from Southwold Corporation to open the engine sheds at Southwold and Halesworth and push the rusting locomotives into the open for photography. The three men, brothers J.M. Jarvis and R.G. Jarvis, who later became Chief Draughtsman for locomotive design on the Southern Railway, and J.H.L. Adams, author and later film maker of the BBC 'Railway Roundabout' programmes in the 1950s, travelled from Harpenden to Suffolk, visiting the London Midland & Scottish Railway engine shed at St. Albans on the way to borrow a pinch bar. Calling in at Halesworth shed the trio managed to prise the reluctant and rusted wheels of *Blyth* into motion, although there were a few anxious moments manoeuvring the engine over the rails beside the inspection pit, which were balanced on rotten sleepers. Having succeeded into getting the locomotive into full daylight, the trio spent the next three hours cleaning and polishing *Blyth* with Carpol until the sun had moved to a favourable position for photographs to be taken. The engine was then returned to the shed for the last time. The party then moved on to Southwold where they encountered failure, for *Halesworth* and *Wenhaston* refused to budge, their cylinders and motion rusted and unable to be freed. After refreshing themselves at a local hostelry and a swim in the sea, the three men returned to Hertfordshire.

Yet another attempt to reopen the railway was made in 1937 when a Mr Parkinson, who had railway connections, produced detailed plans and estimates for running a 3-car diesel train on the line, showing an estimated profit of £1,000 in the first year of operation and over £2,000 in the second year on an initial outlay of £15,000.

In 1936, seven years after closure of the railway, three railway enthusiasts obtained permission to photograph the abandoned SR locomotives at Halesworth and Southwold. They achieved success at Halesworth by pinch-barring No. 3 *Blyth* out of the dilapidated building, over the inspection pit and into the open. The track over the inspection pit was decidedly fragile and the move was fraught with difficulty in case the rails subsided under the weight of the engine. However, the attempt was successful and after photographs were taken the engine was returned to its shelter to await its fate.

LEFT: Having extracted No. 3 they set about giving some attention to cleanliness before taking their photographs. One hardy soul is seen standing on the boiler to clean the rim of the chimney.

After success with No. 3 the trio moved on to Southwold but failed to move either No. 2 *Halesworth* or No. 4 *Wenhaston* out of the shed as they had rusted to the rails.

All photographs J.H.L. Adams/ Kidderminster Railway Museum

DECLINE AND CLOSURE

A general view of the abandoned terminus at Southwold in 1936, with rails still extant among the undergrowth and weeds. The engine shed and associated water tower are to the left, goods shed in the centre and station building to the right. In the background the former Station Hotel, by this time renamed the Pier Avenue Hotel, still flourishes despite the loss of the railway. Bagged and loose heaps of coal belonging to local fuel merchants are to the extreme left.
J.H.L. Adams/Kidderminster Railway Museum

Close-up of the abandoned station building at Southwold in 1936 – seven years after closure of the line. The three doors are labelled LADIES WAITING ROOM, BOOKING OFFICE and PARCELS OFFICE. Note the corrugated iron roof atop the timber-framed brick infill structure.
J.H.L. Adams/Kidderminster Railway Museum

It was envisaged an hourly service would run in each direction, the journey taking about 20 minutes, as the 16 mph speed limit would be eliminated. The new train would have a maximum axle weight of 4 tons compared with 8 tons for the old stock. The scheme also envisaged the refurbishment of the station buildings at Southwold, with a new frontage containing retail outlets on the ground floor and a flat and offices on the first floor. However, by eliminating this work a £500 saving could be made. Infrastructure changes included a new bridge near Halesworth, traffic lights replacing the level crossing gates at Wenhaston, whilst Blythburgh and Walberswick were to be converted to unstaffed halts, tickets being issued on the train by the guard. As with earlier attempts nothing came of the proposal. In the meantime the coaching stock stored at Halesworth attracted itinerants who found the covered accommodation convenient for a temporary home; one tramp made himself too welcome by lighting a fire in coach No. 4, totally destroying the vehicle except for wheels and underframe in the process.

Two years later, in the summer of 1939, Major G.A. Bonce Bruce of Belton Hall, Suffolk, a consulting engineer with an office in Great Yarmouth, prepared a project to reopen the Southwold line. Surveys were conducted and C.D. Brumbley was engaged as draughtsman. The inspection was carried out without fuss but when Bonce Bruce sought Parliamentary sanction to proceed, the L&NER reputedly bought out his interests and nothing further developed. At the outbreak of World War Two much of the boarding of the water tower at Southwold had already been purloined, wheeled beach huts were paraded in the station yard whilst coastal defence work was put in hand. Within days the swing bridge over the River Blyth was positioned at right angles to the railway and parallel to the river as a precaution against invasion by German troops.

The railway continued in its solemnity during the early months of hostilities but in the spring of 1940 the Ministry of Supply instituted a national drive for scrap metal and surplus railway effects were included in the scheme. In June, Southwold Council members passed a resolution to advise the Controller of Iron and Steel at the Ministry of Supply to requisition the assets of the SR for conversion to munitions. The Controller replied stating that a fortnight before receiving the Council letter he had requested the Ministry of Supply to issue the necessary order for the demolition of the Southwold Railway and the requisitioning of all materials, the emergency powers overruling any legalities which for eleven years since closure had protected the assets of the line. Eastern Command of the War Department immediately requisitioned some of the railway, deeming it as high risk in the event of an invasion. In these early stages the swing bridge was removed, the underline bridge at Wenhaston Mill demolished and several sections of track – most notably on Southwold Common – lifted, as they might have proved useful in the event of a landing by German troops. On 3rd January 1941, following the Council meeting of Southwold Corporation, a resolution was sent to R.R. Stokes, MP for Ipswich and P.C. Loftus, MP for Lowestoft that the *'Council desire most emphatically to call attention to the considerable quantity of metal comprising the derelict rolling stock of the Southwold Railway and ask that you will in the national interest call the attention of the appropriate department to get this usefully employed'*. Stokes took action and forwarded to the Council the letter he had received from the Ministry of Supply, and this was read at the meeting on 7th February. Requisitioning would take place as a matter of urgency and tenders invited for the removal and sale of the metal, after which the proceeds would be paid to shareholders.

Ronald Shepherd, the light railway engineer, then took another look at the possibility of reopening the line as an aid to the war effort. Severe cuts in local bus services added to local backing for the scheme and later during February 1941 he inspected the route with representatives of the War Department before canvassing the local authority to petition the Minister of Transport. The chief arguments for the resurrection of the line was the fact that Walberswick and Southwold were only connected by rowing boat after the vehicular ferry had ceased operation; that shipping restrictions had aggravated the supplies of coal and other fuel to the area, which had to be transported by road from Halesworth and Lowestoft, using precious petrol and oil, and that local farmers were experiencing difficulties despatching their much-needed produce to market. In the event of the acceptance of the scheme it was suggested Walberswick station be abandoned and replaced by a new station at Eastwood Lodge Farm, which was nearer to the road leading to the village. Members of Southwold Corporation appeared utterly confused as to their position regarding the future of the railway for only two months

With coastal defence work taking place in 1939, Southwold station yard became the resting place of wheeled beach huts, here seen stored on the trackbed where once the train ran.
Author's collection

The army ensured that enemy troops landing on English shores could not use the railway for they dynamited the swing bridge for national security leaving the structure in this precarious state in 1942. *Southwold Museum*

after wanting the scrap to be recovered as quickly as possible they recorded at their meeting on 4th April 1941, their:

'Strong support to a petition circulating in the district, asking the Minister of Transport to do all in his power to further the reopening of the Southwold Railway. The Council feel this project will be of the utmost benefit to the Borough and neighbouring parishes'.

The damage had been done, however, and the hopes of Southwold Corporation and the petitioners were dashed for in May, Thomas W. Ward Limited was awarded the contract to demolish the railway.

The contractor commenced breaking up the remains of the rolling stock stored at Halesworth in July 1941 and then started lifting the track. By August the Halesworth engine shed had been removed leaving *Blyth* exposed on a short length of track awaiting the cutters torch. A month later the locomotive was gone as the systematic demolition advanced eastwards. The track for the first four miles, entangled in brambles and undergrowth, proved troublesome to remove but the rails were short enough to be manhandled to sites adjacent to road crossings where they were stored before being loaded onto road vehicles. Heaps of dog spikes were also to be found but many were discarded and left by the trackbed. Not all lengths of track were lifted, for a section of rail near Blythburgh in the direction of Walberswick on the embankment overlooking the Blyth was retained and completely covered in earth as the base for an observation post.

Two months after the commencement of demolition a petition in the form of a memorandum dated 26th September 1941 was rather belatedly presented to Baron Leathers of Purfleet, the Minister of War Transport. It suggested the restoration of the railway to working order with stations being tidied up and sidings put in order, but as demolition had started the document was redrafted to reflect the situation. The amended paper proposed the rebuilding of the railway to standard gauge worked by a Sentinel shunting locomotive hired from the L&NER, the engine being based at Halesworth. The map accompanying the report showed the standard gauge line following the original trackbed with two deviations: a short diversion between Corner Farm and Wenhaston Mill to obviate the unnecessary curvature of the original route, and a lengthy re-routing leaving the original track bed just east of Eastwood Lodge Farm and running due east close to Walberswick village before turning north and crossing the River Blyth by a new bridge to join the Harbour Branch on Blackshore Quay before continuing to Southwold. New passenger halts were proposed at Holton, Corner Farm, Heath Farm and Eastwood Farm, with a new station at Walberswick. Sidings were to be installed where necessary, including a connection to Southwold gasworks. Needless to say, the proposal was unsuccessful. The demolition work continued working back towards Southwold; some of the track on the embankment beyond Blythburgh proved too troublesome to drag to the nearest road access and was left in situ. Eventually the contractor's men reached the terminus where the stored engines, *Halesworth* and *Wenhaston*, were cut up and the rails lifted. Not all of the track was removed as about 300 yards of line between Eastwick Lodge Farm and Walberswick remained intact, whilst odd sections of rail were evident in other places. Unoccupied sheds and buildings at Southwold were demolished and by January 1942 the task was completed. Later in the same year the dilapidated Southwold engine shed blew down in a gale. Some of the recovered rail was sent to a Yorkshire colliery for further use, but all other metal including the locomotives were sent for war scrap. Some of the sleepers were acquired by a local retired policeman who cut them up for firewood, when they were sold by a Blythburgh grocer at 2½d per bundle.

The proceeds of the scrap realized about£ 1,500 and after T.W. Ward & Son had paid over the money to the War Office the question was asked of the company to whom the money should be paid. The assets and accounts of the company were still frozen, however, and the War Department after several unsuccessful attempts placed the money on deposit in 1945, pending the time that the company could legally claim it. In the same year the Receiver obtained an order from the Master of the Court to sell land back to former owners and settle outstanding long-term debts. Unfortunately, just as money was forthcoming from the sales, so a newly appointed Master of the Court reversed his predecessor's decision and ordered the earnings to be frozen except for the payment of income tax. The Receiver was thus powerless to act except to pay for the cost of an Abandonment Act.

In the meantime Halesworth Urban District Council complained of the dangerous condition of the bridge spanning the main road, which consisting only of main girders formed a veritable death trap for young children clambering up the bank beside the structure. The bridge had slots cut in the sides during the War for use as gun positions by the local Home Guard. As the railway company was powerless to act and could spend no money, Halesworth UDC was forced to provide safety fences at their own cost and then pass the bill on to the company for settlement in the High Court, where it joined many other claims. The railway company was still in existence but until the High Court chose to act, the UDC and other claimants would have to wait for their money.

After years of fruitless campaigning, Ronald Shephard suggested in 1956 the formation of a railway preservation society to revive the line. He was keen to follow the success enjoyed by the infant Talyllyn and Festiniog railway societies in mid and north Wales but lacked one essential ingredient: whereas the Welsh railways were derelict, the track and infrastructure together with the rolling stock was extant – at Southwold there was nothing except a few sections of track. The plan was to install a brand new railway on the old trackbed and then persuade debenture holders to finance the scheme, allowing some of the frozen assets to be released back to the venture. An able lieutenant was found in Captain J.A. Stedman who had retained a nostalgic interest in the line and had presided at a reunion dinner for former employees of the company back in 1935. An impressive list of sympathizers was drawn up, many who volunteered to build the new railway in their spare time as and when plans were further developed. Initially a miniature railway with 15 inch gauge was envisaged, similar to the Romney Hythe & Dymchurch or the Ravenglass & Eskdale, but this was later abandoned in favour of 1 feet 11 inch gauge as there was a surfeit of secondhand equipment available. It was expected there would be no problems obtaining the land, which legally was still in the ownership of the SR but under the guardianship of Southwold Corporation. Much of the trackbed was overgrown but replacement bridges could be built and the trackbed cleared by mechanical bulldozers and other equipment. Shephard intended to start the venture at Halesworth where there was suitable land for the storage of equipment and facilities for the delivery of materials by rail. Stedman had several meetings with the Receiver and solicitors in 1959 but difficulties emerged. Despite this, considerable interest continued to be shown in the project and several supportive letters were received.

There was optimistic hope that plans which had lain dormant for three years might reach fruition but Southwold Corporation, blind to the potential that a preserved railway might have in engendering tourism to the area, were incensed that large sums of money were owing in rent. The Corporation was anxious to get their hands on the derelict land leased to the railway and forced the hand of the Southwold Company by instituting proceedings against the dormant railway in 1959. Claud Pain was the only surviving Director and in this capacity addressed an Extraordinary General Meeting convened at Haslemere, Surrey on 26th February 1960. The purpose of the meeting was to reduce the number of Directors to three; to elect three Directors; to move the principal office of the company to the Town Hall, Southwold and to register the company under part viii of the Company's Act 1948.

Claud Pain in his address showed no willingness to resurrect the railway between Halesworth and Southwold, instead concentrating his endeavours on stabilizing the company by the appointment of new Directors and obtaining finance to settle outstanding debenture debts.

'This is a meeting of the shareholders of the Southwold Railway Company. As required by the relevant Act of Parliament, notice of the meeting has been given by newspaper advertisements. The present position of the Company is this. It has an issued capital of £49,000, the capital being divided into £10 shares. It has debentures outstanding and unsatisfied and a Receiver was appointed of the Company's revenue on behalf of the debenture holders. I, alas, am the sole survivor of the Board of Directors.

'By way of assets, the Company appears to have a sum of money in the High Court of London, representing compensation for the requisitioning for war purposes in about 1941 of the Company's remaining rolling stock and track. It is in Court because, at the time of requisitioning, there was nobody able, in the name of the Company, to give good receipt for the money to the requisitioning authority, the Ministry of Supply. The Company owns some land, notably the disused stations, sidings and track sites. For many years the Company has been no more than a shell. Its records have been out of date and it has no proper office and no officer except myself. This was a most unsatisfactory state of affairs, not helped by the fact that as the last surviving Director, I am of the age mentioned in the notice of this meeting. It seemed sensible therefore that steps should be taken during my lifetime to put the company affairs in order.

'The Company's special Act of Parliament and the Companies Clauses Acts of 1845 and 1889 are a little out of date and provide no ready and simple means of putting the Company's affairs in order. The present legal code for the Company, however, is the Companies Act of 1948 and Counsel has advised that the Company should apply for registration as a Joint Stock Company under that Act. Counsel is Mr Denys Buckley, long regarded as a leading authority on company matters in this country. Since the date of his opinion, July 1959, he has in fact been made a Judge of the Chancery Division. It is on the authority of his opinion also that the first stage has been taken to bring the Register of Shareholders up to date. I am advised that I ought, before closing these remarks, to make one matter clear at this meeting. By Section 69 of the Companies Act of 1845 it is provided that: "No extraordinary meeting shall enter upon any business not set forth in the notice upon which it shall have been convened". For the moment therefore, however interesting and exciting it may be to hold the first formal meeting of this old Company to be held for many years, the law prohibits us from discussing any business other than that contained in the notice of the meeting.'

Pain concluded:

'You will be aware, however, that once the steps on the agenda have been taken, the Company will live again; the shareholders will have the opportunity of becoming an articulate body again and the board will be reconstituted. There will be a few important decisions affecting the Company which could henceforth be taken without reference to any Extraordinary General Meeting of the Shareholders.'

The resolutions were put and carried. Claud Pain, tired of the company affairs, declined a seat on the new board. Nicholas A.A. Loftus was elected the new Chairman with fellow Directors J. MacLaughlan and Andrew Critten, with H. Townsend the Town Clerk of Southwold, the Company Secretary. The principal office of the company was moved to the Town Hall, Southwold and it was resolved the company be registered under part viii of the Companies Act 1948.

No immediate action was taken and in the same month East Suffolk County Council indicated they intended to widen the road and lower the bridge over the railway at Blythburgh, thus dividing the trackbed in two. Captain Stedman was devastated and was of the opinion it would have a very disturbing effect on any attempt to reopen the line. In the meantime, the editor of the *Railway Magazine*, H.A. Vallance, had been approached to support reopening plans and an article was published in the April 1960 issue. All was to no avail for in the spring the County Council, through the Board of Trade, compulsorily purchased the railway land at Blythburgh so that the railway bridge could be demolished and the A12 main road levelled and widened, the work beginning at Easter. Even at this late stage the BoT were under the impression that the bridge was owned and maintained by British Railways Eastern Region! In the meantime the new Directors stated they had no powers to relinquish the company's statutory rights under the 1876 Act, an odd comment when they were trying to dispose of the company's assets. At a subsequent meeting on 16th June 1960, the Secretary was instructed to register the company and transfer debentures. The board was also to agree with Southwold Corporation the appointment of liquidators. The company was duly registered as a Limited Company on 15th September 1960, with its principal office at Southwold Town Hall and a compulsory winding up order was obtained in the High Court on the application of the Corporation on 17th April 1961.

After the first meeting of the Creditors and Contributories on 11th May 1961, the Official Receiver acted as liquidator, with the task of aggregating the company's assets and distributing any of the remaining money after liabilities had been met. Southwold Corporation was owed £1,600 outstanding rent charges and rates, and whilst debenture holders might benefit, ordinary shareholders would gain nothing. East Suffolk County Council agreed to contribute £150 towards the cost of the winding up process, possibly for being granted permission to demolish the former railway bridge at Blythburgh.

The girders of the Southwold Railway bridge over Holton Road at Halesworth were removed in March 1962, when East Suffolk County Council contracted Butterley Company Limited, who were working on a replacement bridge on British Railways East Suffolk main line, to carry out the task. The actual removal took place on the 19th of the month. In the November 1962 edition of the *Railway Magazine* a short note inferred a winding-up order had been issued and thus the revival plans of Messrs Shephard and Stedman were finished for good. The following year the records of the company were gathered by the liquidator, who in the autumn of 1963 appointed Norcott & Sons of Museum Street, Ipswich to dispose of the railway land, including the eviction of squatters, if any. In October 1963 the Suffolk & Ipswich Fire Authority made a compulsory purchase order on half of the former station yard at Southwold for the erection of a new fire station. Southwold Corporation lodged a half-hearted objection as occupier of the land but did not oppose its use by the Fire Authority. The Ministry confirmed the Fire Authority's compulsory purchase order in February 1964 and the Mayor, Councillor A. Barrett Jenkins JP, officially opened the new building erected in the former coal yard on 23rd November 1965. The former brick and timber station building was also demolished soon after to make way for a new police station and police houses, which were completed in 1968. During the transformation of the former station site the goods shed was moved to the west end of the station yard, where it is now used by Southwold Allotment Holders' Association, whose plots are located on the former track bed. One of the van bodies had found its way to serve as a tool shed on the allotment but on discovery in 1962 it was moved back to stand beside the station building. When that building was demolished the van body was transferred to the East Anglian Transport Museum at Carlton Colville, near Lowestoft, for preservation, where it remains to this day.

The last remaining span of the old swing bridge was finally removed in 1977 to be replaced by a new footbridge, which replaced the temporary bailey bridge erected in 1947.

At a public meeting held in Southwold Town Hall on Thursday 3rd November 1977, A. Barrett Jenkins ascertained opinion as to whether the anniversary of the centenary of the opening of the SR should be celebrated. The majority of the twenty-seven people attending were in favour of the commemoration and a steering committee was formed, with Jenkins as Chairman and including the Mayor E.B. Hurren, David Lee the curator of Southwold Museum and two member of Waveney District Council. In all, fourteen committee meetings were held culminating in a number of functions and souvenirs of the event.

At a ceremony at Southwold on 11th April 1979 to commemorate the fiftieth anniversary of the closure of the line, a commemorative plaque was unveiled on the wall of the police station, marking the site of the former railway station on Blyth Road. The Mayor E.B. Hurren unveiled the plaque at 5.20pm, then at 5.23pm, the time that the last train departed five decades earlier, the hand bell from Southwold station was rung. Attending the ceremony was B. Girling, the last station master at Southwold, then aged 92, 76-year-old W. Upcraft, the last station master at Blythburgh, and 85-year-old G. Burley, a former guard on the line. To commemorate the centenary of the opening and the golden jubilee of the closure, Adnams, the Southwold brewery, launched a special brew called Rail Ale. Other mementos included a brochure jointly written by A. Barrett Jenkins and David Lee giving a short history of the line, together with a sketch map and notes on walking the accessible sections of the formation – 2,000 being printed and selling for 30p each. A commemorative postal cover and stamp cancellation was applied to a decorative cover on 24th September, selling at 30p including a first class stamp, and some 1,300 were returned for cancellation at Ipswich. A costume dance in the 1920s period was also arranged and approximately 120 people attended on 24th September. Between Thursday 2nd and Tuesday 7th August a centenary exhibition was held at the County Primary School in Cumberland Road with over 2,800 attending to view model railway layouts and artefacts from the SR. The events raised £715.27 after expenses, and this was donated to the Southwold Archaeological & Natural History Society for the Museum.

In 1988 Joe Atkinson of Messrs Spicer, Oppenheim & Partners of Newater House, 11 Newhall Street, Birmingham B3 3NY was appointed liquidator of the Southwold Railway Company. The firm was incorporated into the Corporate Recovery Section of Deloitte & Touche of Colmore Gate, 2 Colmore Row, Birmingham B3 2BN. In January 1989 it was announced the assets of the SR amounting to about £20,000 were to be realised, thus more than twenty-five years after the Southwold Railway Company was placed in liquidation and nearly sixty years after the company ceased trading, the affairs of the railway were finally brought to an end, although it was October 1994 before Touch Ross, the liquidators, received confirmation from the Inland Revenue that no Corporation Tax was owing before the company affairs were finally dissolved.

8

The Route Described

The Southwold Railway station at **Halesworth** lay to the east of the Great Eastern Railway station, a few yards to the south of the Up side main line platform and a footbridge (GER No. 466 at 100 miles 48 chains from Liverpool Street) was provided so that interchanging passengers could have easy access to and from the narrow gauge railway. A wheelbarrow crossing was also provided from the Down and Up main line platforms to the SR terminus. The ground level Southwold Railway platform, 200 feet in length, was located on the west or Up side of the single line, with a canopy shelter provided for waiting passengers. In the centre of the platform under the canopy was an office, whilst seats were positioned against the upright supports of the canopy. Fencing backed the platform. Two loop sidings, 350 feet and 270 feet, were located to the west of the platform alongside the GER/L&NER Up side goods yard where coal and other mineral traffic was manually transferred from standard gauge wagons to SR wagons stabled on the outer road. To the north of the station platform the narrow gauge line terminated in a trans-shipment shed where the timber built loading platform was provided for the interchange of goods and parcels traffic with the GER/L&NER.

This structure was 5 feet in width with the platform height slightly below the level of the wagons to facilitate the easy interchange of exchange traffic and permitting the running of barrows between truck and truck. SR staff transferred all commodities. Initially the trans-ship platform was open to the elements but in October 1895 authority was given for a roof to be erected partially over the platform. Originally a second siding 200 feet in length ran parallel with the trans-ship siding but this was removed in 1909. The freight trans-ship shed held four 4-wheel SR wagons and a locomotive. To assist with shunting operations and to give greater yard capacity two new connections south of the station, controlled by Annett's key attached to the single line Train Staff, were installed, the first in 1909 and the second in 1921, between the existing sidings and the main line. Two further connections, also made in 1909, to the south of the platform at a distance of 400 feet from the SR station building between the Halesworth reception road and the main line, incorporated a continuation of the coal/mineral road. An earlier alteration dating from 1909 was the removal of the siding leading from the SR transit shed to a covered shed on the western side of

(Continued on page 112)

The transit shed behind the Up platform at Halesworth in 1911 with footbridge No 466 connecting the GER main line platforms to the SR station. To the right is the SR transship siding and platform between the narrow gauge and standard gauge sidings. *GERS Windwood collection ref 1219*

106 — THE SOUTHWOLD RAILWAY

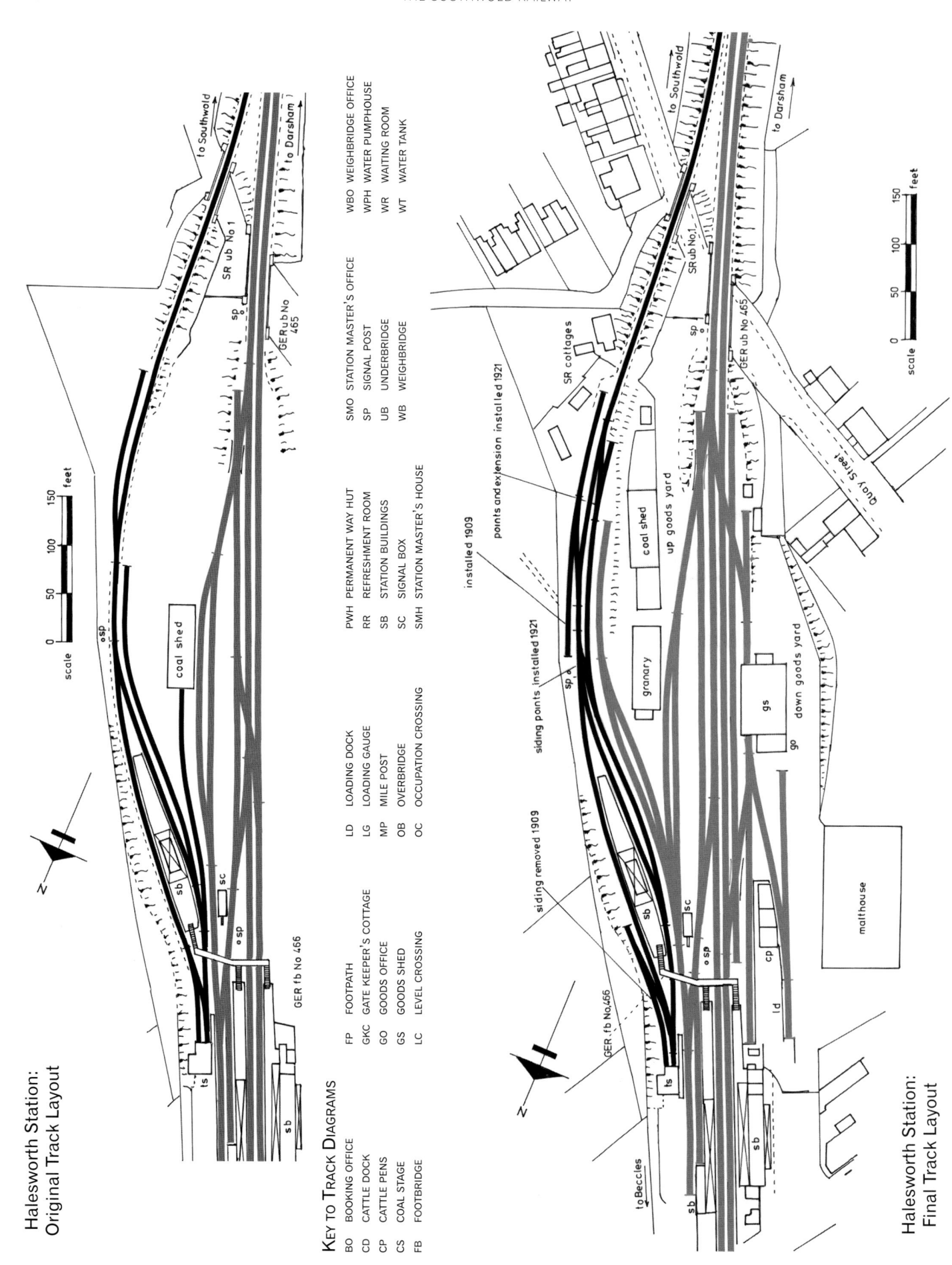

Halesworth Station: Original Track Layout

Halesworth Station: Final Track Layout

Key to Track Diagrams

BO	BOOKING OFFICE	FP	FOOTPATH	LD	LOADING DOCK
CD	CATTLE DOCK	GKC	GATE KEEPER'S COTTAGE	LG	LOADING GAUGE
CP	CATTLE PENS	GO	GOODS OFFICE	MP	MILE POST
CS	COAL STAGE	GS	GOODS SHED	OB	OVERBRIDGE
FB	FOOTBRIDGE	LC	LEVEL CROSSING	OC	OCCUPATION CROSSING
PWH	PERMANENT WAY HUT	SMO	STATION MASTER'S OFFICE	WBO	WEIGHBRIDGE OFFICE
RR	REFRESHMENT ROOM	SP	SIGNAL POST	WPH	WATER PUMPHOUSE
SB	STATION BUILDINGS	UB	UNDERBRIDGE	WR	WAITING ROOM
SC	SIGNAL BOX	WB	WEIGHBRIDGE	WT	WATER TANK
SMH	STATION MASTER'S HOUSE				

2-4-0T No. 2 *Halesworth* shunting wagons from the interchange siding to the trans-shipment platform at Halesworth. The locomotive is in immaculate condition, a vision slightly spoilt by the bucket thrown atop the side tank. *Author's collection*

RIGHT: Looking south from below the footbridge at Halesworth towards the SR/L&NER interchange sidings in 1930. To the left is the passenger station with abandoned coaching stock at the platform. To the west of the platform fence are the SR run round loop and the outer road, the coal and mineral trans-shipment siding, alongside the standard gauge siding. The edge of Halesworth signalbox is to the right. *R. Shephard*

Halesworth GER station from the south circa 1911 showing the Down yard with goods shed to the left and the Up side yard to the right. In the far distance can be seen the signal box and to the right of that the roof of the SR station.
GERS Windwood collection 1224

No. 1 *Southwold* arriving at Halesworth with an evening mixed train from Southwold circa 1910. The station was in a cramped position beside a high embankment, which precluded a run-round loop beside the running line; the latter running at the back of station building and platform fencing. The platform is timber boarded to eliminate muddy conditions in wet weather but could prove a hazard in icy conditions. Two porters advance, one to collect the single line Train Staff from the fireman and the other to assist passengers from the train. *John Alsop collection*

The 10.55am train ex Southwold hauled by 2-4-0T No. 3 *Blyth* pulling into the SR platform at Halesworth on 10th September 1910. The consist of the train includes one of the flat wagons, three open wagons with curved ends to support tarpaulin sheets, and another with straight ends, two luggage vans and the coaching stock. Beyond the fencing at the back if the platform were two loop sidings and the GER Up side goods yard. *LCGB/Ken Nunn*

GER survey of Halesworth station buildings

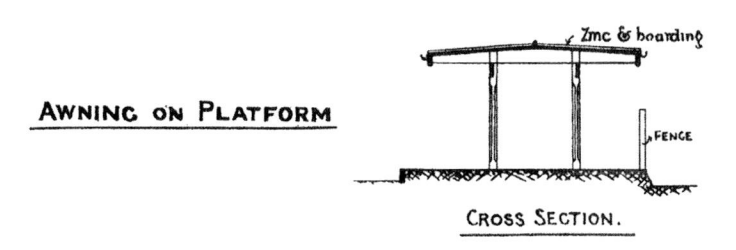

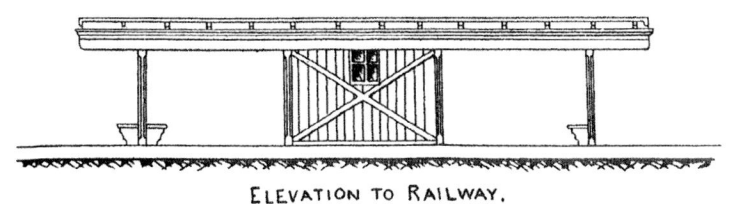

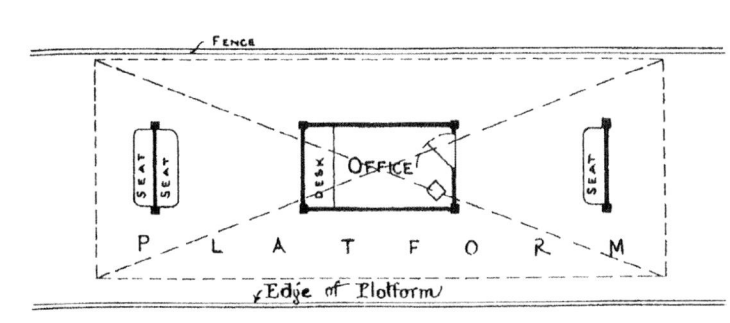

AWNING ON PLATFORM

Zinc & boarding
FENCE
CROSS SECTION.

ELEVATION TO RAILWAY.

FENCE
SEAT | DESK OFFICE | SEAT
PLATFORM
Edge of Platform
From Southwold

PLAN.
Scale of Feet

RIGHT: The faded station nameboard at Halesworth viewed through the window of a derelict SR coach in 1936. Behind the fence is a short wheelbase wagon with curved ends.
J.H.L. Adams/Kidderminster Railway Museum

The SR possessed two cottages at the corner of Limepits Lane, Halesworth and despite the demise of the railway they were still rented out for 1s 6d and 2s 0d per week in 1941. The local council considered them unfit for human habitation but they continued to be occupied until demolition in 1960. *Author's collection*

RIGHT: Transfer between the SR and GER at Halesworth was via footbridge No. 466, at 100 miles 48 chains from Liverpool Street. However, for disabled passengers and those with heavy luggage there was also access on a foot crossing at the south end of the GER Down and Up platforms and through a side gate to SR property, from where there is a glimpse of 0-6-2T No. 4 *Wenhaston* drawing wagons off or coupling wagons to the train in the SR platform.
Author's collection

RIGHT: 2-4-0T No. 3 *Blyth* runs round the train at Halesworth on 10th September 1910. To the left is GER Halesworth signal box and two standard gauge loop sidings, the easternmost serving as a run round loop and the other as an interchange points for the loading and unloading of minerals, coal and coke from standard gauge wagons to SR wagons standing on the outer narrow gauge loop road. The SR signal has arms for each direction of travel mounted on the same post, the fantail spectacle set at a lower level than the arms. The signal lamp is at the base of the post and is probably awaiting the reservoir to be filled with oil before being raised by windlass to be aligned with the spectacle. The points are operated by weighted lever and were interlocked with the signal.
LCGB/Ken Nunn

LEFT: The 3.40pm Halesworth to Southwold mixed train awaits departure at Halesworth behind 2-4-2T No. 1 *Southwold* on 17th January 1920. The leading vehicle, a tarpaulin covered 4-wheel open wagon, has been coupled ahead of the passenger coaches, possibly to be detached at an intermediate station. Note the ornate gas lamp on the left as by this date gas lighting had replaced oil illumination.
LCGB/Ken Nunn

Manning, Wardle 0-6-2T No. 4 *Wenhaston*, with cylinder cocks open, prepares to depart Halesworth with a Down service with open wagons and the two luggage vans fore and aft of a single composite passenger coach. *Ian Pope collection*

THE ROUTE DESCRIBED

With cylinder cocks open and safety valves lifting 2-4-2T No. 1 *Southwold* departs from Halesworth with the 6.30pm train to Southwold on 3rd July 1920. As the train is the last departure of the day no goods wagons were conveyed. To the left of the platform fence is the SR run round loop. *LCGB/Ken Nunn*

Blasting away from Halesworth 2-4-2T No. 1 *Southwold* departs with a heavy train including a 4-wheel wagon as the leading vehicle and then four coaches. To the left is the Up side headshunt and on the right the storage siding normally occupied by coaching stock.
Author's collection

The southern entrance to the joint Halesworth GER/L&NER Up side goods yard and the SR sidings from the Halesworth to Holton/Southwold road. The main line company goods shed is in the Down yard on the left whilst the overgrown SR track is the right. *Author's collection*

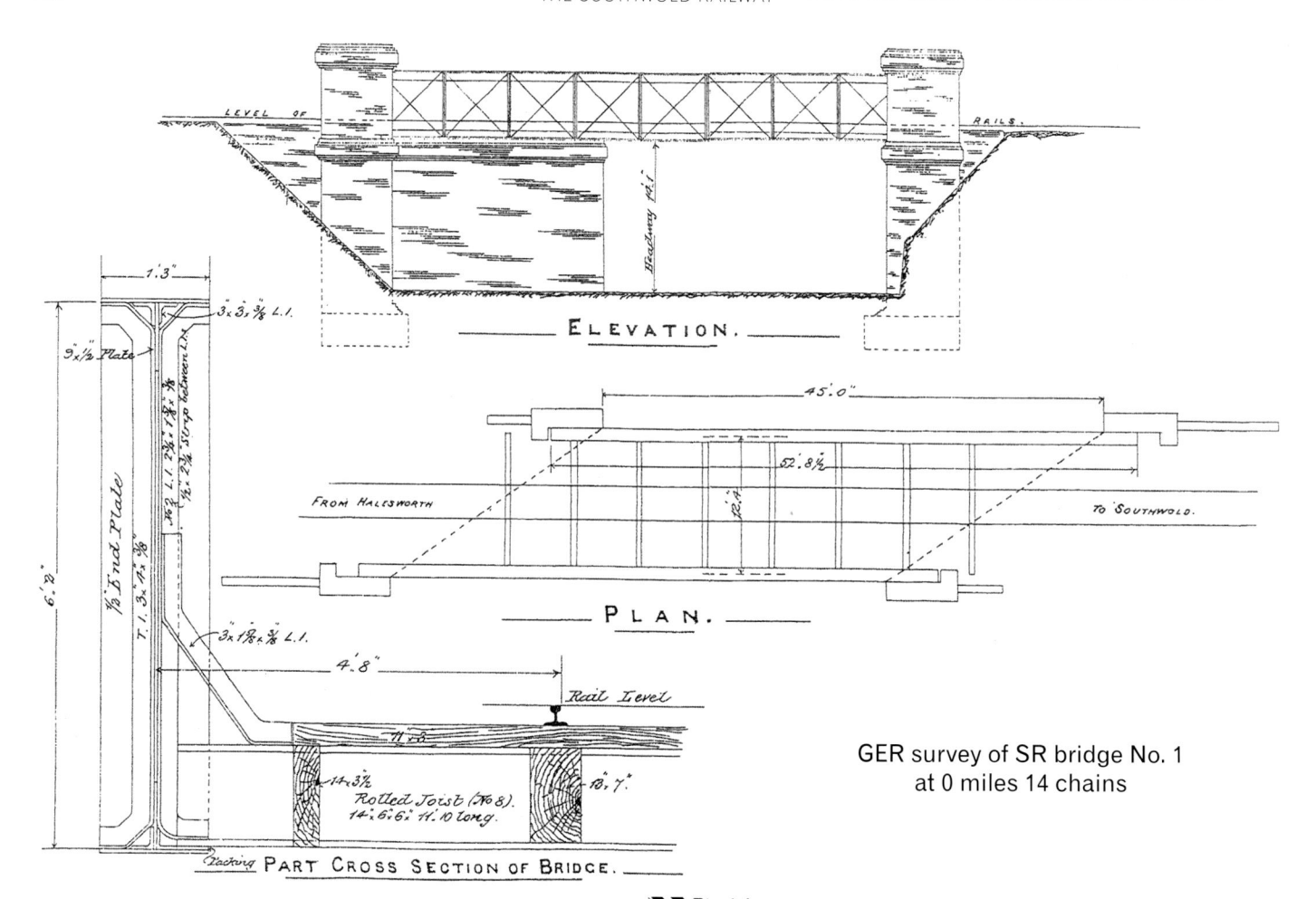

GER survey of SR bridge No. 1 at 0 miles 14 chains

(Continued from page 105)

the run round loop and associated siding. The resultant space was used by the GER installing a loop siding for the interchange of coal traffic proving a better arrangement for both parties.

Away from Halesworth station the SR single main line initially curved sharply to the right past the 280 feet long holding siding (160 feet to the north and 120 feet to the south of the entry points) on the Down or east side of the line, normally occupied by one or two coaches, and then followed a straight course to cross Holton Road underbridge No. 1 at 0 miles 14 chains, constructed of Suffolk White bricks supporting a girder span over the road leading from Halesworth to Blythburgh, situated alongside but separate from GER double line underbridge No 465. The railway then continued parallel to the GER main line for a short distance before swinging away to the south-east and passing over the two-arch Bird's Folly underbridge No. 2 at 0 miles 30 chains, where the planned but never constructed connection to a siding by the River Blyth was to pass beneath the main line by the eastern arch of the structure; the proposed junction being located at 0 miles 33 chains from Halesworth. The narrow gauge line then continued to the east on a 16 chains radius curve before following a straight section, passing the trailing connection leading to the ballast siding at **Bird's Folly** at 0 miles 39 chains; the land for this was purchased in 1904, the junction constructed in July 1906 and the SR Halesworth engine shed constructed of asbestos sheeting on timber framing was built in 1914. The building provided accommodation for the company's fourth locomotive as there was insufficient space in the shed at Southwold. The points leading to the siding were released by Annett's key attached to the Halesworth to Blythburgh single line Train Staff, whilst the connection to the engine shed was formed from an extension of the former trap points. No fixed signals were provided on the main single line to protect the points. In the

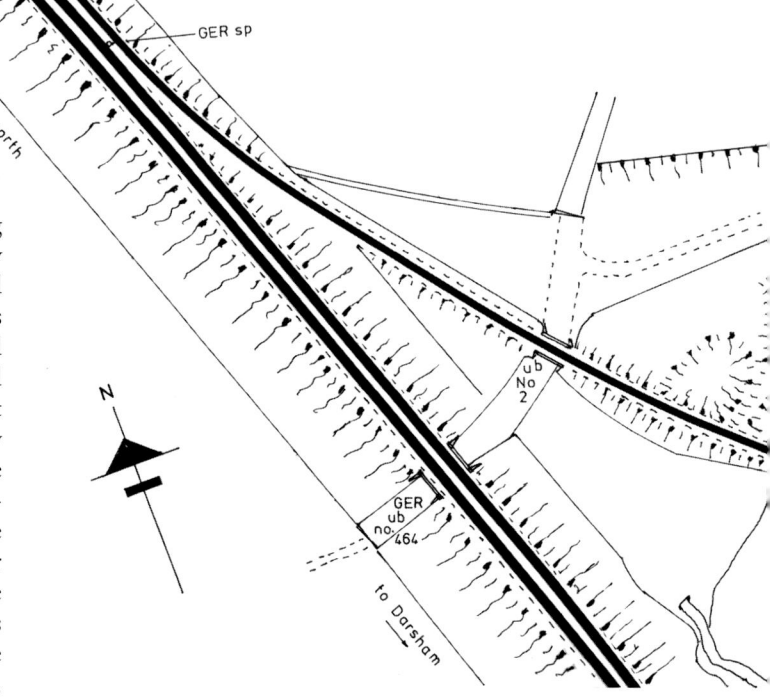

LEFT: Holton Road underbridge No. 1 at 0 miles 14 chains spanned the Halesworth to Holton/Southwold road and being several yards east of the main line bridge gave the SR management ample opportunity to advertise their railway to passengers travelling on the East Suffolk line. This 1930s view facing towards Halesworth station shows the goods yard road entrance on the left. *R. Shephard*

ABOVE: Once over Holton Road underbridge No. 1 at 0 miles 14 chains the SR ran on an embankment shared with the GER East Suffolk main line before diverging to the east near the Up advance starting signal in the distance. In this 1930s view the SR line is barely discernible in the undergrowth. *R. Shephard*

ABOVE: Holton Road underbridge No. 1 was still in place when this photograph was taken in 1945. *Author's collection*

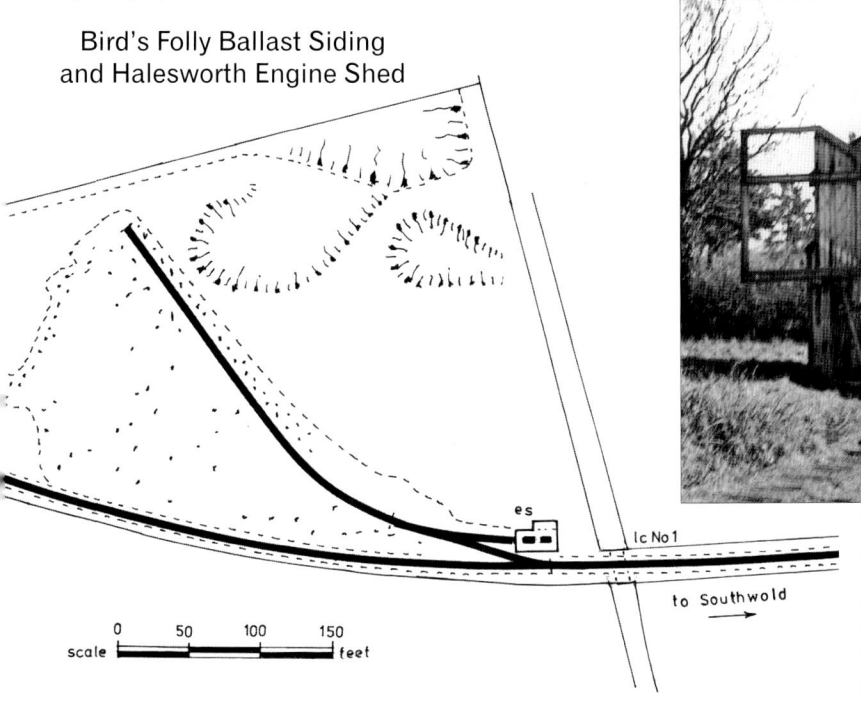

Bird's Folly Ballast Siding and Halesworth Engine Shed

The derelict Halesworth engine shed, with half its timbers missing, in 1939. The points leading from the main single line to Bird's Folly ballast pit siding and engine shed are to the right. 2-4-0T No. 3 *Blyth* stands awaiting its fate within the building. Note the locomotive inspection pit located half in and half out of the shed – similar to the pit at Southwold shed. *Dr I.C. Allen*

absence of locomotive coaling and watering facilities at Halesworth station a tap was provided adjacent to the shed to top up side tanks as well as a chain pump to raise water from the adjacent well, whilst six hods of coal were kept by the workbench in the rear of the shed as an emergency supply.

Beyond the siding connection the railway continued on a straight course away from the environs of Halesworth, bisecting three occupational crossings and entered meadowland and the valley of the River Blyth. Soon after the three-quarter mile post the line negotiated short left and right curves before crossing a culvert by

ABOVE: A full tail load of five coaches, luggage van and an open wagon are well within the capabilities of 2-4-2T No. 1 *Southwold* as the locomotive gets into its stride on the outskirts of Halesworth with the 3.40pm train to Southwold on 3rd July 1920. Permanent way staff have been busy cutting back the undergrowth on this section of line to prevent unnecessary lineside fires but have left the spoils of their work in heaps by the track, possibly for use as cattle or horse fodder. *LCGB/Ken Nunn*

RIGHT: Close up of a section of timber underbridge No. 6 at 1 mile 63 chains where the railway crossed a short length of canal built to by-pass Wenhaston Mill after closure of the line on 20th November 1939. The third lock above the tidal waters of the River Blyth was nearby. *Author's collection*

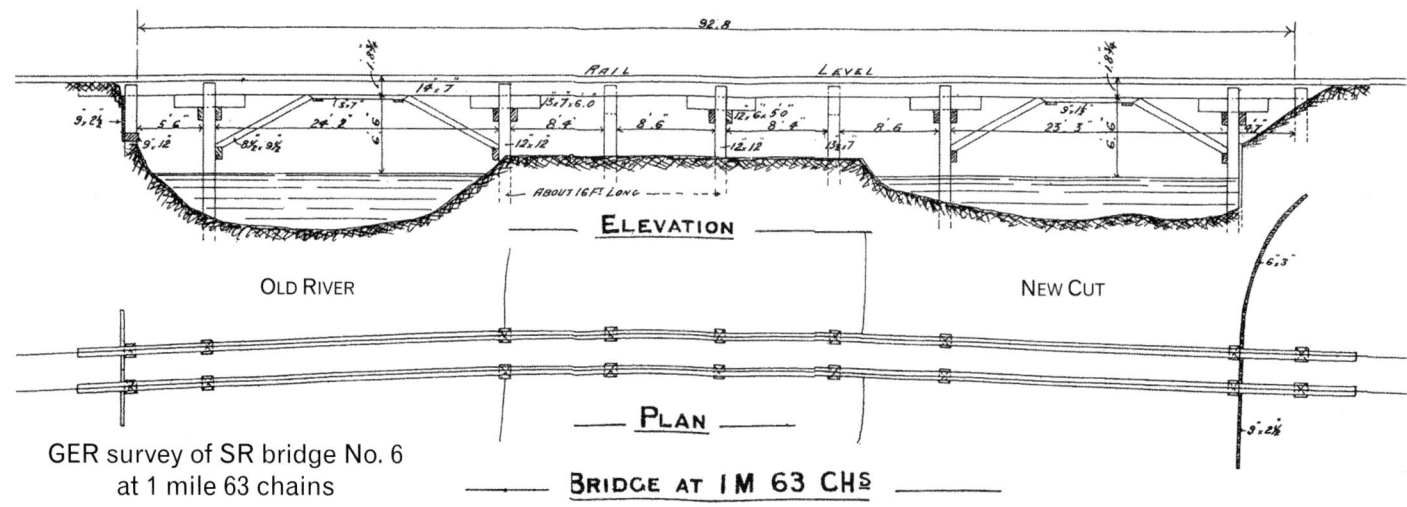

GER survey of SR bridge No. 6 at 1 mile 63 chains

underbridge No. 3 at 1 mile 00½ chain and passing south of the village of Holton St. Peter, which lay astride the parallel road on the Down side of the railway. The line then passed over Corner Farm occupational crossing No. 7 at 1 mile 19 chains; the farm being north of the line, and under Corner Farm Bridge No. 4 also known as Balls Bridge or Mells at 1 mile 22½ chains, a brick and lattice girder structure carrying the road from Holton to Mill Heath and Wenhaston. The railway continued on a short straight section followed by a left-hand curve past the 1½ mile post before negotiating a 25 chains radius right-hand curve to pass over a culvert by underbridge No. 5 at 1 mile 56½ chains and flood opening by underbridge No. 5A at 1 mile 58 chains. Two timber underbridges – No. 6 River Blyth and New Cut at 1 mile 63 chains, and No. 7 Mill Leat at 1 mile 65 chains – took the railway over the waterway and mill pond. Beyond the bridges the line curved to the left skirting the grounds of Wenhaston Water Mill on the Down side and bisecting the associated occupational crossing No. 12 at 1 mile 72¼ chains.

Immediately beyond the crossing on the Down side was **Wenhaston Mill** siding, 55 feet in length, served by points giving a trailing connection for Down trains and located 1 mile 74 chains from Halesworth. Only trains travelling in the Down direction served the siding. The points were protected by a signal with arms for both directions of travel mounted on the same post, which when clear indicated the points were correctly set for the main single line. The 'Patent Locking Box' freeing the connection, catch points and signals were released by Annett's key attached to the Train Staff. This siding was also known as Kett's siding, after the tenant of the mill.

ABOVE: Underbridge No. 6 is seen looking north; the footbridge over the new cut is on the left, with a lock for boat access to the higher river level to the left of that. *Southwold Museum*

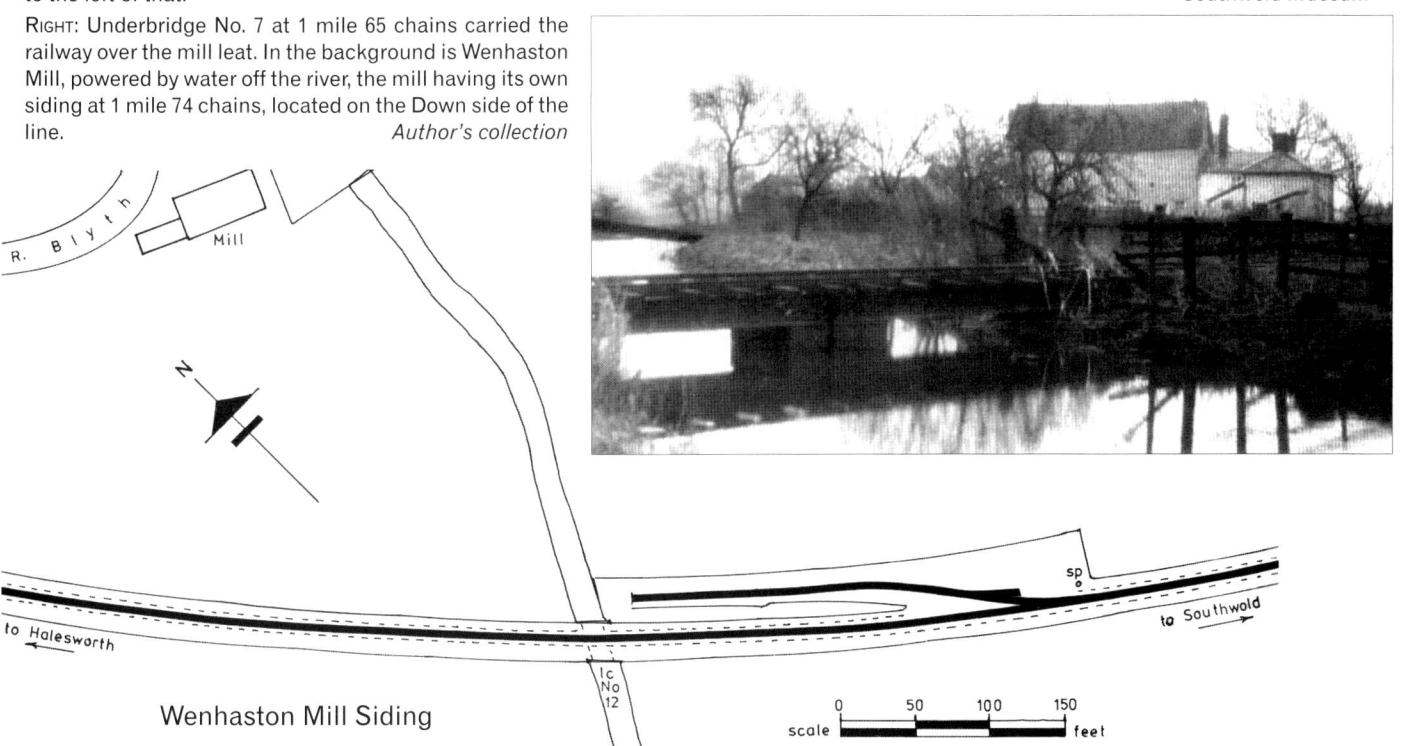

RIGHT: Underbridge No. 7 at 1 mile 65 chains carried the railway over the mill leat. In the background is Wenhaston Mill, powered by water off the river, the mill having its own siding at 1 mile 74 chains, located on the Down side of the line. *Author's collection*

Wenhaston Mill Siding

The only public level crossing on the SR No. 17 was immediately west of Wenhaston station where the road from Wenhaston to Blyford bisected the line and the Blyth Valley. Looking north, the wicket gates on the left were provided for pedestrians who were impatient for the road barriers to open after the passing of a train. Along the road a cart has negotiated the ford through the River Blyth, although a footbridge was provided for cyclists and those on foot.
Author's collection

Wenhaston station, 2 miles 51½ chains from Halesworth, from the level crossing facing towards Southwold. The station master stands on the platform located on the Up or south side of the railway. The platform is boarded in front of the station building and has gravelled surface beyond. To the left are the sidings serving the goods shed and yard, whilst in the background stop signals for each direction of travel are mounted on the same post.
Author's collection

**Wenhaston Station:
Original Track Layout**

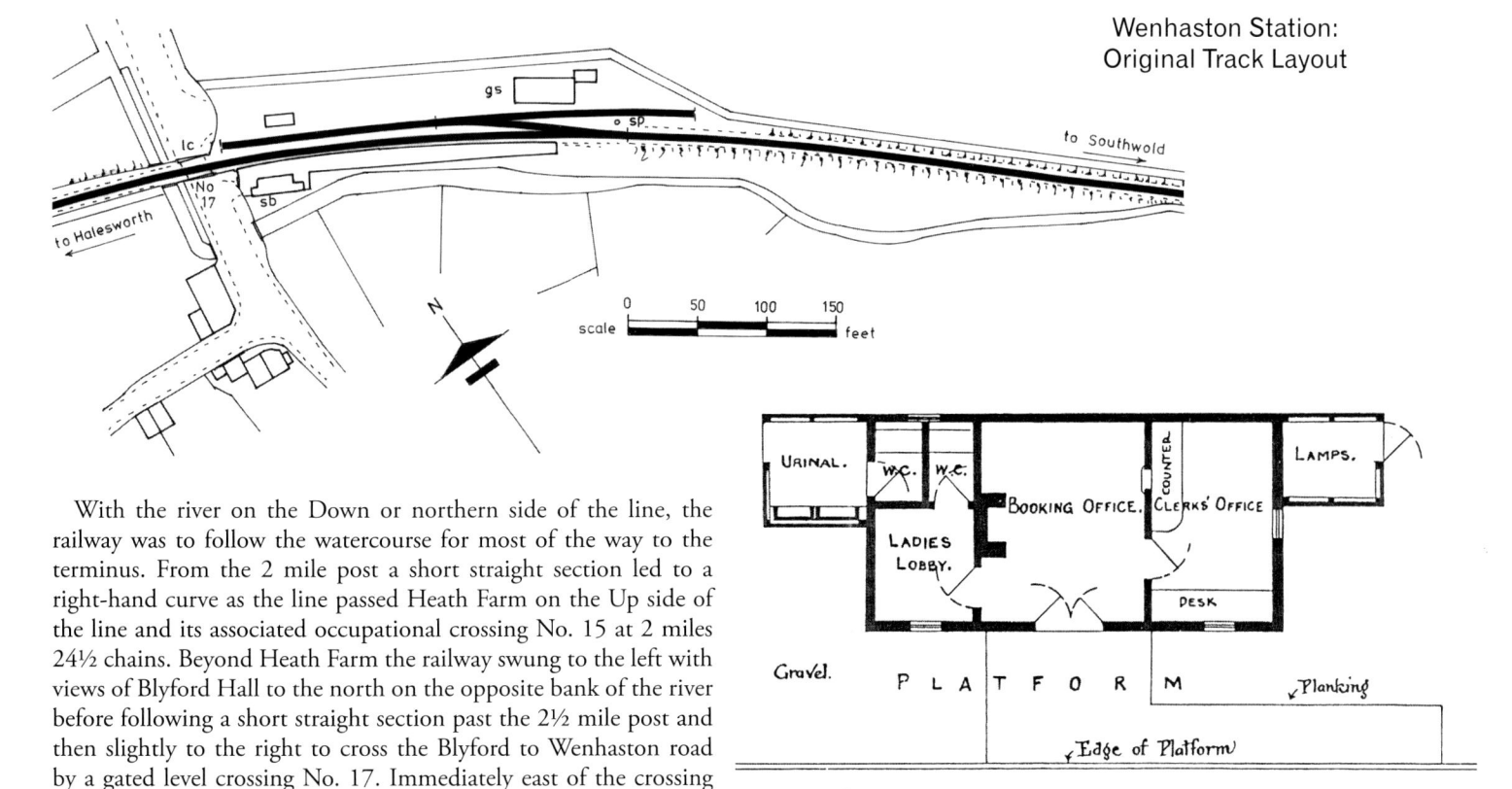

GER survey of Wenhaston station building
(elevation is similar to Blythburgh station)

With the river on the Down or northern side of the line, the railway was to follow the watercourse for most of the way to the terminus. From the 2 mile post a short straight section led to a right-hand curve as the line passed Heath Farm on the Up side of the line and its associated occupational crossing No. 15 at 2 miles 24½ chains. Beyond Heath Farm the railway swung to the left with views of Blyford Hall to the north on the opposite bank of the river before following a short straight section past the 2½ mile post and then slightly to the right to cross the Blyford to Wenhaston road by a gated level crossing No. 17. Immediately east of the crossing the railway entered **Wenhaston** (for Blyford and Bramford) station, 2 miles 51½ chains from Halesworth, with its low single 230 feet long platform on the south or Up side of the line. The station was situated at the foot of a hill between the villages of Wenhaston to the south and Blyford to the north, and the level crossing to the west of the station was the only public road crossing on the line protected by gates. Separate wicket gates were provided for pedestrians too impatient to wait for the road gates to be opened. In the local guidebook Wenhaston was shown as six and a half miles from Southwold, with a 14th century church dedicated to St. Peter in which during restoration a remarkable picture of the 'Doom' or 'Last Judgement' was discovered. The Doom is a painting on wood with Heaven and Hell, saints and demons, popes, cardinals and kings. It is considered unique and a wonderful specimen of fifteenth-century art. The ruins of Mells chapel and Mill Heath were 1½ miles and ½ mile distant respectively. Some very good fishing was available close to the station above Wenhaston Lock, where the Blyth ceased to be tidal, and fishing tickets were available from the station master. The station buildings at Wenhaston were located at the back of the gravel covered platform; they were constructed of brick and timber, with corrugated iron roof, and contained a gentlemen's toilet and urinal, ladies lobby and toilet, booking hall, booking office and lamp room. The station, as with all on the line, owed much similarity to buildings on the standard gauge Culm Valley light railway between Tiverton Junction and Hemyock in Devon, with which A.C. Pain was associated. Two sidings with points in the trailing direction for Down trains 190 feet in length, with 170 feet headshunt, completed the initial track layout; later a second siding was installed at the west end of the yard. A storage shed measuring 40 feet by 15 feet completed the amenities. Originally the station was equipped with a single signal post bearing arms for each direction of travel but in 1921 a connection was provided at the Halesworth end of the layout to obviate the necessity to bring trains travelling in the Up direction from running beyond the signal to attach wagons. The station was then protected by stops signals for each direction of travel, with the arms mounted on single posts located on the approach to the loop.

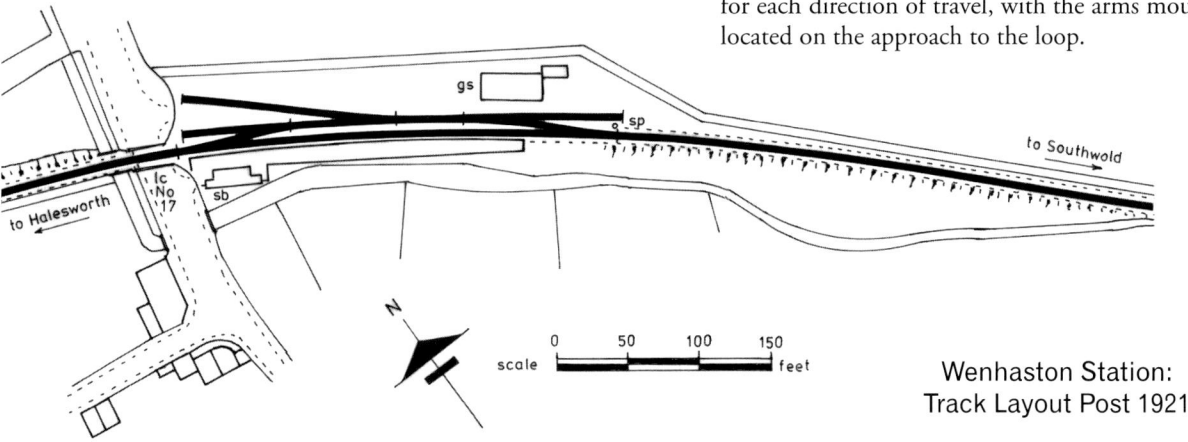

**Wenhaston Station:
Track Layout Post 1921**

A posed view of a train at Wenhaston station used on many postcards. 2-4-2T No. 1 *Southwold* stands at the platform with a Down mixed train whilst passengers and staff attend to loading and unloading at the west end of the station. The white post on the left at the back of the platform supported an oil lamp for night-time illumination. *John Alsop collection*

LEFT: Wenhaston station from the Blyford Road, with the houses and cottages of the village beyond the railway. Level crossing No. 17 at 2 miles 49½ chains is prominent to the right. The Lipton's Tea enamel sign on the platform rather overshadows the station nameboard. *Author's collection*

RIGHT: 2-4-0T No. 3 *Blyth* entering Wenhaston with an Up train. *Author's collection*

BELOW: The 5.23pm Southwold to Halesworth train entering Wenhaston hauled by 2-4-2T No. 1 *Southwold* on 3rd July 1920. The train is formed of two 6-wheel wagons, a 4-wheel wagon, the two parcel vans and five of the six coaches owned by the company, the leading coach being No. 6, recently returned from rebuilding. The Up signal has been cleared to allow the train into the platform and advised the driver the road is clear to Halesworth. *Author's collection*

An Up train from Southwold approaching Wenhaston and passing the solitary signal with the Up direction arm lowered to allow the train into the station. The Down arm to the left of the post was lowered when the line was clear for a Down train to proceed to Blythburgh. Note the lamp and spectacle at the lower position on the post. The permanent way department are using part of the goods yard for the storage of sleepers.

John Alsop collection

THE ROUTE DESCRIBED 121

Blythburgh station, 4 miles 71 chains from Halesworth, was not completed when the railway opened for traffic and was eventually opened in December 1879. This view facing towards Southwold shows the timber frame brick infill station building on the gravel covered platform with sleeper revetment. The main single line passes under bridge No. 11 carrying the London to Yarmouth road over the railway. The siding to the left occupied by an open wagon served the goods shed and goods loading platform provided in 1881. Note the timber cladding on the platform to the right and the sleeper crossing in the foreground provided to enable ease of trans-shipment of heavy items between the platform and the goods yard.
Southwold Museum

Away from Wenhaston the single line initially swung on a 40 chains radius right-hand curve to follow a southeasterly direction running alongside the rushes and foliage of the River Blyth, passing over two culverts by underbridges No's 8 and 9 at 2 miles 64 chains and 2 miles 69½ chains respectively. The railway then swung to the left to follow a straight section to the 3 mile post after which a long arcing right-hand curve took the railway past farm cottages on the edge of Blower's Common on the Up side of the line. Shallow left and right curves carried the line over a succession of occupational crossings and a footpath before the railway passed Beaumur Farm,

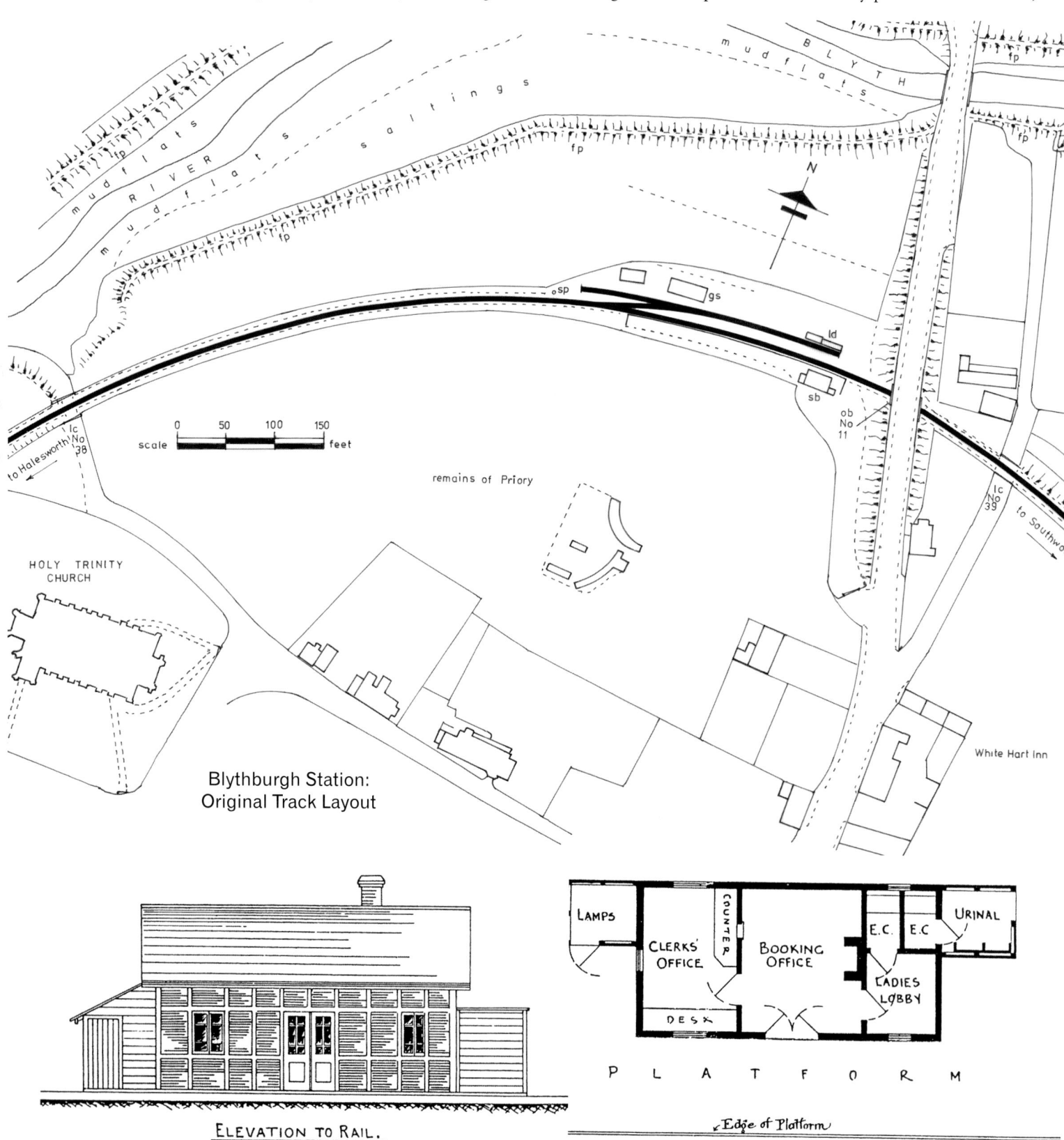

Blythburgh Station: Original Track Layout

GER survey of Blythburgh station building

also on the Up side with distant views of Wenhaston Hall away to the right on higher ground. As the imposing tower of Holy Trinity Church, Blythburgh came into view the line curved initially to the east – bisecting three footpath crossings to pass the 4 mile post and running parallel to Wenhaston Lane, the Blackheath to Blythburgh road, near Young's Bridge – and then to the north parallel to the main London to Yarmouth road, later A12, and the closer Church Lane, with Fen Cottages on the Up side. The railway then swung to the east on a 10 chains radius right-hand curve round the foot of the hill on which the church and village of Blythburgh were sited, and where the outer or north rail was raised so the canted track tilted the coaches at an alarming angle. The line continued on the embankment above the river before entering **Blythburgh** for Wangford station, 4 miles 71 chains from Halesworth.

Blythburgh station had a brick and timber building on the 230 feet long platform located, like others, on the Up side of the line. A single siding 130 feet in length with a 140 feet headshunt was originally provided on the Down or north side of the single line,

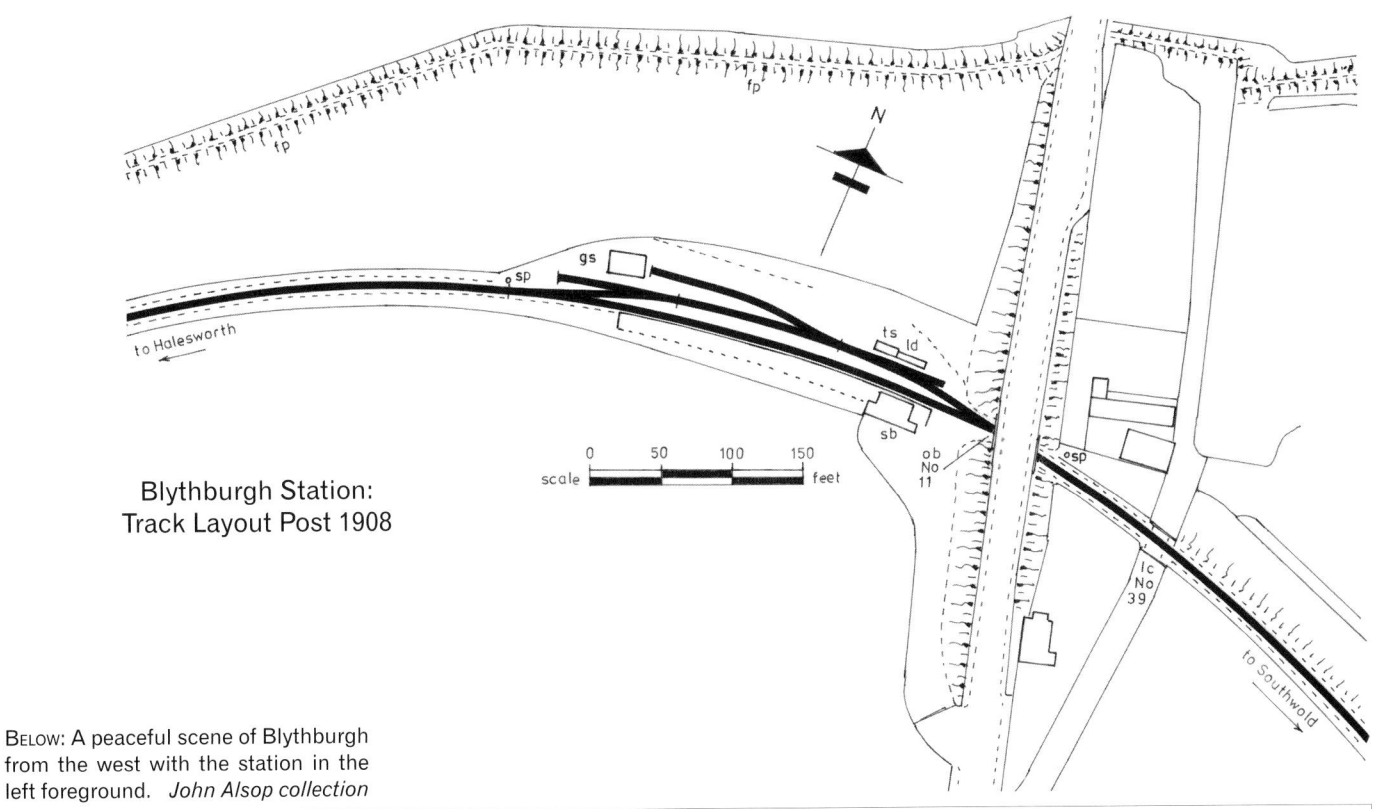

Blythburgh Station:
Track Layout Post 1908

BELOW: A peaceful scene of Blythburgh from the west with the station in the left foreground. *John Alsop collection*

Blythburgh station with 2-4-0T No. 3 *Blyth* at the head of a lengthy train formed of a 6-wheel open wagon sheeted over, two 4-wheel open wagons, a parcels van and five of the six coaches. Although there are milk churns to load the station staff pose for the camera. In the background beyond the station building is overbridge No. 11 carrying the London to Yarmouth road over the railway.

John Alsop collection

Blythburgh station from the over-bridge with a Down train hauled by a 2-4-0T locomotive entering the platform. The view is pre-1908 as the siding to the right has not been converted into a crossing loop but continues to serve a coal merchants store. The timber lean-to building to the left is the lamp store. *Author's collection*

Down train entering Blythburgh. The small loading platform can be seen on the right. Note that by the time this photograph was taken the gravel platform had been replaced by timber
Southwold Museum

CROSS SECTION.

PLAN.

GER survey of loading platform at Blythburgh

accessed by points facing trains in the Down direction, serving the goods shed and yard. An additional siding was installed in 1890 and the original siding extended in 1900. The buffer stops at the eastern end of the siding were removed in 1908 and a connection installed converting it into a loop siding. With the opening of the loop to enable a passenger train to pass a freight train or two freight trains to cross, special instructions were issued giving details of the maximum number of wagons that could be accommodated within the 214 feet clear of the catch rails. A goods loading stage was erected in the yard in 1881 and a second wooden shed erected in the yard. In 1909 the catch points at the eastern end of the loop were removed from directly under the road bridge to a point a few yards west of the structure to obviate derailed vehicles blocking the main single line. In the local guide-book Blythburgh was quoted as five miles distant from Southwold and contained some fine ruins of the once famous Priory of the Augustine foundation, whilst for walkers and ramblers Walberswick Heath and woods were one mile distant from the station.

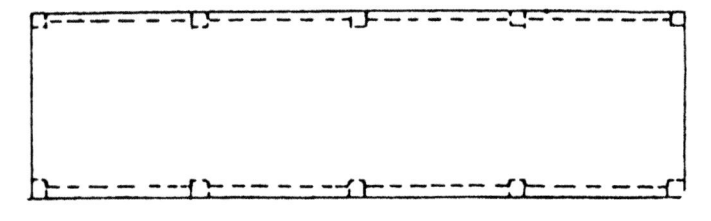

ABOVE: Blythburgh station with a Down train hauled by 2-4-0T No. 3 *Blyth* at the platform. The leading three 4-wheel wagons have sheeted loads with the tarpaulin sheet showing SR ownership. As late as 1929 the company registered a total ownership of 53 of these sheets. The view is post-1908 for in the foreground the run round loop serves the goods shed and goods loading platform. Holy Trinity Church dominates the scene.
Author's collection

ABOVE: An Up train hauled by 2-4-2T No. 1 *Southwold* pulls into the gravel covered platform at Blythburgh station, the driver adjusting the steam braking so that the luggage vans are level with the 17-gallon milk chums awaiting collection for transit to local, Ipswich and London dairies. In the background four 4-wheel wagons stand by the coal storage shed which has a mixture of horizontal and vertical boarding and is still standing. The Up home/Down starting signals on the same post can be seen beyond the road bridge. *Author's collection*

LEFT: The 'signalbox' at Blythburgh was a corrugated iron shed, containing a 5-lever ground frame for operating the Down distant, home and starting signals and Up home and starting signals after the installation of the crossing loop in 1908. The Down home/Up starting signal arms were mounted on the same post east of the station and Up home and Down starting signal arms on the same post west of the station. All points however continued to be operated by weighted levers from the trackside. *Author's collection*

Immediately beyond Blythburgh station the railway passed under the London to Yarmouth road by a girder bridge with brick abutments, No. 11 at 4 miles 72 chains, and curved over level crossing No. 39 before passing mile post 5 to enter the most picturesque section of the route. Running along a narrow embankment above the river the railway, with Lodge Lane on the Up side and Angel Marshes on the Down side, crossed several culverts as it wound initially in a south-south-easterly direction passing reed beds on the Down side and meadow land on the Up side. After straightening out as far as the 5½ mile post the line then negotiated a 12 chains radius left-hand curve to swing east and start climbing through Blythburgh Woods and the Heronry, with its tall pine trees. A right-hand curve led the line past the southern edge of Tinker's Covert on the Down side and Tinker's Walk to the south of the railway.

As river and railway parted company a short right-hand and then left-hand curve over level crossing No. 43 led the line past the southern extremity of Hill Covert and Eastwood. Once through the woodland the railway reached the summit of the line and followed a relatively straight course parallel to the Blythburgh to Walberswick road and Tinker's Walk. After the straight section the line curved slightly to the left through another small area of woodland and past Eastwoodlodge Farm to the south and its attendant occupational level crossing, No. 46 at 6 miles 68½ chains. The long raking curve continued past the 7 mile post as the railway then crossed the open land of Walberswick Common. Heather and gorse were prevalent in season as the line crossed a minor track on Walberswick Cattle Creep concrete underbridge No. 12 at 7 miles 19 chains and swung to the left descending List's Bank and through the shallow List's

ABOVE: Blythburgh station after the track became overgrown, looking towards Southwold. In the background is the London to Yarmouth road bridge No. 11, reconstructed to allow for the possible use of standard gauge rolling stock.
John Alsop collection

LEFT: The western approach to Blythburgh station in 1930 showing the Down home arm and Up starter arm to the left and right of the signal post, both in the clear position. The entry points to the passing loop installed in 1908 are in the foreground, whilst the coal shed is nearest the camera and the goods shed in the distance nearest the road bridge.
Author's collection

A Down train departs from Blythburgh en route to Southwold circa 1920 and crosses occupational crossing No. 39 at 4 miles 75 chains. The view from overbridge No. 11 shows the train from the engine, formed of three 4-wheel wagons with sheeted loads, Composite and full Third coaches in original condition, rebuilt luggage van No. 14 and at the rear 2-plank open wagon No. 9 dating from 1879 conveying a miscellany of items including a perambulator (covered) and a 17-gallon milk churn (probably empty). *Author's collection*

SR occupational crossing No. 42 at 5 miles 49½ chains on the approach to the Heronry protected by the standard 5-bar gate. To allow farm vehicles to cross the line timbers were placed outside and between the rails as well as an additional section of rail on the inside between the running rail and the timbers. View facing towards Southwold. *Author's collection*

ABOVE: A Down train from Halesworth to Southwold formed of two 4-wheel wagons, two coaches, luggage van and a 6-wheel wagon threads its way through the Heronry between Blythburgh and Walberswick. This view was placed on the cover of the SR 48-page timetable published in 1914 priced at 1d. *Ian Pope collection*

ABOVE: A Down train forges up the bank between Blythburgh and Walberswick where the line passed Tinker's Covert and Deadman's Covert near the 6½ mile post. This most densely part of the wooded area was also known as the Heronry. *Author's collection*

RIGHT: With the River Blyth in the background and Scots Firs in the foreground the railway passes close to the Heronry behind fencing. *Author's collection*

No. 1 *Southwold* heads an Up train out of Walberswick and over level crossing No. 50 circa 1923, with the River Blyth in the background.
Southwold Museum

Cutting and away from Walberswick village. The List referred to was a gamekeeper living in nearby Ball's Bridge near Corner Farm, Mells.

At the end of the cutting the line entered **Walberswick** station, 7 miles 46 chains from Halesworth, with its single platform on the Up side of the line. The guidebook recorded Walberswick as a charming village, one mile from Southwold, *'an attractive place for the artist, and indeed all who have eyes for quiet beauty'*. The *'old weather stained and ivy-clad church, perhaps the most picturesque ruin of East Suffolk'*, was only a quarter of a mile from the railway, whilst Southwold Harbour was 1½ miles away. Walberswick Common adjoined the station. The low platform, 230 feet in length, was constructed of ballast with timber revetment, whilst the station building containing a urinal, booking office and staff room was constructed of timber. The original small building was replaced by a larger structure in 1902, containing the clerk's office, gentlemen's earth closet, ladies' earth closet, and ladies' waiting room leading from a central area, which had two pairs of double doors leading onto the platform. Despite the improvements and the platform being provided with at least some lamp standards, complaints were made that the station continued to be illuminated by only one oil lamp during the hours of darkness. Improvements were promised. A single siding was originally installed on the Up side behind the platform, but was later replaced by two sidings – initially inner road 130 feet and outer road 180 feet, later 180 feet and 250 feet in length respectively. The siding points released and locked by Annett's key on the Train Staff were also equipped with a catch point to prevent vehicles running away onto the main single line. Unfortunately Walberswick station was located about a mile from the centre of the village, at the end of a minor track, and was the least used on the Southwold Railway. In 1899 local people petitioned the company to move the station to a more convenient position near the road but further from the village. Needless to say, no action was taken.

Walberswick Station: Second Track Layout

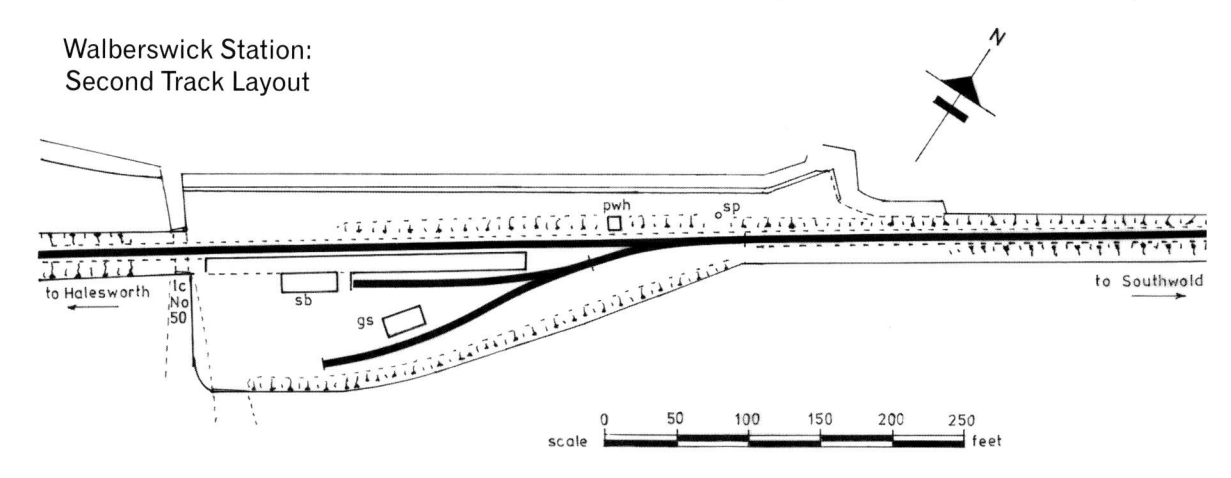

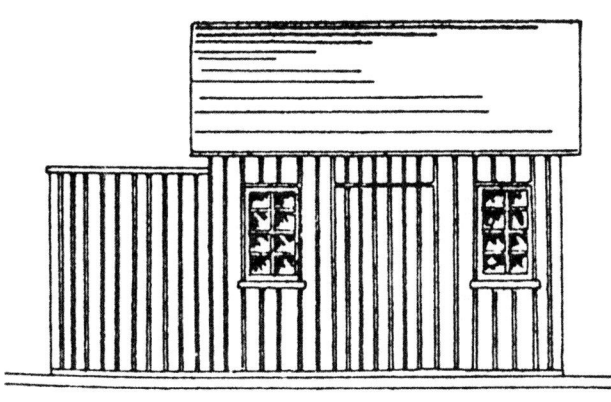

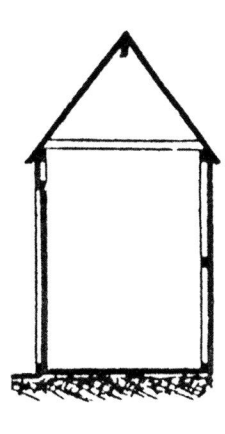

Walberswick station facing towards the Blyth swing bridge and Southwold circa 1902, the year the telephone route was installed but before the station building was rebuilt and fencing placed along the back of the platform, which was gravel surfaced with sleeper revetment facing the track. The station has two platform oil lamps for night-time illumination. The Down and Up stop signals mounted on the same post can be seen by the entry points to the Up side sidings. In both this and a very similar photograph, the lady appears to be patiently waiting her train on the seat provided whilst the porter takes different poses. *Author's collection*

GER survey of the original Walberswick station building

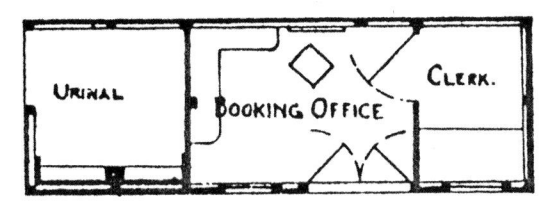

ABOVE: The Walberswick Up signal is lowered for the approaching mid-morning Southwold to Halesworth train as a group of passengers await the oncoming service in 1901. Items of luggage to be loaded on the train include several trunks and a bicycle. The view was taken before the demolition of the original station building whilst in the background the goods shed is adorned with enamel advertisement signs.
Author's collection

UPPER RIGHT: In 1902 the original Walberswick station building was demolished and replaced by a new larger structure. This view facing Southwold shows a pony and trap awaiting passengers from an incoming train – necessary for anybody with a large amount of luggage as the village was a mile distant; the original station nameboard has also been repositioned by the gate. In the foreground is level crossing No. 50 at 7 miles 43¾ chains.
Author's collection

LOWER RIGHT: After the improvements at Walberswick station in 1902 a fence was erected at the back of the platform to prevent passengers straying into the goods yard. A Down train is waiting to depart for Southwold circa 1923 as the leading vehicle is Brake/Composite coach No. 4 which had its First Class compartment rebuilt and ends closed in that year. The new station nameboard is well supported at this exposed location to prevent it blowing down in a high wind.
Author's collection

ABOVE: An early evening view of the rebuilt station building in August 1927, complete with a lamp-stand at each end. On the platform a boy is examining a barrel with his parents and there is a sack barrow outside the closed double doors
Author's collection

RIGHT: Detail from a very similar picture to the earlier photograph of Walberswick station in 1902. The lady continues to patiently await her train on the additional seat provided, apparently oblivious to the antics of the porter and photographer. *Author's collection*

From Walberswick the railway followed a straight course on a shallow embankment with the river gradually encroaching on the Down side and Squire's Hill on the Up side, with distant views of Walberswick village. Descending gradually and then rising, the railway continued on the embankment to cross the **River Blyth** on the swing bridge No. 13 at 7 miles 74½ chains from Halesworth. The approach to the swing bridge over the River Blyth was the steepest on the line at a gradient of 1 in 53/66. The original swing bridge with a span of 146 feet was of wrought iron bow-string girder construction, the turning centre being on a wrought iron cylinder. The swinging part centrally swivelled on a caisson equidistant from the second and third pairs of original supports. The fixed main span was 73 feet 6 inches. The approach openings were of timber construction on timber piles sunk into the river.

Although the authorities insisted on the provision of the swing bridge it was seldom opened, as the maritime traffic was almost non-existent, part blame being attributed to the obstruction of the channel by the central pier. The Blyth Navigation ceased operation in 1884 and thereafter the bridge was seldom opened save for testing. However, the opening span of the bridge was rebuilt in 1907 as part of the widening programme; the fixed span being replaced in 1914. The vibrations of the train as it crossed the river reminded passengers it was time to gather their belongings as they were approaching the end of the journey. Those still gazing from the windows of the carriages would have seen barges unloading at the neighbouring quay and the fishing smacks moored in the river, awaiting their next call to the sea.

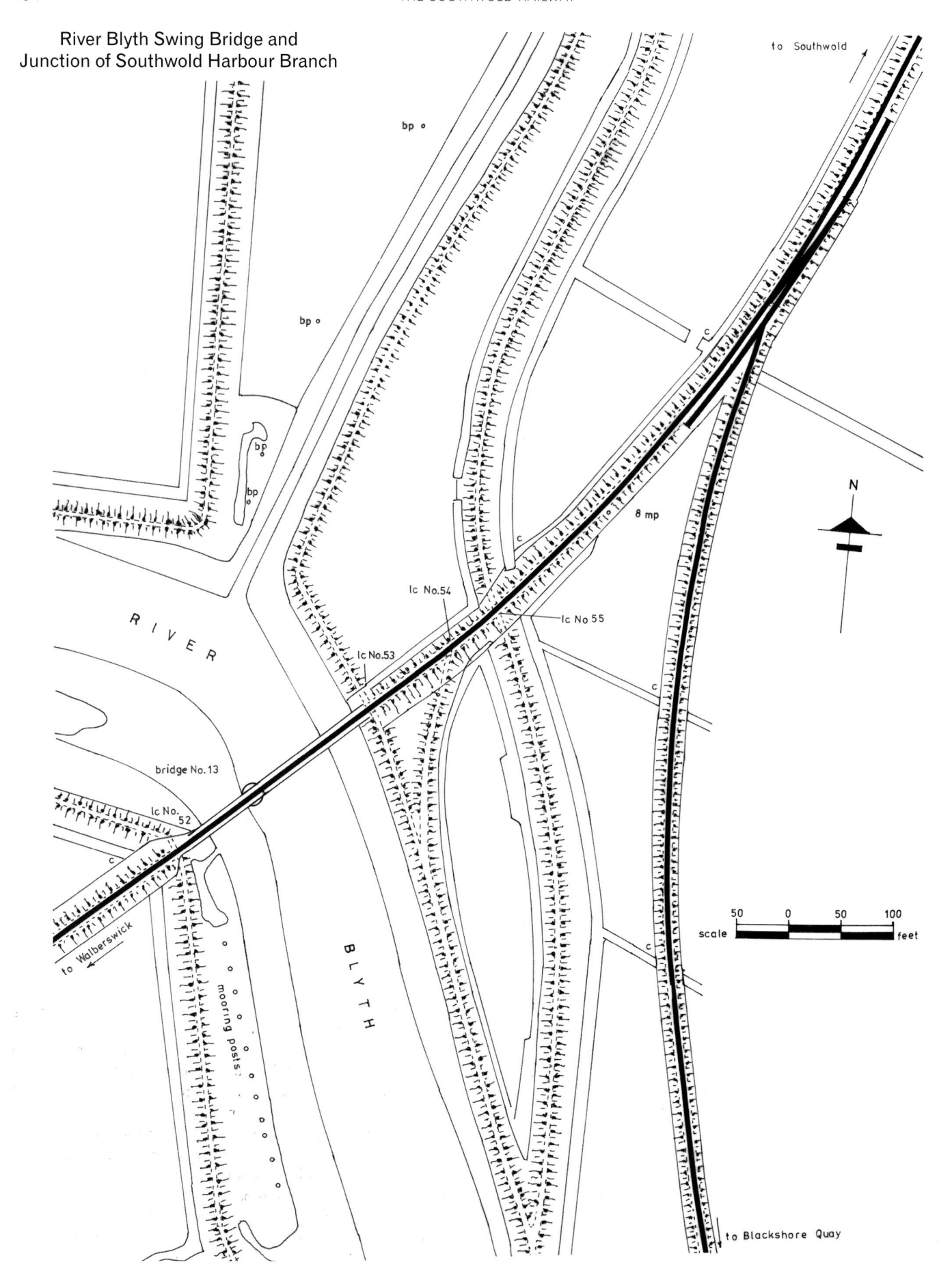

River Blyth Swing Bridge and Junction of Southwold Harbour Branch

A Down train from Halesworth to Southwold hauled by a 2-4-0T runs onto the original bow string girder bridge across the River Blyth between Walberswick and Southwold, No. 13 at 7 miles 74½ chains from Halesworth with an opening span of 146 feet. *John Alsop collection*

An Up train formed of a 2-4-0T locomotive, a 6-wheel open wagon, the two luggage vans and two coaches crossing the Blyth swing bridge, rebuilt in 1907 as part of the possible conversion of the line to standard gauge, and the original fixed span, with the river at low tide. *John Alsop collection*

Although the original bow string girder swing bridge was replaced in 1906/7 by a new structure wide enough to accept standard gauge, the fixed span on the right had to wait until 1914 for modification. The span was considered a 'white elephant', for between 1879 and 1894 it was only opened on one occasion for operational purposes, other than once a year for maintenance checks. These annual checks continued until the line closed but the bridge was again opened on one occasion in 1911 for shipping to pass through. *John Alsop collection*

Beyond the bridge the railway descended at 1 in 53 and 1 in 66 passing the 8 mile post swinging to the left to follow an east-north-east course, from where the connection to the **Harbour Branch** made a trailing connection on the Up side of the line. This siding had a short headshunt running parallel to the main line. The single track Harbour Branch swung sharply to the left initially on a 6 chains radius curve descending at 1 in 66 to level out and run parallel with the eastern bank of the river. The line crossed the road from Southwold Common by an ungated level crossing, bridging ditches on each side of the road by several culverts. Running behind the waterfront houses the branch made a trailing junction to the connection to Blackshore Quay before terminating at a buffer post by the harbour, 1 mile from the junction with the main line and just short of the Walberswick ferry terminal. At the harbour was a siding incorporating facing and trailing points to form a run round loop, a shed constructed of asbestos sheeting and a second-hand Pooley weighbridge built for standard gauge but adapted for the Southwold 3 feet gauge by the insertion of a third rail. The original branch authorised in the 1876 Act envisaged a single line from a point immediately north of the swing bridge and running between the riverbank and the waterfront houses. The only recorded working of a passenger coach across the Harbour Branch was at the time of the BOT inspection by Colonel Druitt on 25th September 1917.

After the Blyth swing bridge the line descended at 1 in 53/66 passing the 8 mile post on the right or Up side. The railway then levelled out, indicated by the gradient post on the left, with Busscreek marshes on the Down side and Wood's End marshes on the Up or south side, before climbing through the cutting bisecting Southwold Common and the golf course. From 1914 a trailing connection with headshunt was located on the Up side beyond the 8 mile post to serve the branch to Blackshore Quay and Southwold Harbour. *Southwold Museum*

ABOVE LEFT: The abandoned Harbour Branch and goods shed in the 1930s with the track much overgrown. *Author's collection*
ABOVE RIGHT: The harbour branch weighbridge with the weighing mechanism housed inside the asbestos clad building. The weighing platform was standard gauge and purchased second hand so an intermediate rail was added to accommodate the 3 feet gauge. The goods shed is in the background. *Author's collection*

ABOVE: An exceptional high tide at Southwold Harbour in 1936 revealed traces of the branch in the foreground leading to the weighbridge hut. The weighbridge was a second hand standard gauge piece of equipment, so to serve SR requirements a third rail was inserted to ensure 3 feet gauge rolling stock could use the facility.
Author's collection

Remains of rails on the Harbour Branch in 1998.
ABOVE: The back of the stop block.
RIGHT: Facing the stop block. The area has become subject to frequent flooding during high tides.

Top: A Down mixed train climbs the 1 in 70 through the cutting near Southwold Common on the approach to the terminus in 1927. The cutting was spanned by a footbridge provided in 1902/3 for the use of golfers on the adjacent Southwold golf course and as a right of way. The western end of the cutting was widened as part of preliminary works for the abortive conversion to standard gauge. *Author's collection*

Middle: Footbridge No 14, at 8 miles 25 chains from Halesworth, spanning the cutting on the approach to Southwold station was built in 1902/3 to provide access between the two sections of Southwold golf course as well as provide public right of way across the Common. The golf club contributed £50 towards the cost of construction. This view facing the terminus is dated 10th July 1911. *LCGB/Ken Nunn*

Right: The footbridge connecting both sides of Southwold golf course and the Common was quite narrow, with steps at each end of the structure. Here Miss A.M. and Master F.H. Jenkins face the camera to record the details of the bridge for posterity. The decking appears to be concrete slabbing and the rails fabricated from wrought iron or steel.

Author's collection

Southwold Station:
Original Track Layout

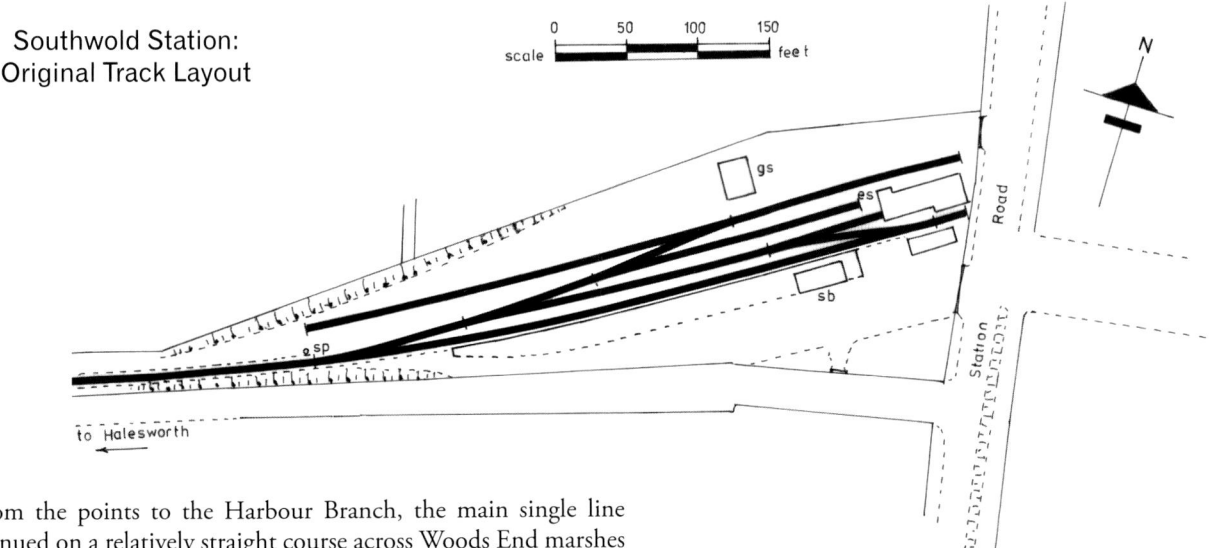

From the points to the Harbour Branch, the main single line continued on a relatively straight course across Woods End marshes on the Up side and Busscreek marshes on the Down side before climbing at 1 in 70 through a deep cutting on a 25 chains radius right-hand curve. The cutting was spanned by a footbridge, No. 14, built in 1902/3 at 8 miles 25 chains from Halesworth, which was provided for the use of golfers on the adjacent golf course. At the western end the cutting was widened at its lowest part as preliminary work for conversion to standard gauge. Some ballast was also removed from this section to replace the ballast lost in the floods of 1894 and 1897. Emerging from the cutting the line levelled out and continued on a straight section, with Buss Creek still away on the Down side of the line and the open land of Southwold Common and the golf course on the Up side. A signal on the Down side heralded the approach to the throat of **Southwold** for Reydon and Wrentham station, and the headquarters of the railway, where the buffer stops were 8 miles 63 chains from Halesworth, located on the west side of the main road into town, appropriately named Station Road. The single platform on the Up or south side of the single main line was host to the station buildings constructed of brick and timber. The 300 feet long platform was initially formed of gravel with a sleeper revetment but the surface was later of timber and finally finished with tarmacadam. Unusually, three horse chestnut trees were planted in a row along the space between the station building and the carriage shed. The original station building was small; in 1895 the waiting room was enlarged and a new booking office and lamp room constructed. Fifteen years later, on 21st September 1910 authority was given for a new ladies' and gentlemen's toilets, whilst W.H. Smith was provided with a new bookstall at the same time. Each rebuilding altered the exterior fascia of the building. Electric lighting was installed in 1905. Other buildings at the terminus included the engine shed, carpenter's repair shed, paint shed, lamp shed and Manager's office, latterly occupied by Henry Ward. Initially there were three sidings at Southwold, located on the Down side of the line: one which formed the run round loop and led to the engine shed, a second parallel siding, and the outside road which had a head shunt at the western end. In 1896 the company acquired additional land to the north of these sidings, which enabled the yard to be extended and enlarged. A new set of facing points was located further west and the run round loop was extended to a length of 540 feet, whilst another connection led to the head shunt of the outside road and formed another extended siding. A facing connection also left the main single line on the Up side and ran to the back of the platform forming a 200 feet long bay, which was protected by catch points. The end of this siding was later covered to form a carriage shed, the upright stanchions consisting of old flat bottom rails. This shed was provided in stages between 1903 and 1904, measuring 40 feet by 14 feet 4 inches, it had six pairs of uprights giving five 8-feet bays, three with sash

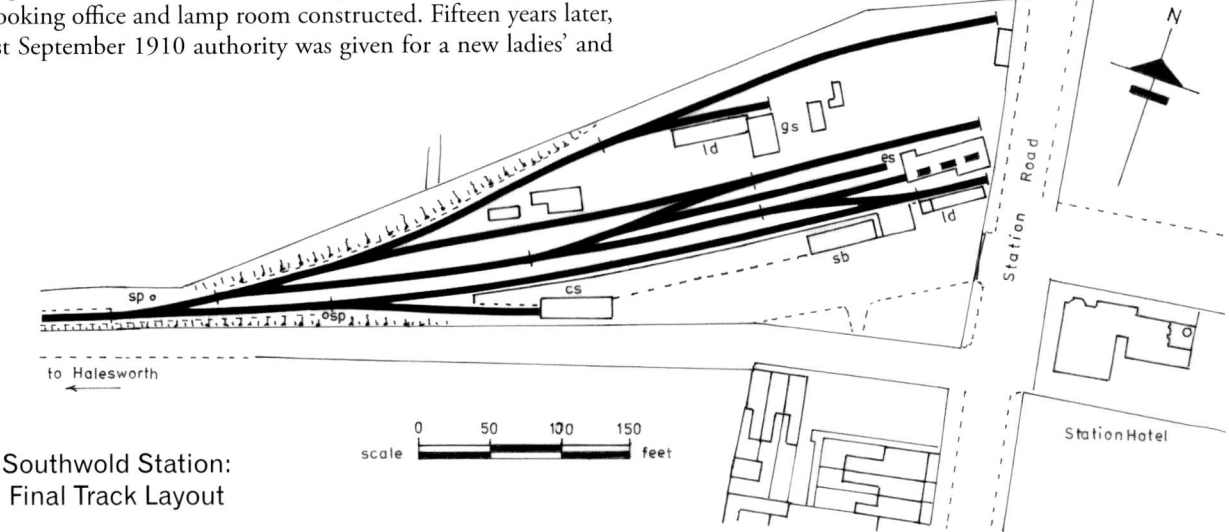

Southwold Station:
Final Track Layout

140 — THE SOUTHWOLD RAILWAY

1927. SOUTHWOLD OLD RAILWAY STATION JUNE 1920

Aerial view of Southwold station in 1920 with the Station Hotel dating from 1900 and the Southwold Hosiery premises dating from 1909 to the left. The station and goods yard covered a considerable acreage but suffered from being located away from the centre of the town.

Ian Pope collection

LEFT: A Down train from Halesworth hauled by 2-4-2T No. 1 *Southwold* approaching the terminus and passing the Southwold inner home signal in the off position, permitting the train into the platform. The connection in the foreground leads to the carriage shed whilst the run round loop and goods yard sidings are to the right. The train is formed of a 4-wheel wagon with tarpaulin covered load, two passenger coaches in cream/white livery and a van behind them. *Author's collection*

ABOVE: Manning, Wardle 0-6-2T No. 4 *Wenhaston* approaches Southwold with a Down train and is passing the outer signal which, as well as bearing the Down outer home and Up advance starting signal arms, also carried a short shunt arm which when lowered authorised movements into the goods yard. The signal oil lamp is at the base of the post near the weighted point lever. The company generously provided a small wooden hut, which appears to have been rotatable to allow it to be faced out of the wind, for the railwayman operating the signal at this exposed location.
Author's collection

RIGHT: Inner signal at Southwold facing towards the station. The left hand arm is the Down inner home signal giving the driver authority to take his train into the platform. The other arm is the Up starting signal; both were interlocked with the points, which were operated by weighted lever.
Author's collection

GER Survey of Southwold Station Building
(Before extensions were made)

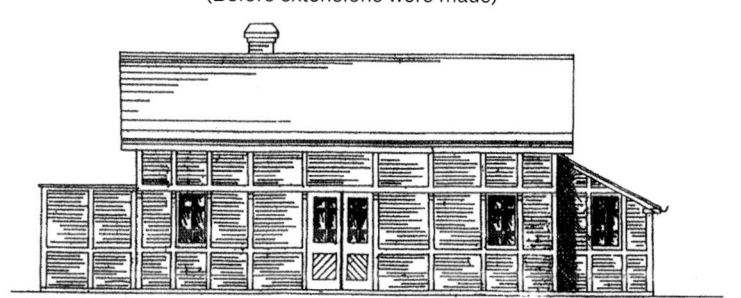

ELEVATION TO RAIL.

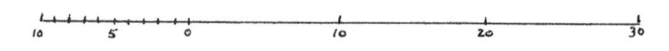

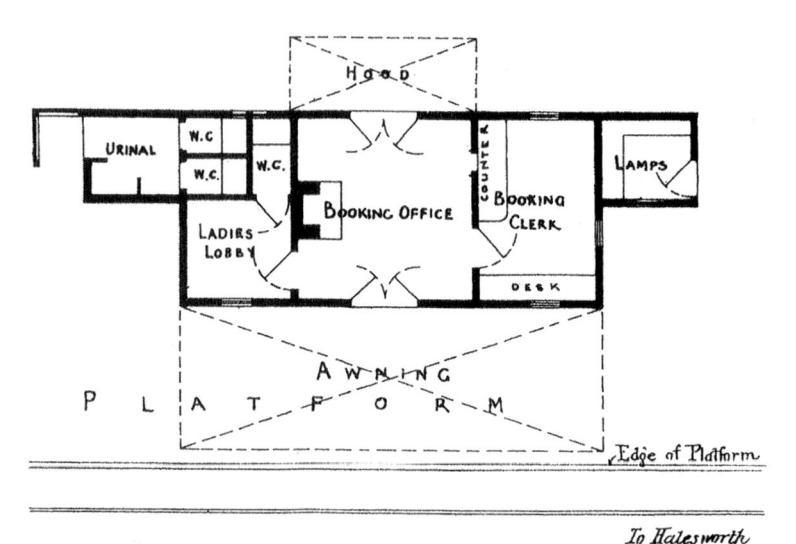

PLAN OF BOOKING OFFICE ETC.

GER Survey of Southwold Engine Shed

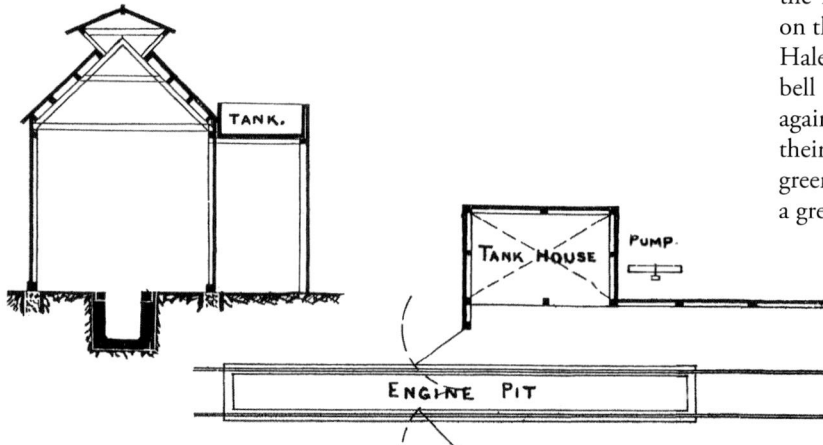

windows and the fourth with a door with the station sign above it, the sign taking up most of one bay and measuring 6 feet by 2 feet; the cladding was probably corrugated iron and the height of the building was estimated at 12 feet.

Southwold was described as:

> 'The Gem of the East Coast, a pretty seaside town, standing on a bold cliff and commanding and extensive views of the North Sea. The climate is most healthy and invigorating, it is appropriately termed "Sunny Southwold". There are miles of golden sands, also an extensive Common. The scenery around Southwold is exceptionally pretty, and the walks and drives in the neighbourhood are numerous and interesting to the pedestrian and cyclist, the surrounding district offers many attractions. There is a well-built pier, from which excellent fishing can be obtained. The drainage and water supply are both good. Mixed bathing is allowed. The golf links consisting of 18 holes, and are situated on the Common, which is close to the town and adjoin the station.'

Some four miles south of Southwold was Dunwich, once the capital of East Anglia, the seat of the Court of Kings, and with the Palace of Bishops. In the 12th century it was one of the greatest and most prosperous of English ports with a population of approximately 40,000 souls. The gradual encroachment of the sea for hundreds of years obliterated the town and church of All Saints, a 14th-century structure, was last used for worship in 1774 before slipping under the waves. Thus the travellers, armed with the above knowledge, having arrived and alighted from the narrow gauge train, would climb into the horse drawn station bus to be driven to the various hotels and boarding houses in the town, whilst another vehicle followed with the luggage. They might have stayed at the Station Hotel located opposite the station which was built in 1900, much of the material being conveyed by rail.

The deepest cutting on the line was 20 feet in depth and the highest embankment 12 feet. Distance posts were located every quarter of a mile from a zero point at the buffer stops north of Halesworth station. They were generally sited on the Down side of the railway. Gradient posts were located on the Up side of the line. It was the normal practice at both Halesworth and Southwold for station staff to ring a hand bell five minutes before the train was due to depart, and again at departure time as a warning for passengers to take their seats, followed by the guard signalling to the driver with green flag and whistle, or during the hours of darkness with a green aspect in his oil lamp.

Southwold Railway Station.

Southwold station seen from Station Road. *John Alsop collection*

Summer shadows from the horse chestnut trees fall across 2-4-0T No. 3 *Blyth* as it awaits departure from Southwold. Station staff and engine crew pose for the camera whilst a number of fruit baskets await to be loaded on the train. *John Alsop collection*

BELOW: In this view of Southwold station the carriage shed had its sides filled in with three windows; the nameboard, Southwold for Reydon and Wrentham, is mounted above the side access door. The 2-4-0T, working cab first, is preparing to start with an Up train to Halesworth. Note the electric lighting columns installed in 1905 on the platform. The centre road is the run round loop.
John Alsop collection

Southwold station facing towards the extreme end of the line 8 miles 63 chains from Halesworth in the 1920s. From left to right is the engine shed, which has been re-roofed, the goods shed beyond the end of the platform, which has been turned and extended, the station building and beyond that the Station Hotel dating from 1900. This view taken just before the line closed shows No. 1 *Southwold*, already withdrawn and cannibalized, raised on blocks to the extreme left beyond the wagon. The hotel had been renamed from Station Hotel to Avenue Hotel by 1924.
John Alsop collection

The area outside Southwold shed, with 2-4-2T No. 1 *Southwold* raised on blocks undergoing repairs whilst 2-4-0T No. 3 *Blyth* is being prepared for the road on 12th July 1911.
LCGB/Ken Nunn

ABOVE: Southwold station building was extended at the western end in 1895 and an additional door installed. Enamel advertisements adorn the structure whilst a locomotive is undergoing boiler repairs or maintenance near the engine shed, with the dome cover on the ground. A coach in cream/white livery also appears to be receiving minor attention.
Ian Pope collection

RIGHT: The east end of the station complex at Southwold; the timber engine shed with original full length ventilator is to the left and the goods shed and loading platform to the right. 2-4-0T No. 3 *Blyth* takes water from the water crane alongside the shed. The water crane was unusual in that there was no flexible piping but a rigid angular pipe similar to continental practice. The points leading to the run round loop are in the foreground. The fireman in the foreground is collecting a bucket of coal to replenish the bunker inside the cab.
Author's collection

A visit to Southwold circa 1939 found the engine shed barred and bolted but containing 2-4-0T No. 2 *Halesworth*, 0-6-2T No. 4 *Wenhaston* and luggage van No. 14 rusted to the rails. The water tower has lost most of the planking to the base of the structure whilst the goods shed on the right, which was turned 90 degrees in about 1912, stands beside the derelict loading platform, itself roofed over shortly before closure. The engine shed subsequently blew down in a gale in 1942. *Author's collection*

9

Permanent Way, Signalling and Staff

Permanent Way

The initial permanent way, constructed to a gauge of 3 feet, was laid in accordance with the tracing approved by the Board of Trade on 17th April 1878, and consisted of wrought iron flat bottom rails weighing 30 lbs per yard, resting on rectangular sleepers measuring 6 feet by 6 inches by 3 inches, laid at central intervals of 2 feet 4 inches. The rails were 21 feet in length and fished at the joints with two plates weighing about 5 lbs, the pair fastened with four ½-inch diameter bolts weighing ¼ lb each. There was a sleeper under each joint to which the rails were secured by a clip sole plate, 3 inches wide by $5/16$ inch thick weighing 2 lbs, fastened by two fang bolts ½ inch in diameter and 5 inches in length. Fang bolts and clips were also used on two intermediate sleepers whilst dog spikes, ½ inch square and 4¼ inches in length, formed the remainder of the fastenings. The sleepers were laid on ballast formed of sand and gravel having a depth of 9 inches. There were nine sleepers under each 21-foot length of rail. At every third sleeper was a single clip sole plate, weighing 1.6 lbs each, attached by one fang bolt and one dog spike, ½ inch square and 4¼ inches long. On some of the curves the outer rail was super-elevated. During construction Ransomes & Rapier of Ipswich were sub-contracted to fabricate nineteen sets of points together with two elbow crossings for installation at Halesworth, Wenhaston and Southwold, the equipment being dispatched by 19th August 1879. It is thought some of the rails used on this work had been returned from Southern Formosa after an ill-fated construction by the firm on the 2 feet 6 inch gauge Shanghai & Woosung Railway in China that had opened in 1876; due to annoyance by the Chinese rulers it was closed on 20th October 1877 and dismantled, all infrastructure and rolling stock then being shipped to Takow where it perished. Only the rails, some of which had arrived too late for use on the venture, were saved and returned to Ipswich and reused. After World War One £1,100 was expended on 50 tons of new steel rails which were used on extensive relaying of the curves on Southwold bank and outside Southwold home signal. The 30 lbs per yard flat bottom rails spiked directly to the timber sleepers were also used for the Blackshore Quay Branch and were still in use along the entire railway when Colonel Trench finally inspected the alterations made at Halesworth in 1928.

The ailing finances of the company resulted in ever-increasing cost cutting methods in the final years when many rails were turned to even out wear on the running surface. Some sections of track were removed from sidings and installed on the main line, with the worn track being placed in the sidings. The management were so concerned at the deteriorating condition of the permanent way that in June 1919 instructions were issued to the effect that, to test the condition of the road, once a week each ganger was to ride on the engine over the length of line for which he was responsible.

There were fourteen bridges on the Southwold Railway and the most important and impressive structure was the swing bridge across the River Blyth between Walberswick and Southwold. The opening and closing of the structure required the services of the permanent way staff, usually a ganger with three men. With the Southwold station master in attendance the locking mechanism was unlocked by inserting the Annett's key on the Southwold to Halesworth, later Southwold to Blythburgh and finally Southwold to Walberswick Train Staff. The bridge was initially pushed with one end of a rope attached to the Southwold end of the opening span, whilst the other end was pulled by a lengthman using the rope standing on the river wall on the Walberswick bank. The operation was completed by a

Above: Track bed of the abandoned railway just beyond Bird's Folly siding and Halesworth engine shed looking towards Southwold. Level crossing No. 2 at 0 miles 47 chains is in the foreground.
J.H.L. Adams/Kidderminster Railway Museum

Left: Trap points in the carriage siding at Southwold inserted to prevent runaway vehicles entering the main line.
Michael Whitehouse collection

GER survey of
SR Swing Bridge No. 13
at 7 miles 74½ chains

The rebuilt swing bridge over the River Blyth, No. 13 at 7 miles 74½ chains, on 10th July 1911. Francis Morton & Company Limited of Garston were awarded the contract for the new span in 1906 and completed the work the following year. The river is at low tide. In the background is Walberswick church.

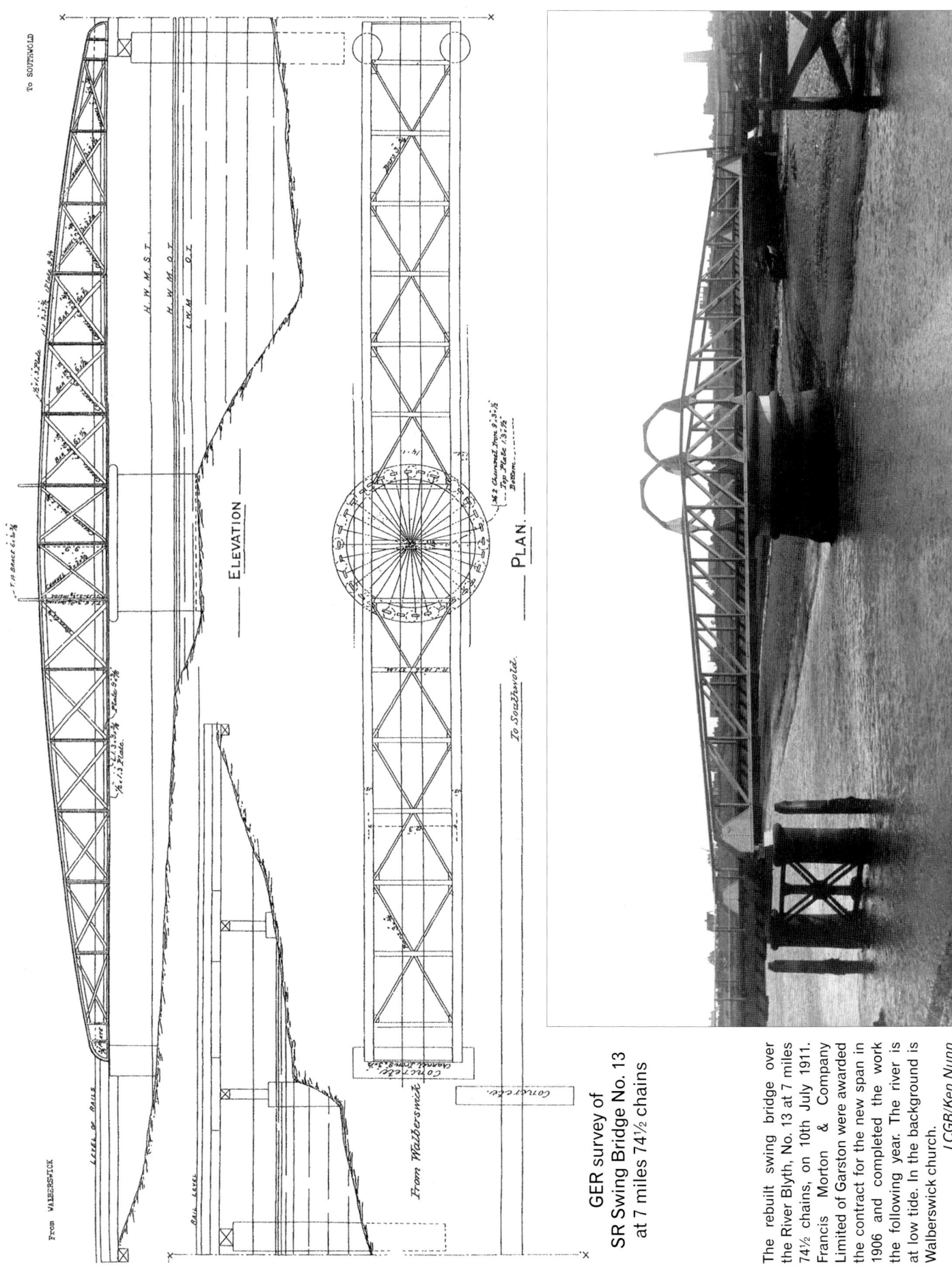

LCGB/Ken Nunn

member of the team in a rowing boat hauling the span for its final movement. The action occupied approximately 20 minutes to complete, as did closure when the operation was completed in reverse. Rule 95 required notice being given by the station master to the Ganger in charge of the length, to open the bridge at the proper time. The ganger in turn was not permitted to remove any wedges, bolts, screws or fastenings on the opening span until the station master was present at the bridge with the Train Staff and key. As soon as any vessel requiring passage had passed up or down stream through the span the ganger was responsible for closing the bridge across the river and properly securing and replacing the wedges and fastenings. Rule 96 stipulated the station master was not to leave the bridge with the Train Staff until the bridge was closed across the river, securely fastened and the mechanism locked, ensuring clear passage for a train to cross the span.

The bridge, with a total span of 146 feet, had a central section of bowstring construction with a pair of brace between the side girders, giving a clear water span of 60 feet and rising to 9 feet 9 inches at the centre, mounted on a central caisson. The approach span were constructed of timber. In 1906/7 the central section was replaced by an angular structure, whilst the approach spans were replaced in 1914 in steel with the Southwold side matching the main span.

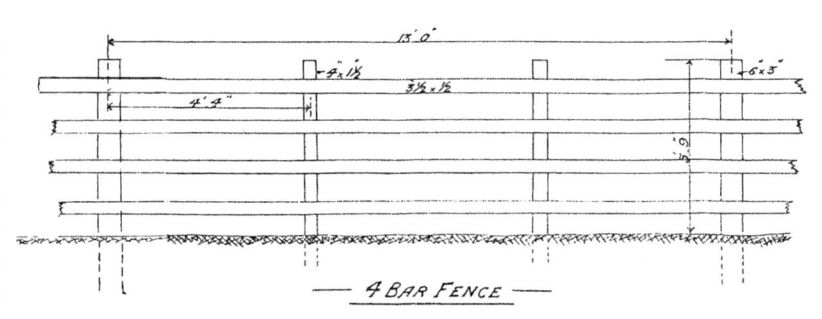

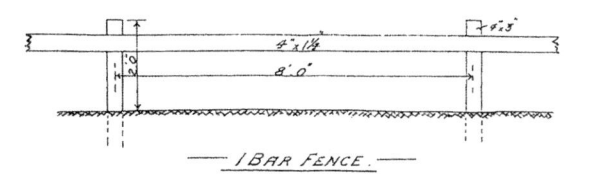

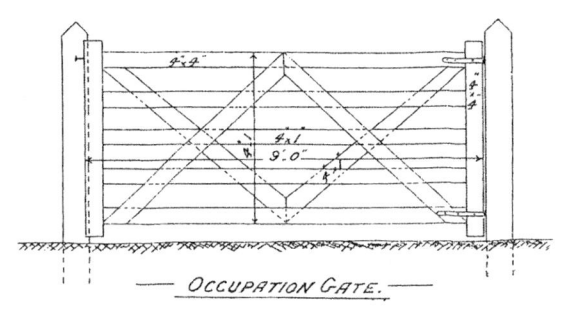

GER survey of SR 4-bar fence, 1-bar fence and 5-bar occupation crossing gate.

ABOVE: Once the railway closed in April 1929 the company abandoned all assets; this view of Wenhaston level crossing facing towards Southwold shows the station building almost hidden by bushes and infant trees. The decking in the foreground spanned a small culvert. *Author's collection*

ABOVE: There was a variation in the fencing of the railway at stations such as Wenhaston, where trellis cross-members adorn the road approach to the level crossing, with the station building in the background. *Author's collection*

LEFT: The sleepers are completely covered in gravel in this view of a Down train near Wenhaston. The lineside boundary fence was formed of three or four horizontal timbers affixed to wooden post. Two vertical lightweight stiffeners were affixed between each wooden post. *Author's collection*

LEFT: Thought to be a group of SR permanent way staff beside the weighbridge office at Southwold Harbour.
Author's collection

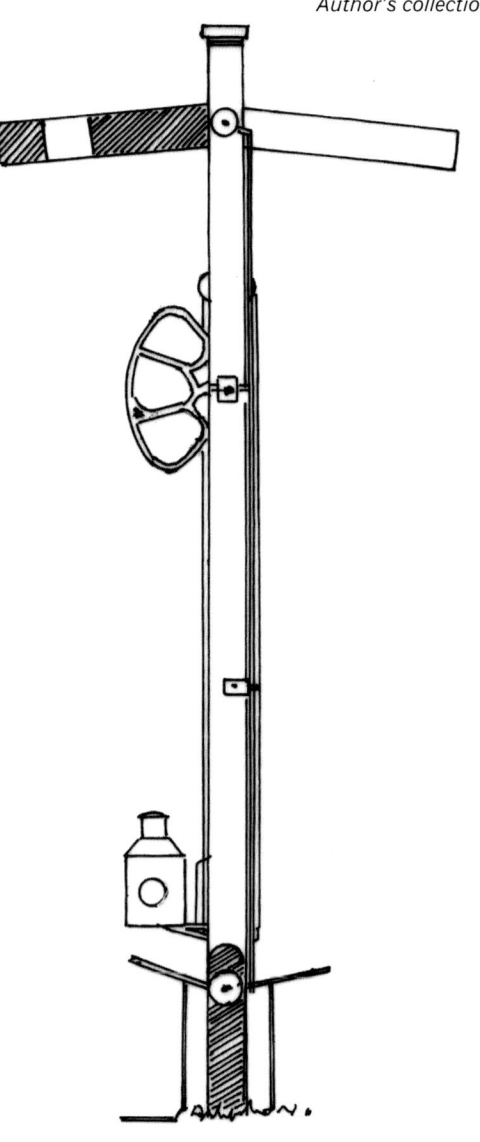

Drawing of SR signal

LEFT: Detail of the Up home and Down starting signal arms sharing the same post at Halesworth in 1936. The spectacles and lamp support cable for night-time illumination are missing. Note the rodding to operate the arms from the balance weights at the bottom of the post and the pulley wheel to raise and lower the oil lamp case.
J.H.L. Adams/Kidderminster Railway Museum

FACING PAGE: Southwold station was protected by two signals in each direction plus a subsidiary shunting arm. Here the inner signal post closest to the camera has the inner starting signal arm on the left of the post and Down inner home right of the post, whilst the far signal on the Down side of the line has the Up advance starting signal on the left and the outer home signal arm to the right of the post. The subsidiary signal is in the clear position. A single lamp with two lenses was used to illuminate the spectacles on each signal; the lamp, shown here in its lowered position, being hoisted up the post by a windlass.
Southwold Museum

In 1884 Ganger Edward Spoor assisted by three platelayers maintained the permanent way and fencing from Halesworth to a point about a mile east of Wenhaston station. The gang worked six days a week with Sundays off duty, with Spoor earning a weekly wage of £1 19s 0d, whilst his staff according to seniority earned between 16s 0d and 13s 0d per week. In 1919 there were two permanent way gangs, each in charge of a Ganger, covering the 8 miles 63 chains of railway, the first gang covering Halesworth to Blythburgh inclusive, and the second gang from Blythburgh exclusive to Southwold. John Nichols, 71 years old and a platelayer, retired from the company on closure of the line having worked on the SR from the opening of the railway. All applications for increase in wages or leave of absence had to be submitted via the station master. John Brabbing, a platelayer, who joined the company in 1895, referred to a staff dinner where a probable cut in wages was announced. Five shillings was mentioned but in the following November a 6s 0d reduction was made followed by two further cuts in subsequent months of 6s 0d and 5s 0d, making 17s 0d in all. For two days' work relaying track on the swing bridge he was paid the princely sum of 6s 8d.

Signalling

Major General Hutchinson found the points and signals on the SR were arranged and interlocked similarly to those on the Culm Valley Light Railway in Devon, which was of no surprise since Arthur C. Pain was Engineer of that line in addition to the Southwold, and later also the Axminster & Lyme Regis Light Railway. Ransomes & Rapier of Ipswich supplied the signalling equipment and pointwork for the SR. The signals were of the lower quadrant slotted semaphore type, with arms for each direction mounted on the opposite sides of the same post. The coloured spectacles, red for danger and green for clear for nighttime illumination or during fog or falling snow, were mounted at a lower position on the post than the signal arms, fixed in line with one another so that one oil lamp with spectacles each side did the duty for both signals. A simple locking apparatus ensured the points were correctly set before the signal could be lowered. When the lamps required refilling with paraffin or rape oil they were lowered down the post by means of a cable running up the post on one side, over the pulley let into the post and down the opposite side to a small winch near the base of the post.

Stop signals mounted on the same post were provided at each of the intermediate stations, operated from ground frames at each station and interlocked with points on the main single line. At Wenhaston Mill siding a signal was provided for both directions of travel, the arms being mounted on a single post adjacent to the entry points to the siding, and if clear denoted the points were correctly set for the main single line. Two signals protected the approach to and exit from Southwold station. On the approach to the station the outer signal upper arm signalled trains into the main platform road and the lower or shorter shunt arm controlled entry to the coal sidings. On the inner post the main arm signalled trains into the main platform line. The starting signals mounted on both the inner and outer signal posts gave trains authority to proceed on the main single line towards Halesworth. Halesworth station was provided with a single signal post with Up home and Down starting arms mounted on the same post. This signal protected the king points at the approach to the station. Initially distant signals were not provided, as the Southwold Railway was subject to a speed limit of 16 mph and worked by one engine in steam only, but later a distant signal was installed in the Down direction on the approach to Blythburgh after the installation of the crossing loop at that station in 1908. At the same time Down starter and Up home signals mounted on a single post were erected east of the station. In accordance with the company's Rule 64 the engine driver and fireman were required to frequently look back during the journey to see the whole train was complete whilst Rule 92 stated a driver was liable to two years imprisonment if convicted of exceeding the 16 mph speed limit.

The single line was worked by one engine in steam or two or more locomotives coupled together, with the single line Train Staff labelled 'Southwold to Halesworth' carried on the locomotive or leading locomotive working the service. The Train Staff had an Annett's key at one end to operate the points at the intermediate sidings and for unlocking the swing bridge over the River Blyth; the arrangement was agreed in a document dated 20th September 1879 signed by R.M. Rapier and J.P. Cooper for the SR, and T.H. Jellicoe, the BoT Secretary. The method of working was adequate for the first two decades of operation when a maximum of six trains ran in each direction during the summer months but by 1902 the

ABOVE: A member of staff at Wenhaston demonstrates how the signal arms are lowered. *Author's collection*

0-6-2T No. 4 *Wenhaston* with a Down train, approaching the outer home signal at Southwold. The porter/signalman sheltering in the small hut at the exposed location, on hearing the sound of the engine whistle lowered the signal to allow the train into the platform. The left-hand arm is the advanced starting signal and the shunt arm to allow a train into the goods yard is mounted at a lower level on the post. The porter/signalman placed the arm back to danger once the engine had passed the signal. *Southwold Museum*

system was found very restrictive when there was need to run a separate goods train. Accordingly application was made to the BOT to introduce Train Staff and Ticket when two trains required to run one after the other in the same direction, the driver of the first train being shown the Train Staff and handed a Train Staff paper Ticket authorizing him to proceed over the single line whilst the driver of the second train carried the single line Train Staff. The BOT approved of the introduction but during the summer months only. The starting of a train from one station was notified by telegraph and later telephone to the next station, on receipt of which the signal at the sending station was lowered. To assist with the working of trains an 'omnibus' telephone line had been installed in 1899 at a cost of £256 0s 0d. To call each station a code of bell calls was introduced. Halesworth was 5 rings, Wenhaston 4, Blythburgh 3, Walberswick 2 and Southwold 1 ring.

As traffic continued to expand it was necessary to facilitate greater line capacity and the crossing loop was installed at Blythburgh in 1908 to enable two trains to pass or cross, but because of the lack of a second platform passenger trains always used the main single line which served the platform. The company had also intended to install a further crossing loop at Wenhaston to handle additional services expected as a result of Southwold Harbour improvements but the BOT disapproved and the inspector suggested the line only be divided into two sections with Blythburgh as the crossing station, each section being worked by Train Staff and Ticket with telephone control. Thus from 1908 the line was divided into the two sections, Halesworth to Blythburgh and Blythburgh to Southwold. The original heavy brass Train Staff with a round head was re-labelled and used on the Blythburgh to Southwold section, with a key to operate the points to the sidings at Walberswick as well as locking and unlocking the swing bridge, whilst a new single line Train Staff with square head was employed on the Halesworth to Blythburgh section and labelled accordingly. This Train Staff had an Annett's key to operate the points at Halesworth, Wenhaston Mill, Wenhaston station sidings and later the siding to the ballast pit/engine shed at Bird's Folly. The paper tickets associated with the Halesworth to Blythburgh Train Staff were blue in colour, whilst the Blythburgh to Southwold tickets were red. The opening of the Southwold Harbour branch necessitated a further revision of single line working arrangements and from 8th August 1914 the railway was divided into three sections, Southwold to Walberswick, including the harbour branch, Walberswick to Blythburgh and Blythburgh to Halesworth. During this period a third single line Train Staff was introduced and paper tickets for the Blythburgh to Walberswick section were green in colour and Walberswick to Southwold were red. When Walberswick station was closed as an economy measure during World War One, officially on and from 2nd April 1917, the railway again reverted to two section operation: Halesworth to Blythburgh, and Blythburgh to Southwold including the harbour branch. The third section was restored when Walberswick station reopened after hostilities, but with the decline in use of the harbour branch this arrangement ceased in 1920 and two-section single line working was reintroduced.

The normal method of operation after 1908 required the driver of a train from Southwold to surrender the Southwold to Blythburgh Train Staff to the staff at Blythburgh, and to collect the Train Staff for the section thence to Halesworth. As stated earlier the Southwold to Blythburgh, later Southwold to Walberswick, Train Staff Annett's key also locked and released the locking mechanism on the River Blyth swing bridge. If trains were to pass at Blythburgh, the locally known 'Ceremony of the Keys' was performed when the driver of an Up train handed over the Southwold (Walberswick) to Blythburgh Train Staff to the driver of a Down train, whilst collecting at the same time the Blythburgh to Halesworth Train Staff. The exchange was officially to be witnessed by the station master but more often than not was transferred whilst he was on other duties. The 'Ceremony of the Keys' was enacted until the passage of the very last train.

The Regulation covering the Train Staff and Ticket method of operation stipulated that when a train was ready to start from a Train Staff station, and no second train was intended to follow or, if relevant, the Train Staff was not required for a train travelling in the opposite direction, the person in charge of the Train Staff station was to give the Train Staff to the engine driver, who was to place it in the Train Staff socket in the cab of the engine. The Train Staff was the driver's authority to proceed over the single line section, provided the starting signal had been cleared. If, however, another train was to follow in the same direction before the Train Staff was required for a train in the opposite direction, the person in charge of the Train Staff working was to show the Train Staff for the section to the engine driver and at the same time hand him a Train Staff paper Ticket authorising him to proceed. The engine driver of the last train through the single line section was to carry the Train Staff. On arrival of the train at the Train Staff station at the end of the section, the Train Staff or Train Staff Ticket was to be surrendered to the person in charge of the Train Staff working. All Tickets given up were immediately invalidated by having the word 'cancelled' written across the documents. They were then sent to the Company Secretary. The Train Staff Tickets were retained in secure Ticket Boxes and were opened by the key attached to the Train Staff for the relevant section of line. The person in charge of the single line Train Staff working was held strictly responsible for the correct working of the system on threat of instant dismissal for any irregularity.

The opening of the siding to serve the ballast pit at Bird's Folly in July 1906, and later in 1914 with the opening of the Halesworth engine shed, necessitated adjustments in the method of single line working. The Annett's key attached to the Halesworth to Blythburgh single line Train Staff released the patent locking box so that the points could be operated. When the ballast siding was shunted it was usual for the engine to run light or with wagons with the driver in possession of the Train Staff. Once shunting was completed and the points secured for the main single line, the engine either propelled the wagons back to Halesworth, where the driver delivered up the Train Staff, or continued through to Blythburgh where the Train Staff was similarly surrendered. Complications arose with

SR Train Staff Ticket.

the opening of the engine shed, especially if the locomotive was returning to shed for stabling. To move an engine from Halesworth station to the shed the driver had to be in possession of the Train Staff; he would then release the points in the main line and back the engine into the siding before reversing the engine over the points and into the shed. The points in the main single line were then returned to normal, set for the main single line and locked, and the Train Staff returned to the station master at Halesworth for safekeeping. This was perfectly acceptable if the same locomotive was to work the first Down train the next day but usually the first train was worked Up from Southwold, and so the Halesworth to Blythburgh Train Staff then had to be taken by road to Blythburgh to enable the train to continue through to Halesworth.

Yet further permutations in single line working were adopted. In a letter to station masters dated 21st October 1915 and headed 'European War', instructions were issued that when the military required a special train on Sundays and there was insufficient time to issue operating notices to staff, Walberswick and Blythburgh stations were to remain closed and the Southwold to Walberswick single line Train Staff was to be used as authority for the train to travel through to Halesworth. Drivers were then authorised to pass signals at the intermediate stations at danger, at a speed of 5 mph. Wenhaston station was to be opened to enable the station master to open and close the level crossing gates for the passage of train or trains. On 18th November 1920 another variation of was issued: in the event of the necessity to run a special fish train on a Sunday, the train was to run without changing the Train Staff at Blythburgh. Then on 20th February 1922 an instruction was issued authorising drivers of special goods trains to stop outside the Home signal at Blythburgh for the purpose of attaching and detaching wagons via a new set of points installed at the Southwold end of the station. These variations in operation appear to have been carried out without the BOT being advised.

STATION MASTERS

At Halesworth, considered an important position because of passenger and goods interchange as well as day-to-day interface with the GER, D. Price, a Yorkshireman born at Newland in 1855 was first station master when the SR opened in 1879. His tenure was not long for he was replaced by Frederick William Hansford who moved from Blythburgh in June 1881 and also stayed but a short while until May 1883, when he transferred to Southwold. The next incumbent was Walter Calver who served at the interchange station from 28th June 1883 until 1901, when he too transferred to Southwold. When Calver took charge at Halesworth he had a staff of two porters for passenger work and a goods porter. Henry Alfred Wright then took over and served from 1901 until closure of the

ABOVE: The final Southwold Railway Train Staffs, one of which still retains its key to the Ticket boxes. *Southwold Museum*

LEFT: The driver of a Down train and station master exchange the single line Train Staffs at Blythburgh – locally and incorrectly known as 'Ceremony of the Keys'. *John Alsop collection*

line in 1929. A company house was provided for the Halesworth station master at 14 Holton Road.

Wenhaston station was the only intermediate stopping point when the SR opened for traffic and it is assumed that George Goldsmith was the first station master – recorded as 'clerk-in-charge', a title favoured by the Great Northern Railway for station master. He was recorded in the 1881 census as living at Chapel Road, Wenhaston and remained in the post until temporary transfer to Halesworth in May of the same year. With Hansford's move to Halesworth (see above) Goldsmith transferred along the line to Blythburgh in July 1881. In February 1883 he married a Miss Remington of Wenhaston, when the station was decorated overall with flags and most of the village turned out for the ceremony. From July Goldsmith was superseded by Henry Alfred Wright, who resided at Southwold where he was employed as a clerk at the station. Wright was issued with a free pass for travel to Wenhaston and back during the period 4th July to 4th August, when he presumably had to find lodgings; the ticket is now in Southwold Museum. He served at the station until 1901 when he was promoted to take charge at Halesworth. Wenhaston must have been an unpopular appointment for no fewer than three station masters served between 1901 and 1913: Percy Frederick Dyer remained until 1907 to be replaced by Albert Henry Sivyer until May 1912 and then John (Jack) Button for a few months until the end of the year, all three leaving the railway service. Harry B. Girling was the next incumbent but on 24th December 1926 he died as a result of injuries sustained in a shunting accident. The SR wasted no time in appointing a replacement and William J.V. Nicholls was transferred from Walberswick on the same day and remained in the post until closure in April 1929 when, as with many others, he was discharged. Nicolls was not the first choice for apparently Henry Ward, the SR Manager, initially offered the position to Henry Wright as an easier job than serving at Halesworth, to save him retiring because of eye problems. Wright declined and this frustrated Ward, who then thought it necessary to find a youth and *'give him two or three months training at one of the stations'*. In the event no youth was employed and Nicholls was allowed to remain in the post. Nicholls attempted to generate interest in reopening the railway after closure by means of electrification but failed through lack of sponsorship.

Blythburgh station was not opened until December 1879 and there is no record of an initial appointment as station master, the position possibly being covered by a relief porter or clerk from Southwold. This was rectified in March 1881 with the appointment of Frederick William Hansford to the position. He had commenced his railway career as a porter at Exeter St. Thomas station on the Great Western Railway and probably answered an advertisement for the post; on appointment he lodged with Mr and Mrs David Harvey at Blythburgh. His tenure was short for he transferred to take charge at Halesworth in June 1881 where he served until May 1883, transferring to Southwold. George Goldsmith, believed to have been a porter at Southwold before being in charge at Wenhaston, then took charge and remained at Blythburgh until 1904 when he was succeeded by William Pullen, who remained until he left the service of the SR early in 1912, going to Manchester to seek his fortune. The new incumbent was Bertie (Bert) Edward Girling who joined the SR at the tender age of twelve as a lad clerk, working in booking and goods offices, and later as a relief clerk before appointment to station master at Blythburgh. He served at the intermediate crossing station until May 1926 when he was promoted to take charge at Southwold. In September 1918 Girling and his wife were summoned for riding bicycles without front or rear lamps and were each fined 2s 6d and 1s 7d costs at Halesworth Petty Sessions. The last station master at Blythburgh W.G. (Wally) Upcraft had a curious career for, being born in 1903, he joined the SR at the age of thirteen in 1916 and served until 1921 when he resigned the company to serve on fishing boats. Whilst on a Lowestoft drifter based at Milford Haven in 1924 he was offered the position of goods clerk by the Secretary and on completion of the voyage rejoined the SR in May. He was appointed station master at Blythburgh in 1926 and served in that capacity until closure of the line on 11th April 1929 when he was discharged. Girling died age 96 in April 1984 whilst Upcraft passed away in February 1984 aged 81 years. He related that in the intervals between trains he would go wild-fowling as the river was so close to Blythburgh station.

As already recorded, when the railway opened there was no intention of opening a station to serve Walberswick but after pressure from local people, and no doubt walkers and picnickers using Walberswick Common, the company acceded to the request and the facility complete with one siding, later two, was brought into use in September 1881. Then the management were loath to appoint a station master at the desolate location and probably a porter took charge. However, Edward Court, a 16-year-old railway clerk at Southwold, was considered a suitable candidate for promotion and was appointed clerk-in-charge at Walberswick in 1882 where duties were not as onerous as other stations. He did not lodge in the village but travelled daily from Southwold, a fact which led to his demise on Wednesday 14th November 1883 when he attempted to join a moving train before it had stopped with fatal results. The management then went from one extreme to the other, for finding no suitable candidate among the clerks employed on the SR they resorted to appointing 74-year-old Edmund Sturley as station master. Sturley had lived in the village for a number of years and was recorded in the 1861 census. The length of his tenure is debatable for William Pullen, a former W.H. Smith newsboy, was appointed clerk-in-charge by 1894, by which time Sturley was 85 years of age; although when he died in Bulcamp Workhouse on 14th May 1902 his occupation on the death certificate was station master. When Pullen was appointed he was 15 years old and served at the station until 1904. William J.V. Nicholls, who had joined the SR earlier the same year as a clerk at Southwold, was Pullen's successor and he served as station master until 1917 when, as result of the decline in traffic and urgent requirements of the War Office for the recruitment of men to replace those lost in the trenches, the Directors decided to close the station officially with effect from 2nd April for the remainder of the period of hostilities, although trains ceased to call from 10th February. One man joined the colours from the SR but his name is unrecorded; the station was not reopened until 1st July 1919. On resumption of the service at Walberswick, no incumbent was initially appointed until William Beard became station master, possibly in November of that year and until 1922 or 1923 when he left the service to be replaced by William Bird who served until May 1926, when he too left the service. Bird was rather reserved in temperament but was considered rather attractive by the local young ladies. One mistakenly took advantage of the poor lighting at the station, where at the time only one lamp provided night-time illumination, when meeting her brother one evening. As the train stopped, amidst clouds of steam, she ran forward and instead of embracing her brother, managed to hug and kiss the unsuspecting station master much to the amusement of the rest of the family. As already mentioned, Company Secretary H. Ward

Group of staff at Southwold station just before the withdrawal of services in 1929. From left to right are George Burley guard, unknown cyclist, Station Master Bert E. Girling, W. Aldis, porter, Albert Edward Self, W. Doy's drayman; in the background are Marchant, General Post Office clerk, N. Fisk, engine driver, and A. Barratt Jenkins, who did much to chronicle the line in its last years. *Author's collection*

offered the ailing H. Wright the position as an 'easy job' in lieu of retiring because of failing eyesight but the offer was declined. The decision was regretted but into the breach stepped William J.V. Nicholls, who since removal in 1917, had probably served as a clerk at Southwold. Within a few months Nicholls was transferred in undue haste to Wenhaston on Christmas Eve to replace the deceased H.B. Girling. Thereafter until closure of the railway, Walberswick station was probably supervised by a clerk travelling daily from Southwold.

When the railway first opened to traffic Johnathan Leigh was appointed station master at Southwold but he departed early in 1881 and was succeeded by Walter George Bridall, who curiously was a schoolmaster by profession. He resided at 14 Station Road Southwold with his wife, two sons and a daughter, and remained in the post until July 1883 when he returned to his profession and took over the Wardens boarding school on the Common at Southwold. He was also Secretary to the River Blyth Ferry Company and remained in Southwold until 1889 when he emigrated to Australia, where he died a year later. The next incumbent at Southwold was Frederick William Hansford, who transferred from Halesworth; he remained until probably 1901, residing at 3 Chester Road and continuing there as an apartment house keeper until his death on 16th January 1908 at the age of 53. Walter Carver, who also transferred from Halesworth where he had served since 1883, succeeded Hansford. Residing at 2 Salisbury Close, Southwold, Calver remained at the terminus until probably early 1905 when

he retired at the age of 54 years. Charles Henry Fitzhugh, formerly a GER booking clerk at Liverpool Street, then took over as station master. He probably came as a result of answering an advertisement in the railway press and initially lived at 6 St. Edmund's Green, Southwold in 1906 before moving on to 28 Station Road and then 9 Station Road. Fitzhugh left the SR in the autumn of 1916 and was succeeded by 37-year-old Henry James Clarke, who had joined the SR in 1913 as a clerk at Southwold station. He, like Fitzhugh, was a member of the National Union of Railwaymen and remained in the post until the Directors terminated his employment on 24th May 1926. The last station master at Southwold was Bertie (Bert) Girling, brother of H.B. Girling at Wenhaston. He transferred from Blythburgh and remained at the terminus until April 1929 when he was probably the last member of staff to be discharged after attending to administrative duties for at least seven days after the withdrawal of passenger and goods services.

The salaries of station masters varied according to the importance of the station: Calver in charge of Halesworth was paid £1 1s 0d for a seven-day working week and received actual payment every fourteen days. No enhancements were paid for working Saturdays and Sundays and on 3rd July 1890 he applied for an increase in salary, quoting as his argument increased traffic and responsibilities. Even by 1913 those in charge of the smaller stations at Wenhaston, Blythburgh and Walberswick only received £1 0s 0d per week, whilst Halesworth and Southwold received £1 3s 0d per week. By 1925 inflation had increased earnings to £1 5s 0d per week rising to £3 5s 0d per week respectively. For these handsome sums the men at Wenhaston, Blythburgh and Walberswick were responsible for issuing and collecting tickets, forwarding and receipt of parcels and goods traffic, preparation of weekly and monthly accounts and statements for all classes of traffic. They were also responsible for the daily cash accounts and remittance of takings to the bank at Southwold. At these stations they also loaded and unloaded goods traffic and advised customers of the arrival and required departure of wagons and raising of demurrage charges in the event of a delay in offloading or loading of wagons. They were also required to assist the guard shunting wagons into and out of the goods yard sidings and operate points and signals. Then because of the deteriorating financial position of the company, from 1925 station master's salaries, along with those of other traffic staff, were drastically reduced.

Traffic Staff

In 1884 two porters were employed on the passenger station at Halesworth earning 18s 0d and 14s 0d weekly respectively for a seven-day week, with no overtime payments for Saturday and Sunday work. A goods porter was employed to handle freight traffic and was paid by the tonnage he handled in a seven-day week. All were paid every fortnight. Wage rises were offered about every two years but in all cases application had to be made to the management via the respective station master. Similarly, applications for leave of absence were directed through the station master. In January 1913 payment for Sunday duty was time and a half for staff in all departments. In 1921 and again in 1923 the financial plight of the company necessitated a wage reduction for all staff, which it was claimed gave one hundred per cent of the 1913 wage claim levels. A typical reduction made to the foreman's rate of pay was from £6 6s 0d every three weeks to £5 5s 0d, a reduction of £1 1s 0d over the period. The traffic staff employed by the SR often reached a venerable old age before leaving the service. Haylock retired in January 1926, recorded as *'too feeble to work'*, whilst Porter Aldis left on 28th October 1927, *'afraid to risk another winter'*. The pair had spent a lifetime working for the company and received a small pension. The dire financial situation meant that neither was replaced and other employees had to cover the duties. Traffic staff uniforms were of blue serge with plain brass buttons and the letters SR on the jacket lapels and caps.

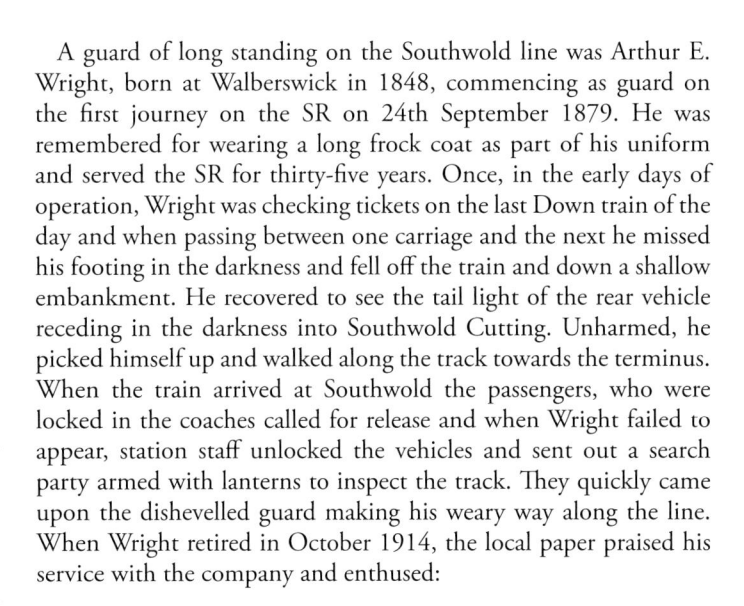

A guard of long standing on the Southwold line was Arthur E. Wright, born at Walberswick in 1848, commencing as guard on the first journey on the SR on 24th September 1879. He was remembered for wearing a long frock coat as part of his uniform and served the SR for thirty-five years. Once, in the early days of operation, Wright was checking tickets on the last Down train of the day and when passing between one carriage and the next he missed his footing in the darkness and fell off the train and down a shallow embankment. He recovered to see the tail light of the rear vehicle receding in the darkness into Southwold Cutting. Unharmed, he picked himself up and walked along the track towards the terminus. When the train arrived at Southwold the passengers, who were locked in the coaches called for release and when Wright failed to appear, station staff unlocked the vehicles and sent out a search party armed with lanterns to inspect the track. They quickly came upon the dishevelled guard making his weary way along the line. When Wright retired in October 1914, the local paper praised his service with the company and enthused:

'We learn that Mr Arthur E. Wright, the veteran Guard on the Southwold Railway, is retiring from that position at the end of the present week. Mr Wright has been connected with the Company since the opening of the line in 1879, his period of service thus extending over thirty-five years. His general disposition and the courteous and attractive manner in which he has, during his lengthy service, carried out his duties, have won the respect and esteem not only of local patrons of the line, but of thousands throughout the United Kingdom who have visited Southwold, and as a tangible recognition of the appreciation of his services a subscription list was opened, and it was hoped that the generous response would be made to that appeal.'

The total amount raised was a creditable £42 5s 6d and a cheque for £41, together with a parchment containing the names of the subscribers, was presented to Wright by Edgar Pipe, the Mayor at a presentation held in Southwold Town Hall in January 1915. Arthur Edgar Wright passed away on 5th September 1924 at his home in Dovercourt after a short illness.

Another guard, John 'Tipney' Palmer, started with the company as a boy of fourteen and was guard for fourteen years. He remembered a passenger joining the 12.50pm train at Halesworth and enquiring, *'Is there time?'* to which he replied *'There'll have to be; I'll have one*

Guard A.E. Wright joined the SR for the opening of the line and served with the company until World War One. On the left he stands with uniform of double breasted jacket and peaked pill-box style cap. In the centre he is seen circa 1910 standing beside a Brake coach in uniform of double breasted frock coat and soft top cap. On the right he is towards the end of his illustrious career, standing beside coaching stock at Southwold. *Author's collection*

Southwold station staff unloading parcels and goods traffic from luggage van No. 14 at the terminus in 1928; on the left is William Stannard, porter, with George Burley, guard, on the right.
Southwold Museum

with you', after which the pair retired to the adjacent Station Hotel. W.J. Blythe remembered the 7.30am train ex Southwold seldom left to time for the guard would look up and down Station Road to see if anyone was hurrying for the train. *'We did keenly appreciate this gesture of the staff – they always made us feel at home.'*

Frederick Leach succeeded Wright and one day, soon after World War One, Leach was in charge of the mid-day goods train which ran during the summer months, when on passing through a cutting he noticed a hare caught in a snare by the side of the line. Unbeknown to the driver he screwed down the handbrake and slowed the train before jumping down and removing the animal from the trap. He then ran after the train and leapt aboard before releasing the handbrake. Another guard employed by the company in the final years of operation was 35-year-old George Burley.

J.A. Steadman, chief goods clerk at Southwold, commenced as a lad clerk at Southwold station in October 1911 at a wage of 4s 0d per week working from 8.00am until 7.30pm, after which he took the mail to the post office. There were no half days and if fish traffic was dispatched on Sundays it was seven days a week work. A. Parker, who became station master at Bentley L&NER, remembered as relief booking clerk he a was at Halesworth on the last day of SR operation. He issued the last ticket to Southwold for the 3.00pm train to enable the ticket issuing ledger to be balanced for the day. For the last trip the SR guard issued the tickets although he doubted if many were sold because of the crowded carriages.

W.J. (Billy) Fisk who was foreman porter/shunter at Southwold when the railway closed told of his early associations with the company when the platelayers advised him if he wanted a share in rabbits caught on the lineside and on adjacent property he would have to purchase his own traps. He assisted with the staking out of the branch line to Blackshore Quay and acted as guard on the BOT inspection special, the only train to traverse the branch with passengers. He also recollected assisting to load the first consignment of fish landed at the harbour, the largest load ever caught and removed by rail. The train consisted of fourteen wagons hauled by 2-4-2T No. 1 *Southwold* and with slippery rails and the rising gradient to the main line the engine stalled. Sand was thrown on the rails under the locomotive wheels to help adhesion and the train reached the main line without further delay.

10

Timetables and Traffic

Before the advent of the Southwold Railway passengers bound for the town alighted from the GER train at Darsham and were conveyed by horse-drawn omnibus via Blythburgh and Henham, a distance of about nine miles to the Swan Hotel, which was the Posting House for the town. The journey was one of rustic scenery through agricultural land interspersed with woodland and clusters of farm buildings. Approaching Blythburgh the travellers obtained wonderful views of Holy Trinity Church standing proud against the skyline with the River Blyth beyond. Passing through the village and the site of the Old Priory the coach passed the small quay where barges loaded and unloaded their wares on the journey between Southwold and Halesworth. Once over the River Blyth the road skirted the woods of the Henham Estate, home of the Earl of Stradbroke, and then swung right and over the Wolsey Bridge to the village of Reydon. Towards the coast passengers would gain their first glimpse of the tower of St. Edmund's Church at Southwold, standing on high land above the river flats. From Reydon the view of Southwold was across marshes with Might's Bridge spanning Buss Creek and fields covering the area north of the church. Once in Southwold the omnibus trundled past the gas works and up the High Street to the Market Place and the final destination, the Swan Hotel. All was hustle and bustle as passengers alighted, ostlers attended to the horses and luggage was unloaded for onward conveyance. After the opening of the SR in 1879 the horse bus service was withdrawn as railway passengers interchanged to and from the narrow gauge line at Halesworth. The new railway certainly provided facilities for the holidaymaker over the fifty years of its existence whilst slowly encouraging a small increase in the population at Walberswick and Southwold, but success in this field was tempered by losses at Wenhaston and Blythburgh. The populations of the places served by the railway were as shown in the table below.

The initial service operated by the SR from 24th September 1879 consisted of four trains in each direction running on weekdays only; each train being allowed 37 minutes running time for the 8¾ miles journey and calling at Wenhaston, the only intermediate station, by request only.

From 24th September 1879					
Up		am	am	pm	pm
Southwold	dep	7.25	10.05	2.20	5.25
Wenhaston	dep	R	R	R	R
Halesworth	arr	8.02	10.42	2.57	6.02
Down		am	pm	pm	pm
Halesworth	dep	9.17	1.42	4.17	7.02
Wenhaston	dep	R	R	R	R
Southwold	arr	9.54	2.19	4.54	7.39
R Calls only if required					

Throughout the operating life of the railway the first Up train from Southwold and the last Down train from Halesworth were designated passenger services. Other trains ran as 'mixed' and shunting was carried out as required at the intermediate stations and sidings. From an early date a conditional goods train ran on weekdays only departing Halesworth about 11.00am to 11.15am and returning from Southwold as required, to enable the locomotive to haul the first Down train in the afternoon. This train ran specifically if seven or more wagons required transit to the intermediate stations or Southwold; six wagons or less were conveyed by mixed trains. If the special goods trains operated the guard was authorized to ride on the engine whilst Regulation 15a of Appendix 1 of the Train Staff Regulations was carried out on the 10.05am train.

By the summer of 1881 the timetable showed a service of five trains in each direction on weekdays and two each way on Sundays. The weekday trains departed Southwold at 7.45am, 11.00am, 2.28pm, 5.00pm and 6.35pm returning from Halesworth at 9.15am, 1.06pm, 3.23pm, 5.43pm and 8.09pm. On Sundays, Up trains departed Southwold at 1.46pm and 6.35pm and Down services returned from Halesworth at 2.26pm and 7.23pm. Trains were allowed 37 minutes running time on the journey and called at Wenhaston and Blythburgh (which had opened in late 1879) by request, whilst passengers wishing to alight at these stations had to inform the guard at the starting station. During August 1881,

Population Figures									
Year	1861	1871	1881	1891	1901	1911	1921	1931	1951
Halesworth	2,521	2,437	2,498	2,316	2,246	2,258	2,060	2,024	2,155
Wenhaston	948	914	877	832	792	831	824	744	738
Blythburgh	832	861	821	746	646	747	673	584	649
Walberswick	315	303	289	270	304	372	408	396	500
Southwold	2,032	2,155	2,107	2,311	2,800	2,655	3,370	2,753	2,473
Total*	4,127	4,233	4,094	4,159	4,542	4,605	5,275	4,477	4,360
Total+	6,648	6,670	6,592	6,475	6,788	6,863	7,335	6,501	6,515
Notes: * Total excluding Halesworth									
+ Total including Halesworth									

passengers arriving on late-running GER trains, finding the SR connection had departed to time, made many complaints to the SR that the connections should be maintained. The Directors were adamant their service would keep correct time and both the *Ipswich Journal* and *Halesworth Times* congratulated the SR for taking the stance and blamed the GER entirely for the late running. In the same year Walberswick station was added to the conditional calling points. The timetable for the summer of 1882 showed the service below.

The following year the railway encountered competition, for Gage's wagonette had started a service between Darsham and Southwold. On Whit Monday in May a special later train was operated departing Southwold at 9.20pm and returning from Halesworth at 10.05pm. Yet more competition followed when Whittaker's four-in-hand Rocket coach commenced a direct service from Southwold to Lowestoft in July, an arrangement that continued through to September. The SR Company also announced that in addition to its normal weekday summer service of five trains in each direction and three each way on Sundays, it would arrange to run additional trains on Bank Holiday Mondays, as on previous occasions passengers had been left behind at Halesworth because of overcrowding. In the same month the SR Manager, A.C. Pain, had written to Southwold Corporation suggesting the reopening of the weekly market *'which had for so many years been dead'*, offering in return single fares for the return journey and one hundredweight of goods conveyed free for each passenger. The Council duly considered the proposal and acted upon it, and the regular Thursday Market, selling mostly perishable items, reopened for the summer season only on 5th July.

The SR for their part introduced an enhanced summer service of six trains each way Thursday excepted, seven on Thursdays only and two each way on Sundays during the months of July, August and September 1883. The additional Thursdays only train departed Southwold at 9.00am, and with two minutes allowed for the engine to run round its train, returned from Halesworth at 9.39am. After much controversy the free conveyance of one hundredweight of goods per passenger on market day was restricted to bona fide dealers. By October there was still demand for a direct road service between Southwold and Lowestoft and H. Goldsmith commenced a daily service with a wagonette pulled by two horses, which was somewhat slower than the Rocket coach. Passengers travelling from Southwold and the branch stations had also benefited during the year, for Arthur Pain had negotiated with the GER for the 8.07am Up train, which had previously run non-stop, to call at Halesworth to connect with the 7.30am train from Southwold. Prior to this, intending passengers had had to wait until the 9.03am GER train. In October the SR timetable showed a reduction to five trains in each direction on weekdays and two each way on Sundays, the latter being reduced to one train each way from November.

In January 1884, the weekday service was reduced to four trains in each direction, when the 4.55pm ex Southwold and 5.40pm return from Halesworth were withdrawn at short notice. Sunday services were also curtailed. Vehement complaints were made, both to the railway company and the local press. Travellers from London arriving at Halesworth on the 2.25pm train ex Liverpool Street, instead of enjoying a reasonable connecting SR service were forced to wait 2½ hours for the last train of the day, the 8.09pm ex Halesworth, in order to reach Southwold. Increased fares were also cause for concern and whilst the SR management reacted rapidly to the comments and reinstated the lower fare structure in February, it was April before the timetable showed an increase to five trains each way with the introduction of the 5.30pm departure from Southwold and the 6.15pm return from Halesworth. Sunday trains were reintroduced on Good Friday and Easter Day for Blythburgh Church restoration services, and then fully from the beginning of May. The 1884 summer timetable of five trains each way on weekdays showed services departing Southwold at 7.30amMO, 7.40amMX, 10.55am, 2.25pm, 5.30pm and 7.10pm, and returning from Halesworth at 9.07am, 1.05pm, 3.25pm 6.15pm and 8.09pm. Trains called at Wenhaston, Blythburgh and Walberswick by hand signal given to the driver, whilst passengers wishing to alight at these stations were required to inform the guard. Trains were still allowed 37 minutes running time for the 8¾ miles journey. The Sunday services were again withdrawn in November. These basic services

Timetable for Summer 1882											
Up		**Weekdays**							**Sundays**		
		am	am	pm	pm	pm	pm	pm ThO	pm	pm	pm
Southwold	dep	7.45	11.00	12.45	2.20	5.00	6.35	9.00	1.50	5.45	7.30
Walberswick	dep	7.48	11.03	12.48	2.23	5.03	6.38	9.03	1.53	5.48	7.38
Blythburgh	dep +	8.00	11.15	1.00	2.35	5.15	6.50	9.15	2.05	6.00	7.45
Wenhaston	dep	8.11	11.26	1.11	2.46	5.26	7.01	9.26	2.16	6.11	7.56
Halesworth	arr	8.22	11.37	1.22	2.57	5.37	7.12	9.37	2.27	6.23	8.07
Down		**Weekdays**							**Sundays**		
		am	am	pm	pm	pm	pm	pm ThO	pm	pm	pm
Halesworth	dep	9.07	11.57	1.30	3.14	5.45	8.09	9.39	2.30	6.30	8.10
Wenhaston	dep	9.16	12.06	1.39	3.23	5.54	8.18	9.48	2.39	6.39	8.19
Blythburgh	dep +	9.27	12.17	1.50	3.34	6.05	8.29	9.59	2.50	6.50	8.30
Walberswick	dep	9.41	12.31	2.04	3.48	6.19	8.43	10.13	3.04	7.04	8.44
Southwold	arr	9.44	12.34	2.07	3.51	6.22	8.46	10.16	3.07	7.07	8.47
Notes: + station for Wangford											
Calls at Walberswick, Blythburgh and Wenhaston by signal only to take up or by telling the guard for setting down.											

SOUTHWOLD RAILWAY.
First and Third Class only.

DOWN TRAINS.

FROM		WEEK DAYS				
		morn	even.	even.	even.	even.
Halesworth	dep.	9 7	1 5	3 25	6 15	8 9
Wenhaston	,,	9 16	1 14	3 34	6 24	8 18
Blythburgh *for Wangford*	,,	9 27	1 25	3 45	6 35	8 29
Walberswick	,,	9 41	1 39	3 59	6 49	8 43
Southwold	arr.	9 44	1 42	4 2	6 52	8 46

UP TRAINS.

FROM		WEEK DAYS							
		morn	Mondays only	morn	Not on Mondays	morn	even.	even.	even.
Southwold	dep.	7 30		7 40		10 55	2 25	5 30	7 10
Walberswick	,,	7 33		7 43		10 58	2 28	5 33	7 13
Blythburgh, *for Wangford*	,,	7 45		7 55		11 10	2 40	5 45	7 25
Wenhaston	,,	7 56		8 6		11 21	2 51	5 56	7 36
Halesworth	arr.	8 7		8 17		11 32	3 2	6 7	7 47

The Trains will stop at Wenhaston, Blythburgh, and Walberswick by Signal only, and Passengers wishing to alight at either of these Stations must inform the Guard at the starting Station.

SR timetable November 1884 from GER public timetable.

continued to run for the next few years with only minor timing changes but in 1887 the Sunday services ran throughout the year, whilst in 1888 the SR ran only two trains each way on the Sabbath during the periodicity of the summer timetable.

By 1889 five trains ran in each direction weekdays only departing Southwold at 7.30am, 10.45am, 2.20pm, 5.25pm and 7.15pm and returning from Halesworth at 9.07am, 1.05pm, 3.28pm, 6.33pm and 8.00pm. All trains were allowed 37 minutes for the 8¾ miles journey and called at Walberswick, Blythburgh and Wenhaston by signal only or by passengers informing the guard. From 1st July the summer service showed an increase to six trains each way on weekdays but no Sunday service was offered. In 1890 the timetable showed five trains in each direction running in the same times as the previous year and services still only served the intermediate stations when required. From 1st July the weekday service was again increased to six trains in each direction and two each way on Sundays, the latter departing Southwold at 9.00am and 5.45pm and returning from Halesworth at 9.48am and 7.25pm. In November the winter timetable showed a reduction back to five trains each way on weekdays, whilst one Sunday train was operated departing Southwold at 6.00pm and returning from Halesworth at 7.25pm.

All too frequently over the years, late running GER trains caused the SR problems. Missed connections in the middle of the day were inconvenient for passengers but manageable by SR staff. A notorious late runner was the GER train from Liverpool Street due at Halesworth just before 8.00pm, which connected with the last Down SR train. Often this arrived up to two hours late necessitating the Southwold Company to arrange a special train to convey passengers to their destinations.

The summer timetable operated in July, August and September 1891 showed a total of six trains in each direction Thursdays excepted, seven on Thursdays only and two each way on Sundays. Up weekday services departed Southwold at 7.30am, 10.12am, 12.05pm, 2.40pm, 5.25pm, 7.05pm and 9.00pmThO, returning from Halesworth at 8.50am, 11.00am, 1.28pm, 3.45pm, 6.13pm, 8.00pm and 9.40pmThO. Sunday services departed Southwold at 9.00am and 5.45pm and returned from Halesworth at 9.48am and 7.25pm. In July 1893 services consisted of six weekday and two Sunday services in each direction with an additional train each way on Thursdays departing Southwold at 9.00pm and returning from Halesworth at 9.40pm.

In January 1895, the weekday services were reduced by one train in each direction with the withdrawal of the 7.15pm train ex Southwold and the return 8.00pm ex Halesworth. Sunday services were also curtailed. The two evening trains were reinstated from June and the Sunday services at the beginning of July. In the same year Station Master Walter Calver was reporting a marked improvement in the running of the late evening GER train, so fewer special workings were required on the SR. The timetable for July 1896, as in previous years, showed calling at Wenhaston, Blythburgh and Walberswick by signal only with passengers wishing to alight informing the guard at the starting station and passengers on the platform giving a clear signal to the driver. With minor changes this footnote appeared for the next eleven years.

Sec., H. Carne.]	HALESWORTH and SOUTHWOLD.—Southwold.	[Man. Director, A. C. Pain.

Fares		Up.	mrn	mrn	aft	aft	aft			Fares		Down.	mrn	aft	aft	aft	aft		
1 cl.	3 cl.	Southwold dep	7 30	10 45	2 20	5 25	7 15			1 cl.	3 cl.	Halesworth dep	9 7	1 5	3 23	6 33	8 0		
0	10	1	Walberswick ∩	7 33	10 43	2 23	5 28	7 18			0	6	0 2½	Wenhaston ∩	9 16	1 14	3 37	6 42	8 9	
0	50	4	Blythburgh * ∩	7 45	11 0	2 35	5 40	7 30			0	10	0 5	Blythburgh * ∩	9 27	1 25	3 48	6 53	8 20	
1	00	6½	Wenhaston ∩	7 56	11 11	2 46	5 51	7 41			1	40	8	Walberswick ∩	9 41	1 39	4 2	7 7	8 34	
1	60	9	Halesworth 136	8 7	11 22	2 57	6 2	7 52			1	60	9	Southwold arr	9 44	1 42	4 5	7 10	8 37	

All 1 & 3 class. ∩ Stop by signal to take up, and set down on informing the Guard. * Station for Wangford.

SR timetable 1890 from Bradshaw.

Fares	Up.	mrn	mrn	aft	aft	aft						Fares	Down.	mrn	aft	aft	aft	aft				
1 cl.|3 cl.												1 cl.|3 cl.										
0 2 0 1	Southwold.........dep.	7 30	10 55	2 20	5 30	7 15						0 6 0 2½	Halesworth...dep.	8 43	1 10	3 38	6 17	8 10				
0 8 0 4	Walberswick a	7 33	10 58	2 23	5 33	7 18						0 10 0 5	Wenhaston a	8 52	1 19	3 47	6 26	8 19				
1 0 0 8½	Blythburgh * a	7 45	11 10	2 35	5 45	7 30						1 4 0 8	Blythburgh * a	9 3	1 30	3 58	6 37	8 30				
1 6 0 9	Wenhaston a	7 58	11 21	2 46	5 56	7 41						1 6 0 9	Walberswick a	9 17	1 44	4 12	6 51	8 44				
	Halesworth 240, 236 arr	8 7	11 32	2 57	6 7	7 52							Southwold....arr.	9 20	1 47	4 15	6 54	8 47				

☞ **All 1 & 3 class.** a Stop by signal to take up, and set down on informing the Guard. * Station for Wangford.

SR timetable 1900 from Bradshaw.

The two evening trains were reinstated for the Easter period 15th, 17th and 19th April 1897, calling only if required at the intermediate stations although services did not run on Good Friday. From 1st June the evening 7.15pm Up and 8.00pm Down workings were reinstated, as were the Sunday services from July. Despite improving connections on Saturday 5th June the situation deteriorated; the 3.20pm ex Liverpool Street GER train was 70 minutes arriving at Halesworth and the 5.00pm from Liverpool Street 50 minutes late. On the SR, Station Master Walter Calver arranged for the 6.30pm and 8.00pm Down SR trains to depart to time with passengers from the 3.20pm ex Liverpool Street catching the later SR service. A special train then ran Up from Southwold to Halesworth to convey passengers off the 5.00pm ex Liverpool Street to their destinations. On Whit Monday 7th June the 8.36am ex Halesworth was re-timed to start at 9.15am whilst an additional service departed Halesworth at 11.35am, arriving at Southwold at 12.12pm and returning to Halesworth six minutes later, essentially running in the path of the normal weekday Q as and when required goods working.

The winter timetable operative from 1898/9 showed a service of four trains in each direction on weekdays only with departures from Southwold at 7.30am, 10.45am, 2.20pm and 5.25pm returning from Halesworth at 8.36am, 1.10pm, 3.13pm and 6.17pm. The interval between the arrival of the 10.45am Up train at Halesworth and the 1.10pm Down departure was used for the Q, as and when required, goods train working to Southwold and return. On 30th March and 1st and 3rd April additional services ran for the Easter holiday departing Southwold at 7.15pm and returning from Halesworth at 8.00pm, both calling at all intermediate stations.

Five return journeys were made in each direction on weekdays but none on Sundays in the winter timetable operative in 1902/3. From March some alterations were introduced: the 7.15pm ex Southwold was re-timed to start at 7.10pm, whilst the return working 8.10pm ex Halesworth started at the earlier time of 7.53pm, thus not providing a connection with the 6.56pm GER train ex Ipswich due at Halesworth at 8.07pm. It is assumed the GER train was frequently late running and even if on time only gave Southwold line passengers a three minutes connection. By departing at the earlier time of 7.53pm punctual running could be achieved on the narrow gauge line to the detriment of passengers alighting from the GE service, who were forced to find alternative arrangements for onward travel.

At a meeting of Southwold Town Council held on 3rd April 1903, a letter from the GER was read stating the service from Lowestoft could be greatly improved if the SR Company would run a train in connection with the 9.48am and 3.50pm trains from Norwich and Yarmouth respectively, and suggesting the Council approach the SR. The Council duly took up the matter but also pointed out the reason for the reduced number of bookings from Halesworth, which they had complained of, was because of the bad service provided by the GER Company! The SR management replied in June with outright refusal but from the beginning of July the summer timetable of six trains in each direction was introduced. No Sunday services operated.

The following winter timetable showed the usual reduction to four weekday trains in each direction but during November and December there was a change of heart and one train ran each way on the Sabbath, departing Southwold at 5.50pm and returning from Halesworth at 7.27pm.

Thereafter the early months of 1904 showed a weekday service of four trains in each direction with an additional late train each way

See page				WEEK DAYS.				SUNDAY
		morn	morn	NS morn	SO even.	even.	SO even.	
36	LONDON (Liverpool St.) dep.	5 9	10 15	11 42	1 0	3 22	4 55	...
	Ipswich — — — —	6 54	11 59	2 27	2 48	5 9	6 26	...
	Halesworth ....arr.	8 10	1 3	3 56	3 58	6 21	7 26	...
37	Lowestoft (Central) ...dep.	7D15	10 7	2 29	2 29	3 45	6 28	...
	Yarmouth (South Tn.) „	7 35	9 51	2 21	2 21	3 39	6 23	...
	Halesworth — — —arr.	8 35	10 51	3 13	3 13	4 30	7 27	...
	HALESWORTH ....dep.	8 40	1 5	3 40	4 0	6 25	7 53	...
	Wenhaston — — —	8 49	1 14	3 49	4 9	6 34	8 2	...
	Blythburgh (for Wangford)	9 0	1 25	4 0	4 20	6 45	8 13	...
	Walberswick — — —	9 12	1 37	4 12	4 32	6 57	8 25	...
	SOUTHWOLD...............arr.	9 17	1 42	4 17	4 37	7 2	8 30	...

A On Saturdays leaves Halesworth 3.58 and arrives Yarmouth 4.56 and Lowestoft 4.41 p.m.
D On Mondays leaves Lowestoft at 7.26 a.m.

SR timetable July 1910 from GER public timetable.

on Mondays and Saturdays. The late Monday train was withdrawn at the end of April. Surprisingly, the SR issued a handy sized timetable booklet in March, which as well as containing local and GER connections included twenty pages of local information and advertisements.

A significant development in 1904 was the introduction of the GER bus service connecting Lowestoft with Southwold via Kessingland which commenced on 18th July giving travellers the opportunity of direct access instead of the convoluted changing of trains at Halesworth. By April 1905 the SR Company was operating a timetable of five trains in each direction on weekdays only. Up services departed Southwold at 7.30am, 10.55am, 2.20pm, 5.30pm and 7.10pm, whilst trains departed Halesworth in the Down direction at 8.43am, 1.12pm, 3.23pm, 6.23pm and 7.53pm. All trains now made mandatory stops at the intermediate stations, although the 37 minutes overall timing for the 8¾ miles journey was maintained. The last Up and Down services had previously operated on Mondays and Saturdays only.

The working timetable for the summer of 1907 showed the services tabled on the left. The following winter, the weekdays only service reverted to four trains in each direction but on and from 1st May 1908 the 7.10pmSO train from Southwold and 7.53pmSO return from Halesworth ran daily. The Sunday service of two trains each way commenced on 10th July. On several occasions in November 1908 trains were halted after starting away from Halesworth for the convenience of late passengers. The Halesworth station master reported that this was often done and instructions were duly issued to train crews and station staff that the practice was to cease and trains were not to be delayed for latecomers.

The timetable for October 1910 showed a service of five trains in each direction on weekdays only. All trains were allowed 37 minutes for the 8 miles 63 chains journey. After complaints were made regarding connections at Halesworth when the GER train arrived and the Southwold connecting service departed at the

Timetable for Summer 1903

Up		MO	MX				
		am	am	am	pm	pm	pm
Southwold	dep	7.25	7.30	10.55	2.20	5.30	7.10
Walberswick	dep	7.28	7.33	10.58	2.23	5.33	7.13
Blythburgh	dep	7.40	7.43	11.10	2.35	5.45	7.25
Wenhaston	dep	7.51	7.56	11.21	2.46	5.56	7.36
Halesworth	arr	8.02	8.07	11.32	2.57	6.07	7.47
Down		am	pm	pm	pm	pm	
Halesworth	dep	8.43	1.12	3.23	6.23	7.53	
Wenhaston	dep	8.52	1.21	3.32	6.32	8.02	
Blythburgh	dep	9.03	1.32	3.43	6.43	8.13	
Walberswick	dep	9.17	1.46	3.57	6.57	8.27	
Southwold	arr	9.20	1.49	4.00	7.00	8.30	

Working Timetable for Summer 1907

Up		Weekdays						Sundays	
		am	am	pm	pm	pm	pm	am	pm
Southwold	dep	7.30	10.20	12.20	2.20	5.40	7.10	9.00*	4.55
Walberswick	dep	7.33	10.23	12.23	2.23	5.43	7.13	9.03*	4.58
Blythburgh	dep	7.45	10.35	12.35	2.35	5.55	7.25	9.15*	5.10
Wenhaston	dep	7.56	10.46	12.46	2.46	6.06	7.36	9.26*	5.21
Halesworth	arr	8.07	10.57	12.57	2.57	6.17	7.47	9.37*	5.32
Down		**Weekdays**						**Sundays**	
		am	am	pm	pm	pm	pm	am	pm
Halesworth	dep	8.40	11.10	1.30	3.40	6.23	7.53	9.44*	7.27
Wenhaston	dep	8.49	11.19	1.39	3.49	6.32	8.02	9.53*	7.36
Blythburgh	dep	9.00	11.30	1.50	4.00	6.43	8.13	10.04*	7.47
Walberswick	dep	9.14	11.44	2.04	4.14	6.57	8.27	10.18*	8.01
Southwold	arr	9.17	11.47	2.07	4.17	7.00	8.30	10.21*	8.04

* Runs 28th July to 8th September only

		WEEK DAYS.						SUNDAYS.
		MO morn	NM morn	morn	even	even	SO even	
SOUTHWOLD	dep.	7 20	7 25	10 5	2 23	5 25	7 10	...
Walberswick		7 25	7 30	10 10	2 28	5 30	7 13	...
Blythburgh, for Wangford		7 35	7 40	10 20	2 38	5 40	7 25	...
Wenhaston		7 46	7 51	10 31	2 49	5 51	7 36	...
HALESWORTH	arr.	7 57	8 2	10 42	3 0	6 2	7 47	...
Halesworth	dep.	8 10	8 10	11 30	3A36	6 21	8 18	
Yarmouth (South Tn.)	,,	9 8	9 8	12 36	4A38	7 21	9 14	
Lowestoft (Central)	arr.	8 50	8 50	12 21	4A23	7 11	9 2	
Halesworth	dep.	8 8	8 33	10 54	3 13	6 26		
Ipswich	arr.	8 54	9 43	12 7	4 16	7 40		
LONDON (Liverpool St.)	,,	10 49	11 12	2 40	5 53	9 20		

MO Mondays only. **NM** Not Mondays.
NS Not Saturdays. **SO** Saturdays only.

Timetable for October 1910

Up

		am	am	pm	pm	pm
Southwold	dep	7.30	10.55	2.20	5.25	7.10
Walberswick	dep	7.35	11.00	2.25	5.30	7.15
Blythburgh	dep	7.45	11.10	2.35	5.40	7.25
Wenhaston	dep	7.56	11.21	2.46	5.51	7.36
Halesworth	arr	8.07	11.32	2.57	6.02	7.47
Liverpool Street	arr	11*30	11.32	6.00	9.25	

*Arrives 10.45am MO

Down

		am	am/pm	pm	pm	pm
Liverpool Street	dep	5.05	10.00	11.45	3.25	5.00
Halesworth	dep	8.40	1.12	3.20	6.24	7.53
Wenhaston	dep	8.49	1.21	3.29	6.33	8.02
Blythburgh	dep	9.00	1.32	3.40	6.44	8.13
Walberswick	dep	9.12	1.44	3.52	6.56	8.25
Southwold	arr	9.17	1.49	3.57	7.01	8.30

Timetable for Winter 1912/13

Up — Weekdays

		am	am	pm	pm	pm
Southwold	dep	7.30	10.50	2.20	5.30	7.13*
Walberswick	dep	7.33	10.53	2.23	5.33	7.16*
Blythburgh	dep	7.45	11.05	2.35	5.45	7.28*
Wenhaston	dep	7.56	11.16	2.46	5.56	7.39*
Halesworth	arr	8.07	11.27	2.57	6.07	7.50*

Down — Weekdays

		am	pm	pm	pm	pm
Halesworth	dep	8.40	1.15	3.20	6.29	7.55*
Wenhaston	dep	8.49	1.24	3.29	6.38	8.04*
Blythburgh	dep	9.00	1.35	3.40	6.49	8.15*
Walberswick	dep	9.14	1.49	3.54	7.03	8.29*
Southwold	arr	9.17	1.52	3.57	7.06	8.32*

* SO after 31st December 1912

RIGHT: Summer 1915 timetable of SR trains arriving and departing Halesworth 1915 from GER working timetable.

BELOW: Winter 1915 SR timetable from GER public timetable.

uniform time of 6.24pm, from 1st February until 28th April 1911 excepting 14th and 17th April every Monday to Friday, the 6.24pm Halesworth to Southwold train was re-timed to start at 6.50pm. The decision was not universally popular and following yet further complaints that intending passengers were forced to wait an extra half hour and delays incurred to the last delivery of letters, from May the departure reverted to 6.24pm although the connection was maintained unless the GER train was excessively late.

The summer timetable for 1911 commencing in July showed six trains each way on weekdays and two on Sundays, with one of the weekday trains in each direction 12.20pm ex Southwold and 3.40pm ex Halesworth covering the journey in 33 minutes by omitting the stops at Blythburgh and Wenhaston. From 26th February 1912 the practice of attaching empty wagons to passenger trains was banned unless specifically requested by Mr Wright. Henceforth wagons were to be attached to the special goods train only. Two years later the winter working timetable showed the following service of four trains in each direction Mondays to Fridays and an additional SO service after 31st December 1912.

In January 1913 the GER bus service between Lowestoft and Southwold was withdrawn without much publicity, much to the delight of the SR management. The summer working timetable for 1913 showed the service tabled above right.

The outbreak of hostilities initially required the SR to make few changes and by October 1915 the weekday service remained at four trains SX and five SO in each direction departing Southwold at 7.20amMO, 7.25amMX, 10.05am, 2.23pm, 5.25pm and 7.10pmSO, returning from Halesworth at 8.40am, 1.05pm, 3.40pmSX, 4.00pmSO, 6.25pm and 7.53pmSO. However, as World War One took its grip on the country, and especially the

Timetable for Summer 1913

Up		Weekdays						Sun
		am	am	pm	pm	pm	pm	pm
Southwold	dep	7.30	10.15	12.16	2.20	5.35	7.10	4.55
Walberswick	dep	7.33	10.18	12.19	2.23	5.38	7.13	4.58
Blythburgh	dep	7.45	10.30	12.31	2.35	5.50	7.25	5.10
Wenhaston	dep	7.56	10.41	12.42	2.46	6.01	7.36	5.21
Halesworth	arr	8.07	10.52	12.53	2.57	6.12	7.47	5.32

Down		Weekdays						Sun
		am	am	pm	pm	pm	pm	pm
Halesworth	dep	8.40	11.33	1.33	3.35	6.26	7.53	7.32
Wenhaston	dep	8.49	11.42	1.42	3.44	6.35	8.02	7.41
Blythburgh	dep	9.00	11.53	1.53	3.55	6.46	8.13	7.52
Walberswick	dep	9.14	12.07	2.07	4.09	7.00	8.27	8.06
Southwold	arr	9.17	12.10	2.10	4.12	7.03	8.30	8.09

coastal areas of East Anglia, so extra troop movements became all too commonplace and from 21st October 1915 special arrangements were made to run trains for military personnel at short notice on Sundays, although this was later extended to any time of the day or night, and entailing the cancellation of normal services, if required, especially in case of emergency.

Commencing on Saturday 2nd September 1916 and every Saturday until further notice the company advised that the 2.23pm Southwold to Halesworth train would not convey local passengers from Blythburgh or Wenhaston. On arrival at Halesworth the train ran ECS back to Blythburgh to form a service to Halesworth calling at Wenhaston. Thus passengers previously enjoying a 2.38pm departure from Blythburgh and 2.49pm from Wenhaston were forced to wait for almost an hour. In consequence, the 3.40pm Down departure was re-timed to 4.00pm. The rearranged times ceased with effect from the October timetable and were probably caused by military requirements.

Two years later the timetable for 1917 showed a reduction in running time to 35 minutes because of the closure of Walberswick station. Only four trains ran in each direction, weekdays only, partly to conserve coal stocks but more importantly to allow paths for military special trains, if required. Service trains departed Southwold at 7.35am, 10.05am, 2.50pm and 5.23pm and returned from Halesworth at 8.40am, 1.05pm, 3.40pm and 6.30pm.

Timetable of SR trains arriving and departing Halesworth May 1916 from GER working timetable.

SOUTHWOLD RAILWAY.

Passenger trains (worked by the Southwold Company) arrive at and depart from Halesworth as under:—

WEEK DAYS.							SUNDAYS
		a.m.	a.m.	p.m.	p.m.	SO p.m.	
Halesworth ... arr.		8 12	10 42	3 37	6 2	7 56	

		a.m.	p.m.	p.m.	p.m.	SO p.m.	SUNDAYS
Halesworth ... dep.		8 40	1 5	3 40	6 30	8 3	

Timetable of SR trains arriving and departing Halesworth January 1917 from GER working timetable.

BELOW: SR timetable 1919 from GER public timetable.

See page		WEEK DAYS.				SUNDAY
14	LONDON (L'pool St.) dep. Ipswich " Halesworth arr.	morn 5 10 7 17 8 34	morn 10 15 12 2 12 52	even. 12 57 2 43 3 53	even. 3 22 5 6 6 21	
15	Lowestoft (Central) dep. Yarmouth (South Tn.) " Halesworth arr.	6 39 7 30 8 28	11 43 11 52 12 53	2 28 2 24 3 13	5 24 5 35 6 23	
	HALESWORTH dep. Wenhaston Blythburgh (for Wangford) SOUTHWOLD arr.	8 40 8 49 9 0 9 17	1 5 1 14 1 25 1 42	4 0 4 9 4 20 4 37	6 25 6 34 6 45 7 2	

The end of hostilities found the railway in a deteriorated condition with competition on the horizon, for by 1919 a bus service operated by Automobile Services Limited was operating between Southwold and Yarmouth thereby draining some traffic from the SR. The summer timetable offered four trains in each direction on weekdays, departing Southwold at 7.40pm, 10.10am, 2.23pm and 5.23pm whilst Down departures from Halesworth left at 8.40am, 1.05pm, 4.00pm and 6.25pm with a 37 minutes timing for the journey. In the same year Walberswick station reopened, whilst during the national railway strike volunteers enabled the SR to operate two return trips, the first departing Southwold at 10.10am. The strike ended on 12th October.

From 18th November 1920 special instructions were issued for the passage of a special fish train on Sundays, when no passenger trains operated. The winter timetable for 1921 continued to show four trains in each direction running on weekdays only. Up services departed Southwold at 7.40am, 10.10am, 2.23pm and 5.23pm whilst Down trains departed Halesworth at 8.40am, 1.28pm, 3.40pm and 6.30pm. The 7.40am Up train and the 6.30pm Down trains omitted calling at Walberswick but like all trains maintained the 37 minutes timing for the 8 miles 63 chains journey. As a result of the accident at Walberswick, revised running times were introduced on and from 21st November 1921 when journey times were extended from 37 to 41 minutes.

The grouping of the railways brought about by the 1921 Railways Act found the GER absorbed into the London & North Eastern Railway but the new ownership had little effect on SR train services.

The summer timetable for 1922 showed a weekday service of six trains in each direction with one return trip on Sunday. Trains were allowed 6 minutes running time on the Down road between Walberswick and Southwold. A minor timetable change made between 10th July and 1st October 1922 saw the 6.37pm train re-timed to 6.35pm, whilst the 8.12pm ran Mondays to Saturdays.

From 9th July 1923 the timetable was as shown here. This summer timetable remained in operation in 1924 with Sunday trains offered from 27th July until 7th September only.

The timetable operative from 21st September 1925 showed five trains in each direction, departing Southwold at 7.30am, 10.05am, 2.24pm, 5.23pm and 7.26pm, returning from Halesworth at 8.40am, 1.00pm, 3.35pm, 6.37pm and 8.12pm. All trains were allowed 41 minutes running time for the journey. From 31st October the service was reduced to four trains in each direction by the withdrawal of the last Up and Down services. From April 1926 a last attempt was made to counteract the loss of trade to the competitive bus company when the service was increased to six trains each way on weekdays and four in each direction on Sundays in the summer months. In 1926 the SR manager instructed that in future when a special goods train was operated Regulation 15a of Appendix 1 of the Train Staff Regulations was to be carried out on the 10.05am mixed train. The working timetable for 1927 showed the same weekday timings as 1923 with two trains operating each way on Sundays from 24th July until 4th September.

Continuing the thrust against the competitive bus services the last summer timetable, operative from 9th July to 23rd September 1928, again showed six trains in each direction on weekdays and four each way on Sundays. On weekdays, Up services departed

Timetable of SR trains arriving and departing Halesworth September 1917 from GER working timetable.

SOUTHWOLD RAILWAY.

Passenger trains (worked by the Southwold Company) arrive at and depart from Halesworth as under:—

WEEK DAYS.

		a.m.	a.m.	p.m.	p.m.	A SO p.m.	SUNDAYS
Halesworth	arr.	8 12	10 42	3 37	6 2	7 52	
Halesworth	dep.	a.m. 8 40	p.m. 1 5	p.m. 3 40	p.m. 6 30	A SO p.m. 8 3	SUNDAYS

A Will not run after September.

	WEEK DAYS				SUNDAYS
	morn	morn	even.	even.	
SOUTHWOLD — — — dep.	7 40	10 10	2 23	5 23	...
Blythburgh, for Wangford	7 55	10 25	2 38	5 39	...
Wenhaston — — — —	8 6	10 36	2 49	5 51	...
HALESWORTH .... arr.	8 17	10 47	3 0	6 2	...
Halesworth — — — dep.	8 34	11 45	3 53	6 25	—
Yarmouth (South Tn.) arr.	9 31	12 40	4 49	7 23	...
Lowestoft (Central) ... „	9 18	12 38	4 36	7 14	—
Halesworth .... dep.	8 28	10 57	3 13	6 26	...
Ipswich — — — — arr.	9 43	12 15	4 16	7 40	—
LONDON (L'pool St.) „	11 22	1 58	5 55	9 29	...

Running Times Between Stations and Station Dwell Times, on and from 21st November 1921		
Up	Running Time	Station Time
Southwold to Walberswick	5 minutes	
Walberswick station		½ minute
Walberswick to Blythburgh	12 minutes	
Blythburgh station		1½ minutes
Blythburgh to Wenhaston	10 minutes	
Wenhaston station		1 minute
Wenhaston to Halesworth	11 minutes	
Down		
Halesworth to Wenhaston	10 minutes	
Wenhaston station		1 minute
Wenhaston to Blythburgh	10 minutes	
Blythburgh station		1½ minute
Blythburgh to Walberswick	12½ minutes	
Walberswick station		5½ minute
Walberswick to Southwold	5½ minutes	

Timetable from 10th July to 1st October 1922

Up		Weekdays						Sun
		am	am	pm	pm	pm	pm	pm
Southwold	dep	7.30	9.45	12.00	2.20	5.23	7.26	5.19
Walberswick	dep	7.35	9.50	12.05	2.25	5.28	7.31	5.24
Blythburgh	dep	7.49	10.04	12.19	2.39	5.42	7.45	5.38
Wenhaston	dep	8.00	10.15	12.30	2.50	5.53	7.56	5.49
Halesworth	arr	8.11	10.26	12.41	3.01	6.04	8.07	6.00
Liverpool Street	arr	11.22	1.20	3.42	5.56	9.22		9.10

Down		Weekdays						Sun
		am	am	am/pm	pm	pm	pm	pm
Liverpool Street	dep	5.00		10.12	1.00	3.18	4.55	4.40
Halesworth	dep	8.40	10.45	1.15	3.45	6.35	8.12	8.00
Wenhaston	dep	8.51	10.56	1.26	3.56	6.46	8.23	8.11
Blythburgh	dep	9.02	11.07	1.37	4.07	6.57	8.34	8.22
Walberswick	dep	9.15	11.20	1.50	4.20	7.10	8.47	8.35
Southwold	arr	9.21	11.26	1.56	4.26	7.16	8.53	8.41

Southwold at 7.30am, 9.45am, 12.00noon, 2.20pm, 5.23pm and 7.26pm, returning from Halesworth at 8.40am, 10.45am, 1.00pm, 3.45pm, 6.37pm and 8.12pm. On Sundays trains departed Southwold at 9.50am, 1.10pm, 5.19pm and 7.00pm, returning from Halesworth at 10.40am, 2.00pm, 6.10pm and 8.00pm. The final timetable, operative from 1st January 1929 showed four trains in each direction: Up trains departed from Southwold at 7.30am, 9.50am, 2.24pm and 5.23pm, whilst Down trains departed Halesworth at 8.40am, 1.00pm, 3.35pm and 6.37pm. All trains were allowed 41 minutes for the journey.

See page		WEEK DAYS.												SUNDAY	
		morn		morn		morn		even.		even.		even.		even.	
24, 25	LIVERPOOL STREET ... dep.	5 0	...		...	10 0		1 0	...	3 18	...	4 55		4 40	
	Ipswich — — — — — "	7 7	—	8 50	—	11 46	—	2 37	—	5 6	—	6 28	—	6 36	
	Halesworth .... arr.	8 24	...	10 0	...	12 39	—	3 38	...	6 28	...	7 28	...	7 50	
26, 27	Lowestoft (Central) — — dep.	7 36	—	9 53	—	11 40	—	2 28	—	5 30	—	6 25	—	5 20	
	Yarmouth (South Town) ... "	7 25	...	9 50	...	11 30	—	2 24	—	5 22	—	6 24	—	5 10	
	Halesworth — — — — arr.	8 24	...	10 41	...	12 31	—	3 14	...	6 26	...	7 27	...	6 9	
	HALESWORTH .... dep.	8 40	...	10 45	...	1 0	—	3 45	...	6 37	...	8 12	...	8 0	
	Wenhaston — — — — "	8 51	—	10 56	—	1 11	—	3 56	—	6 48	—	8 23	—	8 11	
	Blythburgh (for Wangford) .... "	9 2	...	11 7	...	1 22	—	4 7	...	6 59	...	8 34	...	8 22	
	Walberswick — — — — "	9 15	...	11 20	—	1 35	—	4 20	...	7 12	...	8 47	...	8 35	
	SOUTHWOLD .... arr.	9 21	...	11 26	...	1 41	—	4 26	...	7 18	...	8 53	...	8 41	

B On Saturdays leaves Halesworth 8.21, and arrives Yarmouth 9.16 and Lowestoft 9.4 p.m.

ABOVE: SR timetable for May 1923 from the L&NER public timetable.

	HALESWORTH and SOUTHWOLD.—Southwold.								
Miles	Down.	Week Days.	Sundays.	Miles	Up.	Week Days.	Sundays.		
		mrn mrn mrn aft S				mrn mrn aft aft S			
—	864London(L.S.)dep.	5 0 10 3 11A56 3 15 4 55	......	—	Southwold......dep.	7 30 10 52 2 24 5 23 7 26	......		
—	Halesworth....dep.	8 40 1 0 3 35 6 37 8 12	......	1	Walberswick......	7 35 10 10 2 29 5 28 7 31	......		
2½	Wenhaston.........	8 51 1 11 3 46 6 48 8 23	......	4	Blythburgh B......	7 49 10 24 2 43 5 42 7 45	......		
5	Blythburgh B......	9 2 1 22 3 57 6 59 8 34	......	6½	Wenhaston.........	8 0 10 35 2 54 5 53 7 56	......		
8	Walberswick........	9 15 1 35 4 10 7 12 8 47	......	9	Halesworth 864 arr.	8 11 10 46 3 5 6 4 8 7	......		
9	Southwold....arr.	9 21 1 41 4 16 7 18 8 53	......	109¾	864London(L.S.) arr.	11 22 2 4 5 59 9 27	......		

A Departs at 12 25 aft. on Saturdays.   **B** Station for Wangford (2¼ miles).   **S** Saturdays only.

ABOVE: SR timetable 1928 from Bradshaw.

1st JANUARY. 1929, until further notice.

DOWN TRAINS.					UP TRAINS.				
	a.m.	p.m.	p.m.	p.m.		a.m.	a.m.	p.m.	p.m
Halesworth dep	8 40	1 0	3 35	6 37	Southwold dep.	7 30	9 50	2 24	5 23
Wenhaston "	8 51	1 11	3 46	6 48	Walberswick "	7 35	9 55	2 29	5 28
Blythburgh "	9 2	1 22	3 57	6 59	Blythburgh "	7 49	10 9	2 43	5 42
Walberswick "	9 15	1 35	4 10	7 12	Wenhaston "	8 0	10 20	2 54	5 53
Southwold arr.	9 21	1 41	4 16	7 18	Halesworth arr.	8 11	10 31	3 5	6 4

LEFT: SR timetable January 1929.

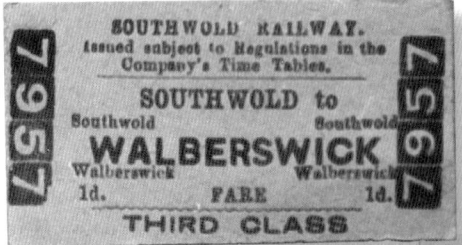

Southwold Railway Third Class single ticket and 2d parcels stamp.

FARES

Tickets issued by the SR were the usual Edmundson design and only First and Third Class fares were offered. A curiosity of the Third Class tickets was the legend *'Actual Fare …'*. In 1879 fares were 2d per mile First Class and 1d per mile Third Class, but from 1st March 1883 Third Class fares were increased to the rate of 1½d per mile. All stations issued tickets but at Halesworth tickets for travel on the SR were issued by the GER booking office. This led to a small amount of fraudulent travel and on 7th October 1885 Station Master Walter Calver asked for permission to examine the tickets of all passengers before the train departed Halesworth as he had no knowledge of who was in possession of a permit to travel because the GER booking office issued the tickets. Then, on 8th July 1886 he again complained to Victoria Street – the booking office had failed to issue tickets on a Sunday and opined the only way to prevent such events was for a periodic check of all tickets before departure of the train. He reported passengers crossing to the

		WEEK DAYS.						SUNDAYS.
		morn	morn	noon	even.	even.	even.	even.
SOUTHWOLD .... dep.		7 30	9 45	12 0	2 20	5 23	7 26	5 19
Walberswick — — — — —		7 35	9 50	12 5	2 25	5 28	7 31	5 24
Blythburgh *(for Wangford)*		7 49	10 4	12 19	2 39	5 42	7 45	5 38
Wenhaston — — — — —		8 0	10 15	12 30	2 50	5 53	7 56	5 49
HALESWORTH .... arr.		8 11	10 26	12 41	3 1	6 4	8 7	6 0
Halesworth — — — dep.		8 24	11 49	1 41	3 38	6 28	8 20	7 50
Yarmouth (South Town) ...... arr.		9 20	12 44	2 32	4 22	7 26	9 25	8 46
Lowestoft (Central) — — „		9 13	12 48	2 22	4 23	7 15	9 12	8 35
Halesworth .... dep.		8 24	10 41	1 9	3 14	6 26		6 9
Ipswich— — — — — arr.		9 40	11 35	2 0	4 17	7 40		7 27
LIVERPOOL STREET... „		11 22	1 20	3 42	5 56	9 22		9 10

SR station from the GER station after the train departure bell had been rung and not having time to book, and some never thought of booking. Headquarters agreed to a purge by inspection, which revealed a number attempting to board the train without tickets and such persons were prevented from travelling until they were in possession of the necessary ticket. Every train was checked for the next eight days when a total of forty-four passengers were sent back to the booking office including twelve passengers returning to Southwold from the Norfolk Show. Calver continued his check for the next seven days and found eight passengers without tickets. The checks evidently had the desired effect but once on the train the company staff were zealous in checking passengers tickets and it was reported on several occasions the guards used their ticket nippers with *'great aplomb'*.

In 1889 the SR single fare structure was:

SOUTHWOLD TO	FIRST CLASS	THIRD CLASS	HALESWORTH TO	FIRST CLASS	THIRD CLASS
Walberswick	0s 2d	0s 1d	Wenhaston	0s 4d	0s 2½d
Blythburgh	0s 6d	0s 4d	Blythburgh	0s 8d	0s 5d
Wenhaston	0s 10d	0s 6½d	Walberswick	1s 0d	0s 8d
Halesworth	1s 2d	0s 9d	Southwold	1s 2d	0s 9d

The following year saw a considerable increase in First Class fares to some stations:

SOUTHWOLD TO	FIRST CLASS	THIRD CLASS	HALESWORTH TO	FIRST CLASS	THIRD CLASS
Walberswick	0s 2d	0s 1d	Wenhaston	0s 6d	0s 2½d
Blythburgh	0s 8d	0s 4d	Blythburgh	0s 10d	0s 5d
Wenhaston	1s 0d	0s 6½d	Walberswick	1s 4d	0s 8d
Halesworth	1s 6d	0s 9d	Southwold	1s 6d	0s 9d

An unusual case of fraudulent travel was brought before Halesworth County Court on Wednesday 20th November 1901 when the GER sought to recover 5s 1d from Claude F. Egerton of Blythburgh. It appeared that Egerton having purchased a First Class cheap return ticket for 13s 9d from Liverpool Street to Southwold, journeyed only as far as Halesworth by train from whence he was driven to his home at Blythburgh by road. The company maintained the defendant had no right to break his journey at Halesworth and ought to have gone on to his destination by train. They were therefore suing him for 5s 1d, the difference between the price paid and the ordinary First Class fare from Liverpool Street to Halesworth. The contention of the defendant was that he, having gone direct to Blythburgh, although not by rail, was justified in breaking the journey at Halesworth. The special conditions, however, under which the cheap ticket was issued, were that it was available for Southwold, Walberswick, Blythburgh, Wenhaston and Darsham stations only and not Halesworth, therefore judgement was for the plaintiff.

During July and August 1909 cheap excursion fares were issued from Halesworth to Southwold every weekday by the 11.10am train, also from Wenhaston and Blythburgh. On Thursdays similar facilities were available from Halesworth only by the 1.30pm train. On Sundays cheap excursion tickets were available from Halesworth, Wenhaston and Blythburgh by the 10.16am ex Halesworth.

The GER also provided cheap return fares from Liverpool Street to Southwold providing Saturday to Monday tickets, Tourist Fortnightly and Weekend Tickets, as well as cheap Residential Season Tickets for clients who lived at Southwold and commuted to London on occasions during the week.

EXCURSIONS AND SPECIAL TRAFFIC

In the Tuesday of the third week of October 1881 the SR ran a special train for the East Suffolk District Sunday School Union convention held at the Congregational Church Southwold, whilst regular services were patronized the following day by people attending the event. The following year on the first Wednesday of July the railway conveyed a party of seventy schoolchildren from Walberswick to Southwold and to round off a memorable day a tea party was provided later in the afternoon by a local farmer.

As a direct result of road competition from various sources the SR offered for Whit Monday 1883 return tickets at single fares and a special later train departing Southwold at 9.20pm, returning from Halesworth at 10.05pm. The company also promised to run additional trains as and when required, after complaints were made regarding previous bank holidays when some passengers were left stranded at Halesworth because of overcrowding on the booked timetabled service. After the resurrection of the regular Southwold Thursday market, return journeys were offered at single fares, with the added bonus of an additional late train departing Southwold at 9.00pm and returning from Halesworth at 9.39pm, apparently achieved with an almost impossible two minutes turn round time. The locomotive crew probably did their best, by uncoupling the locomotive, running round the train and recoupling to the stock, but the 16 mph speed limit must have been exceeded on occasions to achieve a 10.16pm arrival time back at Southwold. The *Halesworth Times* reported in early August *'With a change in the weather and the breaking up of the schools, visitors have been pouring in of late as fast as our limited train service is able to bring them'*. However, the SR and Southwold Council made little effort to welcome the guests, for on Friday 3rd August 1883 the *'town being full of visitors and the night unusually dark numerous passengers arriving by the last train'* it was reported they *'groped their way up Station Road, stumbling into the gutter and over the bank without a glimmer of light'*. On Wednesday 8th August a special late train was operated *'for the convenience of people attending the East Suffolk Sunday Schools Union Annual Meeting at Wenhaston'*, departing Southwold at 9.00pm. The excellent summer weather continued into September when the newspaper reported an extended visiting season and on 17th of the month readers were advised *'the town remains fairly full, the excursion trains have been heavy laden and today an unusually large number of day visitors arrived by rail'*. Saturday 22nd September was also a busy day for the railway, for the Halesworth & Southwold

CHEAP EXCURSION TICKETS
Will be issued to
SOUTHWOLD
Every Monday and Thursday

Stations.		Times.		Fares for Double Journey.	
		a.m.	p.m.	1 Class.	3 Class.
Halesworth	dep.	8 40	1 15	2/-	1/-
Wenhaston	„	8 49	1 24	1/6	9 d.
Blythburgh	„	9 0	1 35	1/-	6d.
Southwold	arr.	9 17	1 52	—	—

The Tickets will be available for Return on day of issue only from Southwold by the 5.25 p.m. during May and the 5.25 and 7.13 p.m. Trains during June.

IPSWICH
Every Monday,
AS UNDER :—

Stations.		Times.		Fares for the Double Journey.	
		a.m.	a.m.	1 Cl.	3 Cl.
Southwold	dep.	7 30	10 50		
Walberswick	„	7 35	10 55	6/6	3/3
Blythburgh	„	7 45	11 5		
Wenhaston	„	7 56	11 16		
Ipswich	arr.	9 1	1 22	—	—

Available for Return on day of issue only from Ipswich at 6.38 p.m.

Cheap Return Tickets
TO
LONDON (LIVERPOOL STREET.)

FROM	FARES for the Double Journey.	
	FIRST CLASS.	THIRD CLASS.
SOUTHWOLD	27/2	12/4
WALBERSWICK	26/11	12/2
BLYTHBURGH	26/3	11/10
WENHASTON	25/10	11/7

The above Tickets will be available for return by any Train only on the Sunday (if Train Service permits) or Monday following the date of issue.

TOURIST, FORTNIGHTLY,
AND
FRIDAY to TUESDAY TICKETS
FROM
LONDON
ARE ISSUED AS UNDER BY ALL TRAINS TO
SOUTHWOLD.

TOURIST. A		FORTNIGHTLY, Available for 15 days. B		FRIDAY or SATURDAY TILL TUESDAY. C	
FIRST CLASS.	THIRD CLASS.	FIRST CLASS.	THIRD CLASS.	FIRST CLASS.	THIRD CLASS.
31/3	18/5	27/6	15/-	22/-	11/-

A—Tourist Tickets are issued by any Train on any day, and are avaliable for return by any of the advertised Trains on any day within Six Calendar Months.
B—Fortnightly Tickets are issued by any Train on any day, and are available for return by any of the advertised Trains on any day within 15 days, including the days of issue and return.
C—Friday to Tuesday Tickets are issued every Friday or Saturday by any Train, and are available for return by any of the advertised Trains on the day of issue, or on any day (Sunday if Train service permits) up to and including the Tuesday following.

A selection of adverts reproduced from an SR Timetable booklet dated 1914, giving special cheap fares for off-peak fares.

Volunteer Corps held a joint company drill and mock battle on 'Blythburgh Walks', as the open heathland on the road to Wenhaston was known. Both companies travelled by train, the 79-strong Halesworth Company taking the 3.14pm departure from the junction and the Southwold Company travelling by the 2.25pm train from Southwold, to form up outside the White Hart Inn at Blythburgh. The railway also carried a *'goodly number of sightseers'* and after the exercise provided a special train for the returning Halesworth Company departing Blythburgh at 7.40pm, whilst the Southwold Company were forced to wait for the last train of the day departing Blythburgh at 8.29pm.

On Saturday 8th March 1884 a *'hare and hounds paper chase'* was run from Halesworth station along Holton Road and across the marshes to Blythburgh, Walberswick and ultimately Southwold. After the event about sixteen of the competitors returned to Halesworth on the 6.35pm train ex Southwold *'very well satisfied by the day's run'*. At Whitsun the weather was hot and sunny and the railway conveyed upward of 700 passengers, some later attending the sports event at Southwold. A large number of holidaymakers also travelled over the 1884 August Bank Holiday when the *'railway arrangements'* were declared *'admirable'*.

In July 1885 the Meteor was advertised to depart from the Inner Pier, Lowestoft at 11.45am on Tuesdays, Thursdays and Saturdays, returning from Southwold the same day, the fare being 1s 6d, less than half the combined SR and GER rail fare.

The band of the Southwold Battery of the 1st Norfolk Artillery was performing on Gun Hill, Southwold on the evening of Saturday 14th August 1886, when a telegram arrived announcing their colleagues had won a gun drill competition at Yarmouth. The band duly marched to Southwold station to meet the 8.09pm arrival and as the train pulled in to the platform they struck up 'See the Conquering Hero Come', only to discover they had been the victims of a cruel hoax. Later, at the Railway Employees dinner held on Friday 24th September, Captain Adnams thanked the company for conveying military parties at reduced fares and especially *'for their liberality of terms in conveying men of No. 8 Battery'*.

Southwold's Marine Regatta encouraged additional travellers to the line but special trains were only operated on 27th August 1889 in connection with a firework display. Then on 24th September 1889 a party of archaeologists arrived at Southwold on the 12.37pm arrival train. They visited Southwold Church and later went by road to Blythburgh church. After the visit the party retired to the White Hart before catching the 5.40pm train to Halesworth en route to Yarmouth.

In June 1890 the SR issued special cheap return tickets in connection with a regatta at Southwold whilst August Bank Holiday found an unprecedented number of visitors at Southwold on the Monday. The *Halesworth Times* reported a number of boats were afloat offshore with the bathing machine proprietors busy all day. The beach was crowded with excursionists and residents alike, the latter in their white tents. *'The railway, which at times has received quite its share of derision, proved on Monday to be quite equal to the demands put upon it'*. One train conveyed nearly 300 passengers during the day, and *'the management at the various stations was so well worked that there was an entire absence of crowding and pressure either at the stations or in the carriages'*. On Thursday 28th August a combined Flower Show and Regatta was held at Southwold, the event concluding with a firework display by *'Messrs Brock of Crystal Palace'*. The SR advertised cheap excursion tickets by the 6.13pm train from Halesworth with a special return working from Southwold after the fireworks, as the last scheduled train departed at 7.05pm. The following Sunday the *'Friendly Societies'* held a parade at Southwold when the SR provided special trains to convey upwards of a thousand people to and from the event. When formed up, the procession, accompanied by two military bands from Halesworth and Lowestoft, was formed four deep and stretched over half a mile in length.

For the 1891 season sports competitions were held at Henham Hall, when cheap day tickets were issued to Blythburgh from all stations. Then in July the SR ran *'frequent and heavy trains carrying upwards of 700 passengers for the Friendly Societies'* Church Parade at Southwold. In the same month, cheap return tickets were issued for Halesworth Horse Fair and in September for a botanical ramble at Walberswick. When the Amusement Committee of the Southwold Ratepayers' Association decided to hold races on the common, the *Halesworth Times* reported the last occasion coincided with the opening of the SR on 24th September 1879.

The SR was again involved in transporting visitors and competitors to the sports event at Henham in June 1892, when cheap return tickets were issued to Blythburgh. Additional late trains had been a feature of many events and usually they were well patronised, but when in the same month a special train was made available for those returning from a *'grand evening concert'* at Southwold, the event failed to attract many patrons and the train departed, calling all stations to Halesworth, with few passengers. Halesworth Horse Show, which included *'a grand military tattoo'*, was more successful when over 5,000 spectators attended the event with the GER and SR issuing cheap return tickets, the latter with especially reduced rate return fares to Halesworth from Southwold and Walberswick at 1s 0d, Blythburgh 6d and Wenhaston 4d. The *Halesworth Times* reported the service provided by both railways as *'admirable'*.

The spring and summer of 1893 found the SR arranging additional trains and offering cheap fares as and when required. March 1893 saw the launching of a new lifeboat at Southwold, whilst Easter bore comparison with the previous year's traffic. On Thursday 6th July a special train departed Southwold at 9.30pm for Halesworth, conveying protesters from their meeting against the Church Suspensory (Wales) Bill, whilst return tickets at single fares were issued for the Halesworth Horse Show on Thursday 20th July. The event included a public auction of horse stock and a grand military tournament. The August Bank Holiday period found large numbers of passenger arrivals and day after day *'the trains have been packed'*. Southwold Marina Regatta on Thursday 17th August included a pyrotechnic display by Messrs Brock of Crystal Palace which encouraged many to travel to the event, and the SR arranged two additional late services departing Southwold at 9.15pm and 11.00pm conveying *'upwards of 600 people'*.

The fifth annual Henham Park Cycle and Athletic Sports event held in early June 1894 was now of sufficient importance for the SR to run a special train to Blythburgh and cheap return tickets were offered. Despite larger numbers attending the event the railway management were disappointed that fewer chose to travel by train. The usual August Bank Holiday visitors availed themselves of the railway facilities whilst on Thursday 16th August a special late departure at 10.15pm from Southwold returned late travellers who had attended the Marine Regatta.

The SR carried *'much additional passenger traffic'* during the 1895 Easter and Whitsun Bank Holiday periods, but three special events at Southwold required special arrangements. On August Bank Holiday Monday 5th August, a lifeboat demonstration attracted 'a very large number of holidaymakers from the surrounding district by road and rail and it is doubtful whether the Southwold Railway has ever carried so many passengers on one day'. The visitors initially watched a procession – including the Volunteer Artillery Band, the Mayor and Corporation, members of the Lifeboat Committee, the lifeboat manned by the crew, the fire engine and brigade, the Ambulance Corps and local fishermen – meander through the town. The Down trains were 'literally crammed' and in the evening the company was obliged to run a special train departing Southwold at 8.30pm. Then for the second event, the Southwold Marine Regatta held on Thursday 22nd August, the grand display of fireworks by Brock required a special train to depart the terminus at 9.30pm, after the company had issued the usual cheap excursion tickets from Halesworth and the intermediate stations. The third event involved a visit by the Ipswich branch of the British Association, who after arriving at Halesworth toured Wenhaston, Blythburgh and Walberswick in 'brakes' before proceeding to Southwold. The return journey was by train and the *Halesworth Times* enlivened the report of the visit:

'Finally a shrill whistle announced the approach of the light engine with its American cars, destined to draw the party to Halesworth, where the scream of the London train was heard, testifying to its impatience to draw them southward to the good town of Ipswich'.

The railway ran late trains as excursions from Southwold in 1896, the first on Wednesday 20th May in connection with a *'variety performance'* at the Drill Hall in aid of the Church Building Fund, which despite a second performance the following day was not repeated. The second late train departed Southwold at 10.00pm on Whit Monday following a demonstration of New Photography, also held in the Drill Hall. The summer months had seen a rapid increase in popularity for cycling and in early June 1896 the Henham Park Cycling and Athletic Sports event was held, with many attendees travelling by train to Blythburgh. Here *'four in hands'* were provided to transport them to and from the grounds, where in addition to extensive accommodation for horses and attendant vehicles, stands had been erected for the storage of cycles. Later in the year on Thursday 20th August 1896 in connection with Southwold Regatta excursion tickets were issued from Halesworth and the intermediate stations and a special train was advertised to depart the terminus at 9.45pm *'sharp'* after a *'Grand Display of Fireworks by Brock'*. The August Bank Holiday encouraged many to the sea and up to 6.00pm on Monday Halesworth GER station had booked 237 passengers to Southwold compared to 296 for Yarmouth and a mere 75 to Lowestoft. The same month had seen an increase in bicycle traffic on both the GER and SR as parties of cyclists toured every road in the area, the *Halesworth Times* reporting *'the ladies being portioned two to one compared with gentlemen'* and *'every train brings in more'*.

Henham Park eighth Cycling and Athletics meeting on Thursday 15th July 1897, attracted over 5,000 people to the event with the GER and SR offering combined and individual return cheap day tickets to Blythburgh. In the same year 415 return and 33 single tickets were issued from Halesworth to Southwold on August Bank Holiday Monday. The No. 9 Company of the Norfolk Royal Artillery Volunteers based at Southwold, used the 7.30am train from Southwold four times on Saturday mornings in 1897, the first occasion on 31st July when a detachment went to a marching camp at Great Yarmouth. On the other occasions in 18th September

On some occasions it was necessary for the SR to utilize all six passenger vehicles to handle large amounts of traffic such as at this summer gathering at Southwold post 1906.

John Alsop collection

and 2nd and 9th October the 10 inch Rifle Muzzle Loading Gun Detachment went to Landguard Fort near Felixstowe.

On Easter Monday 1899, the 8.36am Down service from Halesworth was re-timed to depart at 9.15am and excursion tickets were available to Southwold by this and the later 1.10pm departure, valid for return on the same day. On 10th June the 1st Volunteer Battalion, Suffolk Regiment F Company travelled by the 1.10pm train ex Halesworth to Southwold to undergo the third class of their annual course of musketry. For the Halesworth Horse and Flower Show held on 6th July reduced fares were issued from all SR stations. However, when a record 4,500 people attended the ninth Henham Park Cycling and Athletics meeting only 300 travelled by train. Then on 26th August, in connection with Southwold's Marine Regatta, an extra late train departed Southwold at 9.45pm and was reported as *'well patronised'*. On the following day nearly 100 members of the Royal Archaeological Institute visited the area but unfortunately the GER train was late and their stay at Halesworth was limited. The party then caught the 11.20am train to Southwold and were pleased with *'the homeliness'*, as one elderly gentleman said, *'of this little bit of railway. It was in truth a very agreeable stage of the journey, with an excellent view of Blythburgh church and the marshy valley decked with wild flowers; meadow sweet, willow herb and purple loosestrife and on the common, bracken and heather'*. For August Bank Holiday Monday, 418 passengers booked at Halesworth for Southwold, where it was estimated there were over 5,000 visitors.

The sixty members of F Company of the 1st Volunteer Battalion of the Suffolk Regiment paraded at Halesworth station on the last Saturday in August 1900 to catch the 11.10am train to Southwold for collective practices in connection with the annual course of musketry. They were met on arrival at Southwold station by Lieutenant R.A. Parry and, headed by the town band, marched through the town passing the new pier on the way to the 500 yards range. The group returned to Halesworth on the 5.30pm departure. 1900 also saw the opening of the new pier at Southwold.

The return of Lieutenant Colonel Bonham on Thursday 7th March 1901, invalided home from the Boer War, caused some excitement at Southwold. He had changed at Halesworth on to the 6.23pm train arriving at 7.00pm where he was greeted by the Countess of Stradbroke and a large crowd at the station. After several speeches he departed by coach to Southwold House, the route bedecked with flags.

In May 1901 the local company of 1st Volunteer Battalion of the Suffolk Regiment attended Southwold firing ranges on Thursday and Saturday afternoons travelling by the 1.12pm train ex Halesworth. They were back again on Saturday 13th July, catching the 1.28pm train from Halesworth, and then again on Saturday 12th October travelling by the 1.12pm departure. The Whitsun holiday in the same year was exceptionally fine with many changing trains at Halesworth to travel to the sea; on Whit Monday 240 tickets were issued to Southwold from Halesworth alone. On the same day a party of twenty-eight young people associated with the Norwich New City Men's Christian Guild had their annual outing to Southwold, catching the 8.43am train from Halesworth and arriving at 9.20am. After a tour in horse drawn conveyances to such places as Walberswick, Dunwich and Blythburgh the party returned to Halesworth by the 7.15pm train ex Southwold en route to Norwich. No. 10 Company of the 1st Norfolk Royal Artillery, based at Southwold, often used the railway to travel for exercises and on one such occasion the Breech Loading Gun Detachment was instructed to parade at Southwold station on Saturday 8th June 1901 prior to catching the 7.30am train. Six days later the Company was on parade at the station to welcome Gunner J. Palmer and Lance Corporal Critten on their return from the Boer War, the band playing 'See the Conquering Hero Comes' as the train drew into the station. Early in July over a hundred scholars of Southwold Sunday School travelled by train to Blythburgh and back for games and a picnic. Fine weather over the August Bank Holiday found Halesworth almost deserted as bookings by the GER and SR to the coastal resorts were in excess of those recorded in 1900, 250 passengers travelling from Halesworth to Southwold on the Monday.

On Saturday 13th July 1901 the new paddle steamer *King Edward VII* ran her inaugural trip to Southwold, a luncheon being held at the Grand Hotel in honour of the occasion. The travellers were deprived of a return sailing by sea, however, and after rambling around the town returned by rail via Halesworth. No doubt the inadequacies of the narrow gauge line led to the question of a further development of the railway service between Southwold and Halesworth being freely discussed.

On several occasions following their wedding, happy couples travelled by SR train at the beginning of their married life. On one such occasion Mr and Mrs H. Jaggs, married on 5th February 1902 in St. Edmund's Church Southwold, departed by the 5.30pm train en route to Halesworth, amidst a plethora of good wishes and display of fireworks courtesy of the Mayor of Southwold. Later in the year, on Whit Monday the SR ran a special train from Halesworth to Southwold at 11.45am, returning from Southwold at 12.30pm. Excursion tickets were also available to Southwold by the 8.43am and 1.12pm train ex Halesworth. Then from 2nd June on every Monday and Thursday excursion tickets were available to Southwold from Halesworth, Wenhaston and Blythburgh by trains leaving Halesworth at 8.43am and 1.12pm. Halesworth Horse and Flower Show on Thursday 17th July 1902 also attracted many visitors taking advantage of GER and SR cheap tickets.

For the Easter holiday in 1903 the SR provided on Wednesday 8th April an additional service departing Halesworth for Southwold at 8.10pm connecting with the 5.00pm GER train from Liverpool Street and at the same time on Thursday to connect with the 5.06pm from London. No trains ran on Good Friday but on Easter Monday 13th April excursion tickets were issued to Southwold from Halesworth, Wenhaston and Blythburgh by the 8.43am and 1.00pm trains ex Halesworth. Later in the year, on Thursday 13th August a garden party organised by the Church of England incorporated Society for Providing Homes for Waifs and Strays was held at Halesworth. The SR issued return tickets at excursion fares valid for the day of issue only from all stations to Halesworth for the event with an additional later departure from the junction at 10.15pm, the normal timetabled last train departing at 8.30pm. August Bank Holiday found the railway *'well patronized'*, whilst early in September and mid October the 1st Volunteer Battalions Suffolk Regiment F Company based at Halesworth attended musketry practice at Southwold, travelling by the 11.10am and 1.12pm trains respectively.

At the beginning of April 1904, Halesworth Urban Council applied to the GER to issue Friday to Tuesday tickets from Liverpool Street to Southwold to be available also to Halesworth. Such tickets were already available to stations adjoining Halesworth – Wenhaston on the SR and Darsham on the GE – but the request was turned down in early May. Much excitement was generated in

Southwold on 9th April 1904 when Southwold's Junior Football Team departed by train en route to play Trinity Old Boys of Ipswich, the match being a replay of a drawn game held at Leiston a fortnight earlier. So great were the number of supporters travelling that all carriages and two locomotives were used to get the party to Halesworth. The team was victorious and before they returned the town was decorated with flags. After the train, again hauled by the two locomotives, steamed into Southwold to the strains of 'See the Conquering Hero Comes' played by Southwold Town Band, the team, led by the band and followers, processed through the High Street. On the evening of Thursday 25th August 1904 a Working Men's Club was formally opened at Blythburgh. With the ceremony timed at 6.15pm a number of people travelled by the 5.40pm train from Southwold to attend the event, which included a concert. Unfortunately the rail travellers could not enjoy the full evening for they had to leave to catch the 8.13pm train from Blythburgh arriving at Walberswick at 8.27pm and Southwold at 8.30pm.

Commencing 1st May 1905 cheap excursion tickets were issued from Halesworth to Southwold every Monday and Thursday by the 8.43am and 1.12pm departures. In the same month Ernest Cooper, Town Clerk of Southwold, published a short historical sketch of the borough, which included a full description of train and steam-boat services. The Grand Massed Military Band recital at Southwold found the SR running a special late train to Halesworth on 18th July 1905, to be followed by the Southwold Athletic and Military Sports event held on Southwold Common on 20th July, when the company offered reduced fares and additional trains. Earlier in the month the 1st Volunteer Battalion Suffolk Regiment F Company attended shooting practice on Southwold Common leaving by the 1.30pm train and again on 18th when the Company and recruits were directed to travel by the 11.10am train from Halesworth in order to fire Parts I and II of the Annual Course of Musketry. The month also found the Halesworth Church Sunday School Treat taking the form of an excursion by train to Southwold. Parents wishing to accompany their children were offered a reduced rate return fare of 9d by applying to the Rector not later than the day before travel, when they would be required to present at the booking office. In all 216 children and several adults enjoyed the day, returning by the 7.10pm departure from Southwold. August Bank Holiday Monday 7th August 1905 found 224 tickets issued at Halesworth for Southwold, of which 160 were at excursion fares. Bookings to Blythburgh totalled a mere twenty-five. The Halesworth Church Lads Brigade also enjoyed the bank holiday, assembling at the station before journeyed to Blythburgh and then marching to Wangford to attend the Water Carnival. They returned by train later in the evening.

For 1906 the Easter holiday traffic was reasonable whilst at Whitsun, special excursion fares and additional trains ran on Whit Monday. Halesworth Horse Show held on 5th July found the SR issuing return tickets from Southwold and Walberswick 1s 0d, Blythburgh 7d and Wenhaston 4d, available for the day of issue only. Recent recruits to Halesworth Volunteer Company of the Suffolk Regiment were instructed to travel to Southwold for shooting practice on 19th April by the 1.12pm departure. Later in the same month Southwold's Royal Artillery Volunteers won the final of the Wilson Football Cup at Lowestoft. They travelled back to Southwold by road rather than using rail transport, but later were reported returning from camp by train on Friday 8th June at 7.15pm, being met by *'the band and a number of Southwoldians'*. Sixty members of the Halesworth Volunteers met at Halesworth station on Saturday 15th September and travelled by train to Wenhaston from whence they marched to Thorington Park where manoeuvres were carried out attacking an imaginary enemy.

For the Easter holidays in 1907 the SR ran an extra train departing Southwold at 7.10pm and returning from Halesworth at 7.53pm on Wednesday 27th March to connect with the 5.00pm GER train from Liverpool Street, and on Thursday 28th March to connect with the 5.06pm train from Liverpool Street, although these SR extras did not operate on Good Friday. On Easter Monday 1st April excursion tickets were issued to Southwold from Halesworth, Wenhaston and Blythburgh by the 8.40am and 1.12pm departures from Halesworth. The tickets were available for return only on the day of issue from Southwold or Walberswick by the 7.10pm departure from Southwold. Later in the year, on Thursday 11th July a special late train departed Halesworth at 10.30pm calling all stations to Southwold, returning patrons who had visited the Halesworth Horse and Flower Show. Special cheap return tickets had been issued in connection with the event, priced at 1s 0d from Southwold and Walberswick, 7d from Blythburgh and 4d from Wenhaston. A week later Halesworth Church Sunday School outing used the railway, the scholars marching to the station to catch 11.10am train to spend a day by the sea. The *Halesworth Times* reported *'by the 7.15pm train a tired but thoroughly happy party came back to Halesworth'*. August Bank Holiday traffic on the SR was reported as *'average'*, some 200 cheap day tickets being issued at Halesworth for travel to Southwold. This was double the total issued in 1906 when ordinary fares were charged. An additional late train departed Southwold at 10.00pm with few passengers as rain showers earlier in the evening had resulted in people catching the normal timetabled last train. Three times in 1907 men of the F Company of 1st Volunteer Battalion of the Suffolk Regiment based in Halesworth were instructed to attend rifle shooting at Southwold: on 27th April departing by the 1.12pm train, on 31st August the recruits leaving on the 11.10am train and the remainder by the 1.30pm departure, and lastly on 5th October by the 1.09pm service.

On Sunday 29th March 1908 a large military church parade was held at Henham Hall. Britain was in the process of replacing the old army volunteer system with a territorial system and the church parade was to mark the 1st Norfolk Royal Garrison Artillery Volunteers, which the Earl of Stradbroke had commanded for twenty years. Nearly 700 people attended to commemorate the impending merger of the brigade into the county territorial forces of Norfolk and Suffolk. The Earl chartered a special GER train from Norwich (Victoria) to Halesworth and also arranged for a special service to run on the SR where no Sunday service normally operated in the winter months. On arrival at Halesworth the different contingents were lined up on the SR platform and departed for Blythburgh as promptly as the limited accommodation of the SR would permit. The SR arrangements for the conspicuous occasion were under the direction of Henry Ward, the Secretary, and the first train departed Southwold at 9.30am with about sixty volunteers accompanied by thirty to forty passengers travelling to Blythburgh. After disgorging its passengers the train then ran empty back to Halesworth for the next contingent. The bridges spanning the railway and river at Blythburgh were crowded with spectators as the train formed of all six coaches and hauled by two locomotives passed en route. Arrival at Blythburgh was later than scheduled as about 250 men had to cram into the vehicles with access only available at each end of each car. The train then ran to Southwold to reverse and returned to

Halesworth to pick up the remainder of the Yarmouth men. The company returned the men to Halesworth in the evening, again using all six coaches hauled by two engines.

The Halesworth Horse and Flower Show held on Thursday 9th July 1908 attracted visitors who were offered cheap day tickets and later trains on both the GER and SR, the latter running a service departing Halesworth at 10.30pm to Southwold and calling at all intermediate stations. The Halesworth Lads' Brigade travelled to Southwold on Monday 10th August 1908 for their annual camp. After marching to the station, the thirty-five members joined the 8.40am departure arriving at Southwold at 9.17am and returned the following Friday. For the evenings of Thursday 13th and Wednesday 26th August special late train arrangements were made to cater for patrons attending the Southwold Confetti Fetes, the train departing at 10.00pm with return tickets issued at single fares. The Territorials at Halesworth were instructed to attend Southwold firing range on Saturday 12th September 1908 either travelling on the 11.20am or 1.30pm trains.

For the 1909 Easter holidays the SR ran additional trains on Wednesday 7th, Thursday 8th April and Easter Monday, departing Southwold at 7.10pm and returning from Halesworth at 7.53pm, calling at the intermediate stations if required. On the bank holiday Monday, excursion tickets to Southwold were available from Halesworth, Wenhaston and Blythburgh by the 8.40am and 1.12pm departures from Halesworth, available for return on the day of issue by any train. Unsettled weather resulted in only thirty-five excursion tickets being issued to Southwold from Halesworth. The Whitsun holiday at the end of May produced fine and sunny weather encouraging many to travel to the coast. On Monday 269 tickets were issued from Halesworth to Southwold; not all came by rail for motor buses were equally as busy and many others cycled into town.

The Halesworth Company of the Suffolk Regiment organized rifle shooting at Southwold on Saturday 3rd July 1909, when members were instructed to travel by the 8.40am train from Halesworth. Then on Wednesday 7th July Southwold town centre was decorated with flags and bunting for the visit of four *'first class'* cruisers, HMS *Diadem*, HMS *Niobe*, HMS *Spartiate* and HMS *Andromeda*, which steamed into Sole Bay at noon and remained anchored until 8.00am the following morning. The public were permitted to visit the vessels and the SR announced reduced fares from Halesworth and the intermediate stations for the event available by all afternoon trains, and ran a special late working to Halesworth departing Southwold at 10.00pm, which was *'well patronised'*. The fifteenth Halesworth Horse and Horticultural Show was held the following day, Thursday 8th July 1909, and the Southwold Company issued return tickets available on any train after 7.30am, priced from Southwold and Walberswick 1s 0d, Blythburgh 7d and Wenhaston 4d. A special late train calling all stations departed Halesworth at 10.30pm. For *'Confetti Fetes on the Pier'* afternoon and evening concerts on Thursday 19th August and 2nd September 1909, half-day tickets were issued from Halesworth, Wenhaston and Blythburgh to Southwold by the 3.40pm, 6.23pm and 7.53pm trains ex Halesworth at single fares for the double journey, returning by a special train departing Southwold at 10.00pm.

Additional traffic was always welcome and military activities continued patronage of the railway when on 9th April 1910 non-commissioned officers and men of F Company of the 4th Battalion Suffolk Regiment travelled by the 1.12pm train from Halesworth to Southwold arriving at 1.49pm for shooting practice, returning later in the day by the evening train. Shooting for *'Tradesmen's Prizes'* was conducted on Saturday 7th May commencing at 9.30am when the half company, with the exception of recruits and men who failed to qualify in the Standard Test Table the previous year, travelled by the 8.40am ex Halesworth arriving at Southwold at 9.17am. In June 1910 the Southwold Traders' Association ran their annual excursion from Southwold to Ipswich and thence from Ipswich to Felixstowe along the river before returning by rail. Then on 14th July in connection with Pier Pavilion Concerts at Southwold, a special late train departed Southwold at 10.20pm calling at all stations; excursion fares were available by the 1.12pm, 3.20pm and 6.23pm train from Halesworth. The August Bank Holiday encouraged many to travel to the sea and on 8th August 1910 the *Halesworth Times* reported *'a large number of excursionists arrived by the early train due at Southwold at 9.17am'*. The second train, due at 11.47am, *'discharged more excursionists whose numbers were added to by those arriving by sea, 'bus, pony cart and motor cart'*. After a week camping at Southwold the Church Lads' Brigade travelled to Halesworth by the 7.10pm train on Saturday 27th August 1910, although the entraining must have taken longer than expected for its reported departure was four minutes late.

The Whitsun holiday 1911 found temperatures at Southwold rising to 82 degrees Fahrenheit and the added attraction of a sports meeting and two motorcycle races found the SR accommodation *'taxed to the utmost'*. The Archdeaconry of Suffolk Sunday Association's annual festival was held on Thursday 27th July 1911 at Halesworth followed by a service in the parish church. The GER issued return tickets at single fares by any train from Stowmarket, Ipswich, Lowestoft and intermediate stations on production at the booking office of a programme for the event, or surrender of a voucher signed by the Secretary or surrender of a perforated portion of an admission ticket. The SR, while entering into the spirit of things, wanted no such proof of attendance and issued special return tickets by the 2.20pm train. Fares from Southwold and Walberswick were 1s 0d, Blythburgh 7d and Wenhaston 4d, available for return on the day of issue only from Halesworth, at 6.23pm or 7.53pm.

The company announced that with effect from 17th January 1912 the charge for hiring a special passenger train was increased to £12 10s 0d. Easter 1912 brought a great influx of visitors to Southwold with cheap tickets encouraging many to travel. The *Halesworth Times* reported that on the evening of Maundy Thursday, Southwold station *'looked like the height of the season, the approaches being thronged with vehicular traffic, passengers and friends'*. A fine Whit Monday 27th May proved equally as busy, for a sports day was held in the town and 450 passengers booked from Halesworth. The newspaper advised *'the Southwold Railway was taxed to its utmost capacity, and establishing a record for the largest number of passengers carried in one day'*. The August Bank Holiday also found the trains *'full to overflowing'*.

The Whitsun 1913 holiday traffic was very heavy, the great attraction at Southwold being a promised aeroplane flight and 556 passengers alone booked from Halesworth on the bank holiday Monday. The *Halesworth Times* reported *'in consequence the Southwold Railway Company was taxed to its utmost capacity, the trains were very full being drawn by two engines'*. Then on Wednesday 14th May the Red Cross held a display at Henham Park, the seat of Colonel, the Earl of Stradbroke. For the event the GER issued return tickets at single fares plus one half to

Halesworth and Blythburgh from places as far afield as Ipswich, Framlingham, Aldeburgh, Yarmouth South Town and Lowestoft including intermediate stations, to connect with SR trains arriving at Blythburgh at 12.25pm and 1.45pm, where brakes met both trains to convey passengers to the showground. Competitive buses ran from Southwold every hour. For the occasion the SR ran a normal timetable but used the Q path usually available for the goods train to run a special from Halesworth to Blythburgh with ECS on the return. In the evening the stock was worked ECS from Southwold to Blythburgh to form a special train to Halesworth. The Suffrage Movement paid a visit to Norfolk and Suffolk starting from Yarmouth on 10th July 1913, carrying Yarmouth, Lowestoft and Southwold banners and singing Suffrage Pilgrim songs. The programme on Saturday 12th July included a walk from Wangford via Blythburgh to Wenhaston. An impromptu meeting was held at Blythburgh and another at Wenhaston Green before the party travelled by train to Southwold, where a larger meeting was held in the evening. Another party came by train on 26th July when thirty-nine members of Ilford Church Naval Cadet Corps of Boy Scouts arrived at Southwold by the 2.10pm train. They marched through the town from the station headed by a bugle band to pitch tents on the south-east corner of the Common where they stayed until 9th August. The *Halesworth Times* reported *'other companies of Boy Scouts are expected to pitch their camp on the Common very shortly'*. The influx of visitors to Southwold for the August Bank Holiday found Halesworth booking 220 passengers to the town.

The outbreak of World War One immediately put an end to the spring and summertime events so enjoyed by the travelling public, but throughout hostilities the SR was regularly called upon to operate special trains, probably at very short notice, and one such example occurred on 10th September 1916 when members of the Suffolk Volunteer Regiment, Halesworth Corps were ordered to parade at Halesworth GER station at 12.15pm prior to catching the 12.44pm train to Beccles for inspection. Wenhaston men were advised to catch a special train departing Wenhaston at about noon. The running of such a special would have involved a rearrangement of the normal timetable. The corps was again ordered to parade at Halesworth station on Sunday 1st October at 2.15pm sharp, to travel by special train to Blythburgh to meet up with the Southwold section of the company. The return was made at 5.30pm from Blythburgh to Wenhaston and Halesworth. The SR summer Sunday timetable, which showed one train in each direction departing Southwold at 5.45pm and returning from Halesworth at 7.40pm had ceased, allowing the special train to run as requested.

The Boys' Brigade held their summer camp in the 1920s on the Territorial Army site on Southwold Common, whilst Life Boys, a junior section of the Boys' Brigade, for many years regularly held their summer camp at Southwold on a site near the harbour. All were conveyed by train from Halesworth.

Holiday arrangements for Easter 1922 were published on 27th March. On Thursday 13th April cheap 5, 6 or 9-day excursion tickets would be issued from Southwold, Walberswick, Blythburgh and Wenhaston to London with detailed particulars available at the stations. A train was to run from Southwold departing 7.26pm, returning from Halesworth at 8.12pm, connecting with the 4.55pm GER train from Liverpool Street. No trains were to operate on Good Friday 14th April, whilst on Saturday 15th and Monday 17th the evening service would run in similar times to Thursday, save that on the Monday the train provided a connection off the 5.22pm GER train from Liverpool Street and 7.05pm from Ipswich. Cheap tickets would be issued from Halesworth to Southwold by the 8.40am and 1.32pm trains, available for return by the 5.23pm and 7.26pm trains from Southwold, the Third Class return fare being 1s 10d. Then from Thursday 18th May and every Thursday during May and June 1922 cheap day tickets were issued in connection with half-day closing by the 1.32pm train from Halesworth to Southwold returning by the 5.23pm ex Southwold, again at 1s 10d Third Class.

For a number of years before and after World War One well-healed London City businessmen rented houses at seaside resorts during the summer season, moving their families and servants to the coast so that they could enjoy the sea air away from the metropolis. Southwold was, amongst others, where this arrangement was prevalent and several local families made financial gains before the autumnal weather set in. The head of the family usually joined his wife and children, travelling down on Friday evenings and back to Liverpool Street on Sunday evenings or Monday mornings, and it was therefore highly desirous of the GER and SR to make the best arrangements and thus avoid criticism.

The Whitsun holidays for 1922 were hot and sunny and on the bank holiday Monday Halesworth booked over 200 passengers to Southwold, whilst sixty went to Yarmouth and thirty to Lowestoft. The 22nd Halesworth Horse Show on Thursday 13th July enjoyed return fares at single fares on both the GER and SR. Commencing Thursday 13th July and every Thursday during July, August and September cheap tickets were issued for half-day closing from Halesworth to Southwold by the 1.15pm train ex Halesworth at a Third Class fare of 1s 4d, a reduction of 6d over previous years. Ever keen to encourage traffic, commencing on Monday 10th July and every Monday, Wednesday and Friday until further notice, excursion tickets were issued from Halesworth, Wenhaston and Blythburgh to Southwold by the 8.40am and 10.45am train from Halesworth at single fare for the return journey with tickets available for return by any train after 2.00pm on the day of issue only. August

---

Extra Journey Return Tickets at Reduced Fares

Are issued from the undermentioned Stations to Liverpool Street (not London Suburban Stations) and back, to Visitors holding not less than two tourist or Fortnightly Tickets.

FROM	EXTRA JOURNEY FARES TO LIVERPOOL STREET.	
	FIRST CLASS.	THIRD CLASS.
	S. D.	S. D.
SOUTHWOLD	18 9	11 0
WALBERSWICK		

These Cheap Return Tickets are issued to enable a member of a family to make occasional journeys, for business or other purposes, during the stay of the family at the Sea-side, and will be available for one week from the date of issue. In the event of two members of the family requiring to make the extra journey, the production of not less than four Tourist or Fortnightly Tickets will be necessary. These tickets are not issued to Residents or to other than bona-fide Visitors who have taken up their residence for not less than one week at the Sea-side.

Notice advertising extra journey return tickets at reduced fares, reproduced from the *SR Timetable* booklet dated 1914.

Bank Holiday in contrast was damp and miserable and although additional passengers travelled receipts were disappointing. Then in October excursion tickets were issued from Halesworth, Wenhaston and Blythburgh to Southwold on Mondays and Thursdays by the 8.40am and 1.10pm trains from Halesworth, at single fare for the return journey with tickets available for return by any train after 2.00pm on the day of issue only.

For the Easter holiday in 1923, cheap 5, 6, 8, 10 and 15-day excursion tickets were available, issued from Southwold, Walberswick, Blythburgh, and Wenhaston to London with full particulars obtainable on enquiry at the stations. On Thursday 29th March an extra train departed Southwold at 7.26pm returning from Halesworth at 8.12pm to connect with the 4.55pm L&NER train from Liverpool Street. No services ran on Good Friday but an extra train ran on Saturday 31st March in identical timings as Thursday. For the Southwold Hospital Cup football match held at Southwold on Monday 2nd April between Southwold Town and Old Nactonians, special trains ran, departing Southwold at 12.00 noon and 7.26pm, and from Halesworth at 11.00am and 8.12pm, the latter connecting with the 5.18pm train from Liverpool Street and the 7.02pm from Ipswich. For the holiday cheap tickets were issued from Halesworth, Wenhaston and Blythburgh to Southwold by the 8.40am, 11.00am and 1.10pm trains available for return by any train after 2.00pm. Third Class return fares were Halesworth 1s 2d, Wenhaston 10d and Blythburgh 6d.

Similar arrangements were offered for the Whitsun holiday but with cheap 3, 4, 8 and 15-day excursion tickets issued from Southwold, Walberswick, Blythburgh and Wenhaston to London in association with the L&NER. On Saturday 19th May 1923 an extra train departed Southwold for Halesworth at 7.26pm and returned from Halesworth at 8.12pm in connection with the 4.55pm train from Liverpool Street. On Monday 21st May 1923 the attraction of Southwold Sports was expected to prove an attraction and the SR advised trains would depart Southwold for Halesworth at 7.30am, 10.05am, 12.00 noon, 2.24pm, 5.35pm and 7.26pm, returning from Halesworth at 8.40am, 11.00am, 1.10pm, 3.35pm, 6.37pm and 8.12pm, calling at all intermediate stations if required. Cheap tickets were issued from Halesworth, Wenhaston and Blythburgh to Southwold by the 8.40am, 11.00am and 1.10pm trains, available for return by any train on the day of issue; the Third Class return fares from Southwold being Halesworth 1s 2d, Wenhaston 11d and Blythburgh 6d. Special day trip return tickets at the price of the single fare were available at this period from Southwold to Blythburgh, Wenhaston and Halesworth by the 10.05am, 12.00 noon and 2.34pm trains. The Directors were also desperate to attract patronage to the railway by issuing cheap excursion tickets to Southwold every Monday and Thursday from 7th May until 5th July 1923, departing Halesworth at 11.00am and 1.10pm, Wenhaston at 11.11am and 1.21pm, and Blythburgh at 11.22am and 1.32pm, arriving at Southwold at 11.41am and 1.51pm; the tickets costing 1s 2d from Halesworth, 10d from Wenhaston and 6d from Blythburgh were available for return by any train after 2.00pm on the day of issue only. The Easter holiday arrangements for 1924 were similar to the previous year and with favourable weather both the main line and the SR was well patronised with about 350 excursionists booking from Halesworth the Southwold on Easter Monday.

Southwold Traders Union organised a trip to Wembley Exhibition on 1st October 1924 with fares from Halesworth priced at 11s 6d and from stations on the Southwold Railway at 12s 9d. The SR train was booked to depart Southwold at 5.45am calling at all intermediate stations to connect with the L&NER train departing Halesworth at 6.35am, with arrival at Liverpool Street at 9.33am. Passengers wishing to journey to the exhibition then travelled on to Wembley Park by the Metropolitan Line. The return was booked to depart Liverpool Street at 11.45pm with arrival at Halesworth at 2.22am, where the Southwold was providing a connecting service to the coast. It was a requirement that 300 adult fares would have to be issued to guarantee the excursion. The first run was considered a great success and the *Halesworth Times* reported on the second:

'Some 340 people spent a restless night last Tuesday, being fearful lest they should lose the special train en route to Wembley. The excursionists were ready to catch the 5.45am train from Southwold and at 5.50am the little engine snorted on its way with 240 passengers. At Halesworth the remaining 100 were already seated in the vestibule of the main line train, and with just a stop at Ipswich for refreshments, London was reached at 9.45am. The exhibition grounds were reached at about 10.15am.'

A full day was ensured, for *'at 11.15pm the return journey was started and all felt that the trip had been a really great success. At Ipswich there was a great rush for the canteen before Halesworth was reached at 2.40am.'* A change of train delivered the weary passengers back at Southwold at 3.30am.

On 23rd July 1925 some 200 children, teachers and attendants of Halesworth Church Sunday School travelled by the 10.45am train from Halesworth to Southwold for their annual outing, with a full day spent on the beach and tea provided in the Church Rooms. The party returned on the 7.26pm ex Southwold arriving at Halesworth 8.07pm. The *Halesworth Times* reporting the event was ominous in its remarks, stating *'although several local excursion parties travelled to Southwold for the day, sadly few now travel by train'*.

The excursion to Wembley was repeated in 1925 when on Wednesday 25th September facilities were offered on a special train departing Southwold at 5.45am calling at the intermediate stations if required to connect with the L&NER special train departing Halesworth at 6.35am; the return fare from Southwold was 12s 9d and from Halesworth 11s 6d. After giving participants 14 hours in London, the return special departed Liverpool Street at 11.45pm with Halesworth reached at 3.00am on 26th, where the connecting Southwold train was waiting, reaching the terminus at 3.45am. Similar arrangements continued on a decreasing scale each year until the demise of the railway in 1929.

GOODS TRAFFIC

Before the coming of the railway, carriers' carts conveyed merchandise to and from larger towns and villages, but with the coming of the East Suffolk main line their trade more often than not involved transit to and from the nearest railhead. In 1883 Court ran his carrier cart in connection with the railway service from Southwold daily to Wangford, Blythburgh and Darsham. By 1885 Southwold carriers only travelled weekdays to and from Darsham, with less regular trips to Lowestoft and Yarmouth. Blythburgh had no regular carrier service but the occasional carter called to convey traffic to and from Halesworth. The failure of providing a rail service north of Southwold meant the ground was ripe for connecting carrier services and as late as 1916 Raven was operating daily along the coast to Lowestoft.

The operation of freight traffic on the SR over the years followed a regular pattern. No freight traffic was conveyed on the last Down train at night from Halesworth or the first Up train from Southwold in the morning, although empty wagons could be conveyed on the latter. On arrival of the first Up train at Halesworth any empty wagons on the rear of the coaches were drawn off and shunted to the coal trans-ship road where trans-shippers transferred any incoming traffic from GER or L&NER wagons. The freight trans-ship dock at the end of the line north of the passenger platform could accommodate up to four 4-wheel wagons and engine, whilst the mineral trans-ship platform served by the 250 feet long trans-ship siding (from 1921, 170 feet) was at the rear of the SR passenger platform, alongside the main line about 100 yards south of Halesworth GER signal box and the goods was transferred from and to the GER/L&NER by means of a timber stage five feet in width located between the standard gauge and narrow gauge interchange sidings. The stage was constructed to allow the floor of the respective wagons to be slightly above the stage to permit ease of transit from wagon to wagon. SR staff carried out all trans-shipping by hand. Certainly by the mid 1880s, Rowe was employed as a transfer porter at Halesworth being paid by the tonnage removed from the main line company wagons to the SR wagons. The tonnage of minerals transferred in 1885 was 4,550 for which he was paid £78. In that year he agreed to a reduction of 1d per ton of coals but requested bricks remain at the price agreed. The following rates were suggested by the station master: coal, salt, cement, manure and lime 3d per ton, bricks and coke 4d per ton, pipes and stone 6d per ton. By 1889 it was suggested Rowe be replaced by two men paid 14s 0d or 15s 0d per week as being more economical. In later years two trans-shippers were employed at a wage of £1 1s 0d each per week and who emptied three standard gauge 12-ton open wagons per day.

If luggage vans were used for small goods and parcels traffic, all trains had at least one van at the front of the formation leaving Southwold and one van at the rear leaving Halesworth; if traffic was heavy both vehicles were utilized. The luggage vans, either No. 13 or No. 14, were thus positioned adjacent to the barrow crossing, under the footbridge at Halesworth, so that exchange traffic of parcels and luggage between the SR and GER/L&NER could be transferred with the minimum of effort.

The first Down train from Halesworth conveyed the Royal Mails, originally in the luggage van but later chained up in the guard's compartment of the passenger stock, also newspapers from London and freight from London and the North East in wagons. After arrival at Southwold the locomotive uncoupled before the goods wagons on the front of the train were detached from the coaching stock and manually pushed down the platform to a point near the goods office. The engine meanwhile was taking coal and water before collecting any empty wagons from the coal road and placing them on the front of the next train ahead of the luggage van or vans. Thus on departing, the Up train would convey small items of freight in open wagons covered by tarpaulin, then three to six mineral empties and any other bulk load – sand, sugar beet or vegetables – then the passenger luggage vans and two or three passenger coaches bringing up the rear. The second Up train also conveyed the morning collection of Royal Mail from Southwold.

On arrival at Halesworth the mineral wagons were shunted to the interchange siding whilst vehicles were pushed to the transit shed. It was at this juncture, with nearly three hours to the next mandatory Down passenger working, that the Q, as and when required, freight train was worked at no specific times from Halesworth to Southwold and return, although it nominally departed around 11.15am arriving at Southwold at 11.50am. This conditional working was operated if more than seven or eight wagons required conveyance to any of the intermediate stations as well as Southwold – the guard, in the absence of a brake van, riding on the engine. All shunting and preparation, including the positioning of wagons at intermediate stations, was carried out on the Down journey. On arrival at Southwold the engine ran straight to the goods roads, placing loaded wagons in position for off-loading and preparing empties and other freight for return to Halesworth, the intermediate station traffic being worked via Halesworth until the Blythburgh loop was installed in 1908 and the east end points at Wenhaston in 1921; this Up working was not to convey more than fourteen wagons. On

SR staff or their agents manually trans-shipped coal from standard gauge open wagons to SR narrow gauge stock at Halesworth. This 1920s view shows the GER/L&NER line in the background with the signal box located south of the station and containing a 35-lever Saxby & Farmer rocker frame with 5-inch centres, with 34 working and 1 spare levers.
Author's collection

The goods trans-shipment platform and shed at Halesworth located north of the SR passenger station with the standard gauge sidings at the back of and east of the GER Up platform. Both the GER and L&NER employed horses for shunting their yard – the SR had to rely on locomotive or manpower!
Southwold Museum

arrival at Halesworth the train ran into the goods reception siding, before the locomotive ran round the train and out-sorted stock before backing on to the coaching stock standing at the platform. During this period if any freight required transit from the trans-ship platform, the locomotive collected the wagons and backed the vehicles on to the coaching stock.

After another round trip to Southwold, departing early afternoon on which no coal or mineral traffic was conveyed, empty wagons were collected at Southwold for the Up working and then shunted on arrival at Halesworth. The mid-afternoon Down train then departed. The next Up working in winter was the last train of the day and local carriers were anxious to load their wares for dispatch,

Milk traffic was sent by rail from all SR stations, chiefly destined for Ipswich or London. Here a mixed train enters Blythburgh station with two consignments of 17-gallon milk churns waiting on the platform to be loaded into the two luggage vans, second and third vehicles in the formation. The coaching stock is in the white/cream livery.
Author's collection

A pause during shunting operations at Southwold as 2-4-0T No. 3 *Blyth* in the charge of Driver John Stannard is on the points leading from the run round loop with a well laden and sheeted SR 6-wheel Cleminson open wagon and six 4-wheel vehicles. In the background in this view of circa 1908, Station Master Fitzhugh watches the proceedings from the platform. In the absence of a locomotive, staff often pushed empty and loaded wagons by hand to save precious time.

Michael Whitehouse collection

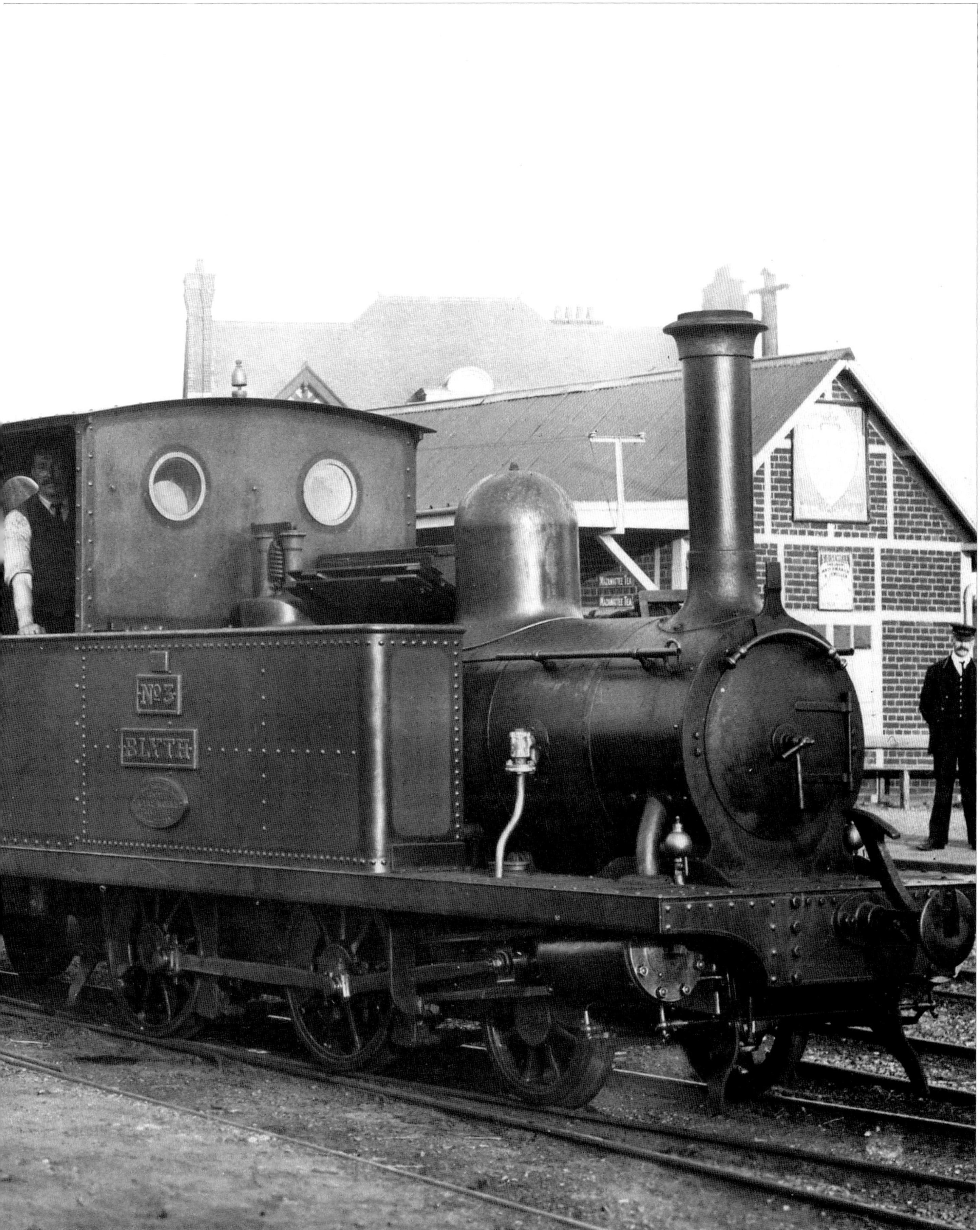
No 3
BLYTH

The guard watches the photographer of a busy scene at Southwold after the arrival of a train at the height of the summer season. Various horse drawn vehicles stand alongside the platform with Doy's carts prominent to collect luggage for onward transit to holiday hotels and accommodation including the portmanteau, clothes hampers and in the centre the obligatory hatbox. Meanwhile, there is great interest at the front of the train, where the engine has been uncoupled and drawn forward. The horse chestnut trees have now grown to a size where they are providing some much appreciated shade.

Southwold Museum

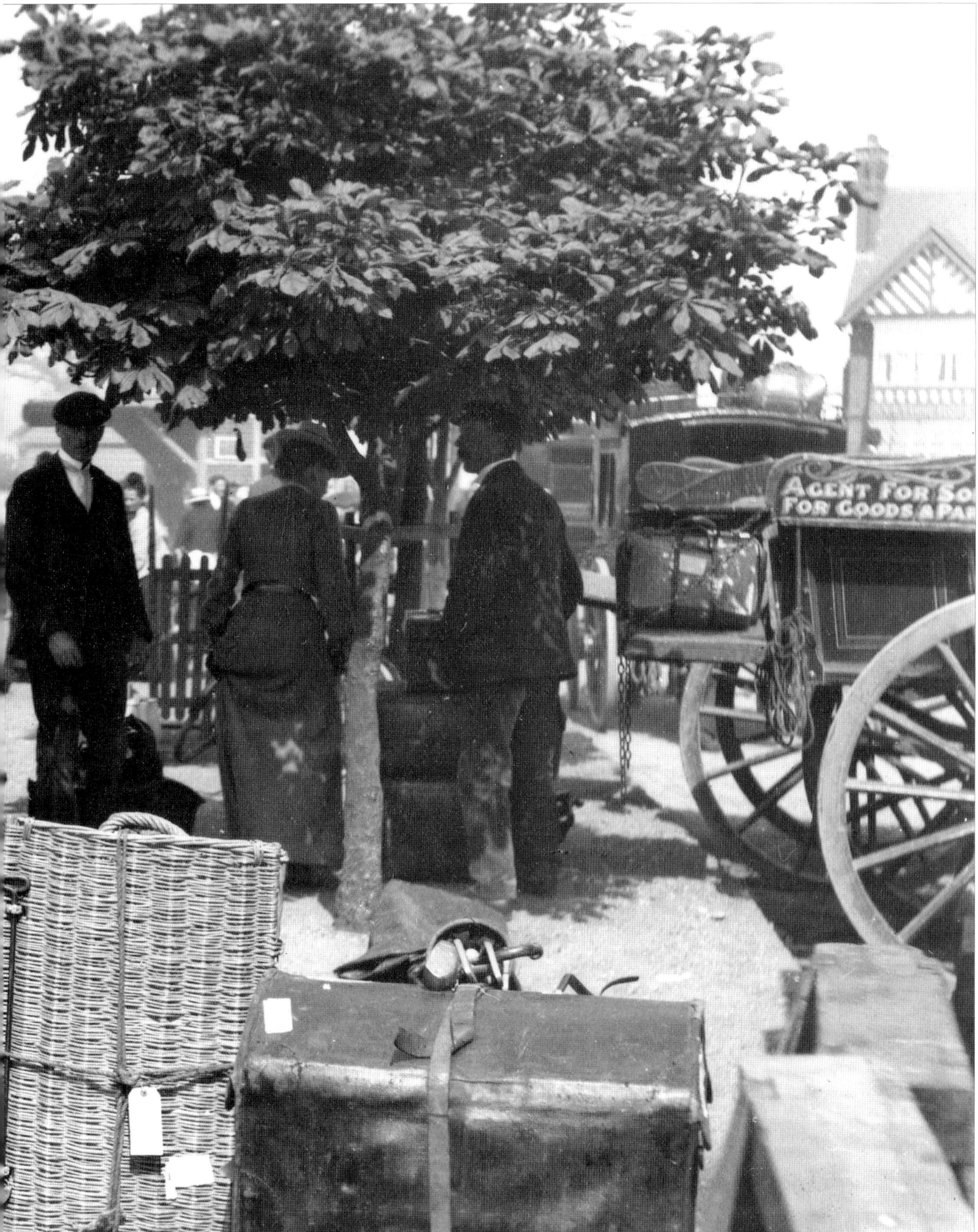
AGENT FOR SO
FOR GOODS & PAR

including Homeknit from Fordux Mill and other industries, and the goods clerk at Southwold was pushed to the limit to write out invoices and trans-ship notes if articles arrived at the last minute. On arrival at Halesworth these wagons were uncoupled from the train and manually pushed to the trans-ship shed. The last Down train conveyed the London evening papers, and on arrival at Southwold the stock was left in the platform exactly as it arrived, before the engine went to shed for disposal.

Wagons of goods for Wenhaston Mill were attached to the front of Down trains for shunting into the 55 feet long siding. Any vehicle collected, whether empty or loaded, remained at the front of the formation and was taken through to Southwold for out-sorting for transit in the Up direction. Prior to 1883 the mill was shown as a steam mill with coal being delivered by sailing wherry up the River Blyth. Similarly, wagons for Halesworth ballast siding were shunted by Down trains and empty vehicles collected. These empties were also taken through to Southwold before being taken back to Halesworth. Wagons for Wenhaston and Walberswick goods yards were also conveyed on the front of Down trains, whilst until 1908 wagons for Blythburgh were conveyed as the front vehicles on Up services, full loads being taken through to Southwold prior to the Up working. Once the crossing loop was installed wagons were placed at the front of both Up and Down services and similar arrangements pertained at Wenhaston after the installation of the points at the west end of the station in 1921. The conveyance of goods vehicles ahead of the coaching stock obviated the necessity to shunt passenger stock into sidings at the intermediate stations, as the locomotive could carry out any movements whilst the coaches remained in the platform.

Fish traffic was regularly conveyed to and from Southwold and as early as 1882, Arthur C. Pain, the SR Secretary, was sued at Halesworth County Court by Richard Lord, a Southwold fishmonger. The grounds for action was that Lord suffered damage estimated at 15s 0d to a box of fish en route from London to Southwold. The judge dismissed the case on two grounds, firstly Lord's contract was with the GER and not the SR, and secondly he should have sued the GER Company and not the SR Secretary – the former having legal identity. The peak period for fish traffic each year was only a short season, when the railway had to call on the services of platelayers to assist with trans-shipment, with record years 1885 when 92 tons were landed and 1888 when 161 tons were conveyed, 40 tons in one night alone. However, the *Halesworth Times* reported on 3rd December 1895:

> 'During the last two or three days extraordinary quantities of sprats have been taken at Southwold, on Sunday 43½, tons being conveyed away by the Southwold Railway Company. This is the largest consignment made on one day in the last 11 years. As usual in such cases there has been a sudden drop in the markets, the price of sprats being only 1s 0d per bushel'.

Then, on 11th December, *'in spite of continual interruptions by gales, the fishing has been fairly well sustained with over 11 tons being conveyed by the SR on Sunday'*. The next year, on 18th November 1896, Southwold beach presented *'a lively scene'* with sprats being landed on the open beach. Subsequently 30 tons of fish were conveyed by train to Halesworth for onward transit to market by the GER. On 24th November 1905 over 16 tons of sprats were dispatched from Southwold by road and rail. Fish traffic landed at Southwold in 1909 and conveyed by rail consisted of 7,125 crans of herrings, 1,202 trunks of trawl fish and 329,600 mackerel, the number of vessels using the port being 100 per cent above the year 1908. Fish traffic was normally sent by the 5.25pm and 7.10pm weekday services ex Southwold and on Sundays by the one evening train. If no Sunday passenger train services operated the fish traffic was taken to Halesworth by special train. Two and a half hours were required at Halesworth to unload SR wagons, check consignments and restack in GER wagons, which were attached to the 7.25pm or equivalent Yarmouth to London express fish train.

Milk traffic was conveyed in the then familiar 17 gallon churns. Two loads were dispatched during the summer months, one by the first Up train and again by the late afternoon train utilizing the luggage van or vans. The churns were sent from Southwold to Blythburgh and Wenhaston, and on some occasions to Halesworth, where some were also forwarded on to Claydon, Felixstowe and London. Milk was also forwarded on the morning train during the winter months and in the early years small quantities were sent to dairies at Lowestoft and Yarmouth.

THOMAS MOY, Ltd.

Contractors to . . H.M. Troops

Coal, Coke and General Merchants and Factors.

Special Low Quotations given on application for all descriptions of Coal and Coke. Delivered to any part of the Eastern Counties.

Order Office: COAL DEPOT, SOUTHWOLD.

ABOVE: Advertisement for Thomas Moy, coal factor at Southwold.
RIGHT: Two lorry drivers employed by the Beccles firm of G.F. Robinson sit on the front bufferbeam of an SR locomotive at Wenhaston in the 1920s. The pair were at the station to collect road-making materials delivered by rail to improve local roads – thereby accelerating the demise of the railway. *Author's collection*

ABOVE: A busy scene at Southwold after the arrival of a train in high summer. As passengers wait, their luggage is being loaded for onward transit by W. Doy's horse drawn carts and wagons. The composite carriage to the left has been painted in the cream/white livery although no lining has been applied to the panelling.
Author's collection

LEFT: A slightly different scene to the picture on the previous pages, but clearly taken at the same time and from the same spot.
Author's collection

Agricultural traffic was forwarded from the intermediate stations, including potatoes, swedes, carrots, turnips, mangold wurzels and other root crops, whilst small amounts of barley, hay, wheat and straw were also handled. Very little fruit traffic was conveyed, the majority incoming for local shops.

Coal and coke formed a large part of incoming traffic and was handled at all stations, the coal being received from Newstead, Bestwood, Kirkley, Hucknall, Sheepbridge, Stanton, Shirebrook and Clipstone collieries amongst others. Thomas Moy was well established as the fuel merchant at Southwold. Of especial significance was the conveyance by the SR of almost 4,000 tons of coal for the Royal Navy along the Harbour Branch in World War One.

Mineral traffic was also an important commodity conveyed by rail including ballast and stone for building sites. When Suffolk County Council undertook a rolling programme of road improvements to eliminate the unmetalled dust tracks of summer and quagmires of winter, the railway unwittingly played a part in its own ultimate demise. From the early 1920s granite chippings and tarmacadam blocks were offloaded at the various goods yards from where they were taken to site by horse and wagon. The granite and tarmacadam was then levelled by steamroller. Over the years brick traffic and the delivery of cement and sand for various building schemes also earned the SR useful revenue. The conveyance of minerals was not without its hazards for on occasions GER staff from Ipswich Carriage & Wagon Department were called to Southwold or Halesworth to assist local staff to clear wagon axleboxes of detritus which had eluded the basic sacking used to protect the wheels and axles.

The local Southwold brewery was taken over by Adnams in 1872 before the opening of the line, and the brewer initially traded locally.

By 1890 expansion was in hand and as public houses at Aldeburgh, Eye and Orford were acquired the company used the railway to dispatch barrels of beer on the SR flat wagons to Halesworth en route to these tied houses via the GER and later L&NER. Beer for neighbouring villages was usually conveyed by road using horse-drawn drays. Loadings, however, were not as prolific as milk churns. An unusual item of equipment destined for Adnams and forwarded on 9th June 1896 was a case containing a chimney glass measuring 7 feet 3 inches in height and 2 feet in length, in all weighing 5 cwt 2 quarters. Station Master Walter Calver advised the SR head office at 17 Victoria Street on 11th June that the commodity could not be accepted as it would not pass under the overbridges on the line unless the load was laid on its side. The item was insured for £25 but if it was laid on its side there was danger of the glass breaking. Mr Scuffinan, the GER station master, had been informed and telegraphed Bishopsgate to negotiate with the senders to see if the

On many occasions goods traffic was loaded and unloaded on the passenger platform at Southwold as the goods shed and platform were small and inconveniently situated. This winter view of Southwold from the 1920s, with the horse chestnut trees devoid of leaves, illustrates the transfer of large items as they are loaded onto Doy's horse-drawn dray for delivery round the town. *Southwold Museum*

item could be laid down. As the chimney would have stood over 10 feet above rail level on the SR with its limited loading gauge, with equal limitations on the GER, an answer was imperative. We are not advised of the response but it is assumed the chimney glass was safely delivered to Southwold by rail and installed in the brewery.

From time to time other special commodities were conveyed. Eager to increase freight traffic receipts the SR management in 1881 agreed to the loading of fencing rails cut from local timber in List's Cutting between Blythburgh and Walberswick. Mr Farrow had approached the company with the unusual request for the loading of two consignments, stating that he wished his own men to carry out the loading of the wagons. On receipt of the request Station Master Hansford, with the threat of Farrow sending his own traction engine to cart the rails to the GER at Darsham and therefore incurring lost revenue to the SR, sought the guidance of Arthur Pain on 6th August, saying because of the short notice he had arranged to drop four or five wagons off the 11.00am train from Southwold on the following Tuesday morning in the cutting, when Farrow would be on hand to supervise the loading by three or four of his men. Once loaded, the engine was to run light Down from Halesworth to collect them and convey them to the junction for the load to be trans-shipped. Pain had earlier suggested the wagons be left overnight to have them loaded by Farrow's men and then collected by a light engine from Southwold before the running of the first Up train at 7.45am on the Wednesday morning. Farrow, who had to advise his company the same evening, agreed to make the three or four men available for loading on each occasion so that he could assess which arrangement was the most convenient.

The SR was also required to handle an unusual item of freight after World War One when a German gun was presented to the town of Southwold by the War Trophies Department. The weapon, a 77mm field gun mounted on a carriage but without other fitments, was probably conveyed on one of the 6-wheel wagons and after arrival and unloading at the station was hauled by Corporation horses to a temporary resting place in the market square.

From the opening of the line parcels traffic was dealt with at every station, although not all categories were initially handled at Walberswick for the GER Appendix to the Weekly Working Timetables No. 43 for May 1904 advised *'the SR Company has intimated that parcels traffic generally is now dealt with at their Walberswick station'*. Pooley & Sons were contracted to maintain the company platform weighing machines.

With the opening of the passing loop at Blythburgh, track capacity on the line was enhanced, although because of the lack of two platforms it was only possible to cross a goods train and a passenger train or two goods trains. The 214 feet length of the loop clear of the catch points at each end necessitated the issue of special instruction dated 1st October 1908 entitled 'Working of Special Goods Through Blythburgh Loop' and giving examples of a full load.

Length

Engine No. 1	19 feet 7 ins
8 long trucks @ 22 feet 4 inches each	178 feet 8 ins
1 small truck	12 feet 10 ins
Total length	211 feet 1 in

Two further tables were provided so that guards could estimate loads and lengths of trains.

Length over Buffers

Truck No's	1 to 8 inclusive, 11 and 12	12 feet 10 ins
	9 and 10	12 feet 8 ins
	13 and 14	12 feet 2 ins
	15 to 23 inclusive	12 feet 10 ins
	24 to 32 inclusive	22 feet 4 ins
	Moy's	22 feet 4 ins
Engine No.	1	19 feet 7 ins
	2 and 3	18 feet 3 ins

Equivalent Lengths of Vehicles

3 small	equals	2 long
5 small	equals	3 long
7 small	equals	4 long
8 small	equals	5 long
10 small	equals	6 long
12 small	equals	7 long
14 small	equals	8 long
15 small	equals	9 long

Walter James Doy & Son, the local carter and milkman at Southwold was employed by the company on payment of a small fee as carting agent at the terminal station. In this role his responsibilities included the collection and delivery of all goods and parcels conveyed on the railway. Albert Edward Self was the carter for Doy.

During a works visit to Stratford between 14th May and 24th July 1895 for cylinder reboring and other unspecified items, 2-4-0T No. 2 *Halesworth* is seen loaded on GER flat wagon No. 12252. A boiler test is in progress as a fire has been lit in the firebox.
John Alsop collection

11

Locomotives

The procurement of locomotives and rolling stock for the Southwold line was first raised in a Directors report to the ordinary general meeting on 28th February 1878 when mention was made of a conditional contract with the Bristol Wagon Works Limited for the supply of engines, carriages and wagons. No immediate action was taken, however, and it was June 1878 before the contractor Charles Chambers submitted to the SR board a proposition from Sharp, Stewart & Company of Atlas Works, Manchester. The offer included the supply of locomotives and rolling stock and in return the company was prepared to accept debentures to the value of two-thirds of the full cost of the order. The board considered the proposal at their meeting on 23rd August 1878 and after due deliberation requested the Secretary to write and ask for a meeting between representatives. These negotiations were successful and on 1st December an order was placed for the supply of three locomotives on the agreed terms of total payment within seven years, despite Sharp, Stewart stating they would not be in a position to supply one or more locomotives before May 1879. The three locomotives subsequently supplied were 2-4-0 tank engines to the makers design, similar to some provided to other light railways, delivered via the GER and Halesworth in May and June 1879. The trio received the following numbers and names on the SR:

No. 1 *Southwold*   (Works No. 2848),
No. 2 *Halesworth*   (Works No. 2849) and
No. 3 *Blyth*   (Works No. 2850).

They had the following principal dimensions.

Cylinders outside	8 ins x 14 ins
Motion	Stephenson with slide valves
Heating surface	189.0 sq feet
Boiler pressure	140 lbs psi
Leading wheels	2 feet 0 ins
Driving wheels	2 feet 6 ins
Length over buffers	15 feet 10 ins,
later registered at	18 feet 3 ins
Total wheelbase	8 feet 0 ins
Coupled wheelbase	4 feet 3 ins
Weight in working order	11 tons 16cwt

Sharp, Stewart official Atlas Works, Manchester photograph of 2-4-0T No. 2 *Halesworth* (Works No. 2849) in photographic grey livery with black and white lining. The trio of locomotives, SR No's 1, 2 and 3, supplied by Sharp, Stewart were delivered to the railway via the GER and Halesworth in May and June 1879. *Author's collection*

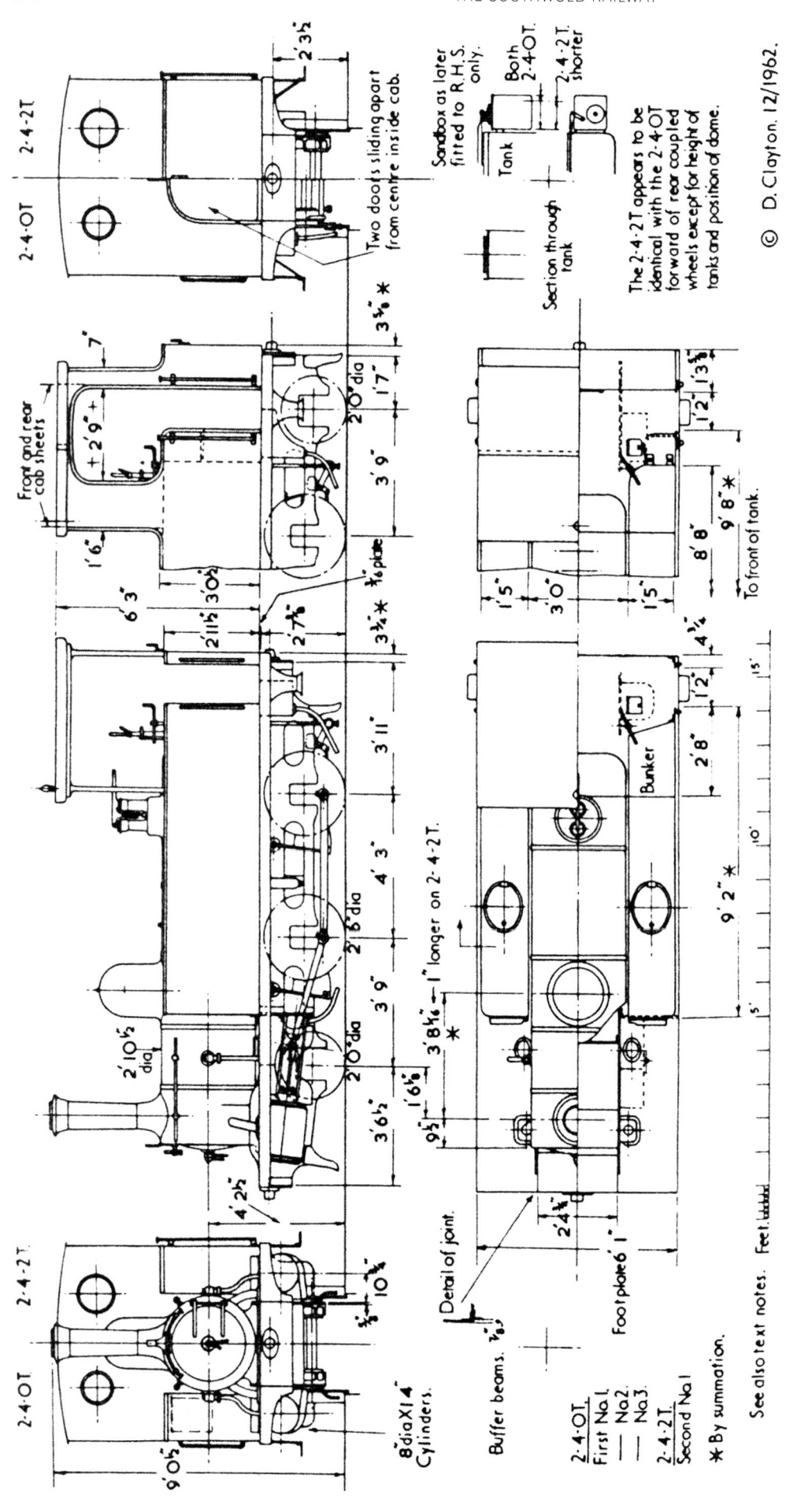

2-4-0T and 2-4-2T Locomotives

This shows the basic outline of 2-4-0 tank locomotives *Southwold*, *Blyth* and *Wenhaston*, and the rear view of the replacement 2-4-2 tank locomotive *Southwold* where different from the 2-4-0Ts. They are based on Sharp, Stewart & Sons drawings 6853 dated 13th March 1874 and 8886 dated 5th April 1893, each of which had only a sectional side elevation and sectional plan perspective. The external views of the ends and some of the plan have been constructed and built up by projection and confirmation from photographs. Each half of the end view views shows either one type or the other as designated, and the section through the tank is of the left-hand side to rear in front of the tank filler. The dimensions as given are from the Sharp, Stewart drawings, except where marked with X, which was obtained by calculation. Details to be noted from the drawings are:

a) Buffer beams were not single plates, but each side of the frame were separate thinner pieces than the central section.
b) As built the 2-4-0Ts had solid bushed ends for coupling and connecting rods but No's 2 and 3 were later modified to marine type as supplied new to the second No. 1.
c) The sand box added in front off the side tank was located on the right-hand side only, the size being estimated from photographs.
d) Front and rear carrying wheels were mounted in radial axleboxes.

The anticipated revenue earned from the undertaking was not sufficient to service the debenture interest payments on the capital and the Southwold Company, incurring serious financial problems by 1883, was unable to pay for the purchase. Traffic levels at that time did not justify the employment of three locomotives and so the financial arrangements with Sharp, Stewart were terminated; No. 1 *Southwold* was declared surplus to requirements and returned to the makers. The locomotive remained with Sharp, Stewart until 1888 when it was modified to 3 feet 6 inches gauge and resold to become No. 1 on the Santa Marta Railway in Colombia, South America. After many years working on banana plantations the locomotive was withdrawn in 1932. During service in Colombia the engine received exterior modifications; cowcatchers were fitted front and back, side chains placed on the buffer beam, rails mounted on top of

The original Sharp, Stewart 2-4-0T No. 1 *Southwold* (Works No. 2848) dating from 1879 is seen (*above*) in fully lined green livery in the early years. Note the wagons in the background are in black livery with white lettering and have Southwold Railway in full on the top plank. No. 1 *Southwold* was returned to Sharp, Stewart in 1883 after the rental payment was in arrears and the SR realized the railway could be operated with two locomotives. It was subsequently re-gauged to 3 feet 6 inches and sold to the Santa Marta Railway in Colombia in 1888 where it is shown (*below*) working a goods train in the early 1930s. The locomotive is easily identifiable but has received several modifications from the new owners: large headlamp, cowcatchers, modified cab and coal accommodation above the side tanks. The locomotive was withdrawn from traffic in 1932 and probably scrapped three years later.
Above, Michael Whitehouse collection; below, Author's collection

Guidance Notes on the Line Drawings of Rolling Stock

Douglas Clayton prepared drawings of Southwold Railway rolling stock between December 1962 and November 1963, and these were originally published in the *Railway Modeller*. They were prepared from various sources, the locomotives from the maker's drawings and the rolling stock from sketches made by A. Barrett Jenkins when the stock was lying derelict at Halesworth. The details were supplemented by careful study of available illustrations and for the luggage van measurements taken from the last surviving vehicle, now at the East Anglian Transport Museum at Carlton Colville.

The preparation of the drawings revealed the various detailed original differences between batches of carriage stock and wagons, and the subsequent modifications made on repair or rebuild. Major differences are shown on the drawings although in the mists of time it is realized many minor details have gone unrecorded, especially ends of vehicles which being closely coupled escaped the photographers lens.

On all drawings the arrow indicates the direction of the end view and all rolling stock wheels are assumed as being 2 feet 0 inches in diameter.

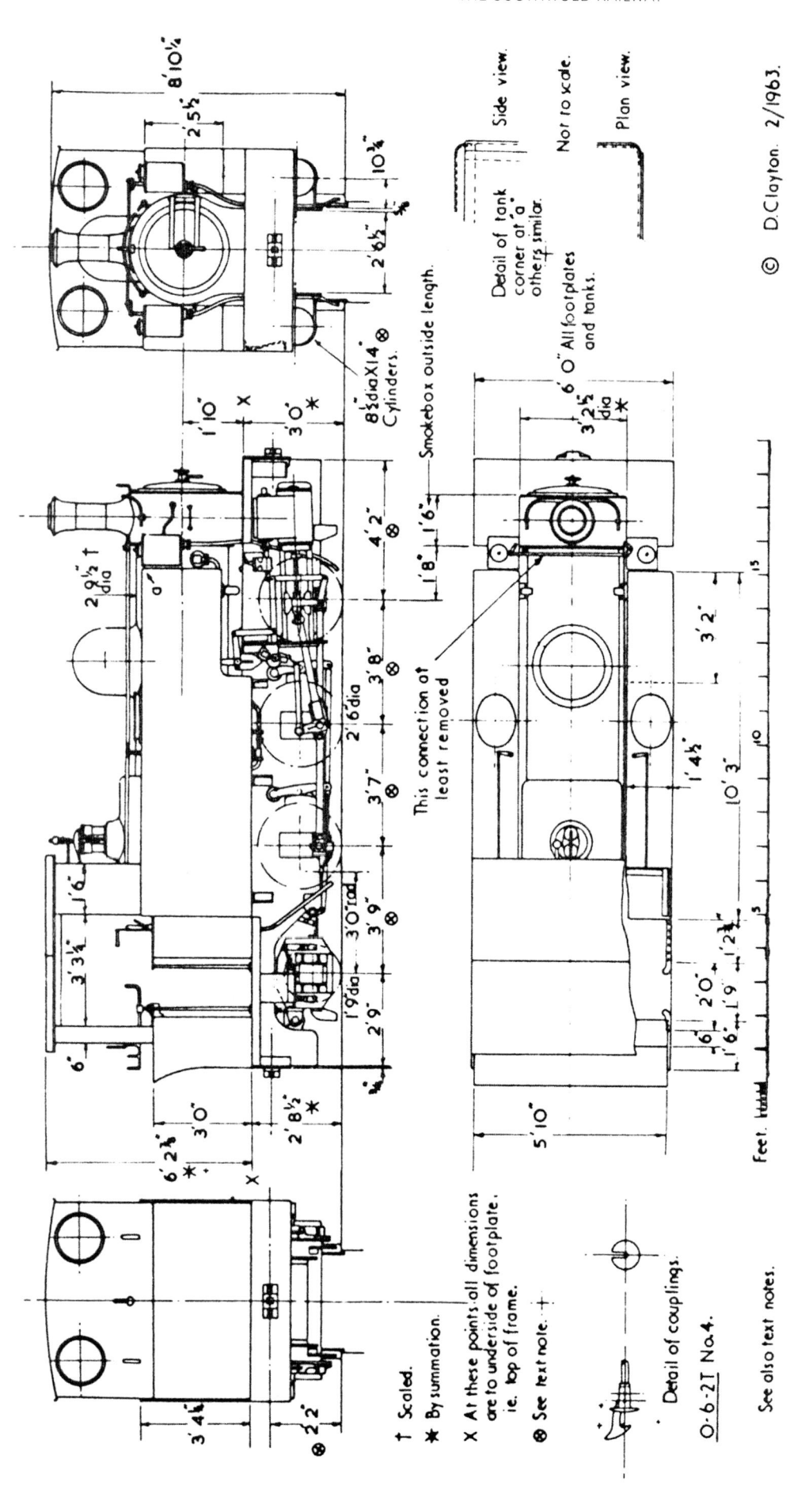

0-6-2T Locomotive

This drawing of No 4 *Wenhaston* was based on an undated Manning, Wardle drawing for order No. 70000, which gave a side view only and half section plan. The external end views and plan were built up by projection with confirmation by photographs where possible, although full details of tank tops and filler were unavailable. The left-hand sandbox and the connection between the sandboxes were removed at an unknown date. Most dimensions were obtained from the Manning, Wardle drawing with some additional calculation. The height of the couplings as shown on the original drawing was 1½ inches different from the Sharp, Stewart locomotives.

The Locomotive dated 15th June 1916, page 120, gave details of the cylinders as 8½ inches by 15 inches, the rigid wheelbase 7 feet 4 inches and the total wheelbase as 11 feet 4 inches. An alternative Manning, Wardle tracing, No. 14647 dated 25th February 1914, showed only the outline of side and front and confirmed the dimensions of drawing No. 70000. However, it differed in many other details and was possibly a proposal, the locomotive being built and completed to drawing No. 70000. Both scale drawings are thus shown in Drawing No 2.

the side tanks and a large headlamp placed on top of the smokebox in front of the chimney. The cab roof was also altered. Back on the Southwold Railway under renegotiated terms, No's 2 and 3 were hired from the makers with money out of revenue between June 1882 and December 1888 at an annual cost of £150, until they were purchased outright early in 1890.

Thus the SR soldiered on with just two locomotives to handle all traffic. By the early 1890s, however, the steady growth in traffic and heavier loads were taxing both engines and the Directors realised that in the event of the failure of one engine whilst the other was undergoing maintenance, it would leave the railway without motive power. Thus in 1893 the company again negotiated with Sharp, Stewart & Company for the provision of another locomotive and settled on a similar design to the original trio but slightly longer in length and having a 2-4-2 wheel arrangement, which allowed a small coal bunker to be placed to the rear of the cab. The locomotive built at the company's Atlas Works, Glasgow (Works No. 3913) and costing £1,020, became the new No. 1 and carried the name *Southwold*. The leading dimensions of the new No. 1 were:

Cylinders outside	8 ins x 14 ins
Motion	Stephenson with slide valves
Heating surface	189.0 sq feet
Boiler pressure	140 lbs psi
Leading wheels	2 feet 0 ins
Driving wheels	2 feet 6 ins
Trailing wheels	2 feet 0 ins
Length over buffers	17 feet 3 ins,
later registered at	19 feet 7 ins
Coupled wheelbase	4 feet 3 ins
Weight in working order	13 tons 7 cwt

Southwold was delivered in time for the summer service and the *Halesworth Times* of 13th June 1893 reported its arrival:

'The friends of this useful and widely popular enterprise will be pleased to learn of each succeeding stage of its development, to which another chapter was added last week in the advent of a new engine of more powerful construction than those at present in use. The Blyth *and* Halesworth *have hitherto carried thousands of passengers attracted by the bracing atmosphere and peaceful calm of the "ancient borough". The No. 1* Southwold *is a larger engine and has eight wheels instead of six.'*

Once the SR was the proud possessor of three locomotives, it was usual to work the trio turn and turn about to keep them serviceable. Normally one worked the timetabled service, the second was standby locomotive at Southwold whilst the third was at Southwold undergoing routine repair, maintenance or boiler washing. On several occasions the SR line was flooded and the company was severely embarrassed at not being able to operate a service on at least one section of the line by having all its stock marooned at Southwold. From 1897 the Directors decided to base one engine with spare stock at Halesworth, on standby in case the line was blocked by flooding and through services were not possible.

Whilst the Southwold shed fitter and boilersmith could undertake most repairs or regular maintenance from the small workshop attached to the town side of Southwold engine shed with occasional assistance from GER maintenance staff from Ipswich shed, heavier repairs were undertaken by the GER at Stratford Works. From 1887 all of the Sharp, Stewart tank engines visited Stratford for attention, the first to arrive, No. 2 *Halesworth*, arrived on 25th March 1887 and received a new left-hand cylinder and other remedial repairs

Sharp, Stewart works photograph of 2-4-2T No. 1 *Southwold* (Works No. 3913) at the company's Atlas Works, Glasgow in 1893 sporting a works grey livery with black and white lining.
Author's collection

Rebuilt Sharp, Stewart 2-4-0T No. 3 *Blyth* standing in front of Stanley Cottages at Southwold circa 1912. On the footplate is Driver H.J. (John) Stannard, whilst leaning on the front buffer beam is W.G. Jackson, the Locomotive Superintendent between 1879 and 1916, who appears to be holding a copy of the *Locomotive Magazine*. *Michael Whitehouse collection*

before being released on 23rd May. She was followed by No. 3 *Blyth*, which entered the shops on 8th June 1887 for general repairs (Stratford Works D&P 232) before being released on 29th July and returned to the SR on 11th August. No. 2 was back at Stratford shops from 14th May 1895 until 24th July to have its cylinders rebored and other unspecified work (D&P 2897), returning to the SR three days later. The following year No. 3 entered shops on 21st January 1896 to have its cylinders rebored and other ancillary work (D&P 3206) before emerging on 12th May, being despatch to the SR three days later. No. 3 received a new boiler at Southwold in 1900 at a cost of £570 10s 7d, whilst No. 2 received a new boiler at Southwold the following year. When No. 1 required a new boiler it was sent to Stratford Works, entering the shops on 22nd January 1904. The work took some time to complete and included reboring of the cylinders (D&P 7187) before release on 8th August. Two days later it was available for return to home territory. No. 3 returned to Stratford in 1909 and entered the works on 13th February for general repairs (D&P 9886) before being released on 8th May. The locomotive required some adjustments and eleven days elapsed before it was returned to the SR. No. 2 followed in 1910, entering shops on 11th March for the cylinders to be rebored (D&P 429) before being released from the works on 24th May and handed over for return to the SR on 6th June. This was the last visit of No. 2 to the GE works but the other locomotives made return visits, No. 3 arriving on 22nd January 1916 for the fitting of a new firebox, cylinder reboring, handbrake repairs and testing of driving wheels (D&P 4852). *Blyth* was ex shops on 26th April and handed over to the traffic department for return to Halesworth on 10th May. No. 1 *Southwold* was sent to Stratford Works in 1917, entering the shops on 28th August where the cylinders were rebored, handbrake repaired, adjustable spring gear fitted and two oil boxes provided for the driving axleboxes (D&P 6112). The locomotive was released from the works on 28th December but was not handed over for dispatch to the SR until 23rd January 1918. No further attention was received at Stratford and so when No. 2 required a replacement boiler in 1920 the work was carried out at Southwold. No. 3 was the last engine to receive a new boiler and heavy maintenance at Southwold in 1925. The reboiling of the locomotives constituted a rebuilding and small plates showing the dates were attached to the side tanks on both sides of the engines. Normally the SR locomotives travelled chimney first to Southwold and cab first to Halesworth, but after returning from Stratford Works No. 3 *Blyth* ran chimney first to Halesworth for a time, to be followed by No. 2 *Halesworth*. This was expected to even out the wear on tyres and flanges but was not a success and before closure of the line all engines had reverted to running chimney first to Southwold.

In the absence of a coal bunker, the original 2-4-0 No. 1, as well as No's 2 and 3, had small coal lockers, one each side of the cab beside the firebox. This enabled the footplate to be kept relatively clear of fuel and allowed the fireman to easily shovel coal through the firehole door in the cramped space available. The replacement No. 1 with its 2-4-2 wheel arrangement had a small bunker for coal and so it was not fitted with the coal lockers, giving the footplatemen slightly more space in the cab. All engines had radial leading wheels; sanding gear was worked by gravity, whilst no continuous power brakes were supplied and the engines had a hand brake operating wooden brake blocks on the driving wheels only. Over the years various minor modifications were made to the engines: the sand boxes originally located below the footplate were repositioned on the right-hand side of the smokebox, with a small steam pipe leading into it; strengthening stays fitted to the front cab sheet and wooden toolboxes carried on the side tanks of No's 2 and 3; No. 1 was fitted with a re-railing jack on the front footplate by the smokebox. As the cabs were draughty for enginemen, detachable wooden side screens were placed in the cabs to protect the staff in times of inclement weather.

The livery of the original trio was in the maker's mid-green livery, lined out black and edged white and the replacement *Southwold* also sported this livery. A tinted postcard by Jarrold's of Norwich shows lining on the side tanks and two bands on the boiler. After early visits to Stratford in 1887, No's 2 and 3 returned in GER in blue livery with red lining and probably red coupling rods; some sources reported they were noted in this livery in the early years of World War One but after visits in 1895 and 1896 the GER painted the locomotives in black livery. Certainly No. 3 in 1916, No. 1 in 1918 and No. 2 in 1920 returned from Stratford painted plain black and in the declining years this was maintained, although throughout their lifespan the brasswork was always polished.

During World War One the locomotives were often overloaded when additional military traffic was conveyed and often struggled on the gradients especially in wet weather. A correspondent writing

Numberplate No. 3 and nameplate *Blyth* still adorn the 2-4-0T at Halesworth shed on 17th May 1937. The Sharp, Stewart builders plate is also evident whilst at the top is the small brass plate attached by the GER after the locomotive received attention at Stratford Works in 1900. *Author's collection*

Manning, Wardle 0-6-2T No. 4 *Wenhaston* was delivered to the railway in July 1914 and retained the green livery until the end. Unlike the Sharp, Stewart tank engines it never visited the GER works at Stratford, all maintenance and repairs being carried out at Southwold. This engine worked the last service train on 11th April 1929 and was subsequently used to ferry rolling stock for storage at Halesworth before returning to Southwold shed. With a life of only fifteen years the Directors attempted to sell the locomotive but as there were no takers it resided at Southwold until cut up for war scrap in January 1942.
Author's collection

in the *Railway Magazine* in 1927 commented that when billeted at Blythburgh he saw *Blyth* on many occasions; she was *'no stranger to overloads for some of her jobs'*. According to Driver Neiley Fisk the 2-4-0Ts were prone to rough riding, *'boxing'* at speed, especially when the leading radial axleboxes were wearing. The second No. 1 with the additional trailing wheels gave an improved ride but was prone to slipping when starting with loads on damp rails.

Anticipating heavier traffic from the Harbour Branch, the SR Directors in January 1914 placed an order with Manning Wardle & Company of Leeds for an additional locomotive. The specification was for an engine that could handle heavy loads and in July 1914 the company delivered the 0-6-2 side tank locomotive (Works No. 1845), which became No. 4 *Wenhaston*; it had the following leading dimensions:

Cylinders outside	8½ ins × 15 ins
Motion	Walschaerts valve gear
Heating tubes	371.0 sq ft (also reported as 223.0 sq ft)
Firebox	35.0 sq ft
Total	406.0 sq ft (also reported as 258.0 sq ft)
Firebox grate area	6.5 sq ft
Boiler pressure	150 lbs psi
Driving wheels	2 ft 6 ins
Trailing wheels	2 ft 0 ins
Weight in working order	19 tons 4 cwt
Coal capacity	14 cwt
Water capacity	650 gallons
Coupled wheelbase	3 ft 8 ins + 3 ft 7 ins = 7 ft 3 ins
Max axle loading	6 tons
Wheelbase	11 ft 4 ins
Length over buffers	21 ft 0 ins
Tractive effort	4,330 lbs

Other special fittings on No. 4 included steam sanding gear with sand boxes above the footplate and a two-way Detroit sight feed lubricator. In the latter years only one sand box was provided as one was removed for use on one of the other locomotives. A handbrake lever operated brake blocks on the centre and rear driving wheels. The engine was finished in dark green livery lined out in light and dark green, with underframe wheels black, lined out in red. This livery was carried throughout its career. The company accounts showed an expenditure of £1,081 4s 0d for the purchase of the locomotive and the agenda for the SR board meeting for 13th September 1914 recorded that the Manager would report on the delivery of the new locomotive, which he duly did at a meeting seventeen days later. The engine was popular with footplate crews, having opening spectacles in the cab, a boon on hot days, and seats for the men. It was less prone to slipping with heavy loads than the smaller engines but had a greater appetite for coal. In the early years of service No. 4 was prone to derailment on the points of the run round loop and sidings at Southwold, and to a lesser extent at Halesworth, until the radius of the offending points were eased. Replacement springs were sent from Manning, Wardle at the end of World War One, both the springs for the leading axle and the control springs for the bissel truck being changed.

Wenhaston never visited Stratford Works and all attention was received at Southwold. Major repairs were carried out in 1928 when a new brick arch, obtained from Manning, Wardle in February of that year, was fitted. This is said to have improved the steaming, provided reduced fuel consumption and running costs. This encouraged the SR board to consider the use of vertical-boilered locomotives, which offered a higher rate of steaming from reduced coal consumption compared with the conventional steam locomotive and in 1928 specifications and tenders were sought from Sentinel, Clayton and Atkinson-Walker but nothing came of the proposal.

As the fortunes of the railway suffered, so fewer locomotives were required to maintain the service. No. 1 *Southwold* was laid aside in 1928 awaiting heavy repairs, but because of ailing finances the company could not afford the cost and the 2-4-2 tank engine was withdrawn from service and cannibalised for spares. It was finally mounted on sleeper blocks, without wheels or motion, and was cut up in May 1929. In the closing months, 2-4-0T No. 2 *Halesworth* was also removed from service, out of use awaiting repairs, leaving 2-4-0T No. 3 *Blyth* and 0-6-2T No. 4 *Wenhaston* to continue hauling services until closure. No. 3 was retired to the shed at Halesworth, whilst No. 4 worked all services on the final day and then for ten days cleared the line of freight traffic and arranged the

Manning Wardle 0-6-2T No. 4 *Wenhaston* was added to the SR fleet in July 1914 chiefly for use on the Southwold Harbour branch and freight services. After initial problems which caused derailments, the locomotive became a firm favourite with enginemen and here stands at Halesworth with a mixed train, which unusually has rebuilt luggage van No. 13 at the head of the formation. *Ian Pope collection*

Sharp, Stewart 2-4-2T No. 1 *Southwold* resting between turns at Halesworth. The numberplate is below the nameplate, whilst the builder's plate is on the small bunker. The absence of leaves on the trees indicates that it is winter, hence the footplate crew have provided a wooden shield to the cab side to minimize the draught. *Author's collection*

In this photograph that possibly dates from the late 1880s, unrebuilt 2-4-0T No. 3 *Blyth* is seen in front of the coal heap at Southwold. The side bunker in the cab is well stacked with coal and the small doors at the rear of the cab are open to give the fireman easy access to the firebox.

Michael Whitehouse collection

Sharp, Stewart 2-4-0T No. 2 *Halesworth* at Southwold waiting to depart with a mixed train. The locomotive has received attention at Stratford Works for in addition to the numberplate, nameplate and builders plate on the side tank, it bears the small brass plate affixed by the GER denoting the visit. By 11th August 1923 a strengthening stay had been fixed in front of the cab attached to the tank top. The engine has a sand box on the right-hand side tank top, whilst the left-hand tank top is host to a re-railing jack. *Michael Whitehouse collection*

2-4-0T No. 2 *Halesworth* with smokebox door removed undergoing boiler repairs outside Southwold shed. Cleminson 6-wheel wagon No. 28 is to the left while the goods loading platform and goods shed are to the right, *Author's collection*

No. 3 *Blyth* at Southwold station on a winter's day with staff wrapped up against the cold. The train has a selection of open wagons ahead of the solitary Composite coach.
Michael Whitehouse collection

stock for storage at Halesworth. Thereafter it retired to Southwold shed to be locked in with No. 2 to await its fate. No. 3 was cut up at Halesworth in December 1941, whilst No's 2 and 4 were cut up at Southwold in January 1942.

FACILITIES AND STAFF

The company provided a single-road timber engine shed with slate roof and full-length smoke ventilator at Southwold to accommodate the three original locomotives. The shed was 64 feet in length and 13 feet in width and had a 32 feet long inspection pit between the rails, located half in and half out of the shed. A small 12 feet by 7 feet workshop with a bench and lathe was provided on the town side of the shed whilst the 12 feet by 7 feet tank house was located on the north side of the building at the west end of the structure, with the pump alongside. The water was pumped into the storage tank and then pumped across the front of the building to serve a continental style water column alongside the platform road headshunt, where locomotives stood to replenish supplies. All heavy and light repairs and day-to-day maintenance were carried out in or around the shed. A violent gale that swept across the Suffolk coastal region on Armistice Sunday 1921 succeeded in blowing part of the roof off the engine shed at Southwold, at the same time demolishing one of the shelters on the pier.

As a result of flooding of the line in 1897 it was decided to outbase an engine at Halesworth so that services could be maintained on at least part of the line in the event of Southwold being marooned and cut off. A timber framed, asbestos clad single road shed, complete with inspection pit and water facilities, was provided at Bird's Folly siding. When the fourth locomotive was delivered in 1914 there was insufficient cover for the engine to be accommodated and so one of the 2-4-0 tank engines was normally outbased at the west end of the line. Originally it was intended to find a site at Southwold and on 24th September 1909 the Chairman reported to the board that for the purposes of erecting a new engine shed, a strip of land measuring 1 rood 7 perches on the north side of the line had been leased from Southwold Corporation for a term of 75 years at an annual rent of £1, the lease being signed and sealed on 28th July. No further action was taken and at the board meeting on 24th March 1915, the manager reported the shed at Bird's Folly, costing £135, was in use. The shed measured about 26 feet by 20 feet with vertical timbers erected at 2 feet intervals reaching to a height of 12 feet at the eaves. A small extension at the south-east corner was a workshop and possibly also for coal storage, the roof over this extension being a continuation of the main roof structure.

William George Jackson, one of Richard Rapier's assistants in China, was appointed the first SR Locomotive Foreman and had the privilege of driving the first public train on the line. He had also had the privilege of driving the first train in China on the Shanghai Woosung Railway in 1876, and soon after arriving in Southwold built 'Shanghai Cottage' in which he and his wife entertained on many occasions. Jackson and his wife dressed in Chinese costume for these soirees and enlightened guests with stories of their time in the Far East and later 'embellished' stories of the 'goings on' on the SR. Jackson retired in 1916 when J.R. Belcher took charge. He had previous experience of narrow gauge railways having served as engineer on the Selsey Tramway in Sussex. Later engineers were F. George who came from the GER at Stratford and, finally, S. Poynter who had previously served at Richard Garrett's works at nearby Leiston.

Normally one engine in steam sufficed for the basic winter service or up to five return workings in the summer. As the engine required to be available for use by 7.00am the first set of men signed on duty a little before 6.00am to prepare the locomotive, continuing to build up the fire by adding oily waste and old chopped up sleepers impregnated with creosote. The basic work had already been started by a shedman on nights who had disposed of the engine the previous evening and prepared the fire in the early hours for the footplate crew. The driver oiled up and between 6.30am and 7.00am the engine was ready for shunting duties prior to working the first Up train. The first set of men were relieved by the 'back shift' men at Southwold after the arrival of the early afternoon train from Halesworth; they then worked the remainder of the services, finishing their shift by disposing of the locomotive on shed and throwing out the fire before handing over to the shedman on nights. At various times on their respective shifts the locomotive men were expected to clean the engine and polish the brasswork. If a more intensive service operated, the first set of men signed on duty around 6.00am working on one locomotive until around 3.00pm whilst the late-turn men signed on around 9.30am to work the second locomotive until 7.30pm or later if necessary. A one-hour physical needs break was permitted when the service and traffic pattern allowed.

Two footplate crews were employed, latterly brothers John and Alfred Stannard serving as driver and fireman on one shift for nearly twenty years, and driver Nealey (Neiley) Fisk and Fireman Adamson on the other turn of duty. The crews worked early and late turns and changed over about 2.00pm. Each engineman was allowed two suits of overalls and two caps per year, with one greatcoat every three years as uniform issue. A.F. (Bert) May, a driver, recollected the occasion when a little girl was spotted on the line. He climbed round to the front of the engine but the child ran clear just in time. On another occasion he and his fireman discovered wagons were missing from the formation of his train and they stopped and reversed back to eventually find the missing vehicles a few miles back. Normally coaling of locomotives was carried out at Southwold where a coal stage was provided, the engines being fully loaded before working the first service and then as and when required during the day between trips. Although the second No 1. *Southwold* and No. 4 *Wenhaston* were provided with bunkers for coal, no such facility was available on the original No. 1 *Southwold*, No. 2 *Halesworth* or No. 3 *Blyth* and coal was heaped into lockers on each side of the firebox in the cab, with replenishment contained in small hods or bags until required to keep the floor free; these three locomotives were therefore required to top up with fuel at more frequent intervals. The shedman on nights was also required to coal the locomotives as part of his duties. In the absence of coaling facilities at Halesworth station up to six hods of coal were retained in the rear of the shed at Halesworth as an emergency supply. It is interesting to find the company conducted experiments in 1912 to find the relative costs of locomotive fuel consumption.

DATE	MILES RUN	FUEL	COST PER MILE
April	494	Coal	2.3d
	494	Half coal and coke	2.59d
	494	Coke	3.06d
May	530	Coal	2.19d
	530	Half coal and coke	2.41d
	530	Coke	2.8d

Sharp, Stewart 2-4-0T No. 3 *Blyth* outside of Southwold shed on 12th July 1911. Fireman A.G. Stannard is in the cab and Fireman F.C. Moore behind the locomotive. Sister engine 2-4-2T No. 1 *Southwold* is alongside, mounted on wooden blocks undergoing repairs.
LCGB/Ken Nunn

2-4-2T No. 1 *Southwold* at rest outside Southwold shed circa 1912, showing the name and number plates on the side tank and builders plate mounted on the side of the small bunker. The chopper type coupling required a protection plate at the back of the bunker, possibly because it had originally punctured the metal. On the footplate is Fireman F.C. Moore with Driver F. (Putter) Collett on the cab footstep, at the front is Fireman A.G. Stannard with oil can during locomotive preparation duties. Note the baulks of timber above the bunker protecting the rear spectacles
John Alsop collection

With cylinder cocks open, 2-4-2T No. 1 *Southwold* departs from the shed. *Southwold Museum*

The April mileage total represented twenty-eight round trips of 17.64 miles whilst the May mileage represented thirty round trips of 17.64 miles. As a result of these tests the company continued to use coal but observed *'when coal used smoke was considerable often entering the carriages when standing at stations. Little smoke nuisance using coke'*.

Locomotive water facilities available at Southwold included a raised tank on the north side of the shed at the west end of the building which served a water column located on the south side of the shed. The watering facility available at Halesworth shed was at the Southwold end of the building, over which there was a timber staging consisted of a tap which was available to top up side tanks, the water being pumped from an adjacent well by a chain pump, the well costing around £25. No watering facilities were available at Halesworth station. At the board meeting of 30th March 1899 the Chairman reported that in order to obviate the necessity of the engines during ballasting etc. having to go to the water mill for water, and the consequent labour attached thereto, a well has been sunk near the main line at the ballast pit, the water mill stream was probably the leat at Wenhaston Mill.

Railway employees, especially on undertakings such as the Southwold, had tales to tell, and whether true to facts or embroidered with anecdotes it is worth relating the story told by Driver Neil (also known as Neiley) Fisk of a special train that was run late one summer's evening in the 1920s. After the arrival of the last Down train at Southwold, Neiley and his fireman were disposing of 2-4-2T No. 1 *Southwold* in the shed when Station Master Bert Girling hurried across to advise a special train was required immediately. The train was to take a very important man to Halesworth where a GER main line train was make a special stop for 3 minutes to allow the VIP to travel to an onward destination. With Southwold's one and only taxi off the road and only 55 minutes until the GER train was due at Halesworth, Neiley agreed to take the service. Unfortunately the fire on No. 1 had been allowed to die down but as the engine was coaled and watered for the next morning's service, he thought 20 minutes would allow steam pressure to be raised thus leaving 35 minutes for the journey to the junction. As one hurdle was cleared so two others became apparent. Wenhaston crossing gates were across the line and it was common knowledge that after the passing of the last train between Wenhaston and Bolton, one of the farmers was in the habit of leaving a set of occupational gates across the line to allow his cows to cross the railway for early milking before the passing of the first Up train. Bert Girling summoned the help of a young lad with a motor cycle to make contact with a member of the Wenhaston permanent way gang who he believed would be spending the evening in the Queen's Head hostelry at Blyford. The man was duly found and conveyed to Wenhaston station where the level crossing gates were opened for the passage of the train. The man then managed to get the permanent way pump trolley onto the line and the pair set off into the darkness towards the occupational crossing to ascertain the situation. The trolley crew duly found the gates across the line and shut them for the passage of the train. While this action was taking place No. 1 had backed on to a Composite carriage so the VIP could travel First Class and set off towards Halesworth with little time to spare. Reputedly, with such a light load, the train was travelling between 35 and 40 mph as it descended the gradient towards Blythburgh and then onto the marshes towards Wenhaston. Having located and shut the occupational gates the trolley crew then had to clear the vehicle from the rails without upending it into a lineside ditch. Time was of the essence as the sound of the approaching train could be heard and the trolley was removed from the main single line near the mill siding, the pair swinging their oil lamp and shouting encouragement as the train passed. Neiley said the special pulled into the Southwold platform at Halesworth, in a timing of 25 minutes from Southwold, just as the GER train drew to a halt at the Up main line platform. The VIP rewarded Neiley and Station Master Girling with a crisp white £5 note before he departed the SR. As the only train of the night, branch line malpractice was evidently rife for the Train Staff and Ticket regulations and associated signalling played no part in the operation.

The SR locomotives were considered to be reliable in traffic but in 1883 two failures occurred at Wenhaston and Halesworth which in both cases resulted in a telegram being sent via the GPO to Southwold station requesting another locomotive to assist. Then on 13th March 1893 the fireman informed Station Master Calver that he considered his driver unfit to carry on his duties, as he was the *'worse for drink'*. Calver, after interviewing the driver, was of a different opinion and allowed the 6.33pm Halesworth to Southwold train to depart to time. In June 1922 the guard of a ballast train was severely admonished for instructing the driver to stop in section on the Blythburgh curve to unload ballast, which was strictly forbidden except in an emergency.

In the latter years drivers were instructed to sound the engine whistle as follows: one whistle when approaching intermediate stations, two whistles when requiring to detach a truck or trucks, and one whistle when approaching Southwold cutting. Drivers also had to reduce the speed of their train when running down the gradient through List's cutting; approaching the bridges near Wenhaston water mill and when passing the curve at the end of Holton Road bridge.

Drivers were required to record station times on a new *'driver's ticket'*, introduced from 21st November 1921, and to include also the names of the driver and fireman. Thus the SR aligned themselves with GER and Colne Valley Railway practice. Drivers were *'strictly cautioned'* that under no circumstances were they to exceed the running times shown or render themselves liable to imprisonment if they did. Station staff were requested not to exceed the time for stops and if shunting took place the lost time was not to be made up; thereby ensuring the 16 mph speed limit was maintained.

Drivers' and firemen's wages were reduced in 1921 and 1923 as the financial plight of the company necessitated wage cuts. The examples of the 1921 reduction were:

Grade	Present	New	Total Reduction	
Locomotive Foreman	£6 0s 0d	£5 5s 0d	£1 1s 0d	spread
Driver	£4 18s 0d	£3 3s 0d	£1 15s 0d	over
Fireman	£4 0s 0d	£2 9s 0d	£1 11s 0d	3 weeks

By the early 1920s the annual leave entitlement for the locomotive department was:

Grade	First year	After 5 years	After 10 years
Locomotive Foreman	6 days	9 days	12 days
Driver	4 days	6 days	8 days
Fireman	3 days	6 days	6 days

ABOVE: Driver Neil (also known as Neiley) Fisk looks back from the cab of 2-4-0T No. 3 *Blyth* at Walberswick in the 1920s.
Author's collection

LEFT: Driver Neil Fisk is in the cab while Fireman A.G. Stannard and an unidentified person stand in front of 2-4-2T No. 1 *Southwold*.
Author's collection

12

Coaching Stock

The passenger coaching stock provided for the SR consisted of six 6-wheel tramcar vehicles built by the Bristol Wagon Works Company Limited. The railway company had invited tenders early in 1879 and the successful contract was awarded with the firm on 6th May 1879. It was rumoured some of the coaches were of an earlier build for the Woosung Tramroad in China, the supposition being made because they were similar in design and bore the same side mouldings. However, they were four wheel vehicles of 15 and 18 feet in length. All six SR vehicles were delivered in 1879 and had Cleminson's patent 'flexible wheelbase' to negotiate the sharp curves on the line, together with combined centre buffer and loose couplings. Being of tramway parentage the six coaches were fitted with longitudinal seats along each side of the body and had end doors for access and egress of passengers. There were two types of coach supplied, Brake First/Third Composites, which were allotted fleet No's 1, 4 and 5, whilst No's 2, 3 and 6 were full Thirds. When delivered No. 1 had the First Class section at the Halesworth end of the vehicle and No's 4 and 5 at the Southwold end. No's 1 and 2 had odd non-opening top lights at the Halesworth end of the coach and No's 3, 4, 5 and 6 the same at the Southwold end. The Brake Composites were fitted with hand brakes for use by the guard. The interiors of the vehicles were spartan and uninviting, with the First and Third Class compartments of the Composite coaches separated by an internal door. The First Class compartments had blue cushions on the seats whilst the Third Class compartments and coaches had bare wooden benches. From 1904 a strip of carpet was nailed to the wooden seats to offer a modicum of comfort. Steps were only provided on the south side of each vehicle, where all station platforms were located. During the hours of darkness the interior of the vehicles was illuminated by oil lamps, which afforded passengers only a very dim light. Regular travellers took advantage of this – on one occasion when a schoolgirl could not find her ticket as the guard came through the train to inspect, she turned up the wick of the nearest lamp causing the glass to blacken. In the ensuing dimness she offered up an outdated ticket, which was duly clipped without comment. No heating was provided and on cold days the floors of the carriages were piled ankle deep in straw to keep passengers feet warm, a measure which was considered a fire hazard by the BOT. The straw also harboured a multitude of insects, not the least fleas, which could cause passengers considerable inconvenience, spiders, which emerged to frighten the fainthearted, as well as flies, woodlice and

Platform view of Southwold station as passengers prepare to join the train watched by relatives, friends or well-wishers, including a baby in the vintage perambulator. The coaching stock, which still retains the open-ended verandahs, appears drab without lining or lettering. On the leading two vehicles some of the side ventilators have been opened because of the warm day. *John Alsop collection*

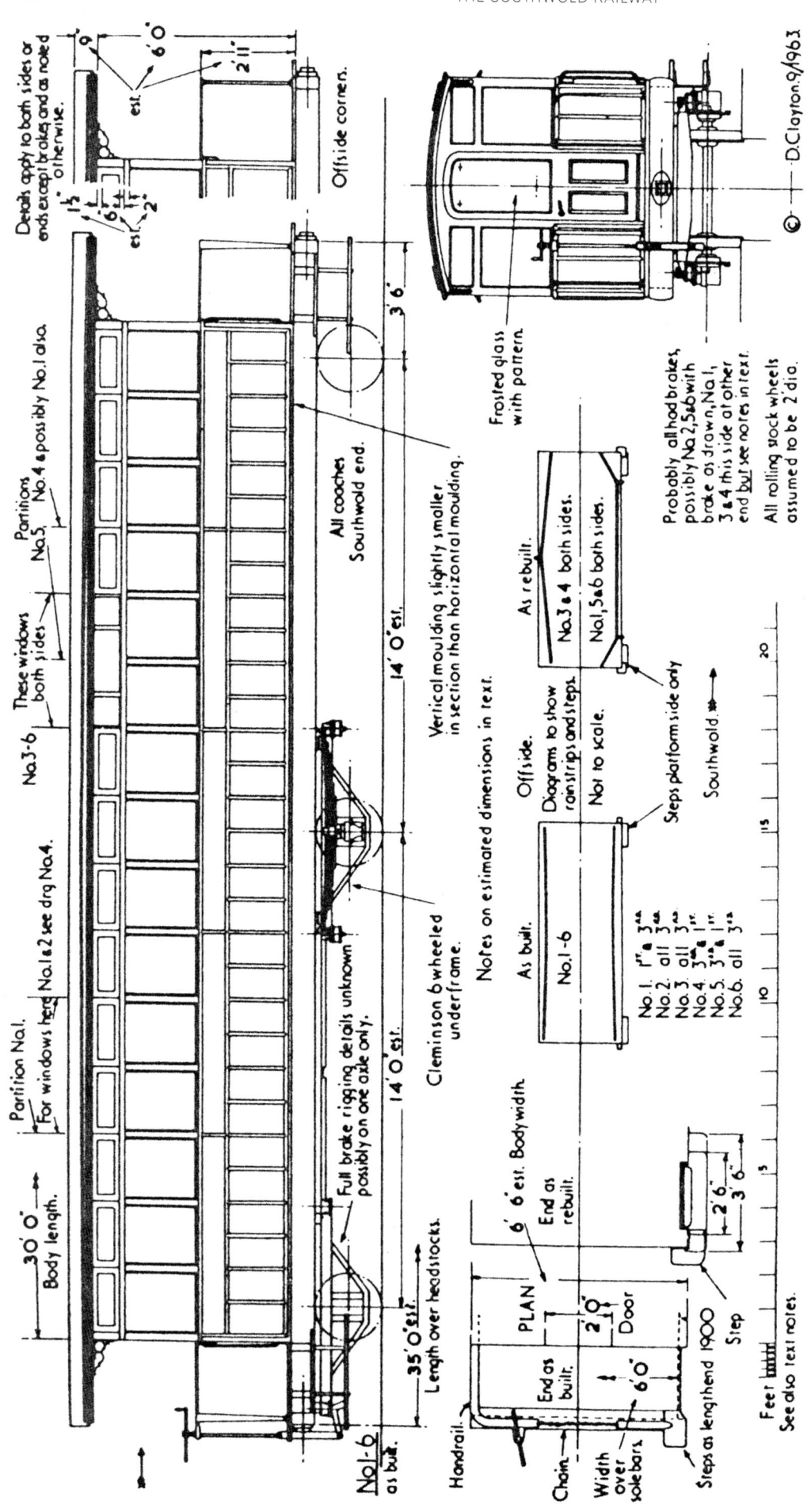

Coaching Stock

These drawings were based on Barrett Jenkins' sketches and dimensions (No. 3) supplemented by close inspection of available photographs. The 6 feet 0 inches height was obtained by calculation; though it was not clear how individual measurements applied, the other dimensions were based on this 6 feet 0 inches and length over headstocks as 36 feet 0 inches, but as the top of the side steps was given as 2 feet 6 inches, with the platform clearly of the same length, the overall length was re-estimated as 35 feet 0 inches. The platform length was confirmed by transposition of the saloon end doors to the platform side of the enclosed vestibule on rebuilding – these doors were understood to be 2 feet 0 inches wide, with the width of the body estimated at 6 feet 6 inches, which was in proportion to the 6 feet 0 inches height. Steps were provided on the south side of each vehicle, the side facing the station platforms, so it was supposed the vehicles were never reversed.

Before rebuilding by Gabriel, Wade & English Limited the main difference on the coaching stock were the odd non-opening top lights on No's 1 and 2 at the Halesworth end and on No's 3, 4, 5 and 6 at the Southwold end, and this feature was retained on rebuilding. The rebuilt coaches No's 1, 3, 4, 5 and 6 showed slight differences and these are shown on drawing No. 4, although variations of moulding were used – some flat, some half round, with some wider which reached the base of the body. These differences were as a result of one coach being rebuilt each year. One of the coaches in No's 3 to 6 group in unrebuilt form ran for time without the vertical moulding.

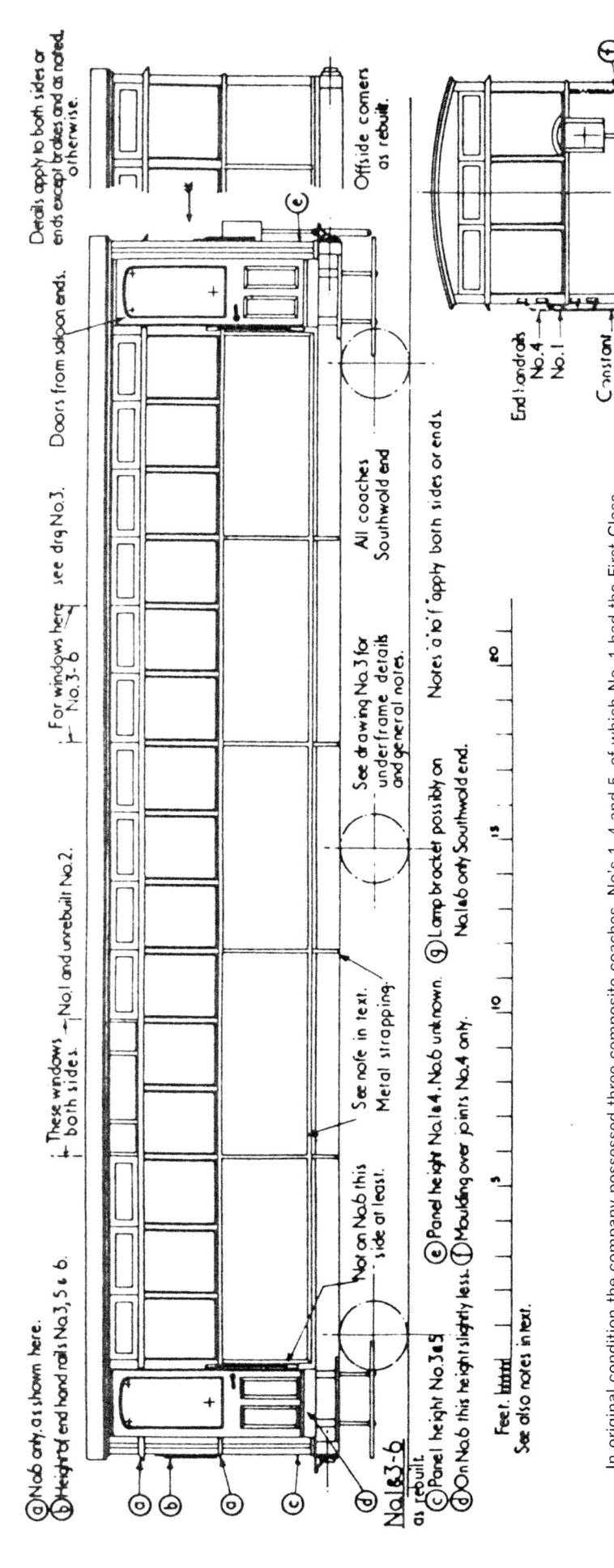

In original condition the company possessed three composite coaches, No's 1, 4 and 5, of which No. 1 had the First Class accommodation at the Halesworth end and the other two at the Southwold end, and this continued after rebuilding. No's 2, 3 and 6 were Third Class only. The position of handbrakes and brake rigging caused considerable difficulty to locate with certainty as no photographs showed these features where the coach number could be deciphered. It was probable that all were equipped with brakes, three at the Halesworth end and the remainder at the Southwold end. A detailed assessment of braking arrangements showed that:

- Coach No. 1 as rebuilt had a brake at the Southwold or Third Class end, and was assumed to have been built as such.
- Coach No. 2, photographic evidence shows no brake at the Southwold end and as a derelict vehicle a view of the Halesworth end showed no brake equipment either, although there were markings on the body. It was thought this vehicle might have had the brake at the Halesworth end but it was removed before the photograph was taken.
- Coach No. 3 had a brake at the Southwold end; a photograph of an unrebuilt vehicle, either No. 3 or No. 6, showed a brake at the Southwold end, while another photograph of No. 6 in rebuilt condition shows that it did not have a brake at the Southwold end of the vehicle.
- Coaches No's 4 and 5 were understood to have been fitted with brakes; before rebuilding one of them had the brake at the Third Class or Halesworth end, presumably as a photograph shows this vehicle with no brake equipment at the Southwold end. No. 4, if fitted, had the equipment at the First Class or Southwold end.
- Coach No. 6 had no brake at the Southwold end after rebuilding but it may have been fitted at the Halesworth end.

The brake fittings in all cases were on the side, i.e. away from the platform; the screwed rod being operated by a vertical handwheel via bevel gears in rebuilt coaches and presumably all similar to No. 1 at the appropriate ends. It was considered unlikely the position of the brakes were altered during rebuilding although an exchange of the 6-wheel Cleminson undercarriage could have taken place.

Unfortunately, after rebuilding there is no quality evidence of the detail of the offside of the coaches; it is believed the drawing gives a reasonable portrayal of the appearance including the closed end corner. The positions of internal partitions has been ascertained from photographs and is common to before and after rebuilding, save that coach No. 1 did not have a partition at the Southwold end and the partition indicated on the drawing is uncertain in its original form. Early photographs show no rain strips over windows or on the roofs and these were presumably added later. The main window pillars have been drawn slightly overscale for clarity.

Barrett Jenkins' sketch showed the windows as 1 feet 9 inches in length with 3 inch timber, but the latter probably only applied to the body corner pillars, the intermediate pillars appearing less – no more than 2½ inches to 2¾ inches wide, which slightly increased the window length. The 3 inch corner panels possibly excluded the ½ inch window moulding and the total of window and pillar dimensions lead to the 30 feet 0 inches body length.

A young boy on the road parallel to the railway admires 2-4-2T No. 1 *Southwold*, with Locomotive Foreman Jackson in the cab and a coach with open verandah at Southwold. The Valentine series card describes the line as the Southwold Miniature Railway. *Author's collection*

Side view of a SR Brake Composite carriage at Southwold before rebuilding. *Author's collection*

Third Class 6-wheel coach No. 2 with open verandah ends at Southwold on 12th July 1911. It was one of six vehicles built by the Bristol Wagon Works Company Limited in 1879, No's 1, 4 and 5 being Brake Composites and No's 2, 3 and 6 full Thirds. Each had the Cleminson patent flexible wheelbase to help negotiate the sharp curves on the line. *LCGB/Ken Nunn*

cockroaches. After a series of complaints instructions were issued to change the straw on a more frequent basis. Foot warmers were provided for First Class passengers. From 1883 to 1890 the vehicles were actually hired, after which they were purchased outright from the manufacturers.

Very little maintenance was carried out on the six coaches, save that Brake Composite No. 1 received attention at the GER carriage and wagon shops at Ipswich in 1888, so that after World War One they were in a thoroughly dilapidated condition. A programme of reconditioning was arranged and during the winter months, when vehicles could be released from traffic, five were sent to Gabriel Wade & English Limited of Wisbech for remedial attention. This work included reconditioning, repanelling the side sheets and the closing in of the open-ended platforms. No. 6 was the first to be sent away in November 1918 and was returned in May 1919. No. 1 was despatched to Wisbech in November 1919 but work was slow and the vehicle was returned in an incomplete state in July 1920, as it was urgently required for the holiday traffic. No such problems occurred with Third Class No. 3 for it went away in November 1920 and returned in April 1921. The next to be sent away for attention was No. 5, which arrived in Wisbech in December 1921 and returned to the SR in May 1922. No. 4 received attention between January and May 1923 but both it and No. 5 were in an unfinished state on return from Wisbech for the First Class compartments of both vehicles were actually reupholstered by L&NER carriage and wagon staff from Ipswich. The last vehicle, No. 2, was not rebuilt but in 1926 the body was braced similarly to the remaining five before their reconstruction. As the vehicles were only released one at a time the modifications showed slight differences in appearance, for whilst some had flat moulding on the body sides, others had half rounded and the remainder had wider moulding which reached to the base of the bodyside. The odd non-opening top lights were, however, retained on all vehicles.

The coaches advanced in a diagonal movement when in motion and tyre wear was above average especially on the outer pairs of wheels. The wheelsets of the coaching stock were regularly sent to Richard Garrett & Sons Limited of Leiston for retyring and deep tyre turning, but the lathe operators frequently objected to carrying out tyre turning as the gravel embedded in the tyres damaged the cutters. The firm actually complained to the SR stating the permanent way ballast covering the rail surface was the cause of the excessive damage to the tyres. Regular passengers were well aware when wheel sets were approaching the time for wheel turning or retyring as the offending vehicle made undulating movements on the rails combined with eccentric vibrations. Visiting passengers were alarmed! The initial livery for the SR coaching stock was almost certainly a dark maroon with gilt or white lettering. The class accommodation was written in full FIRST or THIRD on the upper end waist panels and SOUTHWOLD RAILWAY in the centre waist panel, with the coach number probably on the sole bar. In 1885 working expenses included an amount for painting of carriages and in 1890 two coaches were painted and overhauled, and the livery was changed to cream upper panels and red on the lower panels. Eight years later the Directors referred to extra expenditure in repairs and renewals of carriages as *'all are painted, varnished and retrimmed'*. The work was well overdue for the stock was over twenty years old and had deteriorated in the salty coastal conditions. This in all probability was when the new livery was introduced. The coach body painted white or pale cream with full varnishing was described by a young artist visiting Wenhaston between 1905 and 1914 as

A pair of Brake Composite coaches, No's 5 and 4, at Southwold station showing the maroon livery carried after modification, with the company's title and class of travel lettered on the side of each vehicle.
Southwold Museum

Third Class carriage circa 1923, showing the etched glass in the door. Note the open ventilators.
Southwold Museum

Composite coach No. 1 forms part of a busy train on the approach to Southwold station. Note the variation in the position of the lettering on the side panels shown in these three pictures.

Ian Pope collection

observing *'little yellow carriages'* whilst former GER carriage and wagon staff from Ipswich reported a *'deep cream'*, probably due to weathering. The lettering and lining of the moulding on the lower panels was black with class indication in letters at each end in the large upper waist panels with the fleet number in the centre panel.

The white or cream livery was difficult to keep clean and a further change of livery was made to all-over maroon or deep red. There is no specific mention being made of any painting being carried out locally after 1909 but it is thought the entire fleet was repainted, starting when five vehicles were sent away to Gabriel Wade & English Limited from 1919. White lettering denoting 3RD SOUTHWOLD RAILWAY 1ST, or 3RD SOUTHWOLD RAILWAY 3RD on the bodyside below the side window lights and the running number was again relegated to the solebar. According to one official and several local sources, because of ailing finances from the 1920s, the coaches were painted on the south side only, as all platforms were on the south side of the line, but some protection from weathering was probably afforded by a cheap all-over paint in matt livery on the north side. Throughout their life the coaching stock solebar and below including wheels was black. From the opening of the line until 1903/4 when the carriage shed was provided at Southwold all painting was carried out in the open at Southwold but there was evidence that some work was performed at Halesworth in 1885. In 1921 all coaches were equipped with modified figure-of-eight couplings on the recommendation of the BOT following the accident on August Bank Holiday 1921 when two wagons became detached from a train at Walberswick.

The leading dimensions of the coaches were:

Length over headstocks	35 feet 0 ins
Length over body	30 feet 0 ins
Wheelbase	28 feet 0 ins
Body height	6 feet 9 ins
Body width	6 feet 6 ins

It is rumoured that a 4-wheel coach was tested on the SR but was found unsatisfactory. No firm evidence can be found to verify the statement. In correspondence between the SR and BOT the length

With the rebuilding of five of the six passenger coaches, the guard's were given a small separate compartment in the Brake Composite vehicles, where the handbrake wheel was located, shown here behind the matchboarding. The guard is making his usual ticket inspection, although it was no longer as easy to pass between the stock with the abolition of the open verandah ends.

Ian Pope collection

of the 6-wheel coaches was stated to be over 40 feet, including couplings. Normally one or two coaches were used in service with two spare vehicles retained at Southwold and Halesworth, and these were used for strengthening the formation as and when required.

After closure of the line all six vehicles were stored at Halesworth, No. 6 stabled near the exchange dock and No's 2, 4, 3, 5 and 1 at the station platform in that order. Carriage No. 4 was burnt out by vandals in the 1930s, whilst No's 2, 5 and 1 were damaged by the military in the early months of World War Two, No. 5 having a hole in its side and No. 1 losing its roof and a large part of one side. When bombs fell as a result of enemy action on Halesworth L&NER and SR stations, No. 6 was destroyed and No. 2 further damaged, so that when Ward's staff came to recover the metal for the war effort little was left.

Luggage Vans

The limited accommodation in the coaching stock, especially at busy periods, meant there was no room for passengers' luggage and from the opening of the railway in 1879 it was necessary to load parcels and bulky items of luggage into one or more of the 4-wheel open wagons, suitably sheeted over to protect the contents from the elements. As passenger numbers increased so the use of the open wagons became an operating inconvenience. Early in 1885 the company ordered two 4-wheel covered vans from the Midland Railway Carriage & Wagon Company at a cost of £95 the pair, charged to capital account. They were delivered later the same year and were allocated No's 13 and 14 in the wagon fleet series, although they were shown in official rolling stock returns to the BOT as passenger train vehicles used for the conveyance of passenger luggage and parcels traffic. In July 1885 the *Halesworth Times* erroneously reported the SR had acquired *'much needed covered goods trucks'*, whilst criticizing the lack of cattle trucks. Each of the new vans had sliding doors on either side of the vehicle, which opened towards

Interior of abandoned Third Class coach at Halesworth showing the longitudinal seats, occupied by two enthusiasts in 1936, eight years after the demise of the operational railway.
J.H.L. Adams/Kidderminster Railway Museum

Derelict Third Class coach No. 6 at Halesworth in 1936, the frames and wheels hidden by the trans-shipment platform; main line Up platform ramp to the left and connecting footbridge to the **L&NER** on the right.
J.H.L. Adams/Kidderminster Railway Museum

Full Third Class coach No. 6 standing among the weeds at Halesworth in 1936. This coach has closed ends after rebuilding. The standard gauge/narrow gauge trans-shipment platform is to the left. *J.H.L. Adams/Kidderminster Railway Museum*

Composite Brake Cleminson 6-wheel coach No. 1 abandoned at Halesworth after closure of the line. To the left the small First Class compartment has an internal door leading to the larger Third Class section, whilst at the far end is the small guard's compartment contained the wheel operating the hand brake. *Author's collection*

Halesworth SR station viewed from the connecting footbridge with unrebuilt coach No. 2 in the platform and stored narrow gauge wagons on the former outer interchange siding. *Southwold Museum*

Above: As years progressed after closure the coaching stock at Halesworth provided covered accommodation for itinerants until in 1937 a tramp was believed to have made himself too comfortable by starting a fire in brake/composite coach No 4 with the result the body was totally destroyed. *R. Shephard*

Above: Six coaches and sixteen wagons used on the SR had Cleminson's patent 6-wheel flexible underframe. The outer axles on the vehicles were pivoted and connected by linkage to the centre axle, which was mounted on slides so that it could negotiate curves. All axles were therefore on the radius of the curve thus reducing tyre and flange wear.

Right: The burnt out remains of Brake Composite No. 4 at Halesworth with unrebuilt full Third coach No. 2 beyond. The vertical brake handwheel that replaced the original horizontal cranked type used on the verandahs survived the inferno. *R. Shephard*

Abandoned Third Class coach No. 2 standing at Halesworth in 1936. This vehicle was the only coach not to have been rebuilt and thus retains the open balcony ends. The station buildings on the right darken the scene. *J.H.L. Adams/Kidderminster Railway Museum*

Halesworth station with abandoned stock. Nearest the camera on the weed infested track is coach No. 2, beyond that the burnt remains of coach No. 4 and then No's 3, 5 and 1. *Author's collection*

Four-Wheel Vans

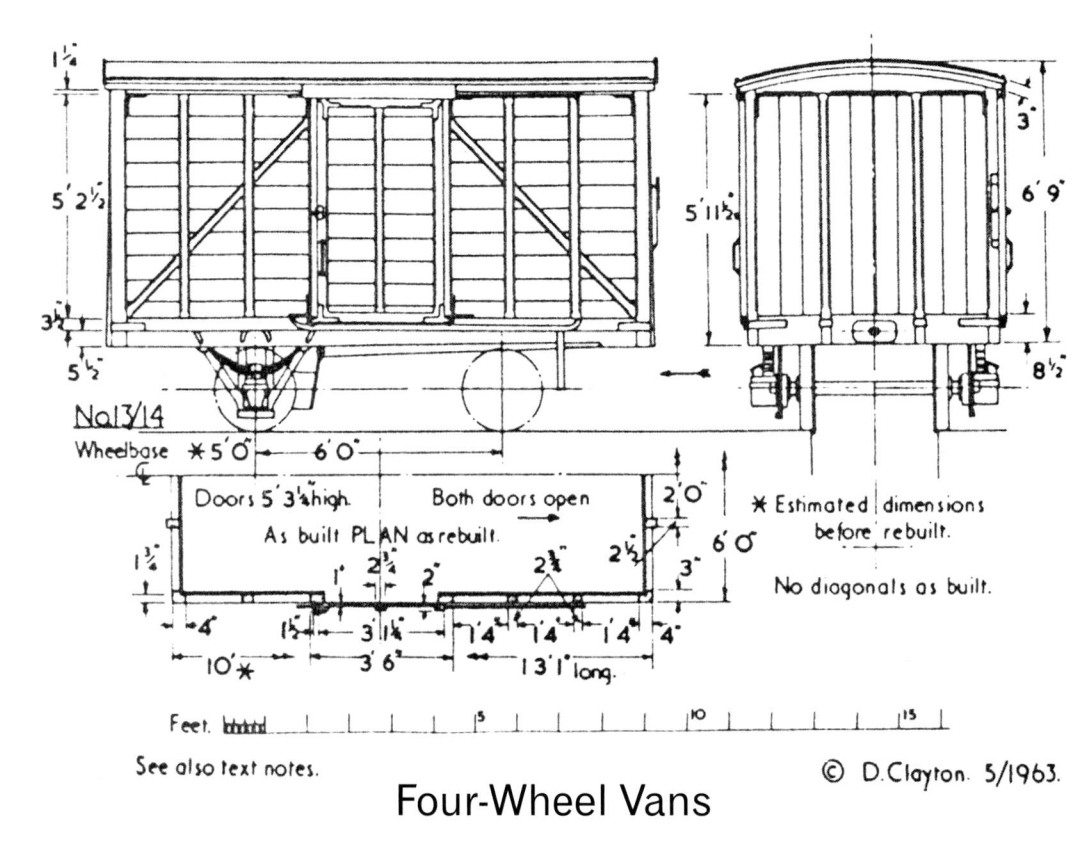

Vans No's 13 and 14. The dimensions were taken from the van body now at the East Anglian Transport Museum at Carlton Colville. The right-hand half of the drawing shows the vehicle after rebuilding, with both doors opening towards Southwold. The left-hand part of the drawing shows the original length, estimated at 10 feet 0 inches, based on the door runner length, assumed to be the original, and also presumably the same length as the wagons for which reason the 5 feet 0 inch length is thought to have applied. As built no diagonal bracing was fitted and on one van at least the lower door runner was inverted for a period. The existing rebuilt van had what appeared to be a lamp bracket at the Southwold end. This might have been fitted to the other van but certainly not before rebuilding.

the Southwold end of the vehicle. As with other rolling stock the wheels had six open bow spokes, whilst a combined centre buffer and coupler was fitted at each end of the vans. These were originally fitted with a chopper type hook coupling secured with a pin, but after the derailment at Walberswick on August Bank Holiday 1921, the pair were fitted with a figure-of-eight coupling as recommended by the BOT but still secured by a pin. Steam heating was not fitted. A brake lever operating a single brake shoe on one wheel was fitted to the south side of each vehicle so that it could be pinned or released from the station platforms. In traffic the vans were found unsteady when running at speed especially when unladen, whilst increasing traffic rendered the vehicles limited in capacity. Instead of purchasing new vehicles the original vans were rebuilt to an increased length by English Brothers & Company of Peterborough, No. 14 being modified in 1918 and No. 13 soon after. Much of the original material would have been retained, notably the running and brake gear, end sections and headstocks, door runners and vertical body frames, but the rest would have been new material. In original and rebuilt condition the vehicle end boarding was vertical with horizontal side timbers.

The two vans No's 13 and 14 were initially painted black with SOUTHWOLD RAILWAY in white on the sides and later received grey livery with black lettering. As the vehicles were normally attached to passenger trains it was decided to paint the vans maroon livery with black ironwork below the sole bar. The company ownership SR and the fleet number were denoted on the sides of the vehicles in large serif white letters and numerals. As with the passenger coaches it was rumoured that in later years the vans were only painted on the south side. Normally the van or vans were placed at the front of the train leaving Southwold and at the rear leaving Halesworth; the reason for this was the accessibility to the barrow crossing at the south end of Halesworth GER and later L&NER station, located by the footbridge. When the railway closed one of the vans, No. 13, was taken to Halesworth, whilst the other languished at Southwold. The former was stored near the exchange dock and was badly damaged when the station suffered from enemy bombing. No. 14, for some time stored in the former engine shed with its wheels and running gear removed, was subsequently bought and placed on an allotment at Halesworth, where it survived as a garden shed until discovery in July 1962 as the only extant item of SR rolling stock. It was subsequently taken back to Southwold, largely by the efforts of W. Barrett Jenkins, and placed in the old station yard. Redevelopment necessitated removal again, this time to the East Anglian Transport Museum at Carlton Colville near Lowestoft, where it remains to this day. The leading dimensions of luggage vans No's 13 and 14 were:

	Original dimensions	Rebuild dimensions
Length over buffers	12 feet 2 ins	
Body length	10 feet 0 ins	13 feet 0 ins
Body width	6 feet 0 ins	
Body height	5 feet 3¾ ins	
Wheelbase	5 feet 0 ins	6 feet 0 ins

The lack of luggage and parcels accommodation in the six coaching vehicles was an embarrassment to the company, especially during the summer months when many visitors travelled to Southwold with much impedimenta. In 1885 the SR increased its rolling stock fleet by purchasing two 4-wheel covered luggage vans from the Midland Railway Carriage & Wagon Company.

ABOVE: No. 13 is at Southwold on 12th July 1911 in company with sister vehicle No 14. The vehicles were fitted with hand brakes on one side only. Most trains ran as mixed passenger and goods and included one or both of the vans for the conveyance of luggage, large parcels and small goods items. In the background are the large heaps of coal and coke brought to the town by rail. *LCGB/Ken Nunn*

BELOW: Southwold station with platform surface timber boarded with the two luggage vans No's 13 and 14 and two coaches waiting their next working. The building to the left is a shed for storage of equipment. *Author's collection*

Southwold station soon after the turn of the century with 2-4-0T No. 3 *Blyth* ready to depart for Halesworth. Passengers gather for final farewells and station staff are on hand to assist with latecomers and see the train away. The locomotive is in immaculate condition with polished hand rails, smoke box hinges and cylinder ends.
Author's collection

Grounded body of the only surviving SR vehicle, luggage van No. 14 at the East Anglian Transport Museum at Carlton Colville, near Lowestoft. The track in the foreground is the 2 feet gauge East Anglian Light Railway.
Author's collection

13

Wagons

The initial twelve wagons were all 4-wheel vehicles supplied by the Midland Railway Carriage & Wagon Company in 1879. No's 1 to 8 inclusive were 3-plank open wagons with curved ends, whilst No's 9 and 10 were 2-plank opens with level ends. The remaining pair, No's 11 and 12, were timber trucks. A further three, 4-wheel 3-plank open wagons with curved ends, were supplied to the SR by the Midland Railway Carriage & Wagon Company in 1892, receiving fleet No's 15, 16 and 17, although the maker's photograph shows No. 16 to be a 4-plank wagon with straight ends. Two years later another six identical wagons were delivered from the same builder and were allocated No's 18, 19, 20, 21, 22 and 23. The leading dimension of the 4-wheel rolling stock was:

4-wheel 3-plank opens No's 1 to 8 and 15 to 23 inclusive:
Length over buffers	12 feet 10 ins
Body length	10 feet 0 ins
Body height at side	2 feet 3 ins
Body height at end	3 feet 3 ins
Body width	6 feet 0 ins
Wheelbase	5 feet 0 ins

4-wheel 2-plank open No's 9 and 10
Length over buffers No. 9	12 feet 10 ins
Length over buffers No. 10	12 feet 8 ins
Body length	10 feet 0 ins
Body height	N/A
Body width	6 feet 0 ins

4-wheel timber wagons No's 11 and 12
Length over buffers	12 feet 10 ins
Body length	10 feet 0 ins
Body height	N/A
Body width	6 feet 0 ins
Wheelbase	5 feet 0 ins

In 1896 Thomas Moy Limited of Peterborough built three, 6-wheel 3-plank wagons with curved ends on the Cleminson's patent 'flexible wheelbase' principle for the railway, which were to be an initial tranche of a fleet of sixteen vehicles. The trio, costing £168 18s 9d, received SR fleet numbers 24, 25 and 26, and were considered so successful in traffic that three years later in 1899 a further six costing £360 0s 0d were added to the fleet, numbered

Evidently a train is expected as Southwold station platform presents an animated scene, prospective passengers milling around talking, luggage is stacked and porters busy themselves. A 4-wheel open wagon stands on the run round loop, possibly to be attached to the outgoing service.
Author's collection

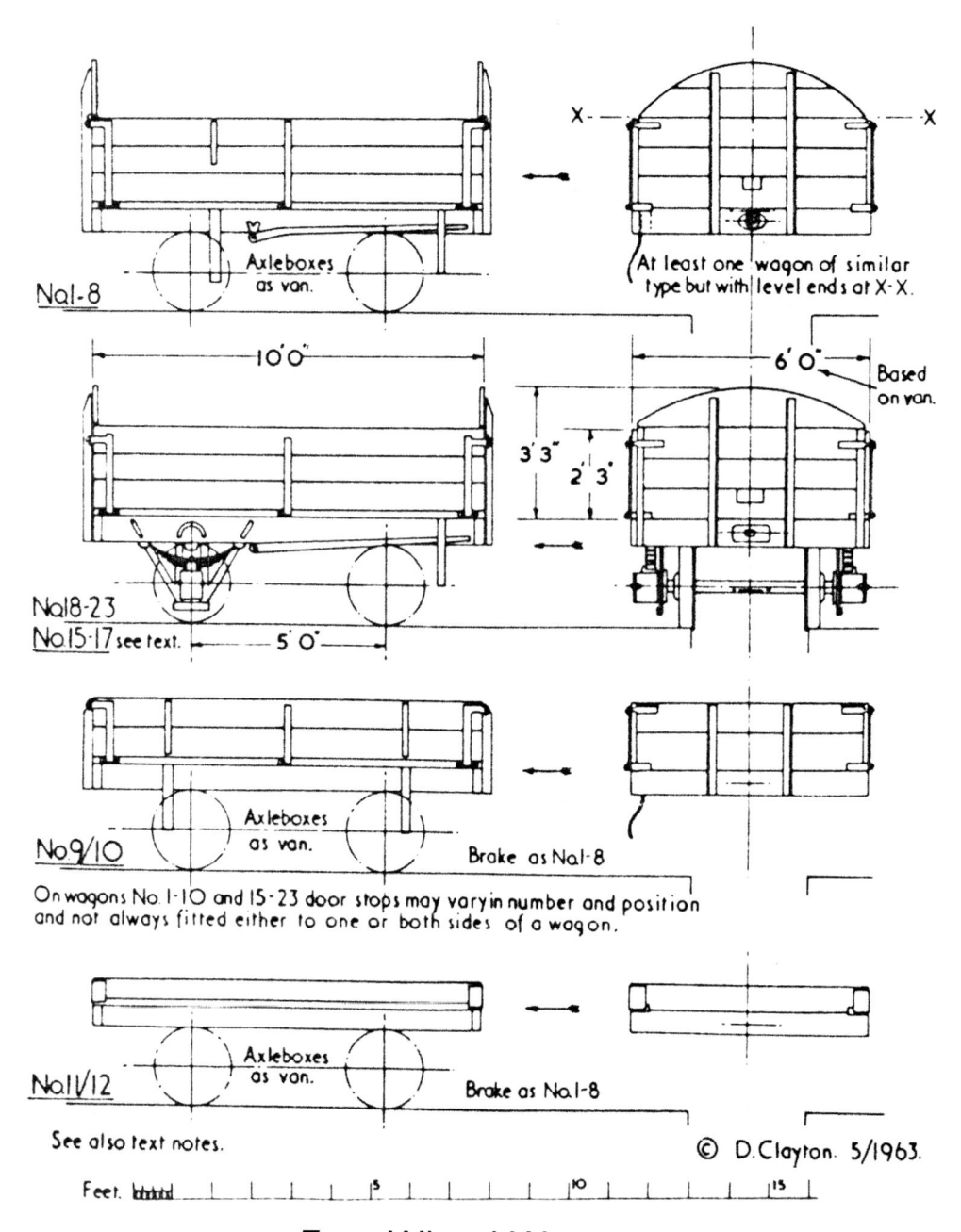

Four-Wheel Wagons

Wagons 1 to 8 and 15 to 23 inclusive
  The dimensions on the drawings are from Barrett Jenkins' sketches supplemented by data from the van body as applicable. The length dimensions quoted for wagon No's 18 to 23 are certain and the height believed to apply, though the vehicle from which the measurements were obtained was not recorded, one end view being sketched apparently for both 4- and 6-wheel wagons. No's 1 to 8 inclusive were similar except for the maximum height of the curved ends, which were higher except for at least one which was either built or rebuilt with level ends as shown on the drawing.
   No widths were shown but all wagons appeared of the same width as the vans. No's 15 to 17 were probably similar to No's 18 to 23 but there might have been variations between individual wagons in height and width of planking, and the dimensions quoted were probably rounded up or down to the nearest inch. Door stops on all the wagons varied considerably, but in all photographs each wagon or its load are covered by a tarpaulin sheet, effectively hiding the identity of the wagon so that details could not be specified. Some wagons ran at times with protective sacking over the axleboxes to prevent loose roadstone, ballast or coal from infiltrating the oil and causing a hot box.

Wagons No's 9 and 10 were 2-plank drop sided vehicles and their dimensions identical to No's 1 to 8 save for the height, which on the drawings are estimated.

Wagons No's 11 and 12 were classified as timber wagons but no bolsters have been evident on known photographs. They always appeared as open wagons and dimensions were assumed as similar to No's 1 to 8 except for height, which has been estimated on the drawings. The coupling sockets for these and No's 9 and 10 were similar to those carried by No's 1 to 8.

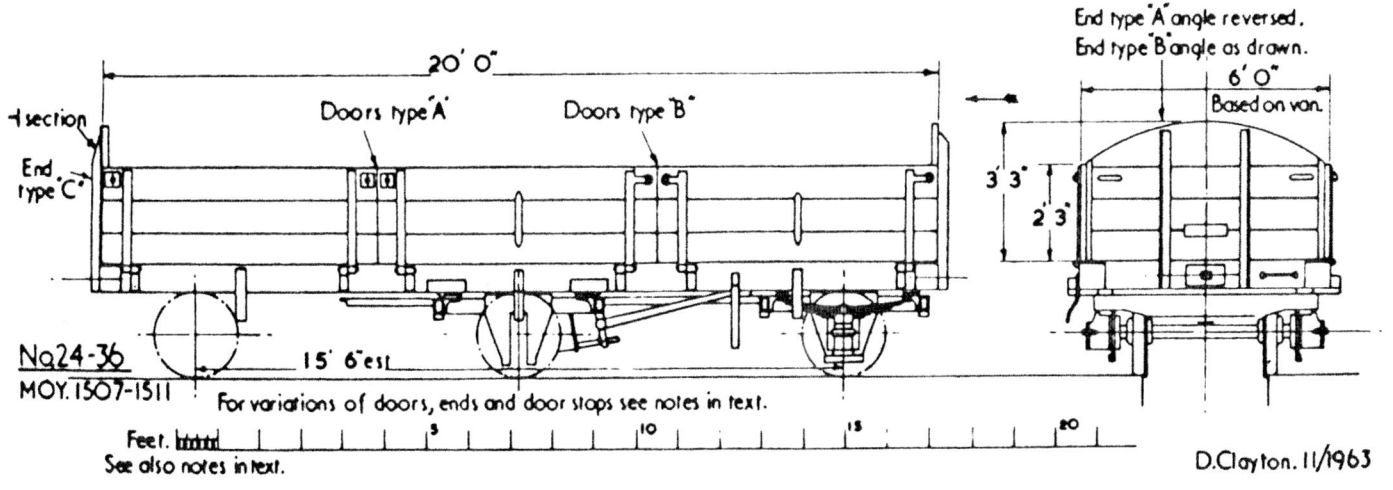

Six-Wheel Wagons

The dimensions on the drawings are from Barrert Jenkins' sketches but unfortunately he made no reference to the actual vehicle or vehicles examined. Variations existed between batches and possibly within batches. The height was probably rounded off to the nearest inch. Two types of door (designated 'A' and 'B' on the drawing) and three types of ends (confusingly also designated 'A', 'B' and 'C') existed and the known variations are shown below.

SR No.	Door	End	Variation
24 and 25	A	B	Square wooden door stop to end doors only (platform side and presumably offside)
27	A	C	No door stops on offside
28	A	C (probably)	Wooden stop to end door only, platform side at least
33	B	B (probably)	
Moy Ltd No.			
1507	A	A	Wooden doorstops as for SR No's 24 and 25
1511	B	B	One steel door stop on each door, platform side at least

It is possible that SR No's 24, 25 and 26 (built 1896), No's 27, 28, 29, 30, 31 and 32 (built 1899) and No's 33, 34, 35 and 36 (built 1914) were similar.

Waiting departure from Southwold 2-4-0T No. 3 *Blyth* stands at the head of a mixed train formed of a flat truck loaded with barrels, an SR 6-wheel open wagon, luggage van, two coaches and at the rear two 4-wheel open wagons and two 6-wheel open vehicles, a load exceeding official limits. The wheel sets in the foreground are unusual in having bifurcated spokes whilst behind them is timber packing and two timber trestles. Behind the locomotive in the carriage shop one of the coaches is receiving attention.

Ian Pope collection

A winter's day finds some staff clad in overcoats against the cold Suffolk wind as 2-4-2T No. 1 *Southwold* prepares to depart with a mixed train to Halesworth. Wagons with tarpaulin covered loads occupy the goods yard to the left while the open sided carriage shed to the right is occupied by at least one coach.
Author's collection

Four-wheel Southwold Railway open wagon No. 4 dating from 1879 with curved ends and a Southern Railway 8-plank open wagon, both displaying the initials SR, are conveniently stabled alongside one another at Halesworth in the 1930s. The fencing in the foreground was typical of the style used by the Southwold Railway at stations.
H.C. Casserley

27 to 32. The railway had to wait until 1914 before the 6-wheel wagon fleet was augmented by a further four vehicles, No's 33 to 36, costing £288 17s 8d. After World War One, No's 37 and 38 were added to the fleet in January 1922 and No. 39 in July 1926; this trio were purchased from Thomas Moy, where they were No's 1507, 1508 and 1509 in the private owner fleet, although the actual order of the individual Moy/SR numbers is not known. Each of the wagons had three hinged doors on each side and a hand brake lever operated a brake shoe on one of the centre wheels. The leading dimensions of the 6-wheel wagons were:

Length over buffers	22 feet 4 ins
Length over body	20 feet 0 ins
Width over body	6 feet 0 ins
Height of body at sides	2 feet 3 ins
Height of body at ends	3 feet 3 ins
Wheelbase	15 feet 6 ins
Tare weight	4 tons approx
Laden weight	7 tons approx

The livery of the initial twelve 4-wheel wagon stock of the SR was black with SOUTHWOLD RAILWAY denoted in white lettering on the top planks on the sides of the vehicles, while the bottom plank carried the inscription 'Load 4 Tons' in script at the left-hand end and the tare weight at the opposite end. The fleet number was painted on the centre of the middle plank. Later vehicles also carried this livery but gradually the fleet was altered, as and when finances allowed, to light grey bodywork and black underframes with black or white lettering, and when repainted the lettering was reduced to SR in approximately 6-inch high letters over the middle side plank with the fleet number in the centre. Running gear was black. The 6-wheel wagons, also painted light grey, were provided with more ornate lettering of white shaded black to the right when delivered with the fleet number in smaller characters placed centrally. As with all small companies in financial distress, in later years repairs to wagons were completed on a piecemeal basis and any shade of grey paint was used for patchwork painting, making for a mottled effect on some vehicles. At this stage the fleet number was placed on the right corner of the solebar on most wagons.

Probably for the opening of the line in September 1879, or soon after, the coal merchant Thomas Moy of Colchester considered it important enough to provide three 6-wheel 3-plank private owner wagons on the railway. These had the Cleminson patent 'flexible wheelbase' and bore fleet numbers 1507, 1508 and 1509. The trio also carried letters A, B and C respectively on the curved ends and

RIGHT: SR 6-wheel Cleminson open wagon No. 25, dating from 1896 built by Thomas Moy at Peterborough, and 4-wheel open wagon No. 1 dating from 1879 built by the Midland Railway Carriage & Wagon Company; both with curved ends. The vehicles are at Southwold in the grey livery with white lettering.
Author's collection

BELOW: SR 6-wheel Cleminson wagons No's 24 and 25, in grey livery with black shaded lettering, en route to Halesworth from Peterborough loaded on two GER flat wagons, No. 13031 on the right. *Southwold Museum*

In 1922 Thomas Moy the fuel distributor with headquarters at Colchester decided to construct an additional two 6-wheel Cleminson wagons for use on the SR as the original vehicles were showing signs of age. No. 1511 is shown before dispatch from Moy's Peterborough works.

Author's collection

the wagons were usually referred to by the letters rather than the numbers. On the Cleminson patent flexible wheelbase system the outer pairs of wheels were in the frame with a centre pivot while the centre pair, also in the frame which was joined to the outer pairs, moved laterally as the wagon negotiated curves and points. In January 1922 two new 6-wheel vehicles were added to Moy's fleet, No's 1510 and 1511, with the letters D and E respectively. In consequence, two of the older wagons were sold to the SR in January 1922 becoming SR No's 37 and 38 and the third in July 1926 becoming SR No. 39, leaving Moy to soldier on with the two most recent vehicles. These wagons were painted red oxide body with black framing, similar to the company's standard gauge vehicles with white lettering shaded to the right: the large lettering MOY occupied the top two door planks while the bottom left was lettered SOUTHWOLD, the fleet number on the middle door and RAILWAY on the right-hand door. Later the fleet number was on the left and SOUTHWOLD RAILWAY on the centre and right-hand door. D and E were on the ends as before. The wagons were sent to Moy's workshop at Peterborough for repairs, the first two believed to be No's 1507 and 1508 on 1st July and 10th August 1885 respectively, followed by No. 1509 on 30th November 1886. The dimensions of these vehicles were the same as the SR wagons. Before delivery of the SR 6-wheel wagons the Moy vehicles were often hired by the SR for the conveyance of long or extra heavy loads and in 1890 two were used to convey the two sections of lantern each weighing 4 tons for Southwold lighthouse.

Locomotive No. 3 *Blyth* with 6-wheel wagons No's 31 and 37 on the run round loop at Southwold in 1928.

Southwold Museum

In the absence of covered goods vans, from the earliest days it was necessary for the company to provide tarpaulin sheets to protect perishable goods conveyed in open wagons. These were normally retained at Southwold when not in use, but Halesworth and Blythburgh usually kept a few to hand. In 1929 the company registered a total of fifty-three wagon sheets on stock.

The locomotives, coaching stock and wagon fleet of the SR were never equipped with any form of continuous brake, either Westinghouse air brake as used by the GER or vacuum brake, despite the Regulation of Railways Act 1889 requiring all passenger stock to be fitted with continuous brake giving instantaneous action when the brake was applied by either the driver or guard. Between 1890 and 1895 there was continuous correspondence between the SR Company and the BOT until the latter threatened to enforce fitting. However, on the advice of Counsel the BOT were advised the case might not be successful as the SR Company had shown it had taken all reasonable precautions for the safety of passengers. The company argued that the expenditure required to equip the continuous brake was far too expensive and that 'traffic had been worked for sixteen years, during which over a million passengers had been carried without a single accident.' A letter to the BOT dated 16th January 1891 strengthened the SR argument, for it confirmed that each coach seated forty passengers and that only two were fitted with handbrakes. It further explained that as no mandatory goods trains operated, freight traffic was carried in wagons attached to passenger carrying services, which ran as 'mixed' trains. To facilitate shunting at the intermediate stations and sidings, on Down services wagons for Wenhaston Mill Siding, Wenhaston and Walberswick were formed at the front of the coaching stock and for Blythburgh and Southwold at the rear of the train. For Up workings the wagon positions were reversed in the formation. Therefore it was argued to achieve full continuous braking of trains it would be necessary to equip all stock. The costly fitting would in turn delay shunting at stations and sidings, as the splitting and recoupling of brake pipes would require additional time and thus extend the running time of the services.

On closure of the line all wagon stock was conveyed to Halesworth for storage where it remained in ever deteriorating condition until the metal was requisitioned for the war effort. During the intervening period most if not all wagons were vandalized of any timber that could easily be removed. Moy wagon No. 1511, standing near the footbridge, was badly damaged as a result of enemy action on Halesworth station and little metal was left for the contractor's men to recover.

The Parliamentary returns submitted to the BOT from 1923 to 1929 showed a total of thirty-eight wagons on stock but this figure incorrectly included the two parcels vans, which were also shown under coaching stock totals. The BOT never questioned the discrepancy.

ABOVE: Halesworth SR station viewed from the connecting footbridge in 1939 with stored narrow gauge wagons on the former outer interchange siding. *Author's collection*

Six-wheel 3-plank Moy private owner wagon No. 1511 photographed at Halesworth 3rd August 1931.
H.R. Norman, John Alsop collection

Front view of abandoned Sharp, Stewart 2-4-0T No. 3 *Blyth* outside Halesworth engine shed in 1936, with the inspection pit in the foreground.
J.H.L. Adams/Kidderminster Railway Museum

Appendix 1

The Reg Carter Postcards

The Southwold Railway was one of the few lines to have a series of cartoon postcards produced to record its so-called eccentricities, let alone two. Two sets of six cards each, the first being issued in 1910, were drawn and originally published by artist Reginald Carter under the title 'Sorrows of Southwold'. As far as is known no legal action was threatened as in the case of Percy French when he wrote and performed a derogatory song listing the shortcomings of the West Clare Railway in the west of Ireland. Carter's postcards were on sale in Southwold up to the outbreak of World War Two and from the date of publishing minor changes were made. In the early days one card entitled 'A slight engine trouble causes delay' incorporated problems associated with the women's suffragette movement and depicted a woman demonstrator sitting in a tree and throwing a bomb at the train with the legend *'Votes for Women'*. After the franchise was granted to married women over thirty years of age in 1918, the woman, bomb and legend were erased from the printing block to produce the picture available today.

Sales recommenced in the 1950s, published by N. Neal, newsagent in East Street and continued until 1967 when C.C. Mack carried on until 1984 and stocks were exhausted by 1987. In 1990, with Mack's agreement, publication was taken over by the Southwold Archaeological & Natural History Society, with three outlets in the town including the museum. Cards printed after World War Two were embossed on the reverse in the lower left corner, *'With Best Wishes'*.

Carter portrayed himself in most pictures usually wearing a broad brim ten gallon hat; he also produced two similar cartoon postcard series of the town, transport and beach, each of six cards, with the same title, which can cause confusion with collectors.

THE SOUTHWOLD EXPRESS. THE DRIVER DOES A ROARING TRADE OWING TO A DELAY CAUSED BY THE PORTER - OVERESTIMATING HIS STRENGTH - THE GUARD MAKES THE MOST OF THIS, AND TRIES TO SPOT A WINNER - THE STATIONMASTER DOES ALL IN HIS POWER TO GET THE TRAIN AWAY.

THE SOUTHWOLD EXPRESS - A HEAVY RAIN PUTS THE FIRE OUT - THE DRIVER FIXES A PASSENGERS' UMBRELLA - THE FIREMAN LIGHTS THE FIRE - THE GUARD DISREGARDFUL OF OF THE WEATHER BRAVELY SUPERINTENDS THE WHOLE UNPLEASANT OCCURRENCE.

THE SOUTHWOLD RAILWAY — A BUSY DAY AT HALESWORTH STATION - COALING UP & OVERHAULING ENGINE FOR THE RETURN JOURNEY - THE SIGNAL BEING OUT OF ORDER CAUSES MUCH DELAY

APPENDICES

THE SOUTHWOLD EXPRESS   A COW ON THE LINE IS LUCKILY SEEN BY THE GUARD - IN HIS EAGERNESS TO STOP THE TRAIN HE PUTS THE BRAKES ON TOO SUDDENLY!

THE SOUTHWOLD EXPRESS - THE GUARD AS A PROFITABLE SIDELINE - PUTS THE DINNERS OF THE COTTAGERS ALONG THE ROUTE ON THE UP TRAIN - THESE BEING DONE TO PERFECTION BY THE RETURN JOURNEY - THE PROCESS OF CURING THE RENOWNED SOUTHWOLD BLOATERS IS SHEWN

THE SOUTHWOLD EXPRESS — THE ENGINE JUMPS THE RAILS OWING TO EXCESSIVE SPEED. THE SKILL OF THE DRIVER ALONE SAVES ALL FROM INJURY.

THE SOUTHWOLD EXPRESS THE FIRST CLASS PASSENGER SUPPORTED BY ALL THE THIRD CLASS, SHEW GREAT ANNOYANCE AT AN UNEXPECTED STOP – TO LEARN FROM THE GUARD, THAT "THE DRIVER SEEING A CHOICE CROP OF GROUNDSEL – IS GATHERING IT FOR HIS CANARY!"

THE SOUTHWOLD EXPRESS :–
THE GOODS TRAIN LEAVES HALESWORTH HALF AN HOUR TOO SOON – THUS MEETING THE 2.20. FROM SOUTHWOLD BETWEEN BLYTHBURGH AND WENHASTON – AFTER MUCH DISCUSSION THE DRIVERS DECIDE TO FIGHT FOR THE RIGHT OF THE ROAD – A SPORTING PASSENGER MAKES THE MOST OF THE SITUATION – THE GUARD WAITS ANXIOUSLY.

THE SOUTHWOLD RAILWAY – WAITING AT THE TERMINUS FOR THE DOWN EXPRESS WHICH IS SOMEWHAT LATE – A VERY UNUSUAL OCCURRENCE.

Appendix 2

Southwold Railway Bridges

Bridge No.	Miles	Chains	Name	Under or Over	Spans	Remarks
	0	00	Halesworth Station			
1	0	14	Holton Road	Under	1	45 feet wrought iron span on brick abutments, span replaced by steel plate girders 1906/7
2	0	30	Bird's Folly	Under	2	20 feet each span, masonry, rebuilt 1906/7.
3	1	00½	Culvert	Under	1	timber, concrete abutments.
4	1	22½	Mells, also known as Balls Bridge*	Over	1	20 feet span masonry, rebuilt 1906/7.
5	1	56½	Culvert	Under	1	timber, concrete abutments.
5a	1	58	Flood Opening	Under	1	timber, concrete abutments.
6	1	63	River Blyth & New Cut	Under	2	93 feet span on 9 timber braced supports.
7	1	65	Mill Leat	Under		timber, concrete abutments.
	2	51½	Wenhaston Station			
8	2	64	Culvert	Under	1	timber, concrete abutments.
9	2	69½	Culvert	Under	1	timber, concrete abutments.
10	3	61	Young's	Under	1	40 feet span, timber, concrete abutments.
	4	71	Blythburgh Station			
11	4	72	Yarmouth Turnpike (A12)	Over	1	29 feet span, masonry, rebuilt 1906/7.
12	7	19	Walberswick Cattlecreep	Under	1	concrete.
	7	46	Walberswick Station			
13	7	74½	River Blyth	Under	1	146 feet span, 60 feet centre span of wrought iron, timber side spans, centre span rebuilt 1906/7, side spans rebuilt from timber to steel in 1914.
14	8	25	Golf Club Footbridge	Over	3	wrought iron and scrap rail, erected 1904, cost of £50 paid by golf club.
	8	63	Southwold Station			

* Also known as Corner Farm
Details and mileages taken from GER survey of 1911 and L&NER survey of 1923 – these show differences to the earlier GER survey of 1894.

THE SOUTHWOLD EXPRESS - THE BRIDGE IS UNABLE TO STAND THE STRAIN OF THE ANNUAL EXCURSION TRAIN - LUCKILY THE LIFEBOAT IS NEAR AND ALL ARE SAVED

Appendix 3

Southwold Railway Level Crossings

No	Location	Miles	Chains	Name	Type
	Halesworth station	0	00		
1	Halesworth & Wenhaston	0	40		occupation
2	Halesworth & Wenhaston	0	47		occupation/footpath
3	Halesworth & Wenhaston	0	58½		occupation
4	Halesworth & Wenhaston	0	72		occupation
5	Halesworth & Wenhaston	1	03½	Cherrytree	occupation
6	Halesworth & Wenhaston	1	06¾		occupation
7	Halesworth & Wenhaston	1	19	Corner Farm	occupation
8	Halesworth & Wenhaston	1	43		occupation
9	Halesworth & Wenhaston	1	52½		footpath/occupation
10	Halesworth & Wenhaston	1	60¾		footpath
11	Halesworth & Wenhaston	1	63½		footpath
12	Halesworth & Wenhaston	1	72¼	Wenhaston Mill	occupation
13	Halesworth & Wenhaston	2	12		occupation
14	Halesworth & Wenhaston	2	13		occupation
15	Halesworth & Wenhaston	2	24½	Heath Farm	occupation
16	Halesworth & Wenhaston	2	30½		occupation
17	Halesworth & Wenhaston	2	49½	Wenhaston	public
	Wenhaston station	2	51½		
18	Wenhaston & Blythburgh	2	67½		occupation
19	Wenhaston & Blythburgh	2	71½		occupation
20	Wenhaston & Blythburgh	3	13½		footpath
21	Wenhaston & Blythburgh	3	15		occupation
22	Wenhaston & Blythburgh	3	33½		occupation
23	Wenhaston & Blythburgh	3	46¼		occupation
24	Wenhaston & Blythburgh	3	51	Beaumar	occupation
25	Wenhaston & Blythburgh	3	54½		footpath
26	Wenhaston & Blythburgh	3	70½		footpath
27	Wenhaston & Blythburgh	3	78½		footpath
28	Wenhaston & Blythburgh	4	03¾		footpath
29	Wenhaston & Blythburgh	4	13¼		occupation
30	Wenhaston & Blythburgh	4	19½		occupation
31	Wenhaston & Blythburgh	4	25½		occupation
32	Wenhaston & Blythburgh	4	33		occupation
33	Wenhaston & Blythburgh	4	37½		occupation
34	Wenhaston & Blythburgh	4	39½		occupation
35	Wenhaston & Blythburgh	4	46½	Fen Cottages (1)	occupation
36	Wenhaston & Blythburgh	4	49½	Fen Cottages (2)	occupation
37	Wenhaston & Blythburgh	4	51	Fen Cottages (3)	occupation
38	Wenhaston & Blythburgh	4	62		footpath
	Blythburgh station	4	71		
39	Blythburgh & Walberswick	4	75		occupation
40	Blythburgh & Walberswick	5	06½		occupation
41	Blythburgh & Walberswick	5	25½		occupation

No	Location	Miles	Chains	Name	Type
42	Blythburgh & Walberswick	5	49½		footpath
43	Blythburgh & Walberswick	6	06	Hill Covert	footpath
44	Blythburgh & Walberswick	6	21½		footpath
45	Blythburgh & Walberswick	6	50½	Tinker's Covert	footpath
46	Blythburgh & Walberswick	6	68½	Eastwood Lodge	occupation
47	Blythburgh & Walberswick	6	79		footpath
48	Blythburgh & Walberswick	7	01¾		footpath
49	Blythburgh & Walberswick	7	31		footpath
50	Blythburgh & Walberswick	7	43¾		footpath
	Walberswick station	7	46		
51	Walberswick & Southwold	7	56		footpath
52	Walberswick & Southwold	7	71½		footpath
53	Walberswick & Southwold	7	75		footpath
54	Walberswick & Southwold	7	76½		footpath
55	Walberswick & Southwold	7	78		footpath
56	Walberswick & Southwold	8	20½		footpath
57	Walberswick & Southwold	8	33		footpath
58	Walberswick & Southwold	8	44		footpath
59	Walberswick & Southwold	8	52½		occupation
	Southwold station	8	63		

Details and mileages taken from GER survey of 1911 and L&NER survey of 1923 – these show differences from the earlier GER survey of 1894.

No. 3 *Blyth* in the snow at Southwold. Note the wooden shield at the cab side to protect footplate staff in such conditions. *Southwold Museum*

Appendix 4

Train Staff Regulations, September 1908, with Amendment of August 1914

NOTE: Original page numbers are indicated within square brackets at the start of each page, thus [1].

[1]

SOUTHWOLD RAILWAY.

Train Staff Regulations

SEPTEMBER, 1908.

KNAPP, DREWETT & SONS LTD.,
Printers,
30, Victoria Street, Westminster.
V 3525.

[3] SOUTHWOLD RAILWAY.

TRAIN STAFF REGULATIONS.

Applicable to Single Lines worked under the Train Staff and Train Staff Ticket System.

1. Single Lines worked under the Train Staff and Train Staff Ticket System are divided into Sections, and the Station at each end of such Sections is called a 'Train Staff Station.' The Train Staff Stations are Southwold, Blythburgh (crossing place), and Halesworth. The Sections are Southwold and Blythburgh, and Blythburgh and Halesworth.

2. A Train Staff or Train Staff Ticket must be carried with each train, and no train must be permitted to leave any Staff Station with a Train Staff Ticket unless the Staff for that portion of the Line over which it is to travel is then at the Station.

3. (*a*) The Danger Signal must always be kept exhibited at all the Fixed Signals at Staff Stations, except when it is necessary to lower them for a train to pass; and, before any Signal [4] is lowered, care must be taken to ascertain that the Line on which the train is about to run is clear.

(*b*) When a Passenger Train and a Special Goods Train, which have to cross each other, are approaching the Blythburgh (Crossing) Staff Station in opposite directions, the Signals in both directions must be kept at Danger, and when the Passenger Train—which has to be first admitted into the Station—has been brought to a stand, the Home Signal applicable to such train may be lowered to allow it to draw forward to the Station, and, after it has again come to a stand, and the person in charge has seen that the Line on which the Special Goods Train will arrive is quite clear, the necessary

[2] **TRAIN STAFF REGULATIONS.**

STAFF STATIONS.

AMENDED REGULATION No. 1.

1. Single Lines worked under the Train Staff and Train Staff Ticket System are divided into Sections, and the Station at each end of such Sections is called a 'Train Staff Station.' The Train Staff Stations are Southwold, **Walberswick**, Blythburgh (crossing place), and Halesworth. The Sections are Southwold and **Walberswick**, **Walberswick** and Blythburgh, and Blythburgh and Halesworth.

H. WARD,
Manager and Secretary.

London,
8th August, 1914.

234

Signal for that train may also be lowered to allow it to draw forward on to the Loop.

4. (*a*) Permission must not be given for a train to approach from the opposite end of the Section when there is any obstruction upon the Line.

(*b*) The Line must not be fouled after permission has been given for a train to approach from the opposite end of the Section.

5. (*a*) A Special Goods Train is not permitted to shunt for another train to pass, except at the Blythburgh (Crossing) Staff Station.

[5] (*b*) An empty Carriage Train may be treated and worked as a Special Goods Train.

(*c*) A Passenger Train is not permitted to pass another Passenger Train at the Blythburgh (Crossing) Staff Station.

6. The person in charge of the Staff-working for the time being is the sole person authorised to receive and deliver the Staff or Ticket.

7. When a train is ready to start from a Station and no second train is intended to follow before the Staff will be required for a train in the opposite direction, the person in charge of the Staff-working must give the Staff to the Engine-driver, who will then place it in the Train Staff Socket provided on the Engine.

8. (*a*) If another train is intended to follow before the Staff can be returned, a Ticket indicating that the Staff is following must be given by the person in charge of the Staff-working to the Engine-driver of the first train, the Staff for the Section being shown to him, the Staff itself being given to the Engine-driver of the last train, as directed in the preceding Rule. The person who hands the Ticket to the Engine-driver must satisfy himself that the train has arrived at the end of the Section before he allows another train to follow. After the Staff has been sent away no other train must, under any circumstances, leave the Station to follow in the same [6] direction, until the Staff for that Section has been returned.

(*b*) The Station Master, or person in charge of the Staff-working, must consider it his first duty to deal with the Train Staff or Ticket on arrival of the train, and at the Blythburgh (Crossing) Staff Station must satisfy himself that the train running in the one direction has arrived complete with the Tail Lamp or Disc on the last vehicle, before handing the Staff or Ticket to the Engine-driver about to travel in the opposite direction.

9. No train must be permitted to leave a Station until the Engine-driver has received the proper Staff or Ticket for that Section of the Line over which he is about to travel, and he must not take the Staff or Ticket from any other than the person in charge of the Staff-working for the time being. After receiving the Staff or Ticket he must not start until the proper Signals have been exhibited, and, when with a train, not until a Signal has also been given by the Guard. On arriving at the Station to which the Staff or Ticket extends, such Staff or Ticket must immediately be given up to the person in charge of the Staff-working. All Tickets so given up must be at once cancelled by the word 'cancelled' being written across them, and the Tickets must afterwards be sent to the Secretary.

[7] **10.** (*a*) An Engine-driver will render himself liable to dismissal if he leaves a Staff Station without the Staff or Ticket for the Section over which he is about to run; or, if he leaves with a Ticket, without having first seen the proper Staff.

(*b*) He must be careful not to take the Staff or Ticket beyond the Staff Station at which it should be left.

(*c*) The person in charge of the Staff-working will render himself liable to severe punishment should he contribute to any irregularity in the Staff-working.

11. Each Staff has marked on it the name of the Staff Station at each end of the Section to which only it applies. The Staffs, Boxes and Tickets for the two Sections are painted and printed in different colours, and the Staffs of the two Sections are different in shape.

12. (*a*) The Tickets must be kept in the proper Ticket Box, the key to open the box being attached to the Staff, for the same Section as the box, so that, if the Ticket Box is kept locked—for which the person in charge of the Staff-working will be held strictly responsible—access to the Tickets cannot be obtained unless the proper Staff for the Section is then at the Station.

(*b*) Only one Ticket must be taken from the Ticket Box at the same time. The box must be [8] locked after each Ticket is taken out, and not again opened until it is necessary to obtain another Ticket for a following train, unless as provided for in Rule 15 of these Regulations.

13. (*a*) The Staff, when at the Station, must not be kept in the box, but on the brackets outside of it.

(*b*) Should a Train Staff be lost, or so damaged that it will not open the box containing the Staff Tickets, the Station Masters at both ends of the Section must communicate with each other and make arrangements to work the traffic over the Section to which the Staff belongs by Pilotman, who must accompany every train until the Staff has been found, or repaired.

(*c*) If the missing Staff be found, it must be handed to the Station Master at either end of the Section to which it applies, who must make arrangements for the ordinary working to be resumed.

14. (*a*) When a Special Train or Engine has to be run, a Red Tail Board must be used by day and an extra Red Tail Light by night, for the purpose of signalling to all concerned that a Special Train is to follow.

(*b*) The Station Master, or person in charge of the Starting Station, will be responsible for seeing that the Red Tail Board by day, or an [9] extra Red Tail Light by night, is attached to the centre of the last vehicle of the preceding ordinary train.

(*c*) The Guard will be responsible for seeing that the Tail Board, or extra Red Light, is under all circumstances exhibited on the last vehicle of the train during its journey, and that it is removed and returned to the Station to which it belongs. A Red Tail Board must be kept at Southwold and Halesworth.

(*d*) In the event of a Special Train having to be run which has not been advised by notice issued by the Secretary, Red Tail Board or Red Light, a telephonic advice must be sent by the Terminal Station Master to each Station on the route.

15. When any train is assisted by a second engine in the front, and such train has to carry the Staff, the first or leading engine must carry a Ticket, and the second engine the Staff. In cases where the train is to be followed by another train, the second, as well as the leading engine, must carry a Ticket.

16. (*a*) In the event of an engine which carries the Staff breaking down between two Stations, the Fireman must take the Staff to the Staff Station in the direction whence assistance can be obtained; and the Station Master at the Station to which the Staff is taken will be held [10] responsible for carrying out all special arrangements necessary during the continuance of the obstruction. Should the engine that fails be in possession of a Ticket instead of the Staff, assistance must only come from the Station at which the Staff has been left, and the Station Master at that Station will be held responsible for making any special arrangements that may be necessary, the Guard of the train being held responsible for -the proper protection of his train until the arrival of the Station Master. But if assistance can be more readily obtained at a Station other than that where the Staff is, immediate steps must be taken to have the Staff transferred to the other end of the Section. The Fireman must accompany the assistant engine to the place where he has left his own engine.

(*b*) When the engine which has failed is carrying a Ticket, the Fireman must take this Ticket with him when he goes for assistance, and the Driver of the engine which has failed must not allow it to be moved until the assisting engine has arrived.

17. Except as shown below, no engine must push a train upon any Running Line, but must draw it.

Exceptions—

(*a*) When within Station limits or where specially authorised by the Secretary.

[11] (*b*) In the case of an engine being disabled a following engine may push the train slowly to the next Station, when the pushing engine must go in front.

(*c*) When the Line is blocked and trains are being worked to the point of obstruction, on both sides.

(*d*) When required to assist in starting a train from a Station.

18. (*a*) When a train or a portion of a train is left upon the Line from accident or inability of the engine to take the whole forward, the Engine-driver must not, if he be in possession of a Ticket, return for it except by written instructions from the Guard, and the Guard must protect his train in the rear, and prevent a following train pushing it ahead. If the Engine-driver be in possession of the Staff, he may return for the rear portion of his train without obtaining instructions from the Guard authorising him to do so.

(*b*) After sunset, or in foggy weather, or during falling snow, before the front portion is drawn forward, a Red Light must be placed on the front vehicle of the rear portion, by the man who divides the train.

19. (*a*) Should an accident occur of such a nature as to block the Line, and the traffic is [12] likely to be stopped for any considerable time, special arrangements must be made for working the trains to and from the Staff Station on each side of the obstruction. The Train Staff must be retained to work trains between the point of obstruction and the Staff Station from which assistance is rendered, and, on the other side, the traffic must be conducted by a Pilotman to be appointed by an order in writing (see specimen Form on pages 13 to 15).

(*b*) The Line on each side of the obstruction must be protected by Hand Signalmen in the usual way.

[13] SOUTHWOLD RAILWAY.

Train Staff and Ticket System.

Working of Single Line by Pilotman during Obstruction.

This Form must be filled up and used whenever it is temporarily necessary, owing to obstruction, to work the traffic by Pilotman.

...................................Station.

....

The Line between .... and .... being obstructed, the traffic between .... and the place of obstruction will be worked by Pilotman in accordance with Rule 19 of the Regulations for Working Single Lines of Railway by Train Staff and Ticket.

.... will act as Pilotman, and must accompany every train to and from .... Station and the point of obstruction.

[14] This Order is to remain in force until withdrawn by the Pilotman.

(Signed)......................................

To ....

*Noted by .... at place of obstruction.

Time .... *Noted by.............................

.... Station.   Time.......................

Noted by .... Pilotman.

* These signatures must be made on the copy held by the Pilotman, who must also sign the Forms held by the person in charge of the obstruction.

Note.—The time at which this Form is cancelled must be written across it.

Six of these Forms must be kept in a convenient place at each Train Staff Station, so as to be available at any moment.

A copy of this Form must be delivered to the person in charge of the Staff Station where Pilot-working commences, the second must be [15] retained by the Pilotman, and the third must be conveyed by the Pilotman to the person in charge of the obstruction. If there is an intermediate Station which is not a Train Staff Station, the person in charge must be supplied with a copy of the Form.

In the event of a Station Master himself acting as Pilotman, he must address and give a copy of the Form to the person he leaves in charge of his Station.

Station Masters and persons in charge receiving this Form will be held responsible that the Foreman, and others concerned at their Station are immediately made acquainted with the circumstances, and are instructed in their necessary duties.

On the other side of the obstruction the Line will be worked by Train Staff, no Tickets being used.

[16] 20. When the Line is again clear, no train must be allowed to pass the point where the obstruction existed without the Staff. The Pilotman must accompany the first train carrying the Staff to the Staff Station, and, after the Pilotman has withdrawn his arrangements for Pilot-working, the traffic must be again conducted according to the Train Staff Regulations.

21. (*a*) When a Ballast train has to work on the Line, the Staff must be given to the Engine-driver in charge of it. This will close the Line whilst the Ballast train is at work. The Ballast train must proceed afterwards to one of the Staff Stations to open the Line before the ordinary traffic can be resumed. But if a Ballast train is required to run over a Section of the Line

from one Staff Station to the other without stopping to work on the way, it may then travel with Staff or Ticket as required; under no circumstances must the Ballast train stop to do work on the Line unless in possession of the Train Staff.

(*b*) The Engine-driver of a Ballast train that has to do work on the Line, must be told, when receiving the Staff, to which end of the Section it is to be taken and at what time it is to be there, in order to clear the Line for the next train.

22. (*a*) Points giving communication between the Sidings and the Running Line controlled by [**17**] the Train Staff cannot be opened without the Train Staff for that Section of the Line where the Siding is situated, and the Train Staff cannot be removed until the Points have been placed in the proper position for trains to pass upon the Running Line, and securely locked so as to prevent vehicles passing from the Sidings on to the Running Line.

(*b*) On arriving at a Siding, the Points of which are controlled by the Train Staff, the Engine-driver must hand the Train Staff to the Guard to enable him to unlock the Points.

(*c*) When the necessary shunting has been completed and the points have been placed in the proper position for trains to pass upon the Running Line, the Guard must return the Train Staff to the Engine-driver, and the latter must not proceed on his journey until he has obtained possession of it.

[**18**]   FORM OF TRAIN STAFF TICKET.

No.

Southwold Railway.

Tram Staff Ticket.

Train............

To

The Engine-driver.

You are authorised, after seeing the Train Staff for the Section, to proceed from .... to .... and the Train Staff will follow.

Signature of person in charge ....

Date ....

This ticket must be given up by the Engine-driver, immediately on arrival, to the person in charge of the Staff working at the place to which he is authorised to proceed. At the end of the day this ticket is to be enclosed by the Station Master to the Secretary.

H. WARD,
Secretary.

September, 1908.

[**19**]   **TRAIN STAFF REGULATIONS.**

STAFF STATIONS.

BLYTHBURGH (CROSSING PLACE).

The Signals at Blythburgh are now as follows:—

On the off side of the line, from Halesworth:—

Down   Distant.
 ,,   Home.
 ,,   Starter.

Facing the line, from Southwold:—

Up   Home.
 ,,   Starter.

The following rules must, be strictly adhered to:—

(1)   When an Engine-driver finds the Distant Signal at Danger be must reduce speed and proceed cautiously towards the Home Signal, being prepared to stop if necessary.

(2)   No train must pass a Home Signal at Danger, or foul the Points to which it applies, unless specially authorised by the Secretary.

H. WARD.

London,
  7th October, 1908.

Appendix 5

Rules and Regulations, 1st November 1918

Note: Original page numbers are indicated within square brackets at the start of each page, thus [1].

[1] **Southwold Railway Company.**

RULES AND REGULATIONS

FOR THE GUIDANCE

OF THE

OFFICERS AND MEN

IN THE SERVICE OF THE

SOUTHWOLD RAILWAY COMPANY.

1st November, 1918.

Printers:
KNAPP, DREWETT AND SONS LIMITED,
30 VICTORIA ST., WESTMINSTER, S.W.1.
11612 v.

[2] At a Meeting of the Board of Directors of the Southwold Railway Company, held at 17, Victoria Street, Westminster, S.W., on the 4th day of October, 1918,

It was resolved—

'That the following Rules and Regulations be, and the same are hereby approved and adopted for the guidance and instruction of the Officers and Men in the service of the Southwold Railway Company, from 1st November next, and that all former Rules and Regulations inconsistent with the same be cancelled.'

[3] **TABLE OF CONTENTS.**

	PAGE
General Rules and Regulations	5
Train Signals	9
Calling-on Signals	9
Signalling in Foggy Weather, or during Snowstorms	10
Station Masters	10
Gatemen	13
Guards	13
Engine Drivers and Firemen	17
Foremen, Gangers, Platelayers and others employed on the Permanent Way	20
Regulations for Working	26

APPENDIX.

I. Regulations For Working Single Lines of Railway By Train Staff And Ticket	28

[4] Every Servant supplied with this Book must make himself thoroughly acquainted with, and will be held responsible for a knowledge of, and compliance with, the whole of the following Rules and Regulations.

[5] **Southwold Railway Company**

GENERAL RULES AND REGULATIONS.

1. Every person employed by the Company must devote himself exclusively to their service, residing at whatever place may be appointed, attending at such hours as may be required, paying prompt obedience to all persons placed in authority over him, and conforming to all the Rules and Regulations of the Company.

2. Every Station Master, Foreman, Engine-driver, Guard, Signalman, Ganger, Shunter, Yardman, Gatekeeper, Clerk, Porter and other servant connected with the working of the railway ; and also every man engaged on the Permanent Way or Works affecting the Running Lines, must be supplied with, and have with him when on duty, and produce when required, a copy of these Rules and Regulations.

3. The address of each person employed in the working of the Railway must be registered at the station to which he is attached or at which he is paid, and must be posted in the Station Master's Office, so that, if required in case of emergency, the men may be readily found. Any change of address must be notified to the Station Master, in order that the record may be kept perfect.

[6] 4. No servant is allowed, under any circumstances, to absent himself from duty, or alter his appointed hours of attendance, or exchange duty with any other servant, without the special permission of his superior officer. In case of illness, lie must immediately report the circumstance to his superior officer.

5. The Company reserve the right to punish any servant at any time, without notice, by fine, suspension from duty, or dismissal for intoxication, disobedience of orders, negligence, or misconduct, or for being absent from duty without leave, and retain the sums which may be imposed as fines, and no wages shall be payable by the Company to any servant during the period of his suspension from duty, or after his dismissal, or during his absence from duly from any cause.

6. No servant of the Company is allowed to trade, either directly or indirectly, for himself or others.

7. No servant is allowed to appropriate to his own use any articles, the property of the Company.

8. No servant when on duty or in uniform is allowed to leave the Company's premises to enter a Hotel or Refreshment Room.

9. No servant of the Company is allowed to leave the Company's premises during his hours of duty except by permission of his superior officer.

[7] 10. No servant is allowed to leave the Company's service without giving the notice required by the terms of his engagement.

11. When a man leaves the service, he must immediately deliver up his uniform and all other articles belonging to the Company, and no money due for wages to any man leaving the service will be paid until his clothing, book of rules, lamps, flags, tools, and all other articles, the property of the Company, which may have been supplied to him, shall have been delivered up in accordance with the Company's regulations. If not delivered up, or if any article be missing or be damaged by improper use, the cost of such articles, or of the repair of such damage, shall be a debt due fiom the man to the Company, and may be deducted from any pay then due, or if such pay be found insufficient to meet the claim, will become a debt recoverable at law.

12. It any servant of the Company lose his copy of the Rules and Regulations, Time Table, or other document of which the Regulations require that he should be in possession, he must immediately obtain another copy from his superior officer.

13. Every servant must assist in carrying out the Rules and Regulations, and immediately report to his superior officer any infringement thereof, or any occurrence which may come under his notice affecting the safe and proper working of the traffic.

[8] 14. The Company's servants must not take charge of luggage or other articles left at the station for the convenience of passengers. All such luggage or articles must be deposited in the Cloak Room in the regular manner.

15. All unclaimed or lost luggage, money, or other property, found in the carriages, at the stations, or upon the Line, must be immediately delivered to the person in charge at the station at, or nearest to, the place where the article has been found, and be dealt with by him in accordance with the Company's instructions upon the subject.

16. (*a*) No person, other than a servant of the Company in the execution of his duty, must be allowed to be, or walk, upon the Railway, unless provided with written or printed permission to do so, signed by a properly-authorised officer of the Company.

(*b*) Unless instructions are issued to the contrary, any person trespassing must be requested to leave the Company's premises, and, on complying, must be warned not to go or pass thereon again. If such person refuses to quit, he must be requested to give his name and address, which must be handed to the nearest Station Master with a report of the circumstances. In the event of the offender refusing his name nnd address, he must be detained and given in charge of the Police.

[9] **TRAIN SIGNALS.**

17. After sunset and during foggy weather every Engine must carry the necessary Headlights, and, when running alone, a Red Tail Disc by day and a Red Tail Light by night. Every train must carry a Red Tail Disc by day and a Red Tail Light by night.

18. The Guard, if there be only one, or the rear Guard, if there be more than one, must see that the Tail Lamp is kept properly burning when necessary.

RED is a signal of 'DANGER,' GREEN is a signal of 'ALL RIGHT.'

CALLING-ON SIGNALS.

19. (*a*) Where short arms are fixed upon the Home Signal posts as Calling-on Signals they are placed below the Home Signal. When a Calling-on Arm is lowered, the Engine-driver must draw forward past the post of the Signal on which the Calling-on Arm is fixed, as far as the Line is clear.

(*b*) Unless instructions are issued to the contrary, the Calling-on Arm must not be lowered until the train has been brought to a stand at the Home Signal.

[10] **SIGNALLING IN FOGGY WEATHER, OR DURING SNOWSTORMS.**

20. During foggy weather, or snowstorms, it is the duty of the Station Master or Person in Charge to take care that Fog 'Signalmen are employed where necessary, at all the places where their services are required, and, where Platelayers are employed for the purpose, to arrange beforehand with the Ganger of the length, the Platelayers who are to act as Fog Signalmen at the various posts.

STATION MASTERS.

21. Every Station Master or Person in Charge of a station is answerable for the security and protection of the office and buildings, and of the Company's property there. He is also responsible for the faithful and efficient discharge of the duties devolving upon all the Company's servants, either permanently or temporarily employed at the station, or within its limits, and such servants are subject to his authority and directions in the working of the Line. He is also responsible for the general working of the station being carried out in strict accordance with the Company's Regulations, and must, as far as practicable, give personal attention to the shunting of trains, and all other operations which in any way affect the safety of the Line.

22. He must take care that all the servants come on duty clean in their persons and clothes, mid in the uniform supplied to them.

[11] 23. The Station Master or Person in Charge must report, without delay, to his superior officer, neglect of duty on the part of any of the-Company's servants under his charge, and forward to him particulars of any complaint made by the public.

24. He must be careful that all stores are prudently and economically used.

25. The Station Master or Person in Charge must take care that immediately on the stopping of each passenger train, the name of the station is called out along the train in a distinct and audible manner, and must pay immediate attention to any indication shown by the passengers of their desire to alight.

26. The Station Master must daily inspect the station, and see that the rooms, offices, lavatories, urinals, and platforms are kept neat and clean. He must also take care that station name-plates or boards, and waiting-room or other indicators, are kept in a clean and satisfactory condition.

27. (*a*) Platforms and steps of overbridges must, when necessary, be strewn with sand, ballast or ashes, or otherwise treated so as to avoid any cause of accident to passengers by slipping.

(*b*) During falling snow, the platforms and approaches to the stations must be kept free from snow by being carefully swept as often as necessary.

[12] (*c*) The. Permanent Way Staff must give as much assistance as possible.

28. The Station Master must frequently inspect the Fixed Signal and other Lamps, and satisfy himself that they are in good working order, and that the glasses, spectacles and reflectors are well cleaned.

29. The Oil burners of Distant and other Fixed Signals and Platform Lamps must he cleaned and trimmed daily and taken to the Lamp-room every morning for the purpose, and not replaced until required to be lighted.

30. Station Masters will be held responsible for keeping their clocks properly regulated, and must, if necessary, at once report any defects in their working, in order that steps may be taken for their immediate repair.

31. No carriage door must he opened to allow a passenger to alight from, or enter, a train before it has come to a stand, or after it has started.

32. When an accident or obstruction of any kind occurs on any part of the Line, it must be immediately reported by telephone, or by the most expeditious means, to the next station on each side of the place where the accident has occurred, so that notice may be given lo the Engine-driver and Guard of approaching train.

33. When a horse is used on the Railway, a man must, in all cases, have hold of its head, whether the horse is drawing vehicles or otherwise.

[13]   GATEMEN.

34. The Lamps on level Crossing Gates of public highways must show a Red light in each direction along the Line when the gates are closed across it, and must be kept lighted from dusk to daylight and during foggy weather as long as the train is running.

35. Traction or other heavy engines, heavy loads of timber, etc., or droves of animals, must not be allowed to cross the Railway when any train can be seen, or is known to be approaching in either direction.

GUARDS.

36. The Guard must be in attendance at the station from which he is to start half-an-hour before the time appointed for the departure of his train, or at such other time as may be specially fixed.

37. The. Guard must have with him his watch, Whistle, and Carriage Key, and take in his van a Red and a Green Flag, a Hand Signal Lamp and a Sprag, and such other articles as may be ordered by te Manager.

38. The Guard must not allow any person to ride outside the carriages or on the platform, nor must he permit any unauthorised person to ride in his van, or in any compartment or vehicle in which parcels or luggage may be placed.

[14] 39. Guards and other servants of the Company are forbidden to carry any description of package, either for themselves, their friends, or the public without proper authority in writing for the free transit thereby, or unless such package be properly entered on the way-bill.

40. When the Engine-driver gives three or more short, sharp whistles, the Guard must immediately apply the brakes.

41. Should any part of the train become detached when in motion, care must be taken not to stop the front part of the train before the rear portion has either been stopped or is running slowly, and the Guard must promptly apply his brake to prevent a collision with the front portion.

42. When the trains are within station limits the Guards are under the orders of the Station Master or Person in Charge.

43. Smoking in the carriages except in the compartments specially set apart for that purpose, is strictly forbidden, and Guards must take care that the bye-law on the subject is enforced.

44. Guards of Passenger trains must, as far as practicable, keep a good look-out ahead and be prepared to take any action that may be necessary. They must also give prompt attention to the luggage, parcels, despatches, and other packages entrusted to them. Parcels which have to be put out must be given by the [15] Guard to the Porter appointed to receive them, who must sign in the Guard's Book for the value parcels delivered to him. The Guard must in like manner sign in the Porter's Book for the value parcels transferred to his care.

45. (*a*) No Passenger train must be started before the time stated in the Time-table.

(*b*) The Signal for starting a Passenger train must be given by the Guard showing a Hand Signal, and, when necessary, blowing his whistle, after obtaining an intimation from the Station Master, or Person in Charge, that all is right for the train to proceed.

If a Flag is used in the day-time as the signal to start, it must be a Green one; at night, when a lamp is used as the signal, it must show a Green Light, and be held steadily above the head.

(*c*) When there are two or more Guards, the signal to the Engine-driver to start must be given by the Guard nearest the Engine after he has exchanged signals with the Guard or Guards in the rear, who must first have received intimation from the Station Master, or Person in Charge, that all is right for the train to proceed.

(*d*) Should a Passenger train be stopped by an accident or from any other exceptional cause, the Engine-driver must not again start until he has exchanged Hand Signals with the Guard, or in the case of more than one Guard, not until he has received the signal from the [**16**] Guard nearest the Engine, who must first exchange Hand Signals with the Guard in the rear.

46. No Passenger train must be stopped at a station where it is not timed to call, for the purpose of taking up or setting down passengers, without the special authority of the Manager.

47. Guards must see that all vehicles are properly coupled up, the cams and pins in order, and the protection lamp or disc is in its proper place at the rear of the train before giving the Engine-driver the signal to start.

48. Guards must see, before a train is due to start, that the doors of the box vans are properly closed, and that no passenger's luggage is conveyed in open trucks unless properly sheeted.

49. Double shunting is strictly prohibited.

50. The Guard must not allow any passenger or parcel to be conveyed by the train unless properly booked; and if he has reason to suppose that any passenger is without a ticket, or is not in the proper carriage, he must request the passenger to show his ticket, reporting to the Station Master, or Person in Charge, any irregularity he may detect. When a passenger is desirous of changing from an inferior to a superior class of carriage, the Guard must have this arranged by the Station Master or Person if Charge.

[**17**] 51. In the event of any passenger being drunk or disorderly, to the annoyance of others, the Guard is to use all gentle means to stop the nuisance, failing which he must, for the safety and convenience of all, remove him from the train at the first station. The Guard must see that the offender's luggage is put out of the train before it proceeds on its journey.

52. At the end of the day the Guard in charge must deliver to the Station Master or Person in Charge, as may be ordered, a journal containing the time of the running of the trains, noting therein every circumstance of an unusual kind and any detentions that have taken place on the journey. In the event of any occurrence having taken place which might have involved, in any respect, the safety of the train or Line, he must, in addition to the notices in his journals, send in a special report thereof.

ENGINE-DRIVERS AND FIREMEN.

50. The Engine-driver and Fireman must be with their engine at such time previous to starting as the Manager may require, and must satisfy themselves that their engine is in proper order.

51. The Engine-driver and Fireman must not allow any other person to ride on the Engine without a written permission from a properly authorised officer.

[**18**] 55. The Engine-driver must keep a good look-out all the time the engine is in motion, and the Fireman must also do so, when he is not necessarily otherwise engaged.

56. The Engine-driver must regulate the running of his engine as accurately as practicable according to the time-table.

57. The Engine-driver and Fireman must pay immediate attention to, and obey all signals, whether the cause of the signal being shown is known to them or not. The Engine-driver must also obey the instructions of the officers in charge of the stations.

58. When an Engine-driver requires the special assistance of the Guard's brake, he must give three or more short, sharp whistles, and the Guard or Guards must immediately apply the brakes.

59. When two engines are employed to draw a train, the Driver and Fireman of the leading engine are responsible for the observance of signals: the Driver of the second engine must watch for, and take his signals from, the Driver of the leading engine, but the Driver of the second engine is not relieved from the due observance of all signals regulating the safe working of the Line.

60. (*a*) The Engine-driver must start and stop his train carefully and without a jerk.

(*b*) In stopping his train, he must pay particular attention to the state of the weather [**19**] and the condition of the rails, as well as the length and weight of the train, and these circumstances must have due consideration in determining when to shut off steam and to apply the brake.

61. (*a*) The Engine-driver must carefully approach all stations at which his train is required to stop, and must not stop short of, or over-run the platform; he must also exercise care in passing stations where he is not required to stop.

(*b*) Should a Passenger train in stopping at a Station, over-run, or stop short of, the platform, the Engine-driver must not move the train back or draw it forward until he receives instructions from the Guard in charge to do so. Station Masters, Guards, and others must at once take steps to prevent Passengers leaving the carriages that are not at the platform; and as soon as the Guard in charge has satisfied himself that all doors are closed and that no passengers are entering or leaving the train, he must instruct the Engine-driver to put back or draw up to the platform as may be required. The Engine-driver must sound his whistle before moving his train.

62. (*a*) Should an Engine-driver or Guard observe any irregularity in the working of Signals, or should he see any cattle or other obstruction on the Line, or any defect in the Signals, Works, Permanent Way, or Telephone, he must report the same at the first station at which the train stops.

[**20**] (*b*) At the end of his journey the Engine-driver must report the circumstance to his Foreman, and the Guard must also report the case in his journal.

63. During shunting operations an Engine-driver must not move his train, although the Fixed Signal may be lowered, until he has received a Hand Signal to do so from the Guard, Shunter, or other Person in Charge.

64. The Engine-driver and Firemen must frequently during the journey look back and see that the whole train is following in a safe, and proper manner.

65. A Green Flag or a Green Light, waved slowly from side to side by Platelayers indicates the trains must reduce speed as may be prescribed, over the portion of Line protected by such Green Signal.

66. The Engine-drivers must so arrange their fires as to avoid any unnecessary emission of smoke from their engines whilst standing at or passing Stations.

FOREMEN, GANGERS, PLATELAYERS, AND OTHERS EMPLOYED ON THE PERMANENT WAY.

67. In each gang of Platelayers or men repairing the Permanent Way, there shall be a Foreman or Ganger; and the Station Master for the district must take care that every such [**21**] Foreman or Ganger is provided with a

copy of these Regulations, a Working Time Table for the current month, and the proper Signals.

68. Each Foreman and Ganger, and every man engaged on the Permanent Way or Works affecting the Running Lines must constantly have with him when on duty a copy of these Rules and Regulations, which he must produce when required. The Foreman or Ganger must read and explain, or cause to be read and explained, the Rules and Regulations, so far as they relate to his duties, to every man who is employed in his Gang, both at the time he comes to work under him and at least twice a year afterwards.

69. Each Gang of Platelayers or Labourers must be supplied by the Station Master for the district with a set of Flags. Each Ganger will be held responsible for having his Flags constantly in proper order and ready for use.

70. Each Station Master must have a register of tho name and place of residence of all the men employed in his district, so that, in case of accident, he may be enabled to summon them immediately to assist in any way that may be required: and should any obstruction take place, caused by snow, frosts, slips, or other sudden emergency, he must immediately collect the number of men required.

71. Before a rail is taken out, during relaying operations, or when the Line is not safe from any cause, a 'Danger' Signal must be [22] exhibited, placed on the Line, at a point at least one quarter mile from the pi .are of obstruction, in both directions.

72. In all cases, before taking out a rail, the Platelayer must have at the spot a perfect rail in readiness to replace it.

73. A Trolley must not be placed on the Line unless the Ganger, or other Man in Charge for the time being is present, and he will be held responsible for seeing it is properly used and protected. It must not be attached to a train, and when not in use must be taken off the rails, placed well clear of the Line, and the wheels secured with chain and padlock.

74. When a Trolley is upon the running Line, a Danger Signal must be placed upon it so as to be distinctly seen by the men in charge of approaching trains.

75. No Wagon, Truck, or Trolley, or other impediment must be allowed to be on any part of the Line within ten minutes of a train being due, and excepting in cases of accidents, or absolute necessity, all repairs must be effected, and the line made clear and safe for the passage of trains, not less than ten minutes before a train is due.

76. In conveying intelligence of, or in summoning assistance to, any accident or failure, a Platelayer must be sent as quickly as possible to the next gang in each direction, from which a Platelayer must in like manner be sent to the [23] next more distant gang, until information of the accident has by this means reached the nearest Station in each direction and the necessary assistance has been obtained; the Platelayers of each gang proceeding without loss of time to the place at which their services are required.

77. Platelayers and others at work on the Line must rely upon their own signals for the protection of themselves and the traffic.

78. (*a*) The Red Signal indicates Danger, and must be used only when it is necessary to stop a train.

(*b*) The Green Signal waved slowly from side to side by Platelayers indicates that trains must reduce speed as may be prescribed over the portion of Line protected by such Green Signal.

70. Each Foreman or Ganger must walk over his length of Line every morning on Weekdays, and once on Sundays, if there are any Sunday trains, and tighten up all fastenings that may be loose; and he must examine the Line, level, and gauge of the road, and the state of the joints, marking, and if necessary, repairing such as are defective.

80. All points and crossings must be carefully examined, and, if necessary, adjusted.

81. In lifting the Permanent Way, no lift must be greater than three inches at once, and then it must be effected in a length of at least [24] twenty yards, in such a manner as not to occasion any sudden change of gradient. Both rails must be raised equally, and at the same time.

82. No ballast must be thrown up to a higher level near the rails than three inches, and it must be thrown as much as possible on the outside of each rail. The rails must be kept clear of gravel, ballast, or any other material.

83. Gangers must close and fasten all gates they find open, and report the circumstances, in order that the persons who are required to keep such gales closed and fastened may be charged with the penalties (*sic*).

84. Each Foreman or Ganger is required in the event of a flood, to examine carefully the action of the water through the culverts and bridges on his length of Line; and should he see any cause to apprehend danger to the works, he must immediately exhibit the proper Signals for the trains to proceed cautiously, or to stop, as necessity may require, and inform the Station Master thereof, and he must take all the precautionary measures necessary for securing the stability of the Line.

85. In the event of any fire taking place upon or near the Line, the men employed on the Line must take immediate measures for putting it out.

[25] 86. Gangers must oil and keep clean the working parts of Points and Signals, unless the duty is otherwise specially provided for.

87. Each Foreman or Ganger must keep his portion of the Line clear and safe, and the fences in perfect repair, and in the event of any sheep, cattle, or other animals getting within the fences he must immediately remove them, and report the circumstance to the Manager.

88. (*a*) Foremen or Gangers must see that all broken Rails, Sleepers, or other defective materials are removed from the road with the least possible delay, and sound materials substituted.

(*b*) All cases of broken rails must be specially reported to the Manager.

89. All Tools, Rails, Sleepers, pieces of Iron, or Wood, or other implement or material, must be carefully placed so as to be quite clear of the Line, and not within two feet of the rails.

90. All Tools and Implements required for the repair of the Line, must, when not in use, be kept locked up in a building, or in boxes, for the security of which each Foreman or Ganger on his own length of Line is responsible.

[26] **REGULATIONS FOR WORKING.**

91. Only one engine in steam, or two or more coupled together, which are then to be treated as one engine or train, must be allowed to be on the Line at one and the same time, excepting in the case of an engine or train becoming disabled and requiring assistance, or an accident occurring which renders it impossible for the engine to proceed.

92. No train shall be run at a greater speed than 16 miles an hour, and the Engine-driver is liable to two years' imprisonment if convicted of so doing.

93. Station Masters or Persons In Charge are responsible for the starting of the trains at the proper limes, as making up time by running at a speed over 16 miles an hour is strictly forbidden.

94. In the event of a masted vessel requiring to go up or down the River Blyth through the Swing Bridge, the Station Master at Southwold shall arrange with the master of the vessel the hour at which the Bridge can be opened, so as to suit the tide and at the same time not interfere with the train service.

95. Notice must be given by the Station Master to the Ganger of the length to open the Bridge at the proper time, who must not permit the wedges, bolts, screws, or fastenings of the opening spans to be unfastened or taken off until the Station Master is present at the [27] Bridge with the staff and key. The Ganger will be held responsible for the proper and securely replacing of the wedges and fastenings as soon as the vessel has passed through.

96. The Station Master must not leave the Bridge with the staff until the Bridge is closed, securely fastened and locked.

97. No train shall be run while such opening is taking place; and on the Station Master's return to Southwold he shall hand the staff and key to the Engine-driver, who is then at liberty to start with the train.

GETTING BETWEEN VEHICLES TO COUPLE OR UNCOUPLE THEM.

98. (*a*) All servants must exercise proper care in getting between vehicles for the purpose of coupling or uncoupling them.

(*b*) Men must not go between two vehicles, or between an engine and a vehicle, to couple or uncouple, until both have been brought to rest.

[28] **APPENDIX I.**

TRAIN STAFF REGULATIONS.

Applicable to Single Lines worked under the Train Staff and Train Staff Ticket System.

1. Single Lines worked under the Train Staff and Train Staff Ticket System are divided into Sections, and the Station at each end of such Sections is called a 'Train Staff Station.' The Train Staff Stations are Southwold, Walberswick, Blythburgh (crossing place), and Halesworth. The Sections are Southwold and Walberswick, Walberswick and Blythburgh, and Blythburgh and Halesworth.

2. A Train Staff or Train Staff Ticket must be carried with each train, and no train must be permitted to leave any Staff Station with a Train Staff Ticket unless the Staff for that portion of the Line over which it is to travel is then at the Station.

3 The Signals at Blythburgh are as follows:-
On the off side of the Line, from Halesworth:-
Down   Distant.
  "   Home.
  "   Starter.
Facing the Line, from Southwold:-
Up Home.
  " Starter.

[29] The following rules must be strictly adhered to:-

(1) When an Engine-driver finds the Distant Signal at Danger he must reduce speed and proceed cautiously towards the Home Signal, being prepared to stop if necessary.

(2) No train must pass a Home Signal at Danger, or foul the Points to which it applies, unless specially authorised by the Manager.

4. (*a*) The Danger Signal must always be kept exhibited at all the Fixed Signals at Staff Stations, except when it is necessary to lower them for a train to pass: and, before any Signal is lowered, care must be taken to ascertain that (he Line on which the train is about to run is clear.

(*b*) When a Passenger Train and a Special Goods Train, which have to cross each other, are approaching the Blythburgh (Crossing) Staff Station in opposite directions, the Signals in both directions must be kept at Danger, and when the Passenger Train—which has to be first admitted into the Station—has been brought lo a stand, the Home Signal applicable to such train may be lowered to allow it to draw forward to the Station, and, after it has again come to a stand, and the Person in Charge has seen that the Line on which the Special Goods Train will arrive is quite clear, the necessary Signal for that train may also be lowered to allow it to draw forward on to the Loop.

[30] 5. (*a*) Permission must not be given for a train to approach from the opposite end of the Section when there is any obstruction upon the Line.

(*b*) The Line must not be fouled after permission has been given for a train to approach from the opposite end of the Section.

6 (*a*) A Special Goods Train is not permitted to shunt for another train to pass, except at the Blythburgh (Crossing) Staff Station.

(b) An empty Carriage Train may be treated and worked as a Special Goods Train.

(*c*) A Passenger Train is not permitted to pass another Passenger Train at the Blythburgh (Crossing) Staff Station.

7. The Person in Charge of the Staff-working for the time being is the sole person authorised to receive and deliver the Staff or Ticket.

8. When a train is ready to start from a Station and no second train is intended to follow before the Staff will be required for a train in the opposite direction, the Person in Charge of the Staff-working must give the Staff to the Engine-driver, who will then place it in the Train Staff Socket provided on the Engine.

9. (a) If another train is intended to follow before the Staff can be returned, a Ticket indicating that the Staff is following must be given by the person in charge of the Staff-working to [31] the Engine-driver of the first train, the Staff for the Section being shown to him, the Stuff itself being given to the Engine-driver of the last train, as directed in the preceding Rule. The person who hands the Ticket to the Engine-driver must satisfy himself that the train has arrived at the end of the Section before he allows another train to follow. After the Staff has been sent away no other train must, under any circumstances, leave the Station to follow in the same direction, until the Staff for that Section has been returned.

(*b*) The Station Master, or Person in Charge of the Staff-working, must consider it his first duty to deal with the Train Staff or Ticket on arrival of the Train, and at the Blythburgh (Crossing) Staff Station must satisfy himself that the train running in the one direction has arrived complete with the Tail Lamp or Disc on the last vehicle, before handing the Staff or Ticket to the Engine-driver about to travel in the opposite direction.

10. No train must be permitted to leave a Station until the Engine-driver has received the proper Staff or Ticket for that Section of the Line over which he is about to travel, and he must not take the Staff or Ticket from any other than the Person in Charge of the Staff-working for the time being. After receiving the Staff or Ticket he must not start until the proper Signals have been exhibited, and, when with a train, not until a Signal has also been given by the Guard. On arriving at the Station to which the Staff or Ticket extends, such Staff [32] or Ticket must immediately be given up to the Person in Charge of the Staff-working. All Tickets so given up must be at once cancelled by the word 'cancelled' being written across them, and the Tickets must afterwards be sent to the Manager.

11. (*a*) An Engine-driver will render himself liable to dismissal if he leaves a Staff Station without the Staff or Ticket for the Section over which he is about to run; or, if he leaves with a Ticket, without having first seen the proper Staff.

(*b*) He must be careful not to take the Staff or Ticket beyond the Staff Station at which it should be left.

(*c*) The person in charge of the Staff-working will render himself liable to severe punishment should he contribute to any irregularity in the Staff-working.

12. Each Staff has marked on it the name of the Staff Station at each end of the Section to which only it applies. The Staffs, Boxes and Tickets for the three Sections are painted and printed in different colours, and the Staffs of the three Sections are different in shape.

13. (*a*) The Tickets must be kept in the proper Ticket Box, the key to open the box being attached to the Staff, for the same Section as the box, so that, if the Ticket Box is kept locked—for which the Person in Charge of [33] the Staff-working will be held strictly responsible—access to the Tickets cannot be obtained unless the proper Staff for the Section is then at the Station.

(*b*) Only one Ticket must be taken from the Ticket Box at the same time. The box must be locked after each Ticket is taken out, and not again opened until it is necessary to obtain another Ticket for a following train, unless as provided for in Rule 16 of these Regulations.

14. (*a*) The Staff, when at the Station, must not be kept in the box, but on the brackets outside of it.

(*b*) Should a Train Staff be lost, or so damaged that it will not open the box containing the Staff Tickets, the Station Masters at both ends of the Section must communicate with each other and make arrangements to work the traffic over the Section to which the Staff belongs by Pilotman, who must accompany every train until the Staff has been found, or repaired.

(*c*) If the missing Staff be found, it must be handed to the Station Master at either end of the Section to which it applies, who must make arrangements for the ordinary working to be resumed.

15. (*a*) When a Special Train or Engine has to be run, a Red Tail Board must be used by day and an extra Red Tail Light by night, for the purpose of signalling to all concerned that a Special Train is to follow.

[34] (*b*) The Station Master, or Person in Charge of the Starting Station, will be responsible for seeing that the Red Tail Board by day, or an extra Red Tail Light by night, is attached to the centre of the last vehicle of the preceding ordinary train.

(*c*) The Guard will be responsible for seeing that the Tail Board, or extra Ked Light, is under all circumstances exhibited on the last vehicle of the train during its journey, and that it is removed and returned to the Station to which it belongs. A Red Tail Board must be kept at Southwold and Halesworth.

(*d*) In the event of a Special Train having to be run which has not been advised by notice issued by the Manager, Red Tail Board or Red Light, a telephonic advice must be sent by the Terminal Station Master to each Station on the route.

16. When any train is assisted by a second engine in the front, and such train has to carry the Staff, the first or leading engine must carry a Ticket, and the second engine the Staff. In cases where the train is to be followed by another train, the second, as well as the leading engine must carry a Ticket.

17. (a) In the event of an engine which carries the Staff breaking down between two Stations, the Fireman must take the Staff to the Staff Station in the direction whence assistance [35] can be obtained; and the Station Master at the Station to which the Staff is taken will be held responsible for carrying out all special arrangements necessary during the continuance of the obstruction. Should the engine that fails be in possession of a Ticket instead of the Staff assistance must only come from the Station at which the Staff has been left, and the Station Master at that Station will beheld responsible for making any special arrangements that may be necessary, the Guard of the train being held responsible for the proper protection of his train until the arrival of the Station Master. But if assistance can be more readily obtained at a Station other than that where the Staff is, immediate steps must be taken to have the Staff transferred to the other end of the Section. The Fireman must accompany the assistant engine to the place where he has left his own engine.

(*b*) When the engine which has failed is carrying a Ticket, the Fireman must take this Ticket with him when he goes for assistance, and the Driver of the engine which has failed must not allow it to be moved until the assisting engine has arrived.

18. Except as shown below, no engine must push a train upon any Running Line, but must draw it.

Exceptions

(a) When within Station limits or where specially authorised by the Manager.

[36] (*b*) In the case of an engine being disabled a following engine may push the train slowly to the next Station, when the pushing engine must go in front.

(*c*) When the Line is blocked and trains are being worked to the point of obstruction, on both sides.

(*d*) When required to assist in starting a Train from a Station.

19. (*a*) When a train or a portion of a train is left upon the Line from accident or inability of the engine to take the whole forward, the Engine-driver must not, if he be in possession of a Ticket, return for it except by written instructions from the Guard, and the Guard must protect his train in the rear, and prevent a following train pushing it ahead. If the Engine-driver be in possession of the Staff, he may return for the rear portion of his train without obtaining instructions from the Guard authorising him to do so.

(*b*) After sunset, or in foggy weather, or during falling snow, before the front portion is drawn forward, a Red Light must be placed on the front vehicle of the rear portion, by the man who divides the train.

20. (*a*) Should an accident occur of such a .nature as to block the Line, and the traffic is likely to be stopped for any considerable time, special arrangements must be made for working [37] the trains to and from the Staff Station on each side of the obstruction. The Train Staff must be retained to work trains between the point of obstruction and the Staff Station from which assistance is rendered, and, on the other side, the traffic must be conducted by a Pilot man to be appointed by an order in writing (see specimen Forms on pages 38 and 39).

(*b*) The Line on each side of the obstruction must be protected by Hand Signalmen in the usual way.

[38] SOUTHWOLD RAILWAY.

Train Staff and Ticket System.

Working of Single Line by Pilotman during Obstruction.

This Form must be filled up and used whenever it is temporarily necessary, owing to obstruction, to work the traffic by Pilotman.

.... Station

.... 19

The Line between .... and .... being obstructed, the traffic between .... and the place of obstruction will be worked by Pilotman in accordance with Rule 20 of the Regulations for Working Single Lines of Railway by Train Staff and Ticket.

.... will act as Pilotman, and must accompany every train to and from .... Station and the point of obstruction.

This Order is to remain in force until withdrawn by the Pilotman.

(Signed) ....

[39] To ....

* Noted by .... at place of obstruction.

Time............   * Noted by ....

.... Station.   Time ....

Noted by..............................Pilotman.

* These signatures must be made on the copy held by the Pilotman, who must also sign the Forms held by the Person in Charge of the obstruction.

Note.—The time at which this Form is cancelled must be written across it.

Six of these Forms must be kept in a convenient place at each Train Staff Station, so as to be available at any moment.

A copy of this Form must be delivered to the Person in Charge of the Staff Station where Pilot-working commences, the second must be retained by the Pilotman, and the third must be conveyed by the Pilotman to the Person in Charge of the obstruction. If there is an intermediate Station which is not a Train Staff Station, the Person in Charge must be supplied with a copy of the Form.

In the event of a Station Master himself acting as Pilotman, he must address and give a copy of the Form to the person he leaves in charge of his Station.

[40] Station Masters and Persons in Charge receiving this Form will he held responsible that the Foreman, and others concerned at their Station are immediately made acquainted with tho circumstances, and are instructed in their necessary duties.

On the other side of the obstruction the Line will be worked by Train Staff, no Tickets being used.

21. When the Line is again clear, no train must be allowed to pass the point where the obstruction existed without the Staff. The Pilotman must accompany the first train carrying the Staff to, the Staff Station, and, after the Pilotman has withdrawn his arrangements for Pilot-working, the traffic must be again conducted according to the Train Staff Regulations.

22. (*a*) When a Ballast train has to work on the Line, the Staff must be given to the Engine-driver in charge of it. This will close the Line whilst the Ballast train is at work. The Ballast train must proceed afterwards to one of the Staff Stations to open the Line before the ordinary traffic can be resumed. But if a Ballast train is required to run over a Section of the line from one Staff Station to the other without stopping to work on the way, it may then travel with Staff or Ticket as required; under no circumstances must the Ballast train stop to do work on the Line unless in possession of the Train Staff.

[41] (*b*) The Engine-driver of a Ballast train that has to do work on tho Lino, must be told, when receiving the Staff, to which end of the Section it is to be taken and at what time it is to be there, in order to clear tho Line for the next train.

23. (*a*) Points giving communication between the Sidings and the Running Line controlled by the Train Staff cannot be opened without the Train Staff for that Section of tho Line where the Siding is situated, and the Train Staff cannot be removed until the Points have been placed in the proper position for trains to pass upon the Running Line, and securely locked so as to prevent vehicles passing from the Sidings on to the Running Line.

(*b*) On arriving at a Siding, the Points of which are controlled by the Train Staff, the Engine-driver must hand the Train Staff to tho Guard to enable him to unlock the Points.

(*c*) When the necessary shunting has been completed and the points have been placed in the proper position for trains to pass upon tho Running Line, the Guard must return the Train Staff to the Engine-driver, and the latter must not proceed on his journey until he has obtained possession of it.

[42]   FORM OF TRAIN STAFF TICKET.

No.

Southwold Railway.

Train Staff Ticket.

Train...............................

To

The Engine-driver.

You are authorised, after seeing the Train Staff for the Section, to proceed from .... to .... and the Train Staff will follow.

Signature of Person in Charge ....
Date..........................

This ticket must be- given up by the Engine-driver, immediately on arrival, to the person in charge of the Staff working at the place to which he is authorised to proceed. At the end of the day this ticket is to be enclosed by the Station Master to the Manager.

Bibliography

GENERAL WORKS
Allen, C.J., *The Great Eastern Railway*, Ian Allan
Gordon, D.I., *Regional History of the Railways of Great Britain: Volume 5, Eastern Counties*, David & Charles
Joby, R.S., *Forgotten Railways of East Anglia*, David & Charles
Taylor, A.R. and E.S. Tonks, *The Southwold Railway*, Ian Allan

PERIODICALS
Bradshaw's Railway Guide
Bradshaw's Railway Manual
British Railways, Eastern Region Magazine
Buses
Great Eastern Railway Magazine
Herepath's Journal
Journal of the Southwold Railway Trust
Locomotive Carriage and Wagon Review
Locomotive Magazine
London & North Eastern Railway Magazine
Railway Magazine
Railway Modeller
Railway Times
Railway World
Railway Year Book
Trains Illustrated

NEWSPAPERS
Daily Express
Eastern Daily Press
Halesworth Times
Suffolk Chronicle
Suffolk Mercury
The Times

MINUTE BOOKS
Southwold Railway
Eastern Counties Railway
Great Eastern Railway
London and North Eastern Railway
Mid Suffolk Light Railway

WORKING & PUBLIC TIMETABLES
Southwold Railway
Great Eastern Railway
London and North Eastern Railway

APPENDICES TO WORKING TIMETABLE
Southwold Railway
Great Eastern Railway
London & North Eastern Railway

MISCELLANEOUS OPERATING AND WORKING INSTRUCTIONS
Southwold Railway
Great Eastern Railway
London & North Eastern Railway

Acknowledgements

The publication of this history would not have been possible without the help of many people who have been kind enough to assist. In particular I should like to thank; The late A.R. Cox, the late W. Fenton, the late E. Blois, the late E. Vaughan, the late K Riley, A. Keeler, the late R.C. (Dick) Riley, the late G. Woodcock, the late P. Morgan, the late Dr I.C. Alien, the late Reverend E. Boston, the late Canon C. Bayes, the late R.H.N. Hardy, David Lee and the late Alan R. Taylor, both of whom have made a great study of the Southwold Railway, Chris Cock for confirmation on signalling matters and Robert Powell for reading through the manuscript; also various members of the Great Eastern Railway Society and the Southwold Railway Trust. The following provided much needed assistance; The National Archives, Kew, British Railways Eastern Region, The House of Lords Record Office, British Library Newspaper Library and last but not least the Suffolk County Record Office.

Index

abandonment of SR assets 95
abandonment of standard gauge conversion 77 *et seq*
accidents and incidents 18, 19, 23, 24, 25, 28, 33, 37, 38, 39, 43, 53, 62, 69, 70, 79, 89
Acts of Parliament 12, 13
agreements between SR and GER 34
attempts to reopen the line 96, 97, 101, 102, 103

ballast siding, Halesworth (Bird's Folly) 56, 112
Blyth Valley Railway 11, 12
Blythburgh:
   opening of crossing loop 59
   station and goods yard 121-8
Board of Trade:
   certificates 18, 19, 29
   inspections 14, 18, 23, 46, 56, 77, 90
   regulations 13, 18
branch to Blackshore Quay 58, 63, 66
   BOT inquiry 67

Calne, Harry secretary 25 *et seq*
Chambers, Charles:
   as chairman 43 *et seq*
   as contractor 13, 14
claims against SR 18, 19 *et seq*

competitive bus services 72, 88, 89, 90
construction of railway 14 *et seq*
continuous brake, fitting of 32, 33, 34, 37, 40, 41, 225
conversion to standard gauge 45, 46, 47, 52
Central Essex Light Railway 77
coaching stock, 6-wheel 205-12

Directors SR 13 *et seq*

East Suffolk Railway 10
Eastern Counties Railway 9 *et seq*
Eastern Union Railway 10
engine and footplate staff workings 201 *et seq*
engine sheds:
   Halesworth 58, 75
   Southwold 201 *et seq*
excursion traffic 171-8

fares 25, 28, 169, 170
fencing and gate dimensions 149
fiftieth anniversary of closure 104
flooding of railway 14, 23, 39, 43, 52, 65, 70, 75
footplate staff, wages 204

gas company 53
government control of railway 73 *et seq*

Great Eastern Railway 11 *et seq*
   acquisition Southwold harbour 33
   agreement with SR 34
   bus service Southwold to Lowestoft 52, 70, 81-5
   Directors visit to SR 14, 65
   possible purchase of SR 35, 36, 37, 46, 47, 65, 67
goods traffic 179-88
Grouping of railways 80, 85

Halesworth:
   alterations at 90
   engine shed 58, 75
   station and goods yard 106-11
Halesworth, Beccles & Haddiscoe Railway 10
Halesworth Light Railway 68, 73
half yearly meetings and financial results 25, 28, 29, 31, 32, 36, 37, 39, 40, 41, 43, 46, 52, 55, 59, 61, 66, 68, 71
Harbour Branch 136-8
Heronry 128-9

Ipswich and Bury St Edmunds Railway 10

Junction for Harbour Branch 136-8

land taken for the railway 16

Sharp, Stewart 2-4-2T No. 1 *Southwold* at Halesworth on 17th January 1920. By the early 1890s the steady growth of traffic necessitated the provision of a third locomotive to replace the original No. 1 that had been returned to the makers in 1883. The company negotiated with Sharp, Stewart & Company in 1893 and settled on a similar design to the original trio but slightly longer in length and having a 2-4-2T wheel arrangement, which allowed a small bunker to be placed to the rear of the cab. The new No. 1 *Southwold* was built at the company's Atlas Works at Glasgow at a cost of £1,020. *LCGB/Ken Nunn*

last train 94
Light Railway Act 1896 41
Light Railway Commissioners enquiry into conversion to standard gauge 47
Light Railway Orders:
  1902 49-51
  1907 57
  Southwold Harbour 72
loading of goods trains 158
locomotive water supplies 203
locomotives:
  No. 1 (original) 189
  No. 1 (replacement) 193,195
  No. 2 189, 195 *et seq*
  No. 3 189, 195 *et seq*
  No. 4 72, 192, 196 *et seq*
London & North Eastern Railway 85 *et seq*, 90, 93
Lowestoft, Yarmouth & Southwold Tramway 11
luggage vans No's 13 & 14 28, 212, 216-18

Mid Suffolk Light Railway 45 *et seq*, 56 *et seq*, 68 *et seq*, 73, 80, 87
Midland Railway 34 *et seq*, 80
motive power staff 201 *et seq*

notice of closure of SR 93

opening, BOT Inspection 14, 15

opening to traffic 17

Pain, Arthur Claude 13, 14, 15 *et seq*
permanent way:
  materials 14
  staff 147, 148, 149
population figures 159
prolongation of winding up of SR affairs 103-4

rail dimensions 147
Ransomes & Rapier, provision of signals 13, 14
Rapier, Richard, Chairman 25, 28, 35, 43
Regulation of Railway Act 1889 32 *et seq*
reparation of foreign citizens 76
requisition of SR assets by Ministry of Supply 101, 102

siding, Wenhaston Mill 19 *et seq*
signalling arrangements 15, 151
single line, method of working 151, 152, 154
snowdrifts 56, 76, 79
Southwold:
  historical survey 9
  station and goods yard 138-46
Southwold Harbour 25 *et seq*, 53 *et seq*
  construction of branch 74
  working agreement with SR 71
Southwold Harbour Co. BOT Order 1907 58

Southwold Railway prospectus 13
Southwold & Halesworth Tramway 11
speed limits 16
station masters 154-7
storage of SR rolling stock after closure 94

telegraphic communication 45
timetables 159-69
traffic staff 157-58

wagons:
  4-wheel 219, 220
  6-wheel 221, 223-4
Walberswick station 23, 130-33
  complaints re location 45, 52
  World War One:
    closure 76
    reopening 77
Wenhaston Mill:
  crossing 115
  siding 16
Wenhaston station and goods yard 116-20
widening works 57 *et seq*
  abandonment of 77
working and public timetables 159-69
World War One:
  incidents 74, 75
  operating alterations 73
  precautions 73
  service alterations 74

Southwold shed on 12th July 1911 with 2-4-2T No. 1 *Southwold* raised on timber blocks undergoing repairs. In the background is SR 6-wheel Cleminson wagon No. 30 in grey livery with white lettering shaded black. *LCGB/Ken Nunn*

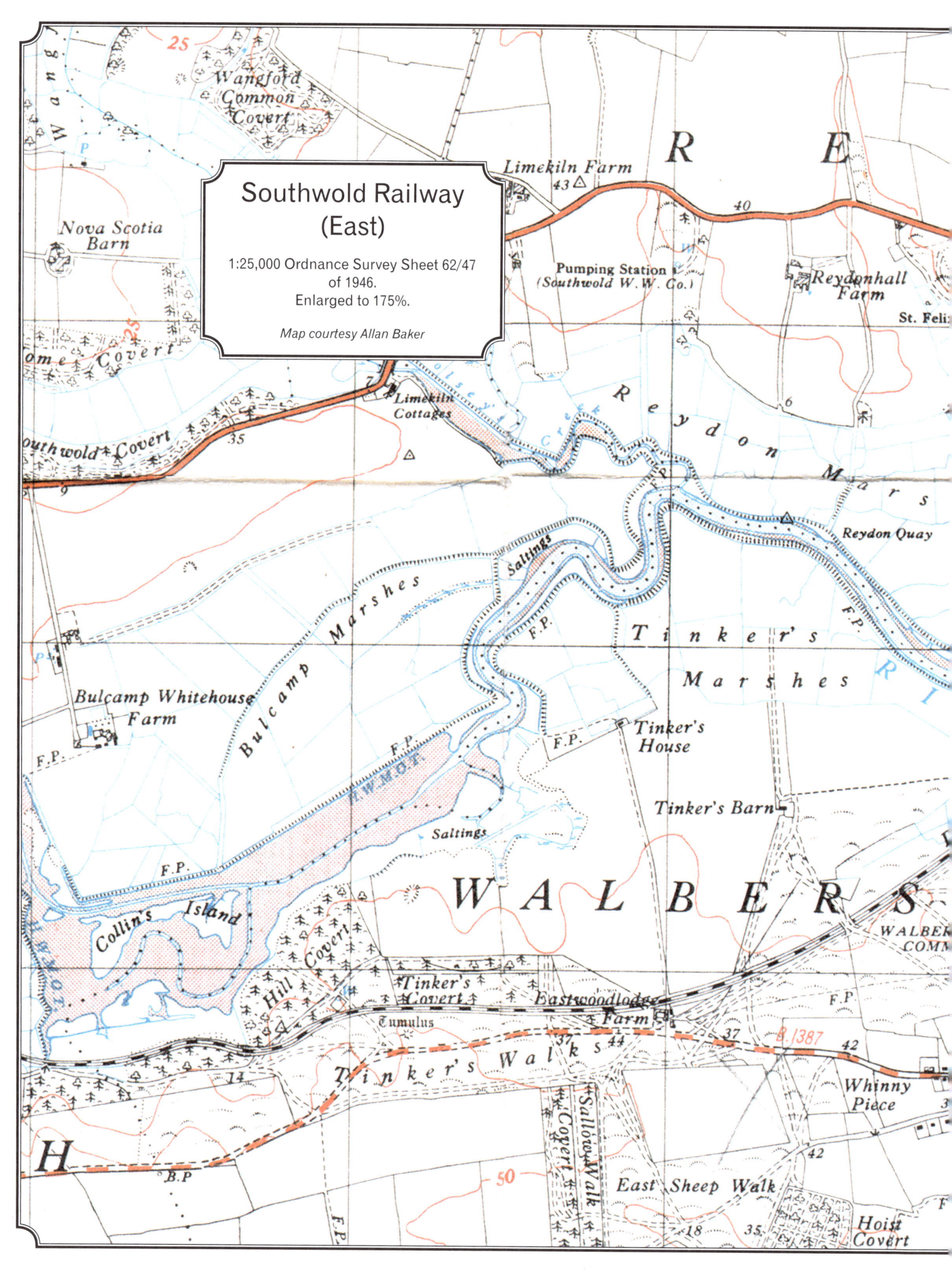

Southwold Railway (East)

1:25,000 Ordnance Survey Sheet 62/47 of 1946.
Enlarged to 175%.

Map courtesy Allan Baker